The Ultimate Bay Book

The Ultimate Bay Book

The Discovery and Delights of San Francisco Bay

by Terry Milne

Photography by Luther Linkhart
Supplemental photography by Terry Milne

A California Living Book

Cover photo courtesy of NASA

Photo on page 134 courtesy of the National Maritime Museum at San Francisco.

Cartography by Terry Milne
"Only Sir Francis Knows for Sure" by Robert H. Power, reprinted by permission from the June 27, 1976 issue of *California Living Magazine*.

Production by David Charlsen

First Edition

ISBN 0-89395-010-6

Library of Congress Catalog Card Number 78-052509

Contents

Ecology — 201

With appreciation to
Arthur W. Upfield
Arthur C. Doyle
and Morte d'Arthur
who have helped me get through
the long work of making this book.

Introduction

"The Port of San Francisco would be twenty times as valuable to us as all Texas." (1845) Daniel Webster, quoted by John C. Frémont in his memoirs.

At this late date it would be a difficult task to dispute, or agree with, Webster's prediction. But it is not hard to appraise the present-day worth of San Francisco Bay. For all who live in the region and the millions who visit every year, the Bay is vital to the quality of life — it is our most precious natural resource. Its great open space is a huge recreation area for sailors, fishermen and shoreline walkers, and it is an incomparable harbor for commerce.

This book reveals the liveliness of the Bay and its many values. It is written with the idea that the better you know the Bay, the more appreciative and protective you can be of its fragile eco-system. This is a discovery guidebook for the long-time resident and for the visitor to the Bay region who wants to do some exploring. It is an activity book about discovering the Bay in various ways and enjoying what you find — where to do something (places) and how to find out about something (information). The book is divided into three parts — Recreation, History and Ecology. It is a comprehensive look at everything that happens on the water and on the shoreline, from Carquinez Strait at the north end, where the rivers of the Delta rush through the narrow canyon to form the Bay, to the town of Alviso at the south end.

The most pleasure this book has given is the discoveries and delights I have found for myself in writing it.

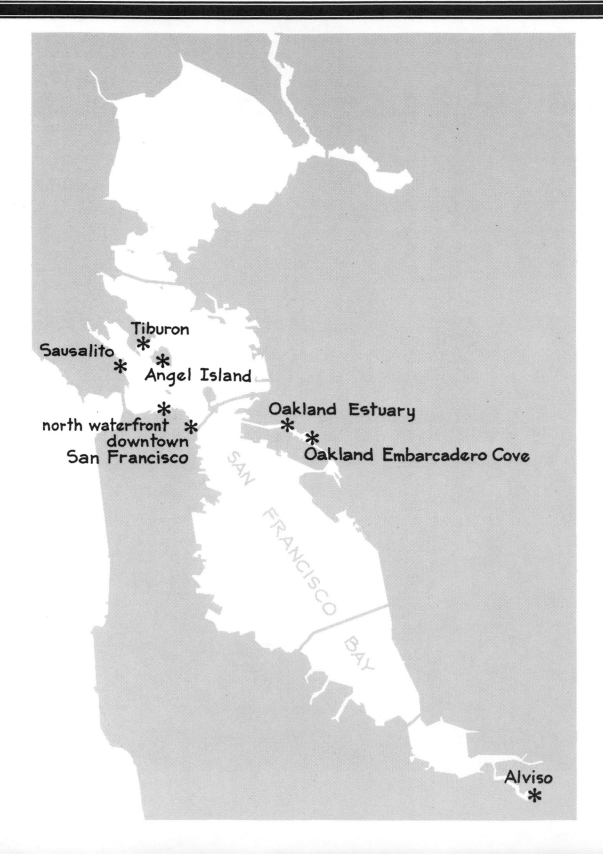

Recreation

Pedestrian Delights

The next several pages portray the waterfront of San Francisco Bay in its full regalia of environments. These bright spots for pedestrians include the small town pleasure boat ports of Sausalito and Tiburon, with marinas and restaurants; the natural beauty of Angel Island State Park, the Bay's finest outdoor experience; two embankment locations on Oakland's urban estuary, with boating as a backdrop; two different sections of the San Francisco waterfront, with downtown and open space activities; and finally, the hidden Bay of Alviso, with its salt marshes and sloughs.

More places for walkers are found in the section *Finding the Bay: Public Parks, Beaches and Shorelines*. For more details about the waterfront activities mentioned here, look in the sections dealing with restaurants, ferry transportation, bicycling, cruising, marinas and sailing.

Promenading in Sausalito

Downtown Sausalito is the snug strip of land where mountain meets the Bay just inside the Golden Gate. This sprawling, salty historical town is one of the oldest settlements across the Bay from San Francisco. Just because it is well-known and popular, you shouldn't miss savoring the stylish delights of a sojourn in Sausalito. Perhaps you can stray away from the crowds and see a little more.

Old Town

The area around the little cove at the south end of town, where the first inhabitants settled is known as "Old Town." Here you can find the Valhalla Inn restaurant (1), and a prim Victorian house (2) on the water at the end of Bridgeway where, for a short time, Jack London lived and wrote.

Town Center

Sausalito, the town that was developed by a ferry company, still has ferry service to the heart of downtown. The ferryboat *Golden Gate* from San Francisco ties up at the same dock (9) that has been in use for years. Adjacent is the Sausalito Yacht Club and Gabrielson Park. Across the way is a slice of landscaping, Viña del Mar Plaza. This park has a fountain and elephant sculpture that were removed from San Francisco's Marina after the Panama-Pacific International Exposition of 1915.

On the inshore side of Bridgeway is a veritable bazaar of shops. You should be able to satiate your shopping instincts in one of these places offering clothes, crafts, books and scrimshaw. The four-story Village Fair, which was a parking garage for ferry commuters in the 1920s, has international items. Beyond the parking lots is The Spinnaker restaurant (10), perched on Richardson Bay.

Esplanade

One of the most delectable things about Sausalito is strolling on its ''Strand,'' Bridgeway, with smart shops, restaurants and saloons, and a sparkling sequence of parks on the Bay's edge. At one end is the bronze sentinel seal statue (3) by sculptor Al Cebrian, reminiscent of Copenhagen's Little Mermaid. A small fishing pier (4) is situated beside two restaurants on the dock — The Trident (5), downstairs, and Ondine (6), upstairs. Next door is Scoma's restaurant (7). Further along, located right beside Princess Park, is the upstairs dining deck of Slinkey's El Monte restaurant (8).

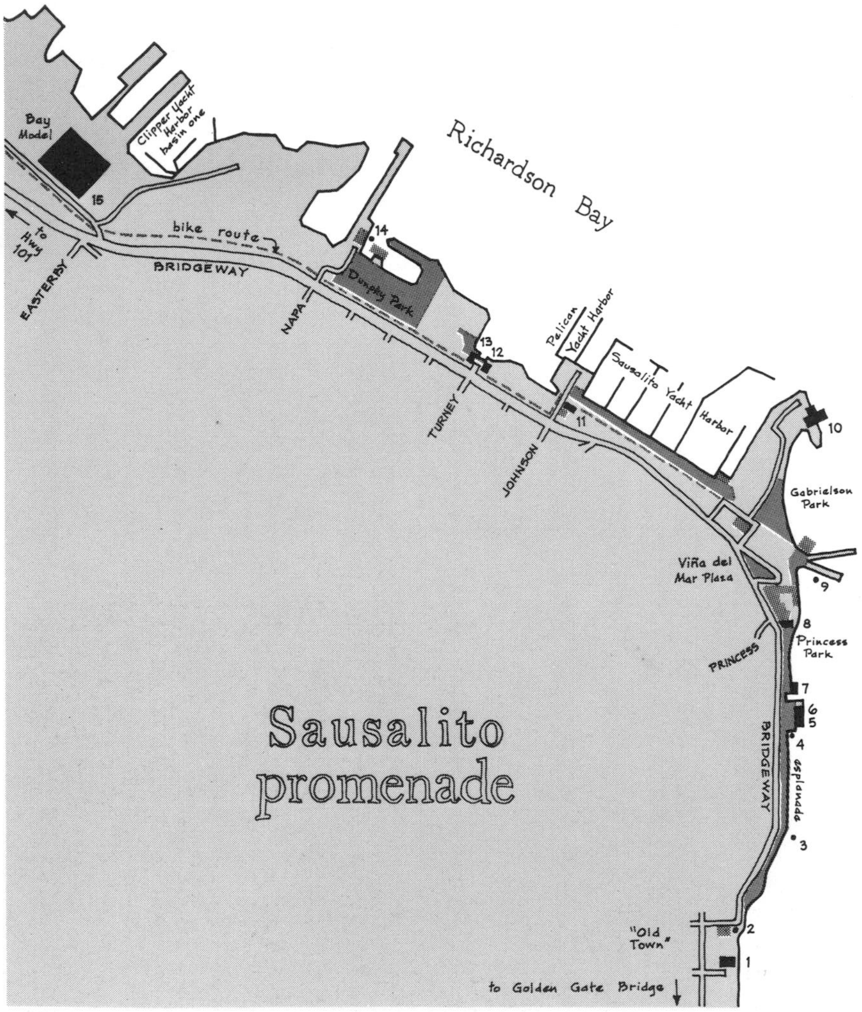

Bay Model
15
Clipper Yacht Harbor basin one
to Hwy 101
EASTBY
BRIGDEWAY
bike route
NAPA
Doughty Park
14
Richardson Bay
13 12
TURNEY
JOHNSON
Pelican Yacht Harbor
Sausalito Yacht Harbor
11
10
Gabrielson Park
Viña del Mar Plaza
• 9
8
Princess Park
PRINCESS
7
6 5
4
BRIDGEWAY
esplanade
• 3

Sausalito promenade

"Old Town"
2
1
to Golden Gate Bridge ↓

Sailing

The northward sweep of Bridgeway takes you by the yacht harbors. A quick browse in the corner chandlery before scouting the sailing craft moored in the basins is enjoyable. Flynn's Landing (11) is a second-floor restaurant that overlooks the boats and Richardson Bay. Further along are two more eating places, Zack's (12), and The Tides (13), with a seldom-used boat launching ramp between them. Across the grass sward of Earl F. Dunphy Park is the Sausalito Cruising Club and Cass' Rental Marina (14). As the name implies, this means sailboat rentals and sailing lessons. A bike route parallels Bridgeway and goes north to Mill Valley.

Bay Model

At 2100 Bridgeway the Army Corps of Engineers operates a model of San Francisco Bay in a huge warehouse (15). The model is open weekdays 9 am-4 pm, and some Saturdays. Surveying the re-created action of currents and tides is an altogether appropriate activity on a nautical visit to Sausalito.

Treat Yourself to Tiburon

Tasty Table-hopping

Neatly tucked away behind the heights of Belvedere and Angel Island sits the tiny port section of Tiburon. Here you can find probably the best selection of waterfront restaurants anywhere on the Bay. You have a choice between inexpensive and expensive and a choice of types of cuisine. Restaurants on the water's edge are Tiburon Tommie's (1), Thirty-nine Main (2), Sweden House Bakery (3), Sam's Anchor Café (4), The Dock (5), Sabella's (6), The Windjammer (7), and The Caprice (8). Some of these have decks for tranquil tête-à-têtes on sunny Sunday afternoons. On the inshore side of Main Street and along Tiburon Boulevard are other inviting eating places.

Main Street

Tiburon's tiny Main Street is pleasant for exploring and not nearly so touristy as Sausalito. You can try the art shops, the lively bookstore, or pop around the corner for some wine tasting at Tiburon Vintners (14). At an upstairs location on the docks is the Sailing Center — lessons and club (13). The Corinthian Yacht Club (one of the oldest on the Bay) with its basin full of boats (15) provides a definite nautical flair to downtown.

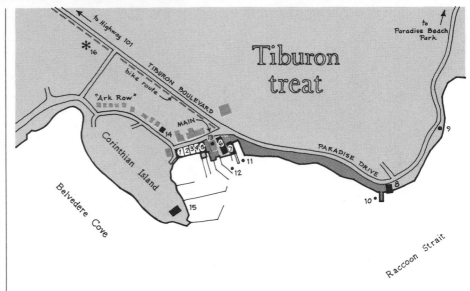

Further Afield

A little further away is the Hygeia tower (9), once used as a lighthouse, in the "Old Town" section. It is a monument to Dr. Benjamin Lyford's dream of almost a hundred years ago to create a community of healthful living that would be a teetotaler's paradise (if that is not a contradiction in ideas). The monument is all that remains.

Tiburon grew up as a railroad town in the 1880s and sent huge ferryboats filled with passengers and railcars across the Bay to San Francisco. Bay-browsing along the public shoreline will provide a glimpse of some of the remnants of the railyards and shops north of Paradise Drive in an area scheduled for development. At the far end of the shoreline is a kid's fishing pier (10). In the other direction is "Ark Row," with its old houseboats and cabins from the early days of Tiburon, some of which are now antique shops. The Boardwalk Shopping Center (15), down Tiburon Boulevard, has the Shorebird Gallery, a delightful shop of crafts and art.

Ride the Ferry

One of the most tempting things about Tiburon is the ferry service. Even though the rail service ended more than ten years ago, the town is still a transportation hub. The ferry from San Francisco, which stops at Angel Island, lands at the end of Main Street (11). You can also travel to the state park across Raccoon Strait on the Angel Island Ferry (12). Both ferries take bicycles for a day of cycling on the island. Another excursion is to follow the bike route to Richardson Bay, where you find a park and the Audubon refuge, or you can go on to further explore Marin.

More of Angel Island is on the following pages.

Blissful Hiking on Angel Island

Angel Island is the largest and most alluring island on San Francisco Bay. Its many years of military use kept it relatively isolated and undeveloped. Now as a state park, its solitude makes it an attractive sanctuary for any adventurer going ashore to seek the many charms of the Bay.

Ferries

The only access to Angel Island is by boat. There is ferry service from San Francisco, Tiburon and Berkeley. The "Red & White Fleet" makes several runs from San Francisco to Tiburon with stops at the island (daily service from Memorial Day to Labor Day, and on weekends and holidays the rest of the year). The Angel Island Ferry from Tiburon operates during the same season — daily in summer, and weekends the rest of the year. A Red & White ferryboat runs from the Berkeley Marina once each way only, on weekends and holidays, from April through October. Private boats may also use the dock and moorings in Ayala Cove on the northwest side of the island.

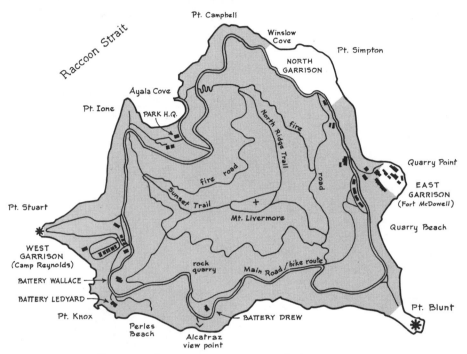

Angel Island for divine hiking

Trails

The focus of activity on Angel Island is Ayala Cove where passengers disembark from the ferryboats and where the Park headquarters is located. But you shouldn't stop there. Trails snake all over the island, providing a lot of walking and enabling you to comb the beaches, explore the old military installations, and ascend 781-foot tall Mt. Livermore. A few areas and certain buildings are off limits. Good Bay-viewing points are abundant. From atop the island you can see across the entire Central Bay, from the Golden Gate to the East Bay Hills. The Alcatraz view point gives a close-up look at that island with the streets of San Francisco as a backdrop. Point Stuart and Point Blunt are crowned by lighthouses. The aquatic spectator can see sailboat regattas that swirl through Raccoon Strait and shipping that turns around the island heading up the Bay. Another way to enjoy the trails is to bring a bicycle on the ferry and explore the island on wheels.

Picnics and Beaches

The main picnic area is at Ayala Cove. Another area near East Garrison is reserved for groups. Almost any place on the island is amenable to picnicking, as long as you find shelter from the wind, but no fires are permitted outside the designated areas. The beach at Ayala Cove is nice, but the finest is Quarry Beach on the other side of the island, sunshiny and protected from prevailing winds. There are a few other small beaches that are good for beach-combing, bird-watching and Bay-viewing. Swimming is definitely not a good idea because of the currents.

The Past

Angel Island represents many facets of the history of San Francisco Bay. The first Spanish explorer to sail into the Bay, Ayala, found island Indian encampments. Traveling around the island you can see reminders of the military which took over in the 1860s and used it as a base during Indian wars, the Spanish-American War, WW I and WW II, and into modern times. At West Garrison (Camp Reynolds) are some buildings, in what could be called Army Victorian, and a large brick warehouse near the shore that is a landmark for Sunday sailors. North Garrison became the chief Immigration Station on the coast, like Ellis Island in New York, and for thirty-five years processed the mostly Oriental influx. In the 1940s a movement began to preserve the island, and in 1954 part of it was first used as Angel Island State Park.

An Intimate Estuary Stroll

The walker's waterfront of Oakland has expanded from the historic precincts of Jack London Square to include access to quite a stretch of the water's edge. From several good spots on decks and docks, you can enjoy the nautical activity close at hand and its echo hard by on the Alameda shore — the real essence of the Estuary experience.

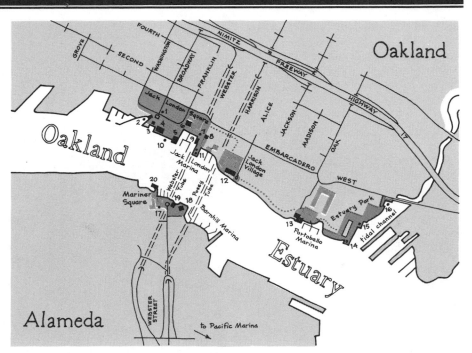

Jack London Square

The whole area where Jack London lurked as a juvenile and sailed as an oyster pirate in the 1890s is surfeited with mementos of Oakland's most famous literary light, starting with the bronze bust (1) at the foot of Broadway. Nearby you can get a good look at the Oakland fireboat (2). One of the smallest eating places in this extended tract of shops and restaurants is the Caffé Lido coffee house (3). More elegant restaurants are perched on the brink of the Estuary — The Sea Wolf, named for London's book (4), The Grotto (5), and The Mast (9). Above El Caballo restaurant (6), The Castaway sits as a penthouse atop the Port of Oakland

office building. Nearby is the dock and disembarkation point for wine and dine cruises (10) to Jack London Square.

Enhancing your waterfront browsing are the Klondike cabin (7) where London lived as a Yukon prospector in '98, a monument to this hometown boy made good; and the mast monument from the cruiser USS *Oakland,* commemorating his hometown; and Heinold's First and Last Chance, a funky landmark saloon (8). The sailboats and power boats of Jack London Marina surround the dock (11) on which are the Spice Box snack bar and Capt. Scotty's bait shop. Next door is the Metropolitan Yacht Club.

Jack London Village

Traversing the parking lot brings you to a confined quadrangle of shops, built in an ersatz style of rough grey boards and ornamental railroad cars, that is reminiscent more of transplanted mine workings from the Rocky Mountains than of anything even vaguely nautical. Two restaurants overlook the water (12) — Spider Healy, downstairs, and Sophies, upstairs. Of the other stalls in the labyrinth, perhaps the most interesting is Sherlock's Home, a smoke shop where you can find Sherlockian items, including a clever poster of Sherlock Holmes' England. At the foot of Alice Street is a landscaped mini-park.

Portobello Development

Following the path across the empty, open property beside Jack London Village, passing a derelict Santa Fe railroad ferry pier, you come to the modern Portobello apartment/office development. The Rusty Scupper restaurant (13) has a deck located beside the docks of Portobello Marina.

Estuary Park

A short walk takes you to the park at the confluence of the tidal channel from Lake Merritt with the Estuary. There is a fishing pier (14) with an ornate picnicking pergola nearby. The stepped wharf (15) has tie-ups for boats, and a boat launching ramp (16) is near the restrooms. Estuary Park will eventually be extended along the channel all the way to Lake Merritt. Crossing the channel leads to the industrial area along Embarcadero.

Mariner Square

So near, and yet so far that you have to drive. From the Nimitz Freeway, travel through the Webster Tube to get to Mariner Square in Alameda. The most engaging thing in the cluster of marine supply stores, yacht sales offices, and railroad car specialty shops (17) is seeing the masts of the sailboats parked on the Estuary. You can find sailing schools and charters. Restaurants are nestled beside the boats and boardwalk — the Ancient Mariner (18), the Barge Inn (19), and the Rusty Pelican (20). Adjacent is Barnhill Marina with its tired, mobile-homey style houseboats.

More of the Estuary is to be found on the following pages.

Embracing Embarcadero Cove

An earnest revitalization of the waterfront of Brooklyn Basin and Embarcadero Cove is underway through efforts of the Port of Oakland. The refurbishing and redevelopment over the next few years will encompass the stretch of shoreline from Ace McMurphy's restaurant at one end, all the way around the cove to Evans Radio Dock. It will consist of expanding a new marina, providing waterfront walkways and fishing piers, and encouraging the opening of more restaurants and boating businesses. The effect will be to enliven the area, make the enterprises already there blossom with activity, and enlarge the walker's scope and enjoyment of the Estuary.

Brooklyn Basin

The waters of Brooklyn Basin have a long maritime heritage. It is continuing in good health — ocean-going shipping stops at the Ninth Avenue Pier, pleasure boats berth at the docks of the marina along the north shore, and boat sales and repair yards flourish along the Embarcadero. Dining places brighten the area — Ace McMurphy's (1), The Ark (2), Barclay Jack's (3), and there is a small café called the Gang Plank (4).

Embarcadero Cove Marina

The Port of Oakland calls its new marina renovation Embarcadero Cove Marina. It is well underway and more berths still to be added. Lani Kai Harbor sits in the middle of this development. Nearby boat yards will be modernized. But the best embellishment is that more of the water's edge will be opened to public access with landscaped paths and fishing piers.

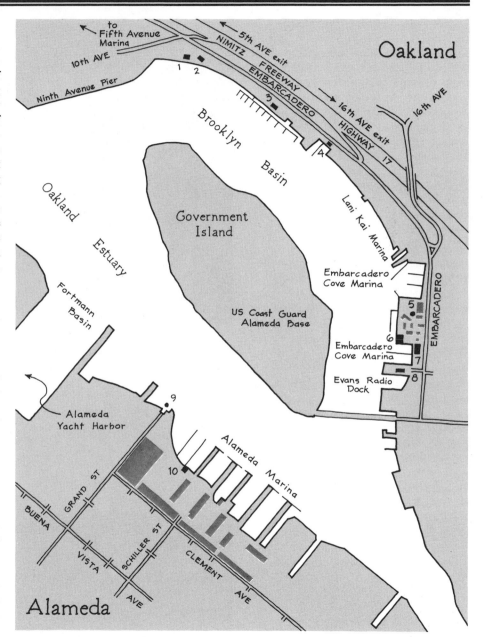

Embarcadero Cove Development

Embarcadero Cove (5) is a collection of buildings, most of them moved to the site from elsewhere and beautified with plantings and pathways. Among the vivid Victorians which have been turned into offices, you can find boat brokers and repair shops, and sailing lessons and rentals. Two restaurants overlook the masses of masts berthed at Embarcadero Cove Marina (privately operated) — Quinn's Lighthouse (6) and Victoria Station (7). Trainees from the Coast Guard base on Government Island sometimes perform their boat drills offshore.

Evans Radio Dock

Oakland's commercial fishing fleet berths at the Evans Radio Dock which is scheduled for remodeling in the grand redevelopment scheme. In the middle of the dock, with its gasoline pumps and fish, is a real waterfront café — The Dock (8).

Alameda Marina

Across the Estuary, beyond Government Island, is the conglomeration of buildings and boats at the Alameda Marina. Boat-building firms and yacht brokerages are represented here, and it is the home of the Island Yacht Club. To one side of the Marina, at the end of Grand Street, is the Alameda Municipal Boat Ramp (9). If you want to spend a little time at the Marina savoring the sailing environment, La Gondola Ristoranté (10), next to the boat basin, provides the perfect stopping place for a bite to eat.

Waterfront Window on the World

San Francisco's northern waterfront offers a waterside walk with a diversity unmatched any place else in the world. This walk takes you through our maritime history, it takes you through the myriad activities of the City, and it takes you from the crowded confines of our major tourist area through open park space to stand under the towering Golden Gate Bridge where the Pacific Ocean meets the Bay. Along the way are many vantage points to see the life, sports, commerce and moods of the Bay.

Golden Gate Promenade

A strip of the Golden Gate National Recreation Area runs along the water's edge from Aquatic Park to Fort Point. This Golden Gate Promenade is heavily used by walkers, runners and bicyclists. At one end is the historic 1860s harbor defense, Fort Point (1). During the bridge construction, a special arch was made to preserve the brick fort with its rickety lighthouse on top. The vista point (2) near the bridge toll plaza offers views of the bridge, a statue of Joseph B. Strauss, the bridge engineer, and you can look down on the fort. The old Navy mine-laying wharf (3) is now a fishing pier, and the nearby beach is good for bird-watching and flower-finding. The promenade continues past Crissy Field to the San Francisco Marina with a tiny beach (4), games area and snack bar. Across Marina Boulevard is the Palace of Fine Arts (5), the restoration of a building by architect Bernard Maybeck and gardens left over from the Panama-Pacific International Exposition of 1915. The Marina Green (6) is popular for fun and games — sunbathing, kite-flying and running the Parcourse. The San Francisco Marina (7) is full of boats, yacht clubs, fishing spots, and offers sailing lessons as well.

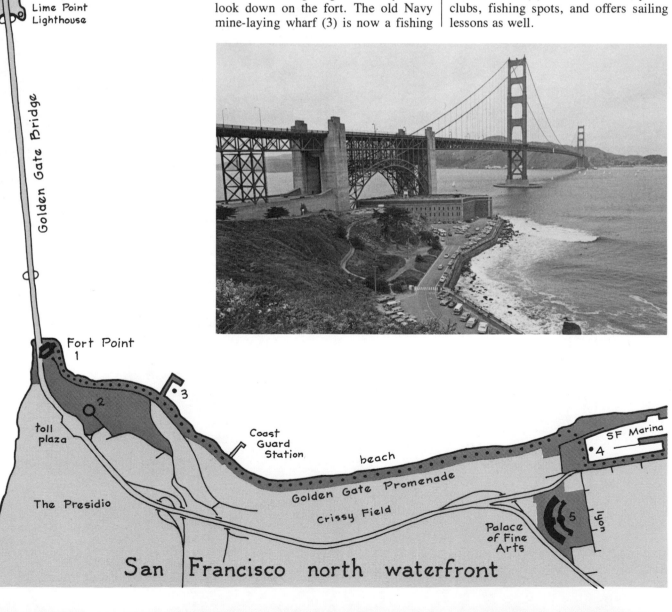

Lime Point Lighthouse

Golden Gate Bridge

Fort Point 1

toll plaza

The Presidio

Coast Guard Station

beach

Golden Gate Promenade

Crissy Field

SF Marina

Palace of Fine Arts

San Francisco north waterfront

Fort Mason

The green hillsides of the old Army base now bustle with the activities of the National Recreation Area. The embarkation piers (8) are used for performing arts, craft festivals and other special events. The headquarters of GGNRA (9) sits in the middle of Fort Mason. Programs are offered, and historic Army houses and the Oceanic Society offices are located nearby.

Aquatic Park

Sloping down the hill from Ghirardelli Square to the beach and lagoon is Aquatic Park, part of the GGNRA. One side of the lagoon is bounded by the curving Muni Pier (10) with its snack bar. Both it and the old Alcatraz Pier that juts west are good for fishing. In the park are the Maritime Museum (11) with its displays of West Coast shipping history, and the cable car turntable (12). At the other side of the lagoon is Hyde Street Pier (13) with five restored historic ships of the National Maritime Museum.

Fisherman's Wharf

The area called Fisherman's Wharf runs from the Cannery to Pier 43. Right in the middle is the basin where the commercial and sportfishing boats tie up. Of the already well-publicized attractions of the Wharf, only two restaurants are noted — Scoma's (14) and The Franciscan (15). At Pier 43½ you can board harbor cruises (for a tour of the world's greatest bay) and the Tiburon Ferry (check schedule). At Pier 43 are helicopter tours, the Alcatraz tour boat landing, and moored alongside, the historic windjammer *Balclutha* (16).

Pier 39

The new shop and restaurant complex has many attractions with dubious attractiveness, but there is a walkway around the pier for Bay-viewing and a small park next to The Embarcadero. On the second floor is perched the Eagle Café (17), and it is well worthwhile to visit this historic and beloved eatery. Down the way is another bar, the Crow's Nest (18), and beyond is Pier 35 where passenger liners berth to the delight of diners at the Peer Inn (19).

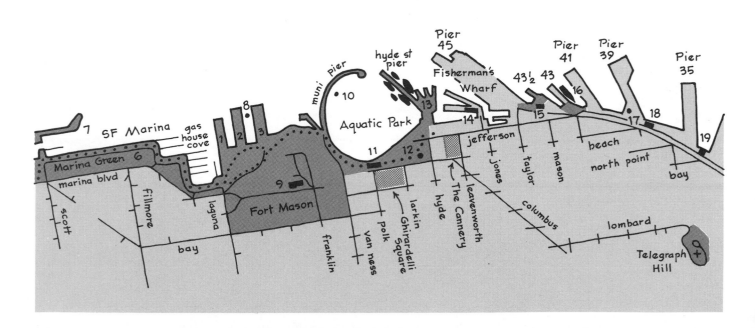

Rambling Round the Ferry Building

At the foot of Market Street, San Francisco's Ferry Building flourishes as it did in the '30s and '40s, the heyday of the ferryboat. A ferry terminal still operates here, close to BART, cable cars, and Market and Mission Street trolleys and buses. Because the Ferry Building is so accessible, it is a focal point for walking around the downtown bayfront of San Francisco. The waterfront of The Embarcadero, as depicted on the map, is a little more than a mile long.

Justin Herman Plaza

Across The Embarcadero from the Ferry Building, almost under the overhead freeway, is dazzling Justin Herman Plaza. An animated doorstep to the City, its paved terraces are filled with street merchants and lunchtime picnickers. Giving strength to its bustle are the stabilizing fixtures in the plaza — statues of Juan Bautista de Anza (1), founder of San Francisco; and Carlos III, the Spanish king who commanded the colonization (2). The impressive (and still controversial) design of the concrete Vaillancourt Fountain sculpture (4) is no longer completed by jets of water splashing in the pool. It has been turned off to conserve energy. You can get snacks at the Café de Wheels (3), and you can find grassy picnicking and frolicking around the stark tetrahedral space-frame gazebo (5). A Parcourse for joggers circumscribes the plaza.

The backdrop of the plaza includes the towering office slabs of Embarcadero Center, with cheerful stores and restaurants on interconnecting levels, as well as the fanciful Hyatt Regency Hotel. On the other side of the Hyatt Regency is the California Street Cable Car terminus (6), beside the stairs down to BART's Embarcadero Station.

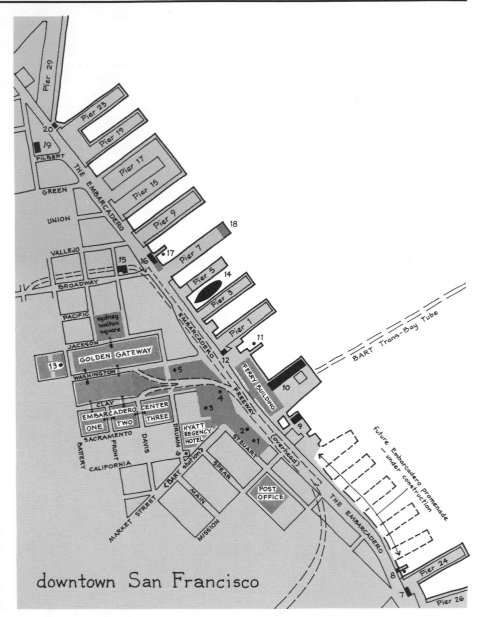

downtown San Francisco

Towards the Bay Bridge

South from the Ferry Building, The Embarcadero is not so pleasurable for walkers. The derelict piers are being removed, so that eventually sparkling views of the Bay will be available from an Embarcadero promenade yet to be built. Beyond, just under the San Francisco-Oakland Bay Bridge, is Carmen's café (7). Next door at a small dock (8), is the San Francisco fireboat, the *Phoenix*.

The Ferry Building

The precincts of the landmark Ferry Building, which survived the '06 fire and served as portal to the City before the advent of the bridges, are lively for waterfront browsing and still serve ferry traffic on the Bay. Inside at the State Division of Mines and Geology office, you can find field guides and pamphlets for geologic explorations. Sinbad's Pier 2 restaurant (9) has outdoor eating space at the edge of the Bay. Behind the Ferry Building is the huge platform surrounding the BART tube ventilator. A new ferry terminal (10) recently opened on it. The ferryboats for Sausalito and Larkspur land here. The Tiburon boats (weekday commuting) land at the stubby dock (11) on the north side of the Ferry Building. The Pier One Lunch (12) is handy for ferry passengers.

Further Feasting

If you roam away from the cafés and restaurants in the downtown office buildings, you can find other dining spots along The Embarcadero: the huddled railroad cars of Victoria Station (15), the elegance of The Waterfront (16), the eccentric Mildred Pierce's (19), and the wharfside Pier 23 Café (20).

Other Favorite Waterfront Haunts

As an aid to your San Francisco Bay explorations, a visit to the fifth floor of the US Custom House (13) is worthwhile. The USGS map sales office has a variety of maps of the Bay (open weekdays, see the section *View Points*). Under the apartment towers of the Golden Gateway is another grassy picnic spot, Sydney Walton Square. Berthed at Pier 5 is the former ferryboat *Klamath* (14), which now serves as an industrial design office. Outside The Waterfront restaurant, the harbor pilot boats are moored (17). These boats put the pilots onboard ships wending their way in and out of the Golden Gate. At the end of parking lot Pier 7 is a section for fishermen (18). Red Stack tugboats tie up on both sides of Pier 9 when they are not towing barges or pushing ships into berths.

Wandering in Alviso

For the seeker of historic spots, the community of Alviso lies at a remote, nearly unknown corner of the Bay. Along the river south of town was *El Embarcadero de Santa Clara*, a thriving seaport in Spanish-Mexican days and a much larger port than Yerba Buena (now San Francisco). It was the shipping point for most of the lands around the South Bay: hides and tallow in the 1830s, quicksilver in the 1840s, and trade in the 1850s when San Jose was briefly the state capital. Alviso was the first incorporated town in California, and the years 1850-61 saw its greatest period of development. At the turn of the century scow schooners like the *Alma* carried crops from the Santa Clara Valley and products from Alviso's fisheries and canneries to all parts of the Bay. A few remnant landmarks quietly mark those times.

The most notable aspect of present-day Alviso is the system of levees and dikes that surround the town. Over the years wells have removed underground water, causing the land to subside as much as ten feet. Now you can stand on the levee at the end of Catherine Street and see where the old shoreline once was near Highway 237. Then turn north and

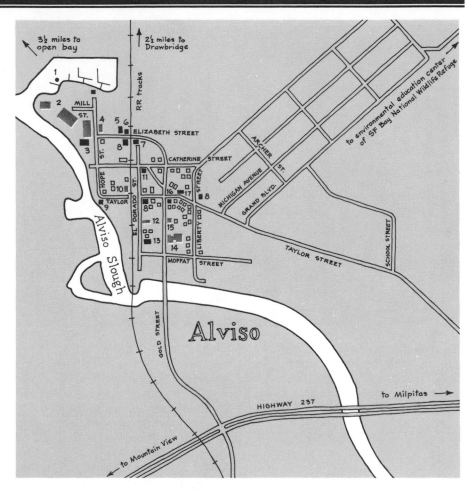

Railroads by-passed Alviso and diverted shipping trade in the 1860s. The old South Pacific Coast Railway ran a line through town in 1876 which briefly halted the town's decline. The small frame railroad station (7) was built in 1904, and is now a residence. Three restaurants (8) may be characterized as seafood grottoes. For simpler fare, there is Rosita's grocery and café (16). The Henry Wade House (11) is an early example of prefab building. It was shipped around the Horn from New England and assembled here in 1851. The brick H.G. Wade Warehouse (13) was built in 1851. It was used to store coaches of the San Jose & East Oakland Stage Line, one of which is now in the Wells Fargo History Room in San Francisco.

Other places in town: the Mudflat Pottery Works (10); a foundry (12); the Alviso Family Health Center (14), built by volunteers in 1966; the fire station (15); and the general store and post office (17). Directly north of town, two and a half miles along the railroad tracks, is the ghost town of Drawbridge, abandoned and sinking into the salt marsh. An environmental education center for the San Francisco Bay National Wildlife Refuge is being constructed at the northeast edge of town.

gaze across three and a half miles of marshland towards the open waters of San Franciso Bay.

The old town has fallen from grace, but it still has vivacity. Along the waterfront of Alviso Slough and the marina you can see enterprising boat building, trimaran construction, and other evidence that sailing is the way of life here. At one end of Hope Street, Alviso Marina (1) has berthing places for boats and a launching ramp. In an area by the slough (2) many boats are being built and berthed — some at JC Boatworks. On the other bank of the slough is a houseboat and cruiser village. Some of the boatworks property has been acquired by the federal goverment for future development as part of the San Francisco Bay National Wildlife Refuge. The Bayside Cannery (3) is a brick warehouse with wood superstructure. This old pickle works, built in 1906, is also included in this federal area. Sitting in faded splendor at the other end of Hope Street, below the levee, is the South Bay Yacht Clubhouse (9).

There are other attractions in the six or nine square blocks of the main part of Alviso. A gallery (4) offers art and antiques. The Tilden House (5) is an incongruous fancy Victorian, built in 1887 by Susan Tilden and still owned by her descendants. Smack beside the railroad tracks is Laine's Grocery (6), built in 1851 and showing every sign of its age. Sometime after it was built, it was moved to the site by Susan Tilden to be Tilden's Store. Now it is Alviso Antiques, offering Lionel Trains and other items — some not so antique.

Dining and Drinking on the Waterfront

When I went looking for the waterfront the easiest first place to find it was over clinking ice cubes in a bar. But to float this project, I had to get past the swinging doors and out to the softer salt water. (Incidentally, I only found one establishment that retains its swinging doors. A couple of other places didn't seem to have any doors at all.)

At first I thought a sort of dining top ten would be possible, to give the absolutely best spots for a waterfront meal. Then, as I discovered more taverns and bistros hidden behind warehouses and boat yards, it became obvious that the list would be very long. (I even left out a few places to keep the list from becoming a "hot one hundred.") With the list looming large, I solidified my criteria. First, the establishment must be on what I consider a shoreline, maritime or waterfront area. Second, it must serve food and/or drink. Keep it simple and you can't go wrong. As you can imagine, the variety in ninety-four eating places on all parts of the Bay is extensive. And vary they do, from the dive to the divine.

Many of the restaurants, bars, cafés and snack bars listed here have Bay views. In fact quite a few derive their custom geographically, from being at a harbor. Others service the needs of adjacent maritime activity and therefore may be stuck at the end of a looming cargo pier and have no view at all. Some shoreline places have boat docking for weekend sailors who often end up awash at the bar.

Like restaurants anywhere, those on San Francisco Bay range in style from merchant kitsch to the unique. Several places are pieces of business empires, likely and unlikely combinations under a single corporate banner with, and without, flagships. Of the Bay's restaurants,

approximately forty percent are all the same. No matter what kind of "instant image" embellishment the interiors display, the food is just what you can get someplace else, just fine thank you, but not worth a special trip for dinner. Several others are definitely worth a special trip from anywhere in the area for the food and the ambience. Others are more utilitarian and give good value for breakfast or for lunch when you're hanging around the docks or a marina.

For further exploration of San Francisco Bay, there are lunch and dinner cruises which are described in the section *Cruising the Bay*. If your're nearby and are desperate for some refreshment, a few marina snack bars are described in the section *Marinas*.

In the more popular visitor precincts, I made no attempt to include all the restaurants, merely the ones near the water. Most of those excluded have no connection with the Bay. And if it's seafood you crave, then look elsewhere, because almost all the really good seafood places are some distance from the water.

Some places changed the menu or the atmosphere to attract more patrons, some remodeled to change the facilities or services, and a few havens vanished while I was doing my survey. Such are the vicissitudes of victualing.

My waistline is in danger, and I have courted liver failure, but the following are the places I found for dining and drinking and testing the moods of the waterfront.

A gastro-geographical footnote to San Francisco: On the City's waterfront, piers are numbered from the Ferry Building at the foot of Market Street. North toward Fisherman's Wharf, the odd numbers go from 1 to more or less 47. South toward Hunters Point, the even numbers (with many gaps) go from 2 to more or less 96.

Marin County

Sausalito

Valhalla Inn

201 Bridgeway. 332-1792. This establishment of Sally Stanford's is a hideaway in the Old Town section of Sausalito in a building erected in the 1870s that has been in turn a beer garden, a saloon and a speakeasy. The menu offers beef, chops and crab legs — dinners include stroganoff, Idaho trout, sole and stuffed pork chops — in a Victorian setting of antiques and leaded-glass lamps. Evening piano music complements the view across the Bay of Angel Island and the Berkeley Hills. Brunch, lunch and dinner are served; reservations are recommended; credit cards are accepted. Closed Mondays; other days 10 am-midnight; dinner served 'til midnight; weekday brunch Tuesdays-Saturdays 11 am-3 pm; Sunday brunch 10 am-4 pm; bar.

The Trident

558 Bridgeway (downstairs). 332-1334. After a lamentable hiatus, this unequaled natural food restaurant and its natural waitresses are once again dispensing delicious food in a hard-core hand-made atmosphere, complete with sunlit deck and a view of Angel Island, the City and all the ferry and sail activity of the Sausalito waterfront. This is the well-known place for celebrity-watching, both major (writers) and minor (movie stars). Extra special lunches and dinners are served; jazz music Tuesday through Friday evenings. No reservations; credit cards accepted. Closed Mondays; weekdays 11 am-11 pm; Fridays and Saturdays 'til midnight; opens Sundays at 10 am; bar open 'til 2 am.

Ondine

558 Bridgeway (upstairs). 332-0791. Easily the classiest of waterfront restaurants, Ondine posts a dress code on the front door. Don't be caught with your denim cuff links on, if you're planning to dine here. The building is a former clubhouse of the San Francisco Yacht Club until it moved to Belvedere in 1927. Award-winning French cuisine (beef, crab legs, pheasant, capon and poissons) is featured, with prices to match. It's worth a special trip. There is a Bay view from the lounge. Dinner is served; credit cards are accepted; reservations are advisable. Open every day 5 pm-10:30 pm; bar.

Scoma's

588 Bridgeway. 332-9551. Another "dock" restaurant, Scoma's building (circa 1904) was once a boat rental office. Italian seafood and steak are on the menu. There is a view of Angel Island from this windowed jewel box. Lunch on Mondays and Saturdays; dinner on the other days; no reservations; credit cards accepted. Mondays and Saturdays 11:30 am-11 pm; Tuesdays through Fridays 6-11 pm; Sundays 2-10 pm; bar.

Slinkey's El Monte

660 Bridgeway (upstairs, hanging over the water). 332-3073. For a restaurant with the worst-sounding name in the region, the food is not so bad. However, you have to keep in mind that you are eating at a "casual dining concept" — if you would rather eat at a restaurant, there are plenty of those down the street. On the overwrought menu you eventually find a list of not-too-expensive items — sandwiches, omelettes, fruit and cheese board, shrimp "louie," quiches and crêpes for lunch, "light dinners," and for dinner fish, veal, steak and their specialty, paella. The deck provides close-up views of the ferry landing, sailboats, and across the Bay to Angel Island and San Francisco. Brunch, lunch and dinner; reservations and credit cards are accepted; jazz music on weekends. Open every day; lunch 11 am-5 pm; dinner 5-10 pm, 'til 11 on Fridays and Saturdays; weekend brunch 10:30 am-3:30 pm; bar 'til 2 am.

The Spinnaker

Off Bridgeway on Anchor Street (beyond all the parking lots). 332-1500. This restaurant is right beside the yacht harbor, stuck out on a point on pilings over the water, like a long glass centipede, near the ferry landing. It has a very close view down Richardson Bay and across to Belvedere and Angel Island. The fare is fish and shell fish, meat and poultry, but the preparation does not match the delicious view. Reservations preferred; credit cards accepted. Open every day for lunch and dinner; lunch from 11 am; dinner 5-10 pm; Saturday, Sunday and holiday bruncheon 11 am-3 pm; bar open 'til midnight.

Flynn's Landing

303 Johnson Street (off Bridgeway, behind the Post Office). 332-0131. On the second floor, overlooking Pelican Yacht Harbor, this restaurant offers seafood and steaks, or you can choose from a different special every day, as well as Boston clam chowder, prawns, crab legs, louis, hot sandwiches, abalone sandwich. Inside you find a casual atmosphere of rough, weathered woodwork, brass ceiling fans, old bottles and decoys. Front windows slide open for a little breeze on warm days. Views are of the marina, Richardson Bay and all the sailboats stretching to Belvedere. An outside deck is planned on the sunny side. Reservations for three or more and credit cards are accepted. Open every day; weekdays 11:30 am-11 pm; Saturday and Sunday brunch or regular menu from 11 am, Sundays 'til 10 pm; bar 'til 2 am.

Zack's

Off Bridgeway at Turney Street. 332-9779. Nestled next to the water, Zack's has large rooms and a patio for alfresco dining. Line-up-by-the-cook cafeteria service for almost anything that cooks on a grill, like hamburgers, sirloin, beef and shrimp teriyaki. No reservations or credit cards; band for dancing nearly every night. Open every day 11 am-2 am; breakfast on Saturdays, Sundays and holidays from 10 am; lunch served 'til 2:30 pm; dinner the rest of the time; bar.

The Tides

Off Bridgeway at Turney Street. 332-0511. A seafood grill that has complete fish and shellfish dinners, house and daily specials, along with hot and cold sandwiches, a couple of steaks, salads and omelettes. The food is as good as the view, which is of the docks and sailboats on Richardson Bay (there is docking for diners). Brunch is fresh fruit, muffins, strudel, pommes frites, omelettes and other egg dishes. They have a nice outdoor patio for fine-weather dining. Upstairs is Wimbledon's disco with music from 9:30-1:30 nightly and Monday night football on a large tv screen. Major credit cards and reservations (including brunch) are accepted. Open every day; weekday food service 11 am-11 pm; weekends from 10 am; Sundays, extensive buffet brunch 10 am-3 pm; bar open 'til 2 am.

Sausalito Food Company

Foot of Harbor Drive (by Clipper Yacht Harbor). 332-0535. Set next to the parking lot of a huge marina, this place provides breakfast and lunch specialties — omelettes and sandwiches — but no view of the water. Sausalito Food Co. is characterized by a very small bar and an attractive solarium dining room which leaks when it rains. Credit cards accepted; no reservations. Open every day for breakfast, lunch and dinner; Mondays and Tuesdays 7 am-6 pm; Wednesdays through Sundays 7 am-10 pm.

Tiburon

Tiburon Tommie's

41 Main Street. 435-1229. Polynesian and Cantonese dishes are served on the waterfront of Tiburon with views of the Corinthian Yacht Club and across the swirls of the Bay. Reservations recommended; credit cards accepted. Open every day; 10 am-2 am; dinners stop at 9:30 pm; bar open later.

Thirty-nine Main

39 Main Street. 789-9867. The regular menu is steak and fish, but Sunday afternoons and evenings hamburgers go with the musical group. On Monday nights from 6 to 10 there is a special spaghetti feed to go with a banjo hootenanny. The other evenings have piano music in the bar. An outside deck lets you watch the tangled sailboats in the cove and Angel Island with the City beyond. Reservations for Tuesday through Saturday nights and credit cards are accepted. Open every day 10 am-2 am; dinner from 6 to 11 on non-special menu nights; bar open 'til later.

Sweden House Bakery

35 Main Street. 435-9767. This small shop with exceptionally good baked goods also has several tables and a small, sunny deck outside. Sample the soups, salads and sandwiches with, of course, a delicious small cake for dessert. Closed Mondays; open 9 am-5 pm on all the other days.

Sam's Anchor Café

27 Main Street. 435-4527. Sam's carries on the traditions of casual atmosphere, unhurried service and quality food (consider the special eggs Benedict sauce) that were started at this same place more than fifty-eight years ago by a Maltese immigrant, Sam Vella. This love for tradition — though it encompasses retaining the original front bar and swinging entrance doors and the hodgepodge but out-of-true carpentry — no longer goes as far as running an extremely fast boat out of the Golden Gate to collect illegal Canadian booze. The

original customers, yachtsmen, have now turned themselves into "boaters," but they still love a good drink. Sam's has a lot of dock space for guests. The primary attraction is an afternoon on the large deck with a terrific view across the Bay. Reservations for inside only (not the deck); credit cards accepted. Open every day of the year except Christmas; lunch served from 10 or 11 am; dinner served 'til 10 pm; Saturdays and Sundays 9 am-10 pm; bar 'til 2 am.

The Dock

25 Main Street (upstairs). 435-4559. A definite nautical flavor dominates this restaurant's décor as well as its menu of hot luncheon entrées, seafood (including cioppino), sandwiches and savory meat dishes (sirloin, duckling). The flavor continues to the large outside deck with a view of the guest dock, the yacht harbor and the San Francisco skyline. Musical entertainment in the lounge every night, dancing Thursday-Sunday evenings; credit cards and reservations are accepted. Open daily (closed Tuesdays and Wednesdays in winter); weekdays from 11 am for lunch and dinner; weekends from 10 am for brunch and dinner; bar stays open later.

Sabella's

9 Main Street. 435-2636. A bright new place decorated with marine artifacts. Going in the front door, you confront the retail fish market, next the oyster bar, then the lounge with a deck outside. The food maintains this piscatorial motif, leavening it with Italian dishes. The dining room is upstairs with an additional deck to take advantage of the view of Angel Island and across the Bay to the City. "Mellow jazz" music in the lounge Fridays-Sundays; credit cards and reservations accepted. Open every day 11 am-11 pm; lunch 'til 3 pm, dinner all day; bar.

Carlos O'Brian's

5 Main Street. 435-3101. The deck of Carlos O'Brian's greets the traveler on the Tiburon Ferry as it eases into its slip. The restaurant is part of a chain which originated in Mexico City. Sauces are emphasized in the cuisine which is described as "continental with a Mexican flair." In addition to appetizers, soups and salads, there are 58 entrees. Credit cards accepted. No reservations. Open every day; lunch from 11:30 am; dinner 6-10:30 pm weekdays, 'til 11:30 on weekends; weekend brunch from 10 am; bar.

The Caprice

2000 Paradise Drive. 435-3400. This highly-rated restaurant is east of the main hub of activity in Tiburon, past the desolate area that was the Northwestern Pacific RR yards, but not far to walk from the ferry. It has a view across the maelstrom of Raccoon Strait past Angel Island to the Golden Gate. The Caprice is luxurious and expensive with specialties that include fresh fish of the season, fresh salmon, prawns, duckling, ox tongue, sweetbreads, veal and scallops. Parking is difficult; credit cards are accepted; reservations are recommended. Open daily for lunch and dinner; noon-3 pm and 5:30-11 pm; bar open 'til 2 am on weekends.

Larkspur

Victoria Station

17 East Sir Francis Drake Boulevard (Ferry Terminal exit). 461-4343. One of a franchise operation with three locations on the Bay waterfront, it features the unusual architecture of cabooses and boxcars with "treasured antiques from British railroading." (Which indicates that there are no longer any trains left in Britain, either.) The company headquarters peers down from the wooded knoll across the road with a cautionary eye. Hamburgers for lunch, prime rib, steak, shrimp and a special salad bar are the highlights for diners. There is no view of the water, but it's across the parking lot from the Ferry Terminal and, while not the only place to walk from there, it is closer than the jumble of the Larkspur Landing development. Reservations are accepted only for more than ten; and you can pop for dinner with plastic. Open every day; lunch 11:30 am-2:30 pm; mid-day 2:30-5 pm; dinner 5:30-11 pm ('til midnight on Fridays and Saturdays): weekend brunch 11 am-3 pm; bar open 'til 1:30 am weekends, 'til 12:30 am weekdays, and 'til midnight on Sundays.

San Rafael

Pier 15 Restaurant

15 Harbor Street (off Francisco Boulevard). 453-9978. A pleasant pub with dark, vaguely Germanic bar and dining rooms attached. The windows in the back room and the deck overlook the San Rafael Yacht Harbor. Boat dock for diners. Reservations not needed; credit cards accepted. Open every day for breakfast, lunch and dinner; 8 am-2 am.

Dominic's Harbor Restaurant

507 Francisco Boulevard. 456-1383. Seafood (from their own boats) and Italian specialties head the menu. Located on the San Rafael Canal with a view of the docked sailboats. There is a guest dock, and during the summer a patio is available for dining and drinking. You are entertained with organ music on Friday and Saturday nights; reservations recommended; credit cards accepted. Open every day 11 am-11 pm; weekday lunch 11:30 am-4:30 pm; weekend brunch 10 am-3 pm; dinner 5-8 pm; bar is open later.

Loch Lomond Marina Snack Bar

At Loch Lomond Marina. 457-2460. A comfortable snack bar with several tables and a counter. You can order sandwiches and beer or the specialties — salads, piroshki and borscht. The marina is right outside the windows. Open every day 8 am-5 pm (open early at 7 am on Saturdays).

Solano County

Vallejo

Harbor House (Remark's)

Harbor Way (at Vallejo Marina). 707-642-8984. A standard menu in a new restaurant with mildly Victorian décor. The view is of the marina and across the Napa River to the Naval Shipyard. Musical entertainment is provided by a quartet or a trio every night of the week. Reservations are accepted; credit cards taken. Open every day; lunch 11:30 am-2:30 pm; dinner 5-10 pm; Sunday brunch 10 am-2 pm; bar.

The Wharf

Mare Island Way. 707-648-1966. The Wharf offers seafood and steaks beside the Mare Island commuter ferry. Vaguely nautical ornamentation, with a view across Mare Island Strait to the Naval Shipyard. Music on Friday and Saturday nights; reservations and credit cards accepted. Open every day; breakfast Mondays through Fridays 6-10 am; lunch and dinner 11:30 am-9 pm ('til 10 pm on Fridays and Saturdays); bar open 'til 2 am.

The Grotto

3 Maryland Street. 707-644-4743. At one end of Vallejo's shoreline promenade by the boat ramp, this restaurant can be termed old-fashioned in the best sense of the word — the atmosphere and service are not easily found any more. It has a sunny dining room with a view across the water to the Mare Island Naval Shipyard. The name implies seafood and you find oysters, crab, lobster, shrimp and fish on the menu as well as steak, sandwiches and ordinary breakfast. You could park your boat at the boat ramp and enjoy a couple of outside tables by the restaurant. Open every day 6 am-10 pm.

Contra Costa County

Crockett

Nantucket Fish Company

Crockett exit becomes Pomona Street, north on Port Street, west on Dowrelio Drive (below Carquinez Bridge). 787-2233. Set beneath the towering bridge, the restaurant has close-up views of the narrow Carquinez Strait and, silhouetted against the heights on the opposite shore, the many passing boats and ships. The seafood has a definite East Coast style and quality, but is not worth a special trip. Outside tables for nice days and occasional entertainment. Reservations for large groups only; credit cards are accepted. Open every day for lunch and dinner; 11:30 am-9 pm ('til 10 on Fridays and Saturdays); weekend breakfast 6-10 am; bar open 'til 12:30 am Friday and Saturday nights.

Rodeo

Rodeo Marina Coffee Shop

Foot of Pacific Avenue, at Rodeo Marina. Plunked down in the middle of a sprawling marina, this is very much a coffee shop, with a counter and several tables that give a view of the edge of the marina. It serves good breakfasts, sandwiches and lunches. Open every day 6 am-2:30 pm.

Richmond

The Galley

At Point San Pablo Yacht Harbor (Point Molate exit off Highway 17 and go to the end of the peninsula). 232-4481. This is a grill hovering at the side of the yacht harbor. It has a view of the boats at the edge of San Pablo Bay. It serves breakfast and lunch along with beer. Closed Mondays; Tuesdays-Fridays 6 am-5 pm; Saturdays and Sundays open from 5 am-6 pm.

Alameda County

Berkeley

The Landing

200 Marina Boulevard (in the Marriott Inn, Berkeley Marina). 548-7920. A typical motel restaurant serving breakfast, lunch and dinner (specialty, medallion steak) with a good view of the marina, the Bay and the Golden Gate from the corner dining room. There is a deck for fresh air imbibing and a guest dock for boaters. Music for disco dancing in The Bridge (bar-lounge) every night. Credit cards accepted; reservations advised for dinner, for lunch more than five people only. Open every day; lunch 11:30 am-3 pm, dinner 5:30-10 pm ('til 11 on Saturdays); Sunday *prix fixe* brunch 11 am-2:30 pm.

Solomon Grundy's

Foot of University Avenue, Berkeley Marina. 548-1876. This restaurant serves breakfast, lunch and dinner from a menu that leaps from prime rib, to a seafood platter, to black bean soup, to bouillabaisse. A wharfy looking place, it has a looming, dark dining room where you have a view of the Bay and one along the Berkeley Pier which plunges like a finger straight toward the Golden Gate. Piano music in the bar every night; credit cards accepted; no reservations. Open every day; breakfast 9:30-11:15 am; lunch 11:30 am-4:30 pm; dinner 4:30-10 pm ('til 11 on Fridays and Saturdays); weekend brunch 10 am-3 pm; bar.

Hs Lordships

199 Seawall Drive, Berkeley Marina. 843-2733. An elaborate restaurant with authentically (''elegant plastic'') English hunt club embellishments, serving blandsville food in a banqueting parlor

(''rubber chicken'') atmosphere. Offerings are of the steak and seafood variety, burgers and omelettes, fish and shish. Views of the magnificent Berkeley skyline and Emeryville. Guitar music in the lounge; credit cards accepted; reservations advised on weekends. Open for lunch and dinner daily; 11:30 am-3 pm; 5-10 pm ('til 11 on Fridays and Saturdays); Sunday brunch 10:30 am-3 pm; bar 'til 2 am.

Emeryville

Angelina's

5901 Frontage Road (near the freeway in Emeryville). 547-2829. A restaurant featuring seafood along with pasta and beef. The view is north up the Bay and of the distant Berkeley Marina. A small wharf is a nice place for walking over the water. Credit cards accepted; reservations may be made. Open every day; weekdays lunch 11:30 am-2:30 pm; oyster bar from 5 or 6 to 9 pm; weekdays dinner 2:30-10 pm ('til 11 on Fridays and Saturdays); Saturdays and Sundays open at 4 pm; bar 'til 2 am weekends.

Charley Brown's

1890 Powell Street (behind Angelina's in Emeryville). 658-6580. Set on the water on the north side of the peninsula, from this place you can see north to the Berkeley Marina and up the Bay. A small wharf is fine for walking over the water. The menu has prime rib, sole, chicken, filet strips, scampi, steak 'n' lobster, sirloin, and crab. This is a tv football watching kind of place. On Friday and Saturday nights music is provided for entertainment and dancing. Reservations are accepted for dinner; credit cards accepted. Open every day; lunch 11:30 am-2:30 pm; Sunday brunch 10:30 am-2:30 pm; dinner 5:30-10 pm ('til 11 on Fridays and Saturdays); bar.

Trader Vic's

9 Anchor Drive (near Watergate Apartment complex). 653-3400. This is merely a branch of the famous restaurant of the same name (the real one is in the City). Only complete dinners are served — Polynesian, Oriental, Continental and Island. You have a beautiful view of Point San Pablo across the Bay. Reservations recommended; credit cards accepted. Open every day; lunch weekdays 11:30 am-3 pm; dinner from 5 pm 'til midnight (Saturdays 'til 1 am); Sundays 3-10 pm; bar.

Casa Maria

Foot of Powell Street at the end of Emeryville peninsula. 654-1794. Boasting an extensive Mexican food menu, this restaurant also has dramatic décor to match. The interesting menu combinations may be more expensive than the usual Mexican restaurant. There are terrific views west across the Bay to the Golden Gate beyond Treasure Island. Reservations and credit cards accepted. Open every day 11:30 am-11:30 pm; dinner from 4 pm; "El Bruncho" Sundays 10 am-3 pm; bar 'til midnight ('til 1 am Fridays and Saturdays).

Oakland

Oyster Pirates Store
(Port View Park Snack Bar)

Foot of Seventh Street (at the end of the Oakland Mole). At Oakland's Seventh Street Terminal in the small park with a viewing tower and a fishing pier. You can get food (sandwiches), beer and bait and take it to the small picnic area to feast and fish. A terrific view of the shipping and sailboats entering the Estuary and the Bay Bridge and the City skyline. Open 9 am-6:30 pm every day.

Oakland / near Jack London Square

In the area are many more eating places with varying culinary accomplishments, but only those next to the water are listed here.

Caffé Lido

At the end of Broadway in Jack London Square. 451-8743. A small coffee shop at the apex of Jack London Square. It serves coffee, sandwiches and beer at several tables inside or to take away by perambulators of the waterfront. Open every day 11 am-4 pm; 'til 6 pm on Fridays and 'til 11 pm on Saturdays.

Sea Wolf

41 Jack London Square, at the Estuary end of the square. 444-3456. Named after Jack London's well-known story, and displaying historical photographs of the author, this restaurant fits well into the scene of Jack London Square. The menu is about equally split between seafood and meat dishes. The view is across the Estuary toward Mariner Square on Alameda. Piano music every night except Monday; reservations recommended; credit cards accepted. Open every day 11:30 am-11 pm; bar 'til 2 am.

The Grotto
(Oakland, Seafood, Fishermen's)

65 Jack London Square, on the south corner. 893-2244. Built on a pier over the Estuary, this restaurant has views of the marina and across the channel to Mariner Square. You can enjoy a drink in the bar or dine on a selection of meats, poultry, veal, crab, fish, prawns and shrimp, oysters, lobster, abalone or pasta. No reservations are taken on Fridays, Saturdays or Sundays; credit cards accepted. Open every day 11:30 am-10 pm ('til 11 on Fridays and Saturdays); Sunday brunch (specializing in omelettes) is served from noon 'til 2 pm.

El Caballo

70 Jack London Square. 835-9260. This Mexican restaurant is in a large building at a corner of the square. It is heavily decorated with antiques, tiles and high arches. A small patio, almost by the waterside, has fair weather views of the boats docked in the Estuary. The menu is large with regular dinners and some delicious specials, although a little pricey for a Mexican restaurant. Music in the evenings from a Mexican guitarist. Reservations accepted for six or more; credit cards accepted. Open every day; lunch 10:30 am-3 pm; dinner 3-10:30 pm; Sunday champagne brunch 10 am-2 pm; bar.

The Castaway

66 Jack London Square. 835-8474. To get a little distance from the eddying Estuary and a better view of the hustling harbor, take the glass elevator by El Caballo and ride up to the Castaway's penthouse dining room. Try an item from their selection of seafood, or steaks, or Polynesian food. Thursdays, Fridays and Saturdays music is provided; credit cards and reservations accepted. Open every day; weekday lunch 11:30 am-2:30 pm; weekday dinner 5-10 pm; weekend dinner 3-10 pm; bar open later than dining room, especially on weekends.

The Mast

75 Jack London Square (on the south side, by the marina). 465-2188. You have your choice of seafood or steaks in this nautically decorated restaurant. For the gourmet, there is even an oyster bar. Music Wednesday-Sunday nights; reservations and credit cards accepted. View of the boats at berth in the adjacent marina. Open every day; 11:30 am-10 pm ('til 11 on Fridays and Saturdays, 'til 9 on Sundays); Saturday and Sunday brunch 10 am-1 pm; bar.

Heinold's First and Last Chance Saloon

South side of Jack London Square. Heinold's announces that it was established in 1883, and when you see it, you will agree that it looks like it. This spavined, authentic relic saloon is well-advertised as a hangout of Jack London in his youth, and this anachronism looks askance at the modern developments that have taken over the waterfront. Inside it's messy and small, so small that you can work up a good thirst, or a good crowd, but not both. (With places this small, no wonder any community of the 1890s had scores of saloons.) It's the kind of place to take visiting tourists for a look in and a quick quaff. Closed Mondays; weekdays 5 pm-1 am; Fridays and Saturdays 10 am-2 am; Sunday 10 am-1 am.

Spider Healy

In Jack London Village, south of Jack London Square (end of Alice Street). 893-8030. This restaurant, named after a colorful wharf rat friend of Jack London's when he was an oyster pirate, features a seafood menu, complemented by nautical decoration. The view is of houseboats afloat along the Alameda shore. Guitar music on Friday and Saturday nights; reservations and credit cards accepted. Open every day; buffet lunch 11:30 am-2:30 pm; dinner 5:30-10 pm; Sunday champagne buffet *prix fixe* brunch 10 am-3 pm; Sunday dinner 4-10 pm; bar 11:30 am-midnight ('til 2 am on Fridays and Saturdays).

Sophies

In Jack London Village (upstairs), south of Jack London Square (end of Alice Street). 893-8020. Rough-sawn funky, with stained glass, fans and an Estuary view, this restaurant offers broil, seafood and chopped meat. The name allegedly comes from a sealer that Jack London sailed on before his writing days, the *Sophia Sutherland*. Credit cards accepted; reservations suggested. Open every day; lunch 11:30 am-4 pm, dinner 5-10 pm ('til 11 on Fridays and Saturdays); Sunday dinner 4-10 pm; bar opens weekdays 11:30 am and weekends 2 pm.

The Rusty Scupper

15 Embarcadero West, south of Jack London Square at Portobello (end of Oak Street). 465-0105. A modern restaurant with redwood beamed ceilings and skylights to let you peer at your choice of prime rib, steak or seafood. However, for my taste the food matches the architecture — overdone. It has an outside deck for drinking with a view across the Estuary to Alameda, and a guest dock for boaters. It sponsors (in conjunction with a radio station) a bathtub regatta in the splash of the Estuary. Country music Thursdays through Saturdays; reservations and credit cards accepted. Open every day; dinner 5:30-10:30 pm ('til 11:30 on Fridays and Saturdays); weekdays lunch 11:30 am-2 pm; bar open at noon.

Oakland / near Embarcadero Cove

Ace McMurphy's

1103 Embarcadero. 893-6700. Your waiter/waitress is your "serving partner," you make selections from a paddleball paddle menu — no sizzling serves, no rippling lobs, no deadly drop shots, just mediocre food. The décor is supposed to be tennis-y, but it is admirably lacking in follow through. The dining room is a light and airy greenhouse overlooking Brooklyn Basin with Campari umbrellas. There are sandwiches, burgers and salads for lunch and dinner; veal, beef, steaks and fish on the menu for dinner; Monday night football and Tuesday dinner specials; and on weekends, a champagne brunch. Open for lunch and dinner every day; 11 am-11 pm; bar.

The Ark

1111 Embarcadero. 893-5900. This restaurant has an extensive seafood menu (fresh fish daily). Also there is a guest dock and a view of the boats in the marina slips, and across the waterway, of Government Island and Alameda. No reservations; credit cards accepted. Open every day; Mondays through Saturdays 11:30 am-11 pm (dinner after 3 pm); Sundays 2-10 pm; bar 'til 12 or 1 am.

Barclay Jack's

1211 Embarcadero. 261-3287. Dine on prime rib, steak or seafood with a view through the marina's wavering masts to Government Island opposite. Music after 9:30 pm Thursdays through Saturdays; credit cards accepted; no reservations. Open every day; lunch weekdays 11:30 am-2:30 pm; dinner 5-10:30 pm (later on Fridays and Saturdays); bar open 'til 1 am.

Quinn's Lighthouse

51 Embarcadero Cove. 536-2050. The Oakland Harbor Lighthouse (built in 1903) was the second lighthouse on the Oakland channel. After automation in 1966 the lighthouse was barged down the Estuary to Embarcadero Cove to become Quinn's Lighthouse restaurant. The verandas that originally surrounded both floors have been modified to casual dining decks that provide an open air view of the marina activities that seem to surround the restaurant. Views across the cove to Government Island. You are presented with a delightfully varied menu of delicious food and seafood. Guest dock for boaters; no reservations; credit cards accepted. Open every day; lunch weekdays 11:30 am-2:30 pm; sandwiches can be had upstairs until dinnertime; dinner 5-10 pm ('til 11 on Fridays and Saturdays); Sunday brunch 11 am-3 pm; bar opens at 11 am.

Victoria Station

55 Embarcadero Cove. 532-1430. Another one of the railroad restaurants, made of boxcars and decorated with British railroad artifacts. Steaks, shrimp, prime rib and ground meat·lunches are attractively served. The special green-house dining room gives a fine maritime view of the sailboats and across the water, Government Island. No reservations are taken; credit cards are accepted. Open every day; lunch 11:30 am-2:30 pm; dinner 5-11 pm ('til midnight on Fridays and Saturdays); weekend brunch 11 am-3 pm; bar 11 am-2 am.

Dock Café

1995 Embarcadero (at south end of Embarcadero Cove). 261-1502. Smack in the middle of the pier where the commercial fishing fleet ties up, this café serves breakfast and sandwiches for lunch. Enjoy your beer in the quivering light of the neon signs. Open weekdays 6 am-2 pm.

Pier 29

300 Twenty-ninth Avenue (foot of Park Street Bridge). 261-1621. Jammed right beside the bridge, this restaurant has a guest dock for boaters. The specialties are steak and lobster and teriyaki steak. The informal atmosphere is enhanced by a glassed-in area overlooking the channel that was cut to make Alameda an island. Friday through Sunday nights there is a guitarist; reservations and credit cards accepted. Open every day; lunch 11 am-2:30 pm (from noon on Saturdays); dinner 5-10 pm; Sunday brunch 11 am-2 pm *prix fixe* buffet; grog 10 am-2 am.

Alameda / north shore

Rusty Pelican

2455 Mariner Square (foot of Webster Street). 865-2166. Supported by piles, sitting over the water with a view across the Estuary of Jack London Square and Village, this restaurant also has a guest dock. Every night of the week they have musical entertainment. Credit cards and reservations accepted. Serving lunch and dinner every day from 11:30 am; Sunday brunch from 10 am; bar.

The Barge Inn

2402 Mariner Square (foot of Webster Street). 522-3325. Most of the dining area at this restaurant is a bright and airy room with lots of windows and a greenhouse roof. Through the close-up masts of sailboats, you have views across the Estuary to Jack London Square and Village. Outside is a small patio with a few tables and umbrellas for nice days. There is an espresso machine from which good coffee flows to complement the extensive menu of good burgers, sandwiches and salads. Specials for weekday lunches, afternoon delights and call-in orders to sail out. Credit cards accepted; reservations accepted for dinner. Open every day; lunch 11 am-5 pm; dinner Wednesdays-Sundays 5-9 pm; brunch weekends 11 am-5 pm; bar usually open 11 am-10 pm.

Ancient Mariner

2400 Mariner Square (foot of Webster Street). 522-0700. A finely-detailed building with an exquisite cupola, reminiscent of the Hotel del Coronado across from San Diego, and a solarium with a view across the Estuary to Jack London Square and Village. The delicious selection of food on the menu matches the setting. Musical entertainment; credit cards accepted; reservations taken for dinner. Open every day; lunch weekdays 11:30 am-3 pm; dinner daily 5-10 pm ('til 11 on Fridays and Saturdays); weekend brunch 10 am-3 pm; bar.

Neptune's Galleon

Pacific Marina (on Galleon Way, at foot of Sherman Street). 522-4653. As the name implies, the fare is mostly seafood, as well as prime rib and steak. The restaurant's interior is arranged to take advantage of the view across the Estuary to the drydock. There is also a deck for enjoying the view and a guest dock for boaters. Music on Friday and Saturday nights; reservations and credit cards accepted. Closed Mondays; open for dinner 5-10:30 pm; Sunday brunch 10 am-3 pm; bar 4 pm-midnight.

La Gondola Ristoranté

Alameda Marina (off Clement Avenue). 521-8640. This restaurant is perched on the edge of the marina where you can get the flavor of all the boating and boat yard activities. Inside are a bar-counter and tables, and there are a few tables on a small outside deck for better views of the boats. The more or less Italian menu even includes good hamburgers. Closed Mondays; lunch weekdays 11 am-3 pm; dinner daily 5-11 pm; weekend breakfast and brunch 7 am-3 pm; bar 11 am-1 am.

Alameda / south shore
Whale's Tail

Ballena Bay Marina (1144 Ballena Boulevard). 865-7552. A presentable restaurant, paneled and antiqued, with a soaring cupola and a view of the adjacent marina. In the "galley" Italian food, seafood and steaks are offered, along with a thorough brunch menu. On a sunny day you might be lucky enough to grab one of the two outside tables. In the separate and appropriately dark bar you can have your "grog." Music on Friday and Saturday nights; reservations and credit cards accepted. Open every day; weekdays, lunch 11 am-4:30 pm; dinner 4:30-11 pm; weekends, brunch 9 am-2 pm, dinner 2-10 pm.

Beau Rivage

1042 Ballena Boulevard (at Ballena Isle Tennis Club, south end of Ballena Bay). 523-1660. The name means "beautiful place by the water," or "beautiful shore," and this restaurant is. The delicious French cuisine, the relaxed atmosphere of couches, antiques and a fireplace, small and uncrowded enough to be intimate, surrounded by the proprietor's pets in the fish tanks, a tiny bar for only eight people, a real brunch for a change (none of this nonsense about eggs Benedict), and seating outside around the swimming pool — all make this truly a beautiful place. Credit cards accepted; reservations accepted, and necessary for Friday and Saturday dinner. Closed Mondays; lunch weekdays 11:30 am-2 pm; dinner 5:30-10:30 pm ('til 9 on Sundays); weekend brunch.

San Leandro

Blue Dolphin

San Leandro Marina (foot of Marina Boulevard). 483-5900. This restaurant offers seafood and steaks and a view of the marina on one side and the Bay on the other. Monday is special family dinner night, and Friday and Saturday nights feature dance music. Guest dock for boaters. Credit cards accepted; reservations accepted only for dinner Tuesdays, Wednesdays and Thursdays. Open every day; lunch 11 am-4 pm; dinner 4-11 pm ('til 1 am on Fridays and Saturdays); Sunday brunch 10 am-2pm; bar.

Casa Maria

San Leandro Marina (5 Marina Boulevard). 351-8825. Boasting an extensive Mexican menu, this restaurant has a view across the water to the Oakland Airport. Interesting décor, but the food costs a little more than it should. Credit cards and reservations accepted. Open every day 11:30 am-11:30 pm; dinner from 4 pm; "El Bruncho" Sundays 10 am-3 pm; bar 'til midnight ('til 1 am Fridays and Saturdays).

San Francisco

Fisherman's Wharf

One of the legends of San Francisco is the historical renown of Fisherman's Wharf as an eating place. This legend may be somewhat tarnished now, but the Wharf remains a locus of activity in the City for out-of-towner and resident alike. However, for various reasons, I have left the task of sorting out the competitive attractions of these varying eateries to you, except for a couple which I will cover here.

Scoma's

Pier 47 (off Jefferson, nearly opposite Jones Street, along alley beside Castagnola's, past the Wharfinger's office). 771-4383. This is the restaurant that visitors remember, or have heard about, because of the good food. The menu has many seafood dishes including "louies" and salads, cioppino and shellfish. Difficult parking; no reservations (which may mean a wait for dinner); credit cards accepted. Open daily 11:30 am-11:30 pm; bar.

The Franciscan

Pier 43½ (on The Embarcadero). 362-7733. The best thing about this restaurant is its upstairs tiered dining room arranged for the view — Alcatraz, Angel Island, shipping and the tour boat slips. Recently it achieved ephemeral fame as the luncheon spot for a president's daughter. The menu has a few things from the broiler (steaks and chops), and a whole page of fish, including my favorite (scallops); the chef's special is "lobster and steak" (for East Coast palates). No credit cards; no reservations. Open every day 11 am-10 pm; luncheon 11 am-1 pm; bar.

San Francisco / City waterfront
Pier 39

Since the opening of this grandiose tourist spot, it has been called a lot of names and a lot of bad things have been said about it, some of which are probably true. More to the point is the concentration of twenty-three restaurants and eating places on the pier. Of course, the Bay views from some of the places are terrific, but that does not necessarily make them worthwhile. The shining exception, which I hope remains undimmed by its neighbors, is the Eagle Café.

Eagle Café

On the second floor corner of Pier 39, near The Embarcadero. 433-3689. Recently the Eagle flew across The Embarcadero (not really, it was hoisted by crane) to its new second-floor perch. The exterior was spruced up with new siding and paint (which was absurd, since its Pier 39 surroundings look so tacky). But inside you find one of the few *real* eating spots on the San Francisco waterfront, and a café with a truly distinctive character. The customers include, but are not limited to, fishermen and cab drivers, employees from the various establishments of Fisherman's Wharf and from the National Park Service, bums and sailors (there's nothing to the reports that they are synonymous), railroad engineers and architects, and even writers. The Eagle started out in 1911 as a ticket office/waiting room for steamship passengers. It became a café in 1928. It is hoped that it won't suffer an overdose of progress at its new perch and see its dedicated customers replaced by indistinguishable tourists. Breakfast dishes and the lunch specials (large portions) which are chalked over the kitchen window are dispensed to a cafeteria line, and the long bar at one side of the room seems to be always open. Open every day; breakfast 6-11 am; lunch 'til 2 pm; bar 'til 9 pm.

Crow's Nest

Pier 37 (The Embarcadero opposite Beach Street). 981-0659. This bar gives a good north waterfront view of the shipping on the Bay and the waters north past Angel Island. In the same location for more than twenty-seven years, it's still holding out against the new Pier 39 development next door. Don't know how long it will last. Open every day 11 am-10 pm (Sundays 'til 6 pm).

Peer Inn

Pier 33 (The Embarcadero opposite Bay Street). 788-1411. Another north waterfront viewpoint, this restaurant involves you with its maritime accouterments. But the best part is the specially constructed Bay-viewing solarium that gives you the feeling of being on a ship's bridge as you watch the tankers and container ships and passenger ships slide by. Serving breakfast and lunch, Mondays-Fridays 6 am-2:30 pm; bar Mondays-Saturdays 6 am-10 pm.

Pier 23 Café

Pier 23 (The Embarcadero opposite Front Street). Do 2-5125. A small, typical waterfront café. From the bar at the back of the room you can see past the pier to Treasure Island and beyond. A brunch/lunch is served, along with the specialty, the Pier Buoy sandwich. The real magic of the waterfront comes alive on Thursday, Friday and Saturday nights when the Pier 23 Jazz Band, Jack Schaefer up front, performs. The raucous blues are sung and played enthusiastically, until the joint is jumpin'. The cabaret atmosphere is enhanced by the mixed audience; tourists just off the boat from Japan, snobs traipsing down from Nob Hill, rendezvousing gays, and carousing nuts from Bernal Heights. On Sunday afternoons there is a Dixieland jam. Closed Mondays; brunch/lunch Tuesdays-Fridays 9 am-2:30 pm; bar, weekdays 9 am-8 pm, weekends from 1 pm, open 'til 2 am on Friday and Saturday nights.

Mildred Pierce's

Across from Pier 23 (Greenwich and Battery streets at The Embarcadero). 392-4850. There's no view of the water from this cafeteria-style restaurant, but a lot of people who work in offices on the piers (particularly architects) lunch here regularly. Breakfast and lunch are served — omelettes, sandwiches and soups with groovy names. The food is good, but the chairs are stupid. The name of the place is derived from the title of a book by James M. Cain, which was filmed as the 1945 "comeback" Academy Award performance by Joan Crawford as an ambitious mother; supported by Ann Blyth, Zachary Scott and Jack Carson, directed by Michael Curtiz. This unprepossessing café is due to be engulfed in denim — it is threatened by a four-square-block development of Levi Strauss and Company. Open weekdays 7:30 am-3:30 pm.

The Waterfront

Pier 7 (The Embarcadero at Broadway). 391-2696. This "seafood & spirits" establishment offers the elegance of oak paneling, ceiling fans, stained glass and brass fixtures. The menu is mostly seafood, a couple of steaks, pasta, and a tepid brunch selection. It provides food that is better than most of the waterfront restaurants, with appropriate prices. The multi-level dining areas enhance the harbor view — the pilot boats docked right outside, and across the Bay, Yerba Buena Island. A small outside deck sits right beside the docked boats. Credit cards accepted; reservations advised for dinner and weekend brunch. Open every day; lunch weekdays 11:30 am-2:30 pm; dinner 6-10:30 pm, weekends from 5 pm; weekend brunch 11 am-3 pm; bar 11 am-2 am every day.

Victoria Station

50 Broadway (at The Embarcadero). 433-4400. Another facsimile of derailed railroad cars, this restaurant of cabooses and boxcars, decorated with treasured antiques from British railroading, is not off the track as far as its menu goes — offering shrimp, steak, prime rib and a special salad bar. It is nestled under the freeway with no view of the water. Reservations accepted for more than eight people; credit cards accepted. Open every day; lunch weekdays 11:30 am-2:30 pm; dinner Mondays-Thursdays 5:30-11 pm, Fridays and Saturdays 5 pm-midnight, Sundays 5-10 pm; bar.

Pier 1 Lunch

Pier 1 (The Embarcadero, north of Ferry Building). 982-3686. When you're hanging around because you just missed the Larkspur or Sausalito ferry and it's a long wait until the next one, here's a place to have a bite or a beer. They serve breakfast and lunch, lox and bagels, and a big selection of drinks from the refrigerators. As a bonus, you have a view of the terrific Ferry Building tower. Open every day; weekdays 6:30 am-6 pm; weekends approximately 8 am-6 pm.

Café de Wheels

Justin Herman Plaza (across from Ferry Building, foot of Market Street, near Hyatt Regency Hotel). 788-0766. What a colossal name for a hot dog stand. You are offered three types — German, Swiss and Polish — along with the proper relishes and pastries and juices. Also on the menu are spinach crêpes, shrimp cocktail and summer salad. You are frankly served for open air seating (several umbrellaed tables) or for walking in the plaza. The entertainment is the *joie de vivre* of the craft merchants and passersby. Winter weekdays 10 am-3 pm; in the summer open on weekends also 10 am-4 pm.

Sinbad's

Pier 2 (The Embarcadero, south of Ferry Building, end of Mission Street). 781-2555. Perched on the pier almost behind the Ferry Building, this restaurant has a large deck for lunching outside with views of the ferries, the Bay Bridge and Yerba Buena Island. The menu offers mediocre preparations of seafood, salads, steaks and chops. Reservations accepted for dinner and for more than five people for lunch; credit cards accepted. Open every day 11:30 am-10:30 pm for food service (including Sunday brunch); bar open 'til 1 am.

San Francisco / south waterfront

Carmen's

Pier 24 (The Embarcadero at Harrison Street). 495-9265. This café is tucked into a corner of the towering front of Pier 24 near the fireboat wharf. There is no view of the Bay, but the Bay Bridge towers overhead, and across the street is Hills Brothers Coffee which offers free aromas on a foggy day. The place is small, five tables and a big counter, and serves breakfast with a Philippine flavor, sandwiches, Philippine-style lunch steaks and beer. Open weekdays 6 am-3 pm and on Saturdays 'til 3 pm.

The Boondocks

Pier 28 (The Embarcadero at Bryant Street). 777-1588. Recently remodeled, this restaurant looks as if it has just been off-loaded from a container ship. Regular waterfront food in a small dining room. There is a view of the Bay between the piers. Closed Sundays; open for breakfast and lunch from 9 am; Saturday champagne brunch 11 am-4 pm; open later into the evening for the bar.

Red's Java House

Pier 30 (The Embarcadero at Bryant Street). Ex 2-9967. Slumped along the front of the pier, this small place is decorated with maritime pictures and pinball machines. Red is a garrulous proprietor who explains that in the twenty years he's been there the business used to be 90 percent from the waterfront, now it's only about 30 percent from the waterfront and about 60 percent from nearby (and not so nearby) offices. Serving breakfast *(sic)* and lunch: donuts, coffee (refills cost extra), dogs, (double) burgers, sandwiches, and beer — "none of this ham and eggs stuff." Open weekdays only 6 am-5 pm.

Java House

Pier 40 (The Embarcadero). 362-9231. Another waterfront café with a view of the Bay and the interesting old boats at the pier next door. Inside are a lot of tables, including one for pool, and outside there is one table. They offer a breakfast selection and hamburgers for lunch, but if you're interested in how your food is cooked, try across the street or down The Embarcadero — here you will see guys eating ketchup on their eggs and bacon, but not on their hash browns. Open weekdays only 6 am-3 pm, breakfast 6-10:30 am.

Pier Head (Hofbrau)

The Embarcadero at Berry Street (opposite Pier 42). 421-7194. This dark waterfront bar and café has a long, busy bar and a separate dining room. The customers are definitely waterfront habitués. A good breakfast and lunch are served. Open weekdays for breakfast 6-10 am and lunch 'til 3 pm; bar open from 6 am Mondays-Saturdays.

Dolphin P. Rempp
(Shipboard Restaurant)

Pier 42 (south end of the Embarcadero at Berry Street). 777-5771. This sailing ship is parked on land, right beside The Embarcadero. Having a long and honorable service on the seven seas, she is newly opened and magnificently playing her role as an addition to the waterfront dining scene. She was built in Thuro, Denmark, in 1908 as the *Ellen*. The 260-ton three-master spent many years in the Baltic trade, carrying lumber and spices; and managed to ply the waters of the South Pacific and reached the coasts of Africa and South America. San Francisco was one of her ports of call. Her present guise is all authenticity — inside there is no phony embellishment to make her look like a ship, since she is one. The décor has the subdued elegance of a European restaurant. But the best part of the story is the restaurant's food — very delicious without being outrageously expensive. The imaginative menu is divided between fish and meats, and the preparation is excellent. The bar opens downstairs at 5 pm, and when the ship's bell rings at 6, diners move upstairs for their repast. Credit cards are accepted; reservations recommended. Closed Sundays; serving dinner only 5 pm-11 pm.

The Wharfside

West end of the big blue monster China Basin Building on Berry Street. 495-0693. A cafeteria serving breakfast and hot plate specials and sandwiches for lunch. It's all good almost-home-made food. Lots of modern plastic room inside and a lot of room and tables outside by the pier to watch the channel, maritime-flavored, and see the drawbridges. Open weekdays 7 am-2 pm.

Blanche's

998 Fourth Street at Mission Channel (at China Basin). Ex 7-4191. Across the drawbridge from the long blue China Basin Building, built on pilings with a large outside deck from which to view the piers of China Basin and the houseboats in Mission Channel. Blanche's has been clinging precariously to the pier for more than twenty years. The unstudied elegance of ''Galerie de Blanche'' offers lunches of shrimp and crab salad. Line up at a counter for lunch (which can include wine in plastic cups), then carry it outside for dining on the delightful deck with trees in tubs, or take one of the few tables inside. Credit cards accepted. Open weekdays for lunch only 11 am-3 pm.

Mission Rock Resort

817 China Basin Street. 621-5538. This is a real waterfront institution, especially for wharf rats and fishermen. (The namesake, Mission Rock, is now submerged beneath Pier 50.) Downstairs is a counter watched over by a pair of pool tables and pinball machines with a deck out back where you can eat their great hamburgers, hot dogs and beer. Upstairs is the ''Top of the Rock,'' another bar and dining room, serving (slowly) sandwiches, soups, salads, fisherman's platters, burgers and daily specials. The popular upstairs deck overlooks the Union Iron Works (now Bethlehem) shipyards and underlooks the Santa Fe switchyard. A lot of activity is generated by the fishing boat rentals, and by the fishing pier next door. There is a guest dock for boaters. Open every day; downstairs, 6 am-9 pm; upstairs, breakfast 8-11:30 am, lunch 11:30 am-3 pm, dinner Thursdays-Sundays 6-9 pm, bar 'til midnight.

The Bounty

End of Cargo Street (off Third Street) at entrance to Pier 96 (India Basin). 826-8925. Serving the waterfront workers and truckers who toil on this isolated bit of waterfront near Hunters Point. Large cafeteria-style dining room with nautical embellishments and a bar off to one side. Good breakfast and lunch, but no waterfront view. Open weekdays; food served 6 am-3 pm; bar 'til 10 pm.

San Mateo County

Burlingame

Saluto's

1600 Old Bayshore Highway. 697-6565. There is a definite Italian flavor to the food found here, presented with a Bay view. The menu features veal, steak and shrimp, pasta, other Italian dishes, shrimp dishes, other seafood, and a prime rib special on Mondays and Tuesdays. Evening musical entertainment; reservations and credit cards accepted. Open every day; lunch weekdays 11:30 am-2:30 pm; dinner weekdays 5:30-11:30 pm, Saturdays from 4:30 pm, Sundays from 4 pm; bar.

Casa Maria

1590 Old Bayshore Highway. 692-3113. An elaborate selection of Mexican food in interesting combinations. They have a special children's menu. From the dining room with its dark and heavy décor, you can watch young and old coots glide by the Bay-view windows. Credit cards and reservations accepted. Open every day; lunch 11:30 am-4 pm; dinner 4-10:30 pm ('til 11:30 pm on Fridays and Saturdays); "El Bruncho" Sundays 10 am-3 pm; bar 'til midnight ('til 1 am on Fridays and Saturdays).

Charley Brown's

1550 Old Bayshore Highway. 697-6907. A Bay view of the airport and Coyote Point. Selections of seafood, steak and lobster, teriyaki and steak. Music on Friday and Saturday nights; reservations and credit cards accepted. Open every day; weekdays, lunch 11:30 am-2:30 pm, "late" menu 'til 5 pm, dinner 5:30-10 pm ('til 11 on Fridays and Saturdays); bar open later.

The Fisherman

1492 Old Bayshore Highway. 697-1490. Located beside Burlingame's Shorebird Sanctuary (a tiny marsh), with a view north for a long distance up the Bay. Fine Italian, seafood and beef dishes are served. Every night except Sunday and Monday there is music and dancing; credit cards accepted; reservations for more than five people. Open every day; Mondays-Saturdays, lunch 11:30 am-4 pm, dinner 4-11:30 pm; dinner Sundays 4-10:30 pm; bar 'til 2 am.

Kee Joon's

433 Airport Boulevard. 348-1122. Ride the elevator to this penthouse restaurant and dine with an aviary of interesting birds. The marine connection is the extensive high-level view of the South Bay. The menu has à la carte and complete dinner Chinese specialties from Canton, Peking, Szechuan and Yanchow. Reservations accepted for four people or more; credit cards accepted. Lunch weekdays 11:30 am-2 pm; dinner every day 5-10 pm; bar.

Diamond Showboat

410 Airport Boulevard. 344-5771. Looking something like a shipwreck, this former US Army ferryboat, the *General Frank M. Coxe*, is beached on the edge of the Bay. The menu features NY steak, prime rib, prawns and sole. On Wednesdays and Thursdays there is a special "all you can eat" dinner of bar-b-que ribs and spaghetti. Cabaret variety dinner show on Friday and Saturday nights (no cover). Credit cards and reservations accepted. Closed Mondays and Tuesdays; open for dinner Wednesdays-Saturdays 5 pm; open Sundays 4 pm; bar.

The Castaway Restaurant

End of Coyote Point Drive in the park (restaurant diners don't pay park entry fee). 347-1027. Nestled in the trees on Coyote Point in San Mateo, the striking architecture includes massive posts and beams, a central fireplace, trees growing through the ceiling, and expanses of windows that present a wide sweep of view north to the airport, San Francisco and Oakland. The menu has been changed from the painfully cute Polynesian fare of the past. Now it's more straightforward — five fish dishes and six steaks. A couple of items invite late evening light eaters. However, the food is not that great, and the service is painfully inadequate. Reservations and credit cards accepted. Open every day; lunch weekdays 11:30 am-3 pm; dinner weekdays 5-10:30 pm ('til 11:30 on Fridays and Saturdays); Sunday dinner 4-10 pm; Sunday champagne brunch 10 am-3 pm; bar.

Redwood City

Harbor House Restaurant

Foot of Whipple Avenue (at Pete's Harbor). 365-1386. Built of piers and pilings, hovering over the marina, set among the sails (or masts, at least), is this large restaurant with good food. It has a guest dock and outside dining on the rooftop overlooking the salt marshes. No reservations; no entertainment, unless the owner happens to be around — he's entertainment! Open every day for breakfast, lunch and dinner 7 am-10 pm; bar.

Charley Brown's

On Harbor Boulevard (at Redwood City Marina). 364-2848. Perched like a pier, on pilings, over the entrance to the marina, with large expanses of overhung glass. There is a view along Redwood Creek of the shipping and Mt. Leslie (salt) across the water. Wednesday nights a jazz group plays and other nights through the weekend there is a piano bar. Reservations and credit cards accepted. Open every day; lunch weekdays 11:30 am-2:30 pm; dinner weekdays 6-9:30 pm, Fridays and Saturdays 5-10:30 pm, Sundays 5-9:30 pm; Sunday champagne brunch 10:30 am-2:30 pm; bar open Saturdays 1 pm-2 am.

Finding the Bay:
Public Parks, Beaches and Shorelines

The ubiquitous natural feature that defines this region and makes it unique is San Francisco Bay. From the portion known as San Pablo Bay in the north to the section named Richardson Bay to the salt evaporators of the South Bay, this body of water has far-reaching influences on the daily life of everyone who lives here. A lot has been written and spoken about the Bay: most of it concerning problems and pollutions, safeguards and solutions. There are many places to observe the Bay as a spectator — from crossings on the six bridges and the ferryboats, from tour helicopters and boats, and from the surrounding hillsides and ridges. Countless thousands zip along the freeways that encircle the Bay without really taking notice of it.

But how do you find the Bay? Despite the relatively few recreation facilities on the Bay shoreline, I made the gratifying discovery that there are many places where you can actually get down and touch the Bay and sample its different moods and waterscapes.

Of the 276 miles of Bay shore, about 73 are now accessible to the public, up from a mere 4 miles just over ten years ago. Several agencies have plans that would open up even more shoreline to provide direct and enjoyable access to the Bay for more people. There are even dreams of connecting parkways to link together parks with continuous shoreline access.

Within the vast lands of the Golden Gate National Recreation Area (GGNRA) in San Francisco and Marin County there are several Bay front areas. Currently being acquired and scheduled for future development is the San Francisco Bay National Wildlife Refuge in the South Bay, headquartered in Fremont. The state is acquiring and planning parks in San Francisco and Marin. East Bay Regional Parks has future developments in store for us on the shores of San

Leandro Bay and other places, and other local agencies have projects for improving shoreline and making the Bay more accessible. Among these agencies, the Port of Oakland is very active. You can get a free "Pleasure Guide" booklet, showing their six parks, from the Port, 66 Jack London Square, Oakland 94607 (444-3188).

The Bay Conservation and Development Commission, through its permit process for private and public development, has encouraged more access to the Bay. Even though it has no power to buy or procure land, BCDC permits have opened up public access to thirteen miles of Bay shoreline and wetlands within its authority (despite the fact that some projects have not yet complied with permit conditions). The Commission has prepared a booklet that identifies all public access sites and parks, established by BCDC permits or by other agencies, within its jurisdiction (some areas are not on the open Bay). This booklet is a comprehensive guide to San Francisco Bay public access and recreation areas, providing a description with a detailed map

of each shoreline site. It is available for free from BCDC, 30 Van Ness Avenue, San Francisco 94102 (557-3686).

I discovered more than fifty places with a diversity of facilities and environments — beaches, marshlands, refuges, piers, islands and rag-tag fills — where you can find the Bay. And the one place where you can see all of the Bay at once: a warehouse in Sausalito where you will find the Bay Model. More elaborate descriptions of many of these areas are given in other sections of the book — *Pedestrian Delights, Shoreline Bicycle Routes and Tours, Marinas, Fishing from the Shore,* and *Birdwatching and Sanctuaries.* Besides sailing or cruising on the Bay, this guide for shoreline exploration of these scattered parks and preserves is the easiest and best way to appreciate the magnificent estuary that is the jewel of this region.

North —
Marin and Sonoma counties

Fort Baker (GGNRA)

Off Highway 101 just north of the Golden Gate Bridge at Alexander Avenue exit, then take first right turn and continue beyond the Army buildings to the water.

A breakwater and pier surround Horseshoe Bay and provide good fishing. From the Cavallo Point promontory above is a vista through the Golden Gate to Lands End, the City in prospect, and an interesting look at the Golden Gate Bridge from under the north end. Road pull-offs en route furnish views to the east — the docks of Sausalito, the hillside houses of Belvedere, Raccoon Strait, the playground of Angel Island, and the East Bay Hills.

Sausalito (City parks)

Off Highway 101 just north of the Golden Gate Bridge at Alexander Avenue exit, then continue into Sausalito on Bridgeway. Or take the Sausalito Ferry from the City (see *Transportation on the Bay*).

Watch the waterfront activities of ferry slips, decks, docks and boats from scattered parcels in Sausalito, including Tiffany Beach, Princess, Gabrielson and Earl F. Dunphy parks. A good walking tour takes you along the Bridgeway esplanade with its landscaping, sculpture, pilings and seating. Views are of Angel Island and across Richardson Bay. The walk culminates at a grassy park (opposite Napa Street) with a playground and the start of the Mill Valley bikepath.

Strawberry Point

Off Highway 101 at Seminary Drive exit, then follow drive around to Richardson Bay.

A wildlife refuge that has good birdwatching possibilities in a marsh area around De Silva Pond. A path continues on the water side of the condominium project around the cove. The drive follows Richardson Bay around the point, with places to park to get down to the narrow shore for fishing or Baywatching. It continues east all the way to Great Circle Drive and the entrance to Brickyard Park which is located at the water's edge.

Richardson Bay Wildlife Sanctuary (Audubon Society)

Off Highway 101 at Tiburon exit, then east towards Tiburon and turn off on Greenwood Cove Drive.

This area of land and much larger water area on Richardson Bay serves as habitat for a wide variety of waterfowl and shore birds. The landmark is the re-located and restored Victorian Lyford House (open Sunday afternoons). You will also find an education center with community-oriented programs and guided nature walks, as well as a self-guided nature trail (small admission fee) through the varied ecosystems of the sanctuary with views across the bay. The Sanctuary is open 9 am-5 pm Wednesday through Sunday. (388-2524)

Richardson Bay Park (City of Tiburon)

Off Highway 101 at Tiburon exit, then east to Greenwood Beach Road.

Large parking lot contains Blackie's Grave, and a bike and walking path along the shore towards Tiburon. You can take a pleasant walk along the natural shoreline that at times is isolated from traffic with grassy spots for picnicking, lots of birds, and views of the City through the slot formed by Sausalito and Belvedere.

Belvedere Park (City of Belvedere)

Off Highway 101 at Tiburon exit, then east to San Rafael Avenue, just before Tiburon.

Landscaped shoreline strip has benches and a gravel pathway for walking and watching birds at the edge of Richardson Bay.

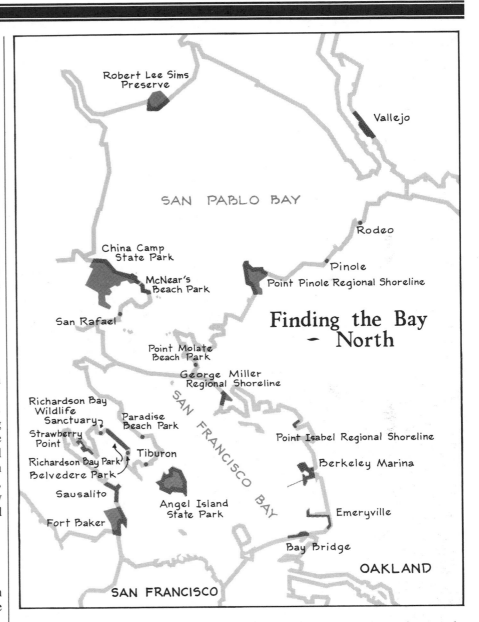

Tiburon

Off Highway 101 at Tiburon exit, then east into the town. Or take the Tiburon Ferry from the City (see *Transportation on the Bay*).

Ragged, undeveloped shore along the waterfront east of the ferry slip, pleasant walking and views with some fishing spots. At the far end, a pier for kids' fishing. A dock area next door to the ferry slip makes a great place for viewing water activities and Belvedere and Angel Island with the City far across the Bay.

Angel Island State Park (within the boundary of the GGNRA)

Can only be reached by ferry: from Tiburon, daily in summer, weekends in winter (435-2131); from San Francisco Pier 43½, daily in summer, weekends in winter (546-2815); and from the Berkeley Marina, one return trip on weekends, April through October (546-2815).

One of the premier weekend picnic places of the Bay region. This largest island in the Bay, a wooded mountain thrusting out of the water, has trails from park headquarters that wind around the whole island, great for circumambulation, riding the ''elephant train,'' or bicycling (bicycles may be brought on the ferries). A snack bar operates in the summer. Linger at the beaches (especially the fine one at Quarry Point), partake of views of the Bay and surrounding hills from atop Mt. Livermore, or sample some of the island's long and varied history at Camp Reynolds and Fort McDowell. Private boats are accommodated at a small pier (for a small fee) and mooring buoys at Ayala (formerly Hospital) Cove. Overnight mooring is allowed (no charge), and you can anchor elsewhere about the island if you want. There are several shoreline fishing spots. The park is open during daylight hours; no dogs are allowed on the island. Park headquarters (435-1915).

Paradise Beach Park (Marin County)

Off Highway 101 at Tiburon exit, then east on Tiburon Boulevard, to cross the peninsula on Trestle Glen Boulevard, and right on Paradise Drive to the park.

Nicely landscaped, well-manicured hillside park on the north side of the Tiburon Peninsula. Various activities are possible — there are picnic tables, a fishing pier, a small beach and restrooms, as well as views of Richmond, the Richmond Bridge and the North Bay. Parking fee: $1 winter; summer, $2 weekdays, $4 weekends. The park is open from 7 to sunset.

San Rafael (City and County)

Off Highway 101 at Central San Rafael exit, then east on Second Street which becomes Pt. San Pedro Road, follow until opposite Main Street.

Park is merely a landscaped strip between the road and the water with benches and a pathway along the rocky shore of San Rafael Bay. Views of Richmond, the Richmond Bridge and the Marin Islands.

McNear's Beach Park (Marin County)

Off Highway 101 at Central San Rafael exit, then east on Second Street which becomes Pt. San Pedro Road, follow along the road, then turn on Cantera Road to the park.

Well-landscaped park with palms and other trees, grassy knolls and artistically placed rocks. Development includes a large beach, a swimming pool, tennis courts, lots of picnic tables and a snack concession. On summer weekends the park usually gets crowded and people are turned away at the gate. Parking fee: $1 winter; summer, $2 weekdays, $4 weekends. Views of The Sisters just offshore and across San Pablo Bay to Vallejo and Pt. Pinole. The park is open 8 am- 5 pm.

China Camp State Park

Off Highway 101 at Civic Center exit in San Rafael, then follow North San Pedro Road three to four miles east.

The site of this brand-new park extends from approximately Buck's Landing all the way east to McNear's Beach with about two miles of Bay frontage. It is a large area, practically the whole north side of the peninsula that faces San Pablo Bay, from the ridges of the wooded hills to the marshland at the Bay. The historic Chinese fishing settlement known as China Camp is included in the tract. At the present time the park is available for day use, hiking, riding, fishing and viewing the scenery. Signs indicating the location of the park have been installed. Further development will await the outcome of public hearings. (456-0766)

Robert Lee Sims Preserve (Nature Conservancy)

Follow Highway 101 north, then turn east on Highway 37 to just past Highway 121-Sonoma junction, cross small bridge to locked gate on right.

This preserve is specially protected, you must obtain permission to visit and the combination for the gate lock. Open marsh area includes a creek and estuary, brackish ponds, and a true salt marsh outside the dikes located at the extreme north end of San Pablo Bay. Several trails start at the headquarters, three miles from the highway. A rich habitat and sanctuary for many species of migrating birds which are best seen during the fall. For permission to visit, call the Nature Conservancy in San Francisco (989-3056).

East —
Solano, Contra Costa and Alameda counties

Vallejo (City of Vallejo)

Off Highway 80 just past tollgate at Highway 29 exit, continue downtown on Sonoma Boulevard, and bear left on Maryland Street.

From the boat ramp parking lot at the end of Maryland Street a landscaped quay stretches for more than half a mile along Mare Island Strait, paralleling Mare Island Way. A paved walk, grassy lawns and wooden benches combine to make this a handsome place for fishing, bicycling, walking or picnicking, with a view across the water to the Naval Shipyard. Following Mare Island Way up the Strait you reach the Vallejo Marina with an elegant promenade that is a good boat-watching vantage point.

Rodeo

Off Highway 80 at Willow Avenue-Rodeo exit which becomes Parker Avenue, then turn at end on San Pablo Avenue to California Street.

Large parking area beside the road with an undeveloped fill area and the water beyond, next to the Rodeo Sanitary District. This is not a particularly attractive place, but the strand line of concrete hunks and mud flat beach is fine for fishing and watching birds offshore. Views of the nearby tank farms and north across San Pablo Bay to Mare Island.

Pinole

Off Highway 80 at Pinole exit which becomes Tennent Avenue, then follow all the way to the end.

Walk from a small parking lot in front of the Pinole Wastewater Plant on the dirt road leading along Pinole Creek out to a jetty of concrete shards. If you arrive at

the right time, you can watch Amtrak zephyr by. On the other side of the plant is a strand of peat, backed by a small marsh. These completely undeveloped areas attract many shore birds and provide a fishing spot and views across San Pablo Bay.

Point Pinole Regional Shoreline (East Bay Regional Park)

Off Highway 80 at Hilltop Drive exit and follow to end, then right on San Pablo Avenue, then west on Atlas Road, and continue on Giant Highway to parking lot.

A headland jutting into the Bay is an extensive park with miles of shoreline for active exploration. Varied terrain — tree-covered slopes, open fields, marshland and beach — which will remain undeveloped invites hikers, bicyclists, picnickers and ecologists. A fishing pier has recently been completed at the end of the point, and it makes a good deep-water spot for fishermen to wet their lines. Shuttle bus (small fee) operates from main parking lot to the pier on weekends during the summer. Parking fee: $1 daily. The park is open from 8 am until dusk.

Point Molate Beach Park (City of Richmond)

Follow Highway 17 through Richmond to San Rafael Bridge, then just before tollgate turn off at Point Molate exit and follow road to beach.

If you turn off Pt. Molate Road toward Redrock Marina before reaching the beach, you find a fishing pier directly below the bridge. The Beach Park has a pretty shingled beach as well as parking, playground, planted trees, picnic area and restrooms. Close-up view of the Richmond Bridge and Mt. Tam in the distance. Occasionally, on weekends, the Castro Point Railway operates steam trains from the park along the shore around the point. The park is open during daylight hours. Proceed through the Naval reservation to off-road parking spots for fishing. Beyond, at the end of the road, on the tip of Pt. San Pablo, is a shorefront area (opposite the East Brother Lighthouse) that would make great parkland.

George Miller Jr. Memorial Regional Shoreline and Keller's Beach Park (East Bay Regional Park)

Follow Highway 17 through Richmond, then turn on South Garrard Avenue through the tunnel to come to the park.

Out in the flat beside the railroad tracks, lies this newly-developed regional shoreline. It has paths and picnic spots, restrooms and recently planted trees. Pleasant views of Angel Island, Marin and Mt. Tamalpais across the Bay; Long Wharf and the Richmond-San Rafael Bridge closer at hand. The park includes grassy Nicholls Knob across the road; from the top you have even better views. Keller's Beach is a small corner of the park just where the road comes out of the tunnel. It sits in a terraced, land-

scaped cove with picnic tables, fire pits, restrooms and a tiny beach. Walk down the rocky sea wall for fishing. Further improvements to the shoreline will include more landscaping and a lagoon. There is even talk of relocating the Castro Point Railway to the park. The park is open from 5 am to 10 pm.

Point Isabel Regional Shoreline (East Bay Regional Park)

Off Highway 80 in Richmond at Central Avenue exit, then follow road to cul-de-sac parking at end.

Good fishing area with access to both the landscaped park area and the rough, irregular shore on pretty much this whole peninsula. Grassy knolls, paths and picnicking spots with views through the Golden Gate, of the City and nearby Brooks Island, a regional preserve. The park is open 8 am-10 pm.

Berkeley Marina (City of Berkeley)

Off Highway 80 at University Avenue exit. Also served by AC Transit.

The peninsula where the marina sits was created by filling the Bay. You can walk all around this peninsula, and an esplanade winds around the berths of the yacht harbor. The rough, open land of the unfinished fill to the north of the yacht basin contrasts with the manicured Shorebird Park on the south side of the peninsula which provides good spots for picnicking and watching the boats of the Cal Sailing Club. The Berkeley Pier juts more than a mile into the Bay. It is popular for fishing and has a cleaning station, restrooms, weekend snack service, and an observation platform with views of two bridges and, with luck, even a sunset through the Golden Gate.

Emeryville

Off Highway 80 at Powell Street exit. Also served by AC Transit.

Walking and fishing along the shoreline at the end of the peninsula, where you find grass and picnic tables near the marina. Views across Treasure Island and Alcatraz to the Golden Gate, and north past the Berkeley Marina to Richmond. Fishing spots along the road on the neck of the peninsula. A path starting where Powell Street dips under the freeway provides access to the "sculpture crescent" of marsh, also called the "mud flats." This is the long-lasting collection of ever-changing driftwood and found-object sculpture that is a pleasing and provocative Bay region landmark for anyone traveling the freeway near the Bay Bridge.

Bay Bridge - Radio Stations

Off Highway 80 at Port of Oakland exit near toll plaza (last Oakland exit), then follow "radio stations" signs to end of road.

From the parking lot walk over steps on the wall toward the bridge. Lots of birds as well as traffic noise mingle on this strip of marshland and beach practically beneath the east end of the bridge. The Port of Oakland calls this area Northport Beach. Views of Angel Island and the North Bay.

Port View Park (Port of Oakland)

Off Highway 80 at Port of Oakland exit near toll plaza, then turn south to follow Maritime Street to end, then follow Port signs along Seventh Street to end and park. Also served by AC Transit.

On a point extending far into the Bay, a well-developed park with fishing pier, snack and bait concession, restrooms and picnic tables. The park is landscaped and has an observation tower with superb views of port action, the Bay Bridge and the San Francisco skyline.

Middle Harbor Park (Port of Oakland)

Off Highway 17 at Jackson Street exit, then turn toward the Estuary on Oak Street, and back to the right on Third Street, then turn west on Middle Harbor Road and follow it to turn across the railroad tracks at the United States Lines Terminal sign, and follow Ferro Street to the end.

A small landscaped park with a fishing pier. Great for watching all kinds of boats — small sail craft beating to windward and huge container ships (after they have finished loading next door) plying the waters of the Estuary on their way to the Bay.

Estuary Park (City of Oakland)

Off Highway 17 at Jackson Street Exit, then turn toward the Estuary on Oak Street, and turn left on Embarcadero West to the park.

A pristine park with a quay on the tidal channel that connects Lake Merritt with the Estuary. It has a boat launching ramp, restrooms, grassy picnic areas, a bizarre modern pavilion and a fishing pier. Views of Alameda across the Estuary and a dry dock across the channel. A walkway goes along the Estuary to connect with the small marina which is located at the Portobello development.

Embarcadero Cove

Off Highway 17 at Sixteenth Avenue-Embarcadero exit, then follow Embarcadero around toward the Government Island causeway.

A commercial development of Victorian buildings, railroad cars and a lighthouse — these structures have been moved to the site and converted into offices, boat shops and restaurants. Paved paths and boardwalks meander through this landscaped jewel beside a large yacht harbor, furnishing views of the boats, Coast Guard training off Government Island, and the Oakland skyline in the distance. An ongoing redevelopment project by the Port of Oakland will eventually provide landscaping and walkways extending from this development all around the cove to the north and west.

Ballena Bay

Off Highway 17 at Alameda exit, then through the tube which becomes Webster Street to end, then right on Central Avenue, then south on Ballena Boulevard to end of peninsula.

From the parking lot, walk around the peninsula and fish anywhere on the undeveloped rip-rap shoreline or along the street. A walkway around the marina provides views south down the Bay and across to the City.

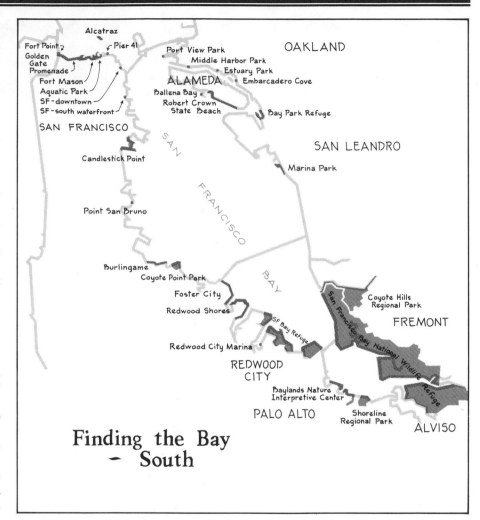

Finding the Bay
— South

Robert W. Crown Memorial State Beach (managed by the East Bay Regional Park District)

Off Highway 17 at Alameda exit, then through the tube which becomes Webster Street to end, then along Central Avenue in either direction to park. Also served by AC Transit.

A well-developed beach recreation area with a long sand beach, picnic areas, summer concessions and a classroom/activity building which will open to the public in the future. The beach extends the length of the south side of Alameda island for long walks in the dunes all the way to the shoreline walkway around the housing development by the mud flats opposite Bay Farm Island. Parking fee is $1/car in summer. The beach is open from 8 am to 10 pm.

Bay Park Refuge (City of Oakland)

Off Highway 17 at 66th Avenue-Coliseum exit and head toward the water, then left on Oakport Street, then right on Hassler Way, then right on Edgewater Drive past the "end" sign to a parking lot.

A small park on San Leandro Bay with picnic tables, a play structure and a fishing pier. Nearby marshlands mean that this is a good bird-watching point. A paved path extends for more than half a mile to the south. East Bay Regional Parks has started development on a plan which will restore shoreline, replenish plantings, and provide more fishing access and bike trails on much more of the shore of San Leandro Bay, including Arrowhead Marsh.

Marina Park (City of San Leandro)

Off Highway 17 at Marina Boulevard West exit and follow to end, then turn on Neptune Drive to park.

Developed, landscaped park with restrooms, picnic spots, playground and horseback riding trail. Walk around the dirt shoreline of the lagoon in the undeveloped part of the park for views up and down and across the Bay. The north arm of the adjacent marina has a small picnicking park at the tip, and the south arm has another park and a fishing pier. Walk across the bridge next to the park and past the landfill area for two miles of Bayside levee with good bird-watching.

Coyote Hills Regional Park (East Bay Regional Park)

Off Highway 17 at Jarvis Avenue exit in Newark, then north on Newark Boulevard to Patterson Ranch Road and follow signs into park.

Coyote Hills are "land islands" that, in the distant past, were actually in the Bay waters, but now are separated from the open Bay by more than a mile of marsh and salt ponds. The park encompasses a variety of wildlife habitat and refuge — salt ponds for gulls, pelicans, shore birds and migrating waterfowl; grassy hillsides for birds and small animals; fresh water marshes for ducks and wading birds; and meadows for song birds, game birds and hawks. From the visitor center, naturalists conduct weekend programs through the marshes and shell mounds. Several trails in the park (including the gentle Bay View Trail) for walking and bicycling; they connect with the Alameda Creek Regional Trails atop flood control levees for hiking, horseback riding and bicycling. Parking fee $1 on weekdays and $2 on weekends and holidays. The park is open 8 am to 10 pm in summer and 8 to dusk in winter. (471-4967)

San Francisco Bay National Wildlife Refuge

Beside the toll plaza at the Fremont end of the Dumbarton Bridge which carries Highway 84 across the South Bay.

On a knoll just above the bridge's toll plaza, the Wildlife Refuge is building a visitor center and administration building. When the center opens in mid-1979, it will offer wildlife exhibits and pictorial presentations. Also there will be three short trails around the little hill and beside Newark Slough. The refuge will include 23,000 acres of Bay, salt ponds and marsh (much of the shore south of the San Mateo Bridge in Alameda, Santa Clara and San Mateo counties) when acquisition is complete. Preservation of habitat for millions of migratory waterfowl and shore birds and rare and endangered species is a principal purpose, and in the future there will be more public access to the various ecosystems of the refuge. An environmental education center on the northeast edge of Alviso and a trail through refuge lands from Coyote Hills Regional Park are expected to be completed soon. At present the National Wildlife Refuge headquarters is in Fremont. (792-0222)

The City and South — San Francisco, San Mateo and Santa Clara counties

Fort Point (GGNRA)

Off Highway 101 at last San Francisco exit near toll plaza, then follow signs to Marine Drive and the point. Also served by Golden Gate Transit and Muni bus to the toll plaza above.

This remnant of Civil War history is situated beneath the south tower of the Golden Gate Bridge at the entrance to the Bay. When the Bridge was constructed, special care was taken to preserve this brick harbor fortification. Guided tours are given on weekends; historic programs and ceremonies are scheduled regularly. The seawall is ideal for fishing and is an outpost for viewing the continual surge of the water from the Pacific through the Golden Gate. The Fort is open 10 am-5 pm. (556-1693)

Golden Gate Promenade (GGNRA)

A walking path stretching for three and one-half miles along San Francisco's shoreline from Ft. Point to Aquatic Park. Easily accessible by Muni bus or car at either end or at several intervals. Signs mark the route, along which you can enjoy the sun, the water, the birds, beachcombing, the sails, the tidepools, piers for fishing, picnic sites, the kites, and striking and forgotten views of the Golden Gate and the Bay. The route crosses Crissy Field, the yacht club and harbor, Marina Green, Ft. Mason, the Muni Pier and Aquatic Park.

Fort Mason (GGNRA)

In San Francisco, at foot of Van Ness Avenue or at Marina Boulevard and Laguna Street are entrances to the promenade through Ft. Mason. Served by Muni bus.

Part of the Golden Gate Promenade traverses Fort Mason, the headquarters for the Golden Gate National Recreation Area. The path beside the piers and along the seawall yields views of the Bay's islands, the Golden Gate Bridge and Marin. Rangers lead guided walks at 1 pm on weekends and holidays. Fishing from two of the old embarkation piers and on the old Alcatraz pier. The walkway is open 10 am-5 pm. The piers are the site of interesting programs, including music, dance and theater. For information about GGNRA programs, call headquarters 556-2920.

Aquatic Park (GGNRA)

In San Francisco, at foot of Van Ness Avenue and foot of Hyde Street, across from Ghirardelli Square. Served by Muni bus and cable car.

Part of the Golden Gate Promenade traverses Aquatic Park, which contains the San Francisco Maritime Museum and adjoins the Municipal Pier with full facilities for fishermen. ''Polar bears'' go swimming at the beach. Adjacent Hyde Street Pier with its old ships forms part of what is now called the National Maritime Museum. The large brick Haslett Warehouse office building across Hyde Street from the cable car turntable now belongs to the GGNRA and they plan to turn it into a museum.

Alcatraz Island (GGNRA)

Reached only by the special ferry from Pier 43 in San Francisco. Reservations are necessary (546-2805).

Guided tours of this mysterious island, lasting about two and a half hours, are conducted by National Park rangers explaining the history of ''The Rock'' — from Spanish discovery through its military fortification and federal prison days to Indian occupation. Be prepared for lots of hiking and some steep climbing; wear a warm coat and good shoes. The views from this Bay vantage point are tremendous, with all the landmarks of the central Bay readily at hand. Boats run daily from 9 am-5 pm, every 45 minutes.

Pier 41

In San Francisco, along The Embarcadero near Fisherman's Wharf.

A small waterfront park space — bland, with bunkers for trees and benches for people, almost overwhelmed by the tawdry Pier 39 development next door. Stretching along The Embarcadero, it is not a pleasant, people kind of park, but merely a green alley to channel consumers to the ersatz tourist mecca that is Pier 39. However it does offer views of the sailboats in the new marina and other Bay vistas. Also there is the chilling promenade around the outside edge of Pier 39 which takes you 1,000 feet out into the Bay. If you can stand the unwelcoming coldness of the backs of buildings, garbage cans and sewer leaks, and if you don't get run down by a maintenance truck that clearly thinks that the promenade is no place for pedestrians, you will find marvelous views of the Bay and its shipping.

San Francisco — Downtown

In downtown San Francisco, at end of Market Street along The Embarcadero.

This section of The Embarcadero is a particularly pleasant walk with little landscaped parcels, shipping and tugboat activities; the Golden Gate Ferries to Sausalito and Larkspur leave from the terminal behind the Ferry Building. The far end of parking lot Pier 7 is a good fishing spot. There are several nooks for lunchtime picnickers on the piers adjacent to the Ferry Building which provide glimpses across the Bay. For a planned promenade, the piers south of the Ferry Building are already being dismantled to open up the waterfront for strollers, fishermen and Bay-watchers.

San Francisco — South Waterfront

In the south waterfront area of San Francisco, off of Third Street.

There are several small land parcels in this, the working part of San Francisco's port, especially at Central Basin, Warmwater Cove and Islais Creek Channel. On China Basin Street is Agua Vista Park (Port of San Francisco) with its fishing pier beside Mission Rock Resort. Nearby, at the foot of Mariposa Street, is a marked public access point with a view of the Bethlehem Shipyard. At the end of Twenty-fourth Street, in the warm water discharge of a PG&E power plant, is a good fishing spot from a shoreline that has been pleasantly refurbished with trees, earth mounds and a small fishing pier. At the lift bridge where Third Street crosses Islais Creek, two mini-parks allow fishing and port-watching.

Candlestick Point (soon to be a State Recreation Area)

Off Highway 101 in San Francisco at Third Street-Bayshore exit, then follow the signs to Candlestick Park.

The rough wasteland of bay fill that surrounds this point, on the shore side of Candlestick Park (the home of the Giants), is scheduled for acquisition and development as a state park. At present, there are some spots suitable for fishing, some for walking. Views across to the East Bay Hills, down the Bay and toward San Bruno Mountain.

Point San Bruno

Off Highway 101 in South San Francisco at Grand Avenue exit, then follow East Grand Avenue and Forbes Boulevard to Pt. San Bruno Boulevard.

Past the parking lot is a small park and shoreline strip, landscaped, with a path. Good for fishing, watching the waterfowl and weekend picnicking. Views of airport action and down the Bay to Coyote Point and the San Mateo Bridge. Atop a hill behind you is the giant sculpture representing Bay bridges with San Bruno Mountain as a backdrop.

Burlingame

Off Highway 101 in Burlingame at Millbrae Avenue, Broadway or Peninsula Avenue exits, then to Old Bayshore Highway and Airport Boulevard.

On Old Bayshore Highway is a rough parking strip on the shore with jumbled concrete rip-rap; there are good views of airport activities. On the Bay side of the Casa Maria, Vagabond and Fisherman restaurants are landscaped walkways, and the small adjacent marsh is the Shorebird Sanctuary. On Airport Boulevard, there is a paved shoreline pathway opposite Burlingame's Bayside Park that extends south behind the airport parking lot as a bikeway beside Burlingame Lagoon; on the Bay side of the boulevard, a huge dirt fill area surrounds Anza Lagoon where you sometimes see small boat sailing, or you can just walk for some Bay-watching. The Diamond Showboat restaurant parking lot has fishing from its rough edge on the Bay. And Fishermans Park (San Mateo County), near Coyote Point, has benches, tables and is a good fishing location. Views of San Bruno Mountain, the airport and north across the Bay.

Coyote Point Park (San Mateo County)

Off Highway 101 near Burlingame on Peninsula Avenue and Coyote Point Drive.

One of the few places on the west side of the Bay where there is anything like a beach (with summer lifeguards). The park occupies a wooded knoll and extends along the shore in both directions, the half mile of artificial beach on one side and a marina on the other. South of the marina a biking and walking levee path extends for a mile to Third Avenue. Along with a restaurant, picnic areas and a playground, there is a Junior Museum nature center. Entry fee is $2/car, except there is no charge for those going to the restaurant or marina. The park is open from 8 am to dark. (573-2592)

Foster City

Off Highway 101 at Highway 92, go towards the San Mateo Bridge, then turn right on Foster City Boulevard, and turn left on Hillsdale Boulevard.

Just under the south side of the San Mateo Bridge is the San Mateo County Fishing Pier which sticks far out into the Bay. It has restrooms and benches and is open 24 hours. Walk and bird-watch along Beach Park Boulevard where the parallel Bay shoreline consists of shell beach, marshland and a roadway along Belmont Slough. Views of the bridge and across the Bay.

Redwood Shores

Off Highway 101 in Redwood City on Marine World Parkway to end, then either turn left into rough undeveloped land or turn right on Bridge Parkway and follow Tiller Lane and Spar Drive to cul-de-sac.

Walk on a dirt and gravel road and path that skirts the edge of the peninsula for five and a half miles along Belmont Slough, the Bay and Steinberger Slough. From these levees surrounded by wasteland, you can see across the Bay and find waterfowl, willets, sandpipers, avocets, herons and egrets — the sentinels of the sloughs.

Redwood City Marina (Redwood City)

Off Highway 101 at Harbor Boulevard exit, then follow toward the port to marina.

The marina has a small park area. A picnic deck beside the water, a small fishing pier and the sailboats in the basin are attractions. Around you are mountains of salt and a restaurant.

Baylands Nature Interpretive Center (City of Palo Alto)

Off Highway 101 in Palo Alto at Embarcadero Road exit, then follow road to end and bear left past yacht harbor.

This environmental center has regularly scheduled programs and nature walks. It is surrounded by marsh preserve, sloughs and mud flats that are typical of much of the Bay's shoreline. Explore the marsh on boardwalks or on perimeter levees. At the recycling center, south of the yacht harbor, there are signs for a nature walk which takes you around the levees of a flood control basin for miles of hiking along Mayfield and Charleston sloughs and the Bay. The Center is open 2-5 pm weekdays and 10 am-6 pm weekends. (329-2506)

Shoreline Regional Park (City of Mountain View)

Off Highway 101 at Stierlin Road exit in Mountain View, then follow road past landfill site to end.

This large park is being developed on landfill beside some salt ponds. It is accessible now on weekends (when construction is not going on) for walking over the dirt hills and beside the salt ponds with views of the Bay. They hope to have an environmental center relatively soon. Eventually the park will have a golf course, a small sailing lake and a reconstructed marsh area. Also planned is a trail through the park that would connect with shoreside access at Stevens Creek and Palo Alto Baylands.

San Francisco Bay Model (Corps of Engineers)

Off Highway 101 at Marin City-Sausalito exit, then right on Bridgeway past second light, then immediately turn left to 2100 Bridgeway.

A Bay tour would not be complete without seeing the Bay Model. This is the one place in the Bay region where you can see the entire Bay from a single vantage point. In a huge, dark warehouse is a hydraulic model of San Francisco Bay (including the Delta) molded in concrete, rising only a few feet off the floor. In its scale operation, a tidal cycle of 14.9 minutes surges under the six-foot-long Golden Gate Bridge. The model is open 9 am-4 pm on weekdays and the first and third Saturdays of the month. (332-3870)

Transportation Under, On and Over the Bay

Historically, the Bay has been an impediment to commerce and travel. The basic problem now is the same as it was then — how to cross to the other side. From the era of sporadic transbay sailing ventures, to the fledgling mass transit period of river steamers and grandiose ferryboats, to mass production-inspired spanning of the waters by mighty bridges for individual propulsion units, we seem to be closing the circle by a return to modern modes of mass transit. However the comparison does not quite fit — riding in the flickering darkness of BART's tube is not nearly the same as the sea air, fog, sea gulls, sparkling sunshine and beautiful views of the bygone ferryboat time.

Whether your trip is for business or pleasure, you can find information in this section about crossing the Bay. Everything is covered — so-called ''space age'' rapid transit trains beneath the Bay, ferries (San Francisco's traditional mass transit), bridges (for today, but maybe not tomorrow) that cross the Bay, buses across the bridges. For bicyclists, tips are mentioned in the section *Shoreline Bicycle Routes and Tours*.

Under the Bay

Bay Area Rapid Transit (BART)

After fifteen years of planning and construction, BART finally got off to a fitful start, opening sections of its route to service and ultimately the transbay tube in 1974. BART's bond with the Bay is the submarine tube that connects San Francisco and Oakland (there's no truth to the story that this tunnel was dug by the Oakland Mole). The electric trains of BART connect stations in San Francisco, Alameda and Contra Costa counties with seventy-one miles of track. The trains operate from 6 am to approximately midnight on Mondays through Saturdays, and 9 am to midnight on Sundays. Transfers to bus systems for service to waterfront areas are available in San Francisco and the East Bay. Restricted bicycle access to the trains is permitted. In San Francisco, the Embarcadero Station is very near the waterfront activities of Justin Herman Plaza and the Ferry Building. The first station across the Bay is Oakland West, and the Lake Merritt Station is near the Oakland Museum, Lake Merritt, and several blocks from the Estuary. (As an example of BART's "space age" character, it now takes two minutes longer to cross from Berkeley to San Francisco than it did using the Key System's trains and ferries in 1903.) Fares on the system vary by distance; there is a special excursion fare. Bay Area Rapid Transit (San Francisco 788-BART — East Bay 465-BART)

The Bay's other underwater passages are a pair of tunnels beneath the Estuary that separates Oakland and Alameda. In fact this is the major auto traffic link that joins Alameda to the mainland. The Webster Street Tube and the Posey Tube plunge underground near Jack London Square (Alameda exit from Highway 17) and surface as Webster Street near Mariner Square in Alameda.

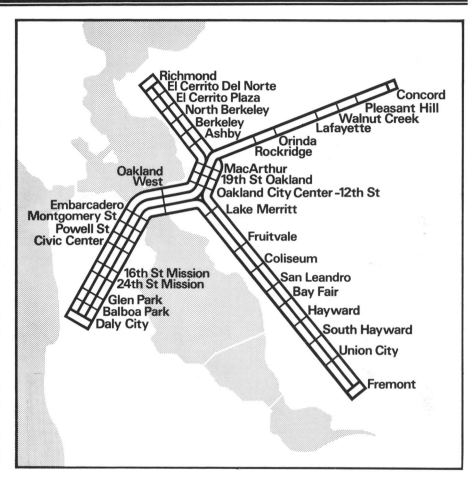

On the Bay

Ferryboats

The classic image of San Francisco is a view from the water, and there are millions who still remember the venerable Ferry Building as the entrance, the gateway, to the City. Travelers journeying to the City and commuters of the workaday world approached on ferryboats in the days before the bridges.

That golden age is gone, but there are revitalized ferry operations on San Francisco Bay. The focus has changed. There are no longer East Bay routes like those that carried millions of passengers each year, bringing them from transcontinental trains and from home to office. Now the emphasis is the suburb to the north, Marin County, and ferries for recreational pursuits. Ferryboat rides have now come to be characterized as floating cocktail parties. (Actually, you have to be quick to down two drinks.) The last of the stately ferryboat routes to die was the Richmond-San Rafael, replaced by the bridge in 1956. Still in service is what has to be considered the last of the large ferryboats, *Las Plumas,* the railcar ferry of the Western Pacific.

New ferry routes also function to deliver passengers to parks for recreational relaxation. A ride on almost any of these ferryboats is as good as a harbor tour excursion, and it's less expensive. For information about the special tour boats to Alcatraz, which is not precisely a ferry operation, see the section *Cruising the Bay.* Bicyclists, and their bicycles, are more or less welcome on all the ferry runs listed below, except the Mare Island Ferry.

Mare Island

For the real ferry freak, this route is the only remaining historic route on the Bay that has been in continuous operation up to the present time. Begun in 1855, it was one of the first ferry services on the Bay. One of the hoary vessels that served on this line, the *Issaquah* which retired in 1948, now lies mouldering at the Gate 5 houseboat area in Sausalito. The Mare Island Ferry now runs modern motor launches across the waters of Mare Island Strait. Boats operate during commute hours, transferring workers to the Navy Yard from the terminal beside the Wharf restaurant in Vallejo. If you feel constrained to partake of this bit of history, the service is open to the public, but the Navy Yard is not. Mare Island Ferry (707-643-7542)

Larkspur

The Golden Gate Bridge District has initiated a new ferry route, from San Francisco's fine old Ferry Building to the new tetrahedron terminal at Larkspur on an inlet near San Quentin. The purpose is to connect commuter buses from points in Marin to the ferry for a speedy trip to downtown San Francisco.

Since the idea's inception, it has been controversial, primarily because of expense. Tolls from the Golden Gate Bridge are being used to cover ferry system deficits (and the toll may be going up). Before the GT *Marin* took to the water in December 1976, to inaugurate this route, there were two and one-half years of escalating costs and mechanical set-backs. Three months later the GT *Sonoma* joined the fleet. It's not fair to guess, considering past delays, but the GT *San Francisco* may be in service by the end of 1979.

These sleek, gas turbine-powered boats have been criticized as too luxurious — which isn't true, they are just right. The interiors have been described as being as plush as an airplane, but they are not that crummy. Actually the boats are very attractive, and they provide a fast, smooth, enjoyable ride, one of the nicest rides on the Bay. Despite being half the size (165 feet from stem to stern) and half the capacity (750 passengers) of the magnificent ferryboats of the past, they still house many amenities — an adequate bar, lots of windows for sight-seeing, historical pictures for decoration, and plenty of deck space for walking. Some special excursions on the Larkspur Ferry are mentioned in the section *Cruising the Bay.* Service at approximately hourly intervals, 6 am to 8 pm weekdays, 9 am to 6 pm weekends. Fares — one-way $1.50, children 75¢ ($2 and $1 on summer weekends). Golden Gate Transit (San Francisco 332-6600 — Marin 453-2100)

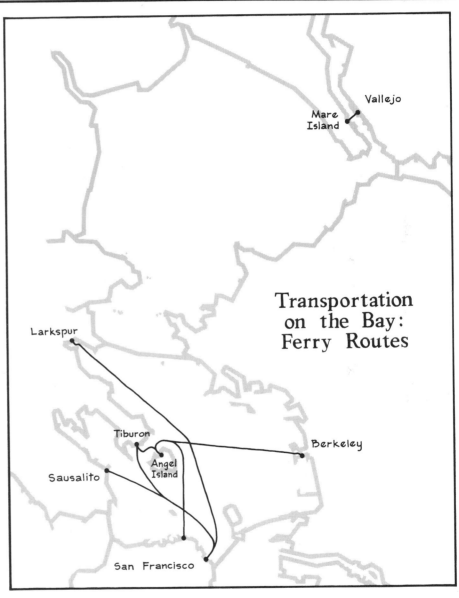

Transportation on the Bay: Ferry Routes

Vallejo

Mare Island

Larkspur

Tiburon

Berkeley

Sausalito

Angel Island

San Francisco

Sausalito

If your pleasure is an excursion that includes a cruise on the Bay and then a stroll around a fascinating petite port that is historically reminiscent and scenically alluring, then Sausalito is your goal. The attractions are many — boutiques enough to make a bazaar, comestibles for hearty consumption, promenades for pedestrians, and, not least, passage on the ferryboat which crosses the busiest part of the harbor and accords the most revealing sightseeing opportunities.

Sausalito was the terminus of the first ferry to Marin. The North Pacific Coast Railway pioneered a route to San Francisco's Ferry Building that lasted more than sixty-five years, with its successor, the Northwestern Pacific RR, running the last old-time ferryboats on this route in 1941. As you cruise to Sausalito on the *Golden Gate,* perhaps you can barely glimpse this last-run floating palace, the *Eureka,* tied up at the San Francisco Maritime Historic Park near Ghirardelli Square. Nearly thirty years later, in 1970, the Golden Gate Bridge District revived a ferry operation as part of a commuter service of buses and ferryboats from Marin to the Ferry Building in San Francisco.

On weekdays the boat runs approximately from 7 am to 8 pm, on weekends from 9 am to 9 pm. Embarking in Sausalito you buy your ticket on the boat. Fares — one-way $1.50, children 75¢ ($2 and $1 on summer weekends). Golden Gate Transit (San Francisco 332-6600 — Marin 453-2100)

Tiburon

Another delightful destination that furnishes comfortable walking and browsing within a very small area is Tiburon. You can check out the charming shops or treat yourself at one of several restaurants, on a sunny day enjoy the decks (see section *Dining and Drinking*). Commuter service on the "Red & White Fleet's" *Harbor Queen* from Tiburon to the City (Ferry Building) is run on weekdays (approximately 6:30 to 8 am), with reverse service in the evenings (a couple of the evening returns dock at Fisherman's Wharf).

This is a restoration of the route operated by the San Francisco & North Pacific RR in the 1880s and 1890s — this direct route was dropped in 1909. The ferryboat fleet included the *Ukiah* which was rebuilt as the *Eureka* and now reposes at the San Francisco Maritime Historic Park.

The more recreational ferry service operates as the San Francisco-Angel Island-Tiburon route (see below) on weekends and holidays, also weekdays during the summer. Departures from Pier 43 at Fisherman's Wharf.

Buy tickets on-board when bound for the City. Fares — one-way $2. Harbor Carriers (546-2810)

Angel Island

The largest island on the Bay, Angel Island is the region's leading pleasure ground. Approachable only by boat, its isolated status protects it from intrusion by autos and other facts of urban life. This state park is reserved for walking, playing, picnicking, observing, bicycling, sightseeing and other activities suitable to the environment. The best part of an excursion to Angel Island is the ride on one of the ferries to get there. Angel Island State Park; for information about the park (435-1915)

from San Francisco

The "Red & White Fleet" operates ferryboats to Angel Island from Pier 43 at Fisherman's Wharf. Departures start at 10 am and continue at approximately two-hour intervals. The boats stop at Angel Island and then go on to Tiburon before returning to San Francisco. Be sure not to miss the last returning boat, which can be as late as 6:15 pm on summer weekends. Season: daily, Memorial Day to Labor Day; weekends and holidays the rest of the year. Fares — round-trip $4.25, children $2.25. Harbor Carriers (546-2815)

from Berkeley

The "Red & White Fleet" also sails from the Berkeley Marina to Angel Island. This weekend service departs from the Marina at 10 am only and leaves the island at 5 pm only. Season: first Saturday in April to last Sunday in October, weekends and holidays only. Fares — round-trip $3.50, children $1.75. Harbor Carriers (546-2815)

from Tiburon

Another ferry route, which could be of interest to Marin bike riders, operates from Tiburon. The small launch departs hourly from the dock on Main Street between the Dock and Sabella's restaurants. Season: daily in summer (June to Labor Day) 10 am-4 pm ('til 6 on weekends); weekends and holidays only in winter (Labor Day to June) 10 am-4 pm. Fares — round-trip $1.75, children $1, bicycles 25¢. Angel Island Ferry (435-2131)

Over the Bay
Bridges

To many, San Francisco Bay means its bridges. The glamourous Golden Gate, the business-like Bay, the rolling Richmond, the duplex Carquinez, the serviceable San Mateo, and the dumpy Dumbarton — these six bridges are the jewels in the sparkling, encircling crown of the Bay. They are the steel sinews that bind the area into one place. The bridges provide the most powerful images of this region.

If you are tied up on a bridge during a rush hour traffic jam, you probably are not admiring the beauty of the bridge, but probably damning its function as a bottleneck, and even regretting the passing of the ferryboats that the bridges replaced. As a mark of our mechanized age, the traffic use of the bridges has been, in general, underestimated. This traffic ''problem'' has given rise to many schemes to cope with it. Among them are a paltry revival of our once comprehensive ferry system and a study for a second deck for the Golden Gate Bridge. Designs have been considered for additional crossings of the Bay — a very characteristic Frank Lloyd Wright plan for a soaring arch to Oakland; several plans for routes from the south waterfront of San Francisco to Oakland or Alameda, including the long-lived Southern Crossing (some involved a combination bridge and tunnel); even a couple of plans that for extent would beat any bridge we now have, a crossing from the City to Richmond, and another from the City to Tiburon via Angel Island.

One curiosity about bridges, and our bridges in particular, which may never be satisfied is comparative length. When

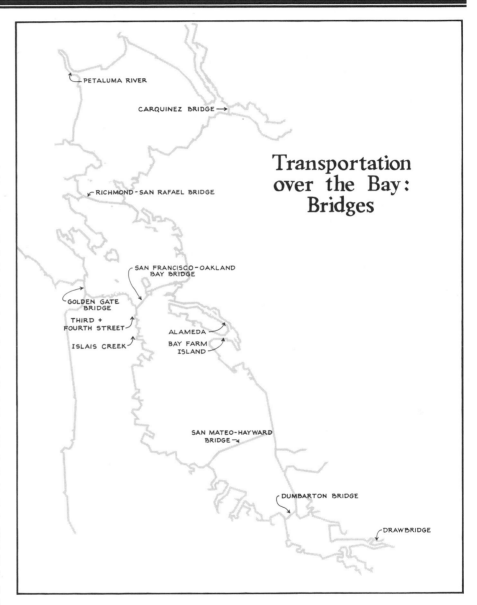

Transportation over the Bay: Bridges

you delve into the world's longest, you are confronted with categories. Historically, there is the longest ''at time of construction'' (our Carquinez, Bay and Richmond bridges qualify). When type of construction is considered, it becomes even more complicated. For suspension bridges, length is determined as ''single, or center, span'' (the Golden Gate is second, and either one of the twin spans of the Bay Bridge is sixth), or it is determined as ''anchorage to anchorage'' (the Golden Gate is third), or it is determined as ''end to end of approaches.'' In cantilever construction, consideration is given the ''main span'' (the Bay Bridge is third, and the Carquinez is tenth), and ''end to end of approaches.'' When gauging total length, as in ''the longest bridge in the world,'' judgment is even more perplexing. On some lists of this classification, our bridges are noted: in fifth place San Mateo, in seventh place Bay Bridge, and just outside the top ten, Richmond-San Rafael. But to accept this placing, you must convince yourself that the San Mateo Bridge is actually two (a pair of) bridges, and furthermore that ''end to end of approaches'' applies to low-level bridges (and causeways) which hop over islands and slide through tunnels. To all that, I say pfui. Comparing a high-level marvel like the Bay Bridge to the San Mateo Bridge is like comparing apples and avocados. By disregarding all the ''non-bridge'' entries and adopting a strict ''shore to shore'' stance, the Richmond-San Rafael Bridge becomes the longest bridge in the world, and the Bay Bridge is a close second (subtracting its tunnel through Yerba Buena).

None of these lengthy debates is likely to come to mind when you're zooming across one of the bridges. More likely that you can recognize the surroundings and relate them to the Bay as a whole. For many travelers, the Carquinez Bridge is a principal entrance to the Bay Area and their first glimpse of San Francisco Bay. Even a glance at freeway speed gives you some sense of the rivers emptying into a

large basin and the Bay stretching away toward the ocean. From the Richmond-San Rafael Bridge you can note the extent of the Bay in both directions. It is a demarcation between the remote northern Bay and the urbanized central Bay, with Mt. Tamalpais looming over it all. The Bay Bridge is a trip between two metropolises, with proximity to intense development and maritime activity. You have a sense of being where everything's happening. The Golden Gate Bridge is a perfect connection between seething (SF) and serene (Marin). The open sea is beyond with world commerce flowing out of the harbor (gateway). The San Mateo-Hayward and Dumbarton are flat bridges across marsh, mud and salt with dredged levees. They connect the flat sprawl of South Bay suburbs. It is my recommendation that you travel all of our bridges, because in a way each presents and represents some facet of the character of San Francisco Bay.

Carquinez Bridge

Carquinez Strait marks one boundary of San Francisco Bay. It is where the waters of the Sacramento and San Joaquin rivers, since ancient times, have tumbled through the narrow opening that they carved and flooded the valley between coast mountain ranges. For some years transportation across the channel was provided by several ferry lines. The Rodeo-Vallejo Ferry lasted less than ten years on the Strait, closing in 1927 when the bridge opened. This privately-financed bridge was the second to span a portion of San Francisco Bay, and its construction paved the way for building our other bridges in deep, swift water. At the time it opened it was billed as "the world's highest bridge" (135 feet above the water). It was advertised in an age of motor car enthusiasm — "this mighty

span makes it possible for the motorist to drive from Tia Juana, Mexico, to Vancouver, Canada, a distance of 1775 miles, without use of ferries." In a remarkable outburst of foresight, it was the Rodeo-Vallejo Ferry company which formed a subsidiary, the American Toll Bridge Company, to build the Carquinez Bridge, and thus built themselves out of the ferry business.

As a condition of the franchise, the bridge reverted to Contra Costa and Solano counties and the State in 1948. In 1958 the State built a very similar (but not twin) bridge alongside that carries Sacramento-bound traffic.

The pair of bridges now carry the traffic of Interstate 80, west to San Francisco and east to Sacramento. The toll for automobiles is 40¢ and is collected only eastbound.

Richmond-San Rafael Bridge

The newest of the Bay's six bridges is the Richmond-San Rafael Bridge. When it opened in 1956, traversing almost exactly the Richmond-San Rafael Ferry route, it brought to an end the last of our auto ferries.

With a description that is full of qualifiers, it is the world's longest (uninterrupted), high-level (not causeway), over-water (continuously) bridge at a little over four miles. (Some less than authoritative listings have it as the world's thirteenth longest.) It has a sag in the middle that gives a "roller coaster" effect (it rises to 185 feet above the main shipping channel) and a pronounced bend as it approaches the Marin County shore. The double-decked bridge was built by the State, and bears Highway 17 between Richmond and San Rafael. One of the traffic lanes now carries an emergency water pipeline to Marin. When you're zipping across, you can see Red Rock (a boundary point of San Francisco County) and also The Brothers lighthouse.

The bonds have not been paid off yet, so you're still paying for the bridge. The toll for automobiles is $1 and is collected only westbound.

San Francisco-Oakland Bay Bridge

For many years, since the 1860s, schemes for crossing the Bay were concocted to connect San Francisco with the eastern shore and thus the rest of the country. Several routes were advanced, including at least one that combined a bridge and tunnel. One long-lived plan called for a bridge to cross from the east shore to Yerba Buena Island with ferry service continuing to the City. Another of the early plans was revived in recent years as the State Highway Department's dream of a "southern crossing" — the Hunters Point-Alameda route. However, thanks to vehement local opposition and state political moves, this dreadnought may have been scuttled once and for all.

Work on the San Francisco-Oakland Bay Bridge that we now have, the central crossing, got under way in July 1933. Construction required the leveling of Rincon Hill in San Francisco for one approach and anchorage, the tunneling of Yerba Buena Island, and the placing of bridge supports parallel to the Key System pier for approaches from Oakland. Built simultaneously to the Golden Gate, the Bay Bridge was commenced later and completed earlier. It opened November 12, 1936.

The bridge is composed of twin suspension spans on the west side of Yerba Buena and one main cantilever span and five truss spans on the east side, carrying Interstate 80 across nearly four miles of water. It is double-decked with one-way traffic on each deck and exits in the middle to Yerba Buena and Treasure Island. The top deck is City-bound. Originally the lower deck carried trucks and interurban tracks, but train service was discontinued in 1958. Each of the twin cable suspension spans soars 2,310 feet. The towers rise 474 and 519 feet above the water, and the roadway clearance over the shipping channel is in excess of 200 feet.

The San Francisco-Oakland Bay Bridge is not the phenomenon that the Golden Gate is. The celebration of its opening was not as big as the Golden Gate's, and its birthdays are not noted as enthusiastically. However, because of its location, its presence is probably displayed to more of the population of San Francisco and Oakland. It doesn't have the dash or glitter, but it makes no pretensions. It performs its function with authority, carrying a greater number of travelers and commuters on their journeys than any of the other bridges on the Bay. The best part of a trip on the bridge is the memorable image you command from its height, the dignified water entrance to the City, descending to the shore.

If you have any car trouble on the bridge, there are convenient call boxes scattered along the side. There is emergency gas service, and if you need a tow it's free to whichever end of the bridge you choose. Unlike the Golden Gate, you can't leave any miscellaneous items for security if you forget the toll.

The tolls have recently been raised — you are now financing mass transit. Car pools (three or more people) are toll free, 6-9 am and 3-6 pm. The toll for automobiles is 75¢ and is collected only westbound.

Golden Gate Bridge

The headlands at the mouth of San Francisco Bay were given the name Golden Gate by Frémont, even before the city was called San Francisco. For 160 years after the first settlement of this now-populous peninsula, there was no bond across the strait. Now we have a bridge which is at the same time a symbol, a tourist attraction, a congested trafficway, and a menace to lives.

Usually a representation of San Francisco includes a picture of the Golden Gate Bridge to make it instantly identifiable. And appropriately the bridge is a symbol of San Francisco — more than any other this is *our* bridge. Born in vision, nurtured in controversy, matured in progress and celebrated as destiny, the bridge is a fitting product of engineering and architecture to be the colossus that stands at the edge of a continent.

The popular myth that one of San Francisco's first bizarre characters, Joshua A. Norton (Norton I, Emperor of the United States and Protector of Mexico), commanded that the Golden Gate be bridged has no basis in fact. In 1869, from his summer capital in Oakland, he ordered a suspension bridge built from Oakland to Yerba Buena Island to Sausalito to the Farallones for the Central Pacific Railroad. (Now that was a vision, but not of a Golden Gate Bridge.) This hare-brained scheme of Emperor Norton's blocked serious discussion of Bay crossing proposals for many years. In 1872 and again in 1916 suggestions were made about the desirability of bridging the Golden Gate. Then along came Joseph B. Strauss, the mighty man with the magic imagination that it took to finally erect the bridge. He came to San Francisco in 1919 to survey

the problem presented by the Golden Gate. In 1922 his plan for a bridge was published. The dream was adopted in 1923 by Frank P. Doyle, of Santa Rosa, who became known as "the father of the Golden Gate Bridge," because of his campaign for construction and service on the bridge's board of directors. Then came the obstructions — political maneuvering, bonding hassles, engineering recriminations, re-bids for construction and a series of court litigations. Given the opportunity, people of four counties and part of two others overwhelmingly voted to pledge their property to back the construction bonds for the bridge. Through it all, the chief engineer, Strauss, with the financial help of A. P. Giannini's Bank of America, pressed on, and ultimately the will of the people prevailed. So there is a basis for the esteem and pride of ownership that makes it *our* bridge — we helped build it.

Construction started on the Marin side of the bridge on January 4, 1933. Opening day, reserved for the huge crowds of pedestrians, was May 27, 1937. The first automobiles crossed the following day. Celebrations lasted for more than a week, and Hollywood entertainers Robert Taylor, George Jessel and Al Jolson appeared in the City to participate in the festival. The bridge's anniversaries are periodically commemorated (the fortieth was in 1977). It has now become the world's number one man-made tourist attraction, so it is being constantly saluted every day.

The Golden Gate is no longer the world's longest suspension bridge, although it was for many years. The suspension span of 4,200 feet is surpassed by a mere 60 feet on the Verrazano-Narrows Bridge in New York. The twin towers, the gate of the Golden Gate, spring 746 feet from the water and the roadway structure has a clearance of 220 feet at mid-span. The bridge was built as a flexible structure which is affected by temperature and air movement. On cold days the tops of the towers move away from each other (as much as 22 inches) and the roadway arches upward; on hot days the effect is the opposite (towers may move 18 inches). The tower tops may move 12 inches side to side. A stiff wind can set the roadway in motion and blow it as much as 16 feet up and down and sway it 27 feet back and forth. Contrary to some expectations, the bridge is not painted gold. An early plan was to paint the bridge a multi-hued rainbow effect with the towers gold to symbolize the Golden Gate. Less colorful heads prevailed — the coating is a specially mixed International Orange paint, perhaps just the right color to capture the many moods of lyric beauty in different light and weather to make it truly a "span of gold."

The Golden Gate Bridge has become a hazard to life as an alluring magnet for suicide. The first confirmed suicide leap was less than three months after the opening. To date there have been more than six hundred known suicides off the bridge. Eleven who leaped have survived. A couple of stuntmen have successfully jumped and told the tale, but there have been a few unsuccessful ones also. Despite efforts of the Bridge District to prevent self-destruction and other calamities, proposals have been made to erect barriers and to ban walking and cycling on the bridge. Any suicide-prevention fence can only detract from the bridge's well-conceived architecture. Bicycle riding was prohibited in the 1960s (then restored), and the suggestion was made again in 1977. But too many people bike across the bridge to make that a good idea. (Besides, bicycles may be the commuter vehicles of the future.)

In addition to the magic span that it is, the bridge offers other attractions to the sightseer. At each end of the bridge, in San Francisco and Marin, there are vista points, parking lots with good views of the Bay, and surrounding hillsides and skylines of the cities. The Golden Gate is also the only bridge on the Bay that you can walk or bicycle across. During daylight hours, you can take a stroll on the east (Bay side) walkway which is a mile and a half long observation deck from one vista point to the other. However, it is often quite windy and cold, but you get a magnificent view of the scenery and the cables of the bridge. The bicycle route is on the east side on weekdays and on the ocean side on weekends.

The Golden Gate Bridge conveys north-south Highway 101 from San Francisco across to Marin and the northern redwood country beyond. If you have any car trouble, a free tow service will get you off the bridge. If you have a flat, you're supposed to keep driving on the flat tire to get off the bridge. Too many people have been run over to make it something to have doubts about. The bridge office at the toll plaza has amassed wondrous stuff that people have left as security when they didn't have the toll. Some come back to redeem their pawn, some do not.

The tolls were raised a few years ago, and there has been discussion since about raising them again. Needless to say, this action has sparked heated protest, since the bridge bonds were paid off in 1971. The Bridge District now uses the income to support a system of buses and ferryboats. Car pools (three or more people) are toll free, 6-10 am. The toll for automobiles for now is $1 and is collected only southbound.

San Mateo-Hayward Bridge

The San Mateo Bridge was the third span across the Bay. Built through private initiative, the San Francisco Bay Toll Bridge Company, it opened in 1929. It was a low-level crossing with a vertical lift span above the navigation channel. The bridge has since been taken over and operated by the State.

The channel is now spanned by a concrete arching orthopropic span that gives the bridge a definite incline section and a sinister bend toward the western end. The cities of San Mateo and Hayward are connected by highway 92 across seven miles of water.

The tolls have recently been raised — you are now financing mass transit. Car pools (three or more people) are toll free, 6-9 am and 3-6 pm. The toll for automobiles is 75¢ and is collected only westbound.

Dumbarton Bridge

The first auto span to cross part of San Francisco Bay was the Dumbarton Bridge. It was built by the Dumbarton Bridge Company in 1927. These private entrepreneurs barged pre-built spans down the bay from Oakland. It is a mile-long, low-level crossing (six and one-half miles total) with a drawbridge over the shipping channel. At the present time, the State, which now owns the bridge, has an active scheme afoot (or is that awash) to replace this bridge with a brand new one. Delaying lawsuits and planning contingencies have extended the construction several years into the future.

About a hundred years ago the name Dumbarton (for a county in Scotland) was given to a railroad stop where the community of Newark is today. Subsequently the name was transferred to the

bridge. Someone has suggested that to be fair, it should be called the Reasonably Intelligent Barton Bridge.

It carries Highway 84 between Palo Alto/Menlo Park and Newark/Fremont. Crossing the bridge, you seem to be surrounded by salt evaporation ponds.

The tolls have recently been raised — you are now financing mass transit. Car pools (three or more people) are toll free, 6-9 am and 3-6 pm. The toll for automobiles is 75¢ and is collected only westbound.

Other Bridges

There are several other interesting bridges that cross creeks and channels of the Bay. Most of them are drawbridges that are opened only occasionally to let boats in and out of berths. They are for real bridge enthusiasts.

In San Francisco, on the south waterfront:

Third Street Bridge. The most intriguing of these subsidiary spans is the bridge that carries Third Street and railroad tracks across China Basin (Mission Creek). This metal monster is a Strauss trunnion bascule bridge, named for

Joseph B. Strauss (engineer for the Golden Gate Bridge) who invented this type of counter-weighted bascule lift for drawbridges. It has been in operation since May 1933, replacing a bridge built by Atchison, Topeka & Santa Fe RR in 1904. Operation of the bridge is such a curiosity that special weekend demonstrations of the "draw" or lift have been performed. The best opportunity to see it up is on a weekend, but then purely by chance.

Fourth Street Bridge. Just a block away from its more impressive sister (above), this plain Jane sibling is much smaller. It carries Fourth Street across China Basin (Mission Creek). This small trussed span was built in 1917. Often it is opened at the same time as its bigger sister.

Islais Creek Bridge. This modern roller-bearing drawbridge carries Third Street across the Islais Creek Channel. It began operation in 1950.

crossing to Alameda:

Three automobile bridges carry traffic across the portion of the Estuary that was once a land connection with Oakland. Years ago it was dredged out to form a channel to San Leandro Bay, making Alameda an island. The Park Street, Fruitvale and High Street bridges cross this channel. Beside the Fruitvale Bridge is a railroad "lift" bridge that carries the Southern Pacific to Alameda.

Another, more modern, crossing is the Bay Farm Bridge that spans the outlet of San Leandro Bay between Alameda and Bay Farm Island.

North Bay:

There are a pair of bridges over the Petaluma River where it flows into the north end of San Pablo Bay. The Highway 37 bridge is a new swooping arch of concrete. The Black Point railroad bridge is a rickety-looking "swing" span carrying Northwestern Pacific (SP) tracks across the river.

South Bay:

The Dumbarton railroad bridge, a little more than half a mile south of the Dumbarton auto bridge, is actually the oldest bridge on the Bay. It was built in 1909, exclusively for rail cars, by the Southern Pacific as the "Dumbarton Cut-off." It is a low-level "swing" operated drawbridge, opening for boats bound for Palo Alto or Alviso. From your car, it's easy to spot the big trusses rising up out of the salt flats and mud flats that characterize the South Bay.

There are a pair of railroad bridges on the Southern Pacific right-of-way that few people ever see. Carrying the tracks from Alviso toward Fremont across Mud Slough and Coyote Creek, they spawned the community of Drawbridge (on Station Island) which is now a ghost town that is sinking into the marshland. The only way to see the bridges or the ghost town is to walk out two miles on the SP tracks from Alviso.

Buses

Another way to get across the bridges of the Bay is on scheduled public bus routes. Buses handle more commuters than all other forms of rapid transit combined and in many cases make a good substitute for that ubiquitous form of personal transportation, the car. Transit service in the Bay region could hardly be called unified however, although all the bridges have bus service across them. Some shoreline and waterfront areas are served by city buses — southern Marin has Golden Gate Transit; Richmond, Albany, Berkeley, Emeryville, Oakland, Alameda and San Leandro have AC Transit; a few points in San Mateo County have samTrans; and San Francisco has the Muni bus system.

Alameda-Contra Costa Transit

Frequent bus service across the San Francisco-Oakland Bay Bridge is operated by AC Transit. From numerous points in the East Bay, the buses reach the Transbay Terminal in San Francisco for connections with Golden Gate Transit and the City's Muni. Although the service is adequate, it is a far cry from the interurban electrics that operated transbay from the time the Bay Bridge Terminal opened in 1939 until the trains shut down in 1958. AC Transit (653-3535)

Golden Gate Transit

Buses across the Golden Gate Bridge between San Francisco and most communities in Marin County are provided by Golden Gate Transit. The system is operated by the Golden Gate Bridge District (the bridge tolls subsidize the mass transit), and connects with the ferries at Sausalito and Larkspur, and offers weekend service to recreation areas in western Marin. Golden Gate Transit (San Francisco 332-6600 — Marin 453-2100)

Greyhound

Greyhound Lines operates bus service from its downtown terminal in San Francisco to major points in the Bay region. It crosses the Carquinez Bridge to Vallejo, the San Francisco-Oakland Bay Bridge to the East Bay, and the Golden Gate Bridge to San Rafael and the North Bay. Greyhound (San Francisco 433-1500 — Oakland 834-3070 — Vallejo 707-643-7661)

Traveler's Transit

The only bus service across the Richmond-San Rafael Bridge is Traveler's Transit. Most runs are on weekdays during commute hours, but there are a couple of midday trips and a few on weekends. It operates from San Rafael to the Greyhound and BART stations in Richmond. Traveler's Transit (457-7080)

San Mateo Transit

The San Mateo-Hayward Bridge is crossed by the buses of samTrans. The service operates on weekdays during daytime hours. It runs from First and B streets in San Mateo to the Hayward BART station. samTrans (871-2200)

Peerless Stages

The only bus service across the Dumbarton Bridge is operated by Peerless Stages between Palo Alto and the Fremont BART station. Peerless Stages (444-2900)

Shoreline Bicycle Routes and Tours

The peripatetic routes and tours described here may be short and some are discontinuous, but the emphasis is on the Bay and its shoreline. You have a choice of twenty shoreline routes and park tours for recreational roaming. Using your own imagination or with the aid of a good map, you can make up more continuous trips for yourself. The state highway department (CalTrans) puts out a lot of information (brochures, booklets) for cyclists. Also, East Bay Regional Parks has information leaflets available about their bike trails.

Biking across the Bay

You can only bicycle across one bridge on San Francisco Bay. It is the bridge that is all things to all people, the Golden Gate. The walkway is open to cyclists, and walkers, during daylight hours, 6 am-9 pm. On weekends and holidays the ocean side walkway is for cyclists, and on weekdays the Bay side. Golden Gate Bridge (921-5858)

Getting across the Richmond-San Rafael Bridge has finally been made possible. A bike shuttle service using a van and trailer zips you and your bike across the bridge for a measly ten cents. It operates on weekends and holidays and is shut down for three months in the winter. Leaving from Point Richmond near the gas station on Standard Avenue (Highway 17 and Castro Street) just before it becomes a freeway, the service runs every hour on the hour, 8 am-7 pm. The pick-up point in Marin is at the San Quentin freeway entrance (near the main gate), and it runs on the half-hour, 8:30 am-7:30 pm. CalTrans (232-9444)

AC Transit has service to take cyclists across the San Francisco-Oakland Bay Bridge. The specially modified "pedal-hopper" bus operates on Saturdays, Sundays and holidays only. It follows the B "Grand Avenue" line in the East Bay, and comes to the Transbay Terminal in San Francisco. The fare is 60¢ plus 25¢ for a bike, but they don't take tandems. AC Transit (653-3535)

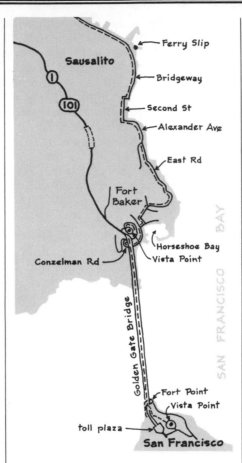

Recently a van and trailer service started across the Bay Bridge during commute hours. This experimental operation will last at least through 1979. Bicyclists and their vehicles are carried between the MacArthur BART Station in Oakland and the pick-up point at Main and Folsom streets in San Francisco. It runs from 6:30-8 am and 4-6:30 pm — fare 25¢. CalTrans (557-1611)

Bay Area Rapid Transit also provides bicycle service across (or under) the Bay with the "bikes on BART" program, and you can ride the train to any station on the line. With a special permit (to get the permit you go through a little hocus pocus and pay $3), you can take a bike on BART during off-peak hours — weekdays only, 6-6:30 am, 9 am-3:30 pm,

6:30-11 pm (midnight on some lines). On weekends, you can go without a permit, and at all hours. Combined with the AC Transit and CalTrans service (above), you can cross the Bay, San Francisco to Oakland, at almost any time. BART (465-4100 for recorded message — ask for ext 510 for more info)

The other way to have a bicycle outing across the Bay is by ferryboat. The section *Transporation on the Bay* gives a rundown of ferry routes which will present you with a recreational cornucopia of ferry/bike trips to Marin from San Francisco.

Routes and Tours
Marin County
Golden Gate Bridge and Sausalito

Perhaps the most rewarding waterfront ride on the Bay is this one — across the celebrated Golden Gate Bridge and down a winding hill into the well-favored town of Sausalito. Information about bicycling over the bridge is given above, and other sections of the book carry on about the charms of Sausalito. Starting from the vista point at the San Francisco end of the bridge, you might have to use the tunnel depending on available access. This trip is most delightful on a squeaky clean day, free of smog and the encroaching sea fog, because the scenery will be at its very best. Fog cuts down visibility, and the wind from the Pacific can make cold and hazardous cycling. You reach the vista point at the Marin end of the bridge for more sightseeing tableaus. From there, wind through the tunnels and Conzelman Road beneath the bridge down to Horseshoe Bay at Fort Baker. Next proceed along East Road and Alexander Avenue with more Bay views to the "old town" section of Sausalito along Second Street. Then you follow Bridgeway and the promenade for some explorations in the tourist/business quarter of town. A great way to make this a circle tour is to take the ferry *Golden Gate,* from its slip at the end of El Portal, back to the Ferry Building in San Francisco.

Sausalito to Mill Valley

This excursion is a nautical delight for cyclists, a continuation of the above tour. (You can start this trip on the ferry from San Francisco.) Taking your time, you can browse among several marinas along this route, admiring the sailboats and denizens, checking out the chandleries and bars. From central Sausalito at *Viña*

del Mar Plaza, the course continues north along Bridgeway. When Bridgeway rises on the hillside, the special bike path takes Marinship and goes by the Bay model. Near Waldo Point the paved trail again parallels Bridgeway. You pass the Gate 5 houseboat area (where some derelict ferryboats are beached), which is still remarkable and fascinating as well as more controversial than ever. Continuing northwest along the edge of the Bay, the path passes under Highway 101 as it bridges up to cross the water. You travel beside the shoreline marsh of Richardson Bay teeming with feeding water birds. The marked route follows Almonte Boulevard and Miller Avenue five miles into Mill Valley.

Mill Valley and Strawberry Point

This is a spin along marsh and shoreline that evokes the original environment of the Bay. Shore birds and waterfowl are prevalent in refuge areas along the route, making this a good tour for ecology and bird-watching, a five-mile continuation of the one above. At the end of Strawberry Point is an elevation with good outlooks across to Sausalito and the City skyline beyond. From Miller Avenue in Mill Valley, turn on Camino Alto, then turn right on Sycamore Avenue to find unpaved paths, a Parcourse, and a small bike/pedestrian bridge that carries you across the head of Richardson Bay, past Shelter Bay, to eventually discover Highway 101's frontage road. Following the frontage road toward the water, you make a U-turn under the Highway 101 bridge and go north to find Seminary Drive. Along Seminary is De Silva Pond and quite a bit of shoreline access to a quiet part of Richardson Bay. At the junction with Great Circle Drive is a path leading down to Brickyard Park at the shore. Continue on Great Circle for the postcard vista of distant San Francisco, or cut across the peninsula on East Strawberry Drive, past condos and a piece of bay, to Tiburon Boulevard. Going towards Tiburon you turn off on Greenwood Cove Drive to the Audubon Society's Richardson Bay Wildlife Sanctuary and Education Center. An admission fee lets you take the nature walk, do some bird-watching and tour the Victorian mansion.

Tiburon

Most of this bicycle journey is via the extensive Richardson Bay Park and shoreline path. It generally follows the edge of the Bay for three miles and has grassy picnic areas with splendid views. Continuing the tour above, you leave the Sanctuary and Education Center, following Greenwood Cove Drive to the park and paved bike/pedestrian pathway. When the route leaves the shoreline it threads its way to the end of Tiburon at Main Street. On the way to Main Street you may take a side trip up through Belvedere to inspect the elegant architecture of the spiffy houses and the environs of the yacht club. The dwarf downtown of Tiburon is another browsing area of shops and restaurants. If you want to make this outing in reverse, catch the Tiburon ferry in San Francisco.

Angel Island

This state park is accessible by ferryboat and makes a good destination for a weekend ride. Information about the ferries is in the *Transportation* section of the book. It's very easy to spend an entire day in this non-motorized environment, exploring every peak and point of the island — and you may return again and again. From the headquarters at Ayala Cove where the ferries disembark, a road circles the island for more than five miles with plenty of opportunities for side trips. There are concessions and lots of picnic spots. At one time the island was denuded of foliage for firewood. But now it has been reforested by Army personnel importing exotic plants. The further you roam away from the cove, the fewer people you will meet. On your tour you will find inviting beaches, an overabundance of deer, panoramic views of all parts of the central Bay, and remnants of the island's convoluted past.

Tiburon Peninsula

Away from the populous side of the peninsula, this is a venture to a fairly remote section of shoreline. From the ferry slip at the end of Tiburon Boulevard, this is a continuation of the Tiburon tour above, or the start of the bicycle portion of a combined ferry/bike trip. Begin this ten-mile circuit by heading east out of the tourist center of Tiburon on Paradise Drive. The winding road rises on the hillside past Dr. Lyford's tower to Hygeia above Raccoon Strait. The road curves through woods away from urban civilization and turns north past Bluff Point and then back west to Paradise Beach Park. The park is a great place to take a break. The winding route holds high on the hillside and provides a northern prospect up the Bay past the Richmond Bridge. You can prolong the trip along Paradise Drive past the lagoons of Paradise Cay, with glimpses of more Bay scenery, all the way down to the Highway 101 frontage road near Corte Madera. Or if you want to curtail the jaunt, you can make a cut-off on Trestle Glen Boulevard to cross the peninsula to Richardson Bay Park and Tiburon.

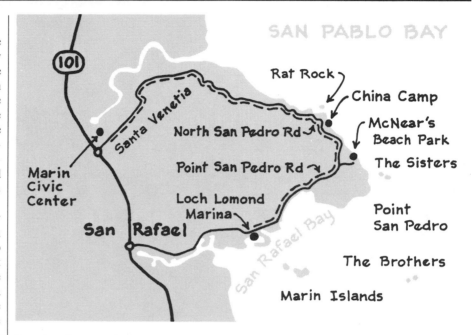

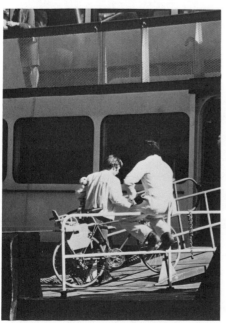

San Rafael and China Camp

This out-of-the-way excursion might be called a cyclist's island tour. A shoreline ramble for nine miles around Point San Pedro lets you see several small islands of the North Bay and at the same time gives you country solitude that is not easy to acquire. Depending on how much traffic you want to avoid, you can start this trip as far out from downtown San Rafael as the Loch Lomond Marina. Following Point San Pedro Road north, you trace the shore of San Rafael Bay. Close at hand are the wooded Marin Islands and on the other side of the Bay, near Point San Pablo, are two rocks called The Brothers. On one of the Brothers is mounted a fascinating old-style lighthouse. Continuing past the quarry, you come to the turn-off for McNear's Beach Park with swimming pool, beach and snack bar. Turning west around the point, you will be on narrow, winding North San Pedro Road which passes through land that is being acquired for a new state park. There should be some signs of this. Next you come to China Camp where they still catch shrimp. Stop for a look at the ramshackle pier and notice Rat Rock just offshore. From the elevated road you have good views of San Pablo Bay to the north. Past China Camp the road descends and travels by extensive marshland and mud flats. You can keep on the road through Santa Venetia to end up at the lagoon and park of the Marin Civic Center.

Contra Costa County
Crockett to Port Costa

This ramble is east, away from the Bay, high above mile-wide Carquinez Strait. The eminence gives you sweeping views of the Strait and the double Carquinez Bridge. There are numerous scenic turnouts to stop and observe the ocean-bound maritime commerce, Benicia on the far shore, and other activities of this busy waterway. The Crockett exit off Highway 80 becomes Pomona Street in downtown Crockett, then turns into winding Carquinez Scenic Drive. Following this for four miles, you can wend your way down to Port Costa which was a huge, bustling port for the trans-shipment of the Valley's grain on "limejuicers" in the 1880s. Today it is a shadow of its former self, being a remote village that exists as a mecca for antique-ophiles and restaurant aficionados. You can continue this trip east on the scenic drive six miles more to the attractions of Martinez.

Rodeo and Pinole

An excursion from Crockett in the opposite direction from the one above gives you a view of Carquinez Strait and Bridge and leads you through small communities surrounded by Bay-based industry. From the Crockett exit, San Pablo Avenue heads west with good high-level views of the Strait. Then the road swoops down through refineries and tank farms (why does anyone want to grow tanks?) to the town of Rodeo with its marina on the shore of San Pablo Bay. Continuing south, you reach Pinole after seven miles and can find the shore across the railroad tracks where Amtrak trains sometimes zephyr by. You can examine the mud flats at Rodeo and the small marsh at Pinole at the shoreline access.

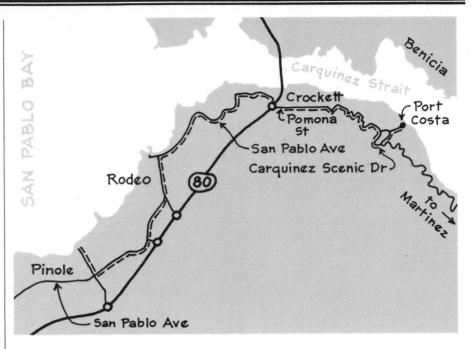

Point Pinole

Point Pinole Regional Shoreline, operated by East Bay Regional Parks, is a good place for a weekend adventure on two wheels. The Point is an attractive park, a large area of land jutting into San Pablo Bay with diverse natural environments. It is an isolated destination with a Bay shore that seems untouched by man. From the entrance parking lot ($1) a paved path runs through the middle of the park for a little more than a mile to the point. Side trips can be made, and there are picnic facilities. The meadows, groves, marshes and mud flats are habitat for a wide variety of birds. You can try fishing from the new pier, or just do some sightseeing, picking out the landmarks of the North Bay as it stretches uninterrupted before you.

Point San Pablo

Another intriguing remote section of Bay shoreline is north of the Richmond-San Rafael Bridge on Point San Pablo. The only way to get there is by car from Richmond over the Highway 17 freeway approach to the bridge. Take the Point Molate exit and follow the road to Point Molate Beach Park. If you're at the park on the right weekend, you'll see the steam museum Castro Point Railway in operation. From the park an history-evoking bicycle venture can be made along Point San Pablo. Following the road north through the Naval Fuel Depot, you will find curious-looking castellated buildings. Many years ago this was Winehaven, a resort destination for weekending San Franciscans. Now the Navy uses the buildings. The road continues very near water level two miles to the end of the point. On the hills above are oil tanks, mostly belonging to Standard Oil, but a few hold molasses. At the end of the point is a pier that used to be a sardine reduction plant in the heyday of the Bay's purse seiners in the 1940s. Across a short breadth of surging water are the Victorian buildings of The Brothers light station. Just around the point are buildings that remain from the last whaling station on the Pacific Coast — long closed, thank goodness. Across the strait is Point San Pedro in Marin. This terrific viewpoint with "no trespassing" signs is a bit of land owned by the City of Richmond and should be converted to a park with a bit of public access to the Bay.

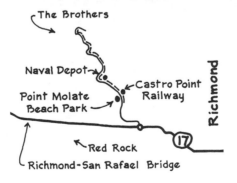

Alameda County

Berkeley

There really is not a shoreline tour in Berkeley, although the marina is a nice place for some pleasant pedaling. And you can follow the freeway frontage road south along the shore crescent to the Emeryville peninsula. The bicycle situation here may improve as more park development takes place. East Bay Regional Parks has a dream of a bike path from the Berkeley Marina all the way around to the foot of the Bay Bridge.

Oakland

An adventuresome expedition can be mounted along the Estuary from the central location of Jack London Square. Any trip from here is on busy city streets, so the best time for this venture is a weekend when the traffic should be fairly light. After checking out the four corners of Jack London Square, you might be interested in seeing some of the industrial sites of the Port of Oakland. Ride up Broadway to Third Street, then left on Third through the warehouse area to Cypress Street, then right on Cypress to Seventh Street and turn left. Following Seventh Street four miles west past trucking and container storage to its end may be a trial because of the railroad tracks and rough paving, but Port View Park at the end is worth the effort. There is an observation tower for a good look at the maritime traffic leaving the Estuary and the skyline of San Francisco not very far across the Bay. Head in the other direction from Jack London Square if you want to relate to flotillas of sailboats and gangs of waterfront restaurants.

Going through the parking lot to Jack London Village and following the shoreline gravel path past the ill-fated Portobello development, you come to Estuary Park, passing marinas and eating places on the way. The park has a gazebo and grass and a stepped quay. From the park you can continue a mile southeast on Embarcadero to Brooklyn Basin to come to Embarcadero Cove — more sailboats berthed in marinas, and restaurants taking advantage of views of the water.

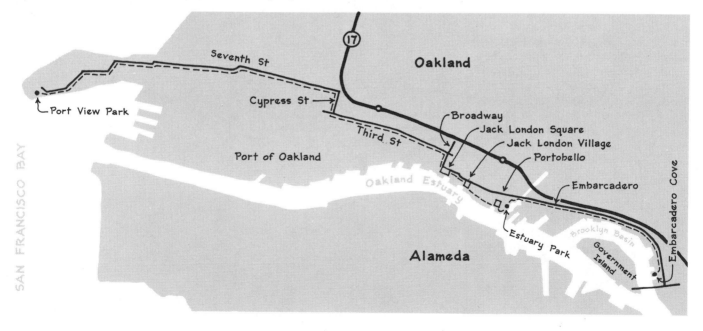

San Leandro Bay

To find the location of this ride, you'll have to find Bay Park Refuge (see section *Finding the Bay*). San Leandro Bay is between Alameda, the Coliseum complex and the Oakland Airport. At the present time there is a short paved bike path along the shore of the bay. As part of the East Bay Regional Parks effort to develop a shoreside park on San Leandro Bay, the path is being extended along the east and south edge of the bay into Arrowhead Marsh.

San Leandro

The San Leandro Marina is a pleasant place to wander on a bike. There is a fleet of boats to look over, and just to the south is Marina Park with grassy picnic areas. As land fill garbage is covered over with park development, the bike path will be further south on the Bay-edge levee.

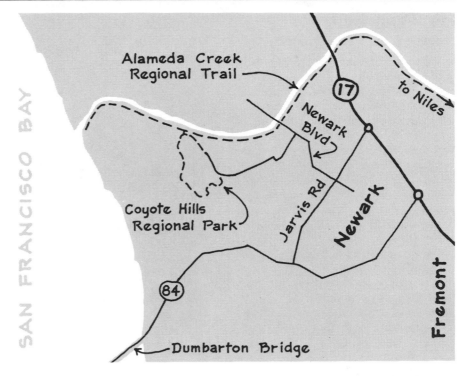

Alameda Creek

The Alameda Creek Regional Trail is a fairly level levee path running through Fremont along the Alameda Creek Flood Control Channel. One side of the channel is for equestrians and the south side is for cyclists (and hikers). One end of the trail is at Vallejo Mill Park in Niles, which is pretty far inshore for a shoreline trail. But it's all downstream, about nine miles, heading toward the Bay, with at least four other spots to get on the trail conveniently, until you get to Coyote Hills Regional Park. There is a connection to the trails in the park, and approximately three miles beyond is San Francisco Bay.

Coyote Hills Regional Park

Activities in this park are described in other sections of this book. The Bay View Trail is a paved bicycle circuit of the hills. You can observe the salt ponds and bird life of the Bay. At the north end of the park, a connection with the Alameda Creek Trail (above) takes you through the marshland and salt evaporators to the edge of the Bay.

San Francisco
Golden Gate Promenade

This jaunt is over 3½ miles of mostly paved path for bicycles or walkers. The pathway is the Golden Gate Promenade, part of the Golden Gate National Recreation Area, a scenic setting that offers solitude on the northern waterfront of San Francisco. Starting from the developed portion of the City's waterfront, which still retains some spots of historical significance, your explorations take you to some less built-up areas of natural beauty. At Jefferson Street, you turn your back on the restless hurly-burly of Fisherman's Wharf and head west for this trip. You will notice the Hyde Street Pier, formerly the ferry dock for boats from Sausalito and Berkeley, now the home of a collection of Pacific Coast ships in the San Francisco Maritime Historic Park. Next you cross Aquatic Park, which also includes a cable car turntable in Victorian Park, and is the locale for rowing and swimming clubs on the lagoon, the Maritime Museum, a small beach, and the sweeping curve of the Muni Pier on the far side. As you pass from Aquatic Park and go by the old Alcatraz Pier up into Fort Mason, you pick up the signs of the Golden Gate Promenade route. The tree-shaded environs of Fort Mason encompass the headquarters of the GGNRA and the old Army embarkation piers now used for many public activities, as well as some old Victorian dwellings of pre-War-Between-the-States vintage. Exiting from the fort, you pass the myriad masts of the boats at the San Francisco Marina and you range across Marina Green, all built on Bay filled for the Panama-Pacific International Exposition of 1915. A side trip is possible across Marina Boulevard at Lyon Street to the gardens of the Palace of Fine Arts, the restored remnant of the exposition. At the end of the marina, this excursion takes you to the

sand dunes and marshes of the Bayshore beside Crissy Field (another landfill for the exposition) where you can find abundant birdlife, spring wildflowers and fishing spots. Continuing, you pass the Coast Guard station, a fishing pier and the seawall of the Golden Gate. Finally you end the trip at Fort Point, specially niched beneath an arch of the Golden Gate Bridge, built before the War between the States and now a National Historic Site. Views of the Bay from the fort are special, a wind-blown perspective of the bridge and close-up inspection of the traffic through the Gate.

South Waterfront

Properly, anything south of the Ferry Building at the foot of Market Street can be called the south waterfront, but it usually applies to anything south of China Basin. On the City's Bayfront, piers are numbered from the Ferry Building. South towards Hunters Point the numbers are even, from 2 to more or less 96. Following this route provides interesting glimpses of the maritime face of San Francisco; and it does present some hazards to the bicyclist — railroad tracks, poor paving and bridge crossings. From the pedestrian precincts of Justin Herman Plaza near the Ferry Building, The Embarcadero extends south to China Basin. You pass by piers in stages of disrepair, various kinds of oceangoing ships tied up or refitting, the San Francisco fireboat at Pier 24, a motley collection of boats around Pier 42, and several cafés for a beer or a bite. At the end of The Embarcadero, turn along Berry Street for a couple of blocks to cross Mission Creek (China Basin) on the behemoth bridge at Third Street. Just across the bridge, turn left and follow China Basin Street past piers, boat clubs, a launching ramp, railroad yards and the Santa Fe railcar ferry slip at Pier 52, a

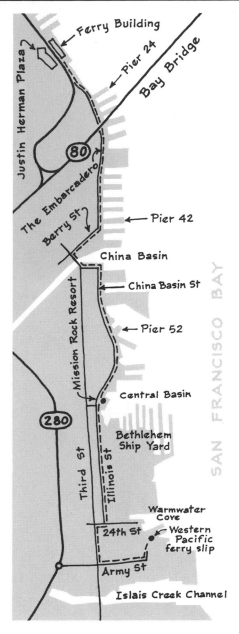

fishing pier, and the invigorating atmosphere of Mission Rock Resort. Two and a half miles brings you to a stop at Mission Rock for some lively eating and drinking action which also provides the ambience of fishing and fishing boats, docks, and a close look at the Bethlehem Ship Yard across the Central Basin. If, after this nautical hullabaloo, you feel like continuing the trip through sparse but still interesting maritime activities, keep south on China Basin and Illinois streets — at the end of Twenty-fourth Street is a park for fishing in Warmwater Cove in the PG&E plant's water discharge. Go back down Twenty-fourth to Third Street and head left to Army Street. Out at the end of Army near the shipping terminal is an open, gravel parking lot next to the Western Pacific rail yards where you can see their car ferry, *Las Plumas,* tied up, the last of the enormous old-time ferries still operating on the Bay. You can extend this trip to four miles, down Third Street to the Islais Creek Channel, with drawbridge, fishing spots and more shipping movements.

San Mateo County
Burlingame and San Mateo and Foster City

This is a bicycle tour that picks its way between several of the Peninsula's Bayshore access points. These include large and small Bayside parks and wildlife habitat and refuges. You will have abundant opportunity to search for a variety of wading birds and waterfowl in the marshes and sloughs. The route also passes by picnic areas, a couple of sailing lagoons, fishing spots, and even a beach for swimming. Plans are in the works for construction of a continuous special bikeway connecting all of these shoreline places. For the present, you will have to make do with the combination of marked bike trails and city streets to make this tour. At the south end of the San Francisco Airport there is a parking lot for airport viewing (Millbrae Avenue exit from Highway 101). From the park cycle down Old Bayshore Highway past the waterfront restaurants of Burlingame — tucked in between a couple of them is the miniscule Burlingame Shorebird Sanctuary. Beyond Bayside Park on Airport Boulevard, the bike path turns inshore along Burlingame Lagoon, while bayward of Airport Boulevard is Anza Park Lagoon with occasional sailing action. Crossing the lagoon at Beach Road, a side trip toward the shore reveals tiny Fishermans Park and nearby the old Bay ferryboat, *General Frank M. Coxe,* beached as a restaurant. Continuing on Airport Boulevard takes you into Coyote Point Park with its long swimming beach, the only one on this side of the Bay, and a wooded knoll above the marina. Through the park, past the end of the marina, a levee path goes south to the postage-stamp Ryder Court Park. You get on Third Avenue here, but head west towards the freeway for a couple of blocks (taking the other direction past the city dump brings you to a bridge that is prohibited to bicycles and pedestrians). Turn left on South Norfolk Street and pass through the residential area to turn left on Kehoe Avenue and find signs for a

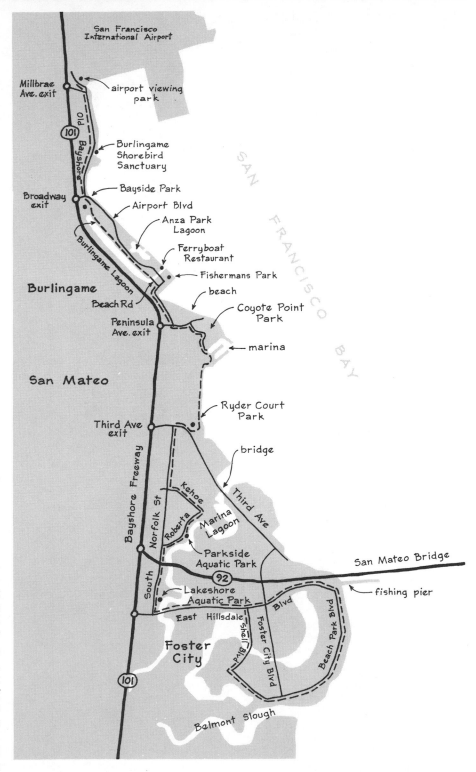

bike route along San Mateo's Marina Lagoon on Roberta Drive. Pass Parkside Aquatic Park and return to South Norfolk and follow it past Lakeshore Aquatic Park to East Hillsdale Boulevard. Then you can make a terminating loop of the shell beach, marshy slough and central lagoon of Foster City by following East Hillsdale, Beach Park and Shell boulevards. On this circuit you will notice the public fishing pier beneath the San Mateo Bridge, birdlife in the mud flats, and perhaps some Sunday sailors on the lagoon.

Organizations

These groups sponsor occasional bicycle trips along the shoreline of San Francisco Bay, and of course to many other destinations. Non-members are usually welcome.

Golden Gate National Recreation Area
Fort Mason
San Francisco 94123
(556-2920)

East Bay Regional Parks
11500 Skyline Boulevard
Oakland 94619
(531-9300)

American Youth Hostels
625 Polk Street
San Francisco 94102
(771-4646)

East Bay Bicycle Coalition
Box 1736
Oakland 94604

San Francisco Bicycle Coalition
1405 Seventh Avenue
San Francisco 94122
(664-8193)

Cruising the Bay

The absolutely best way to appreciate San Francisco Bay is from the water. If you're a resident or if you're a visitor, cruising about this noble harbor lets you find its images of unmatched beauty. It's even enjoyable when the mysterious fog floats in. Here are some suggestions to let you sample the sparkling waters of this immense estuary and to see the familiar landmarks from the water.

These cruises operate in the central Bay and provide memorable views of the Golden Gate and its bridge, Fort Point and the Presidio, Marin's hillside towns, Angel Island, Alcatraz, Treasure Island, the San Francisco-Oakland Bay Bridge, and the skyline and waterfront of San Francisco.

Other cruises which may be of interest are described in the sections *Charter Cruises* and *Ecology Cruising*. Another trip which provides a cheapie cruise is a point-to-point ride on one of the ferries listed in *Transportation on the Bay*. You can make a real sightseeing trip by combining a ferry cruise and a walking tour of your destination (see section *Pedestrian Delights*).

Sightseeing Cruises

These five tours embark from San Francisco, four from the Fisherman's Wharf area and one from the Ferry Building. The vessels can carry hundreds of passengers, with open top decks for tasting the salt air and glassed-in lower decks to retreat to if you need to warm up or want refreshment at the snack bar. They are the basic scenic tours, including souvenir postcard shots for your camera, with a couple of extended trips thrown in.

Gold Coast Cruises

The *Gold Coast* sails from Pier 45 at Fisherman's Wharf for a two-hour sightseeing cruise. It is a smaller boat than its competitors, but the tour route is more extensive and it lasts longer. Season: Memorial Day through October. Trips depart daily — 10:30, 1 pm and 3:30. Tickets: $4, children (5-12) $2. (775-9108)

Harbor Tours

The large "Red & White Fleet" offers many sightseeing and touring opportunities on its boats — the *Harbor Emperor* (named for San Francisco's weird but wise character, Emperor Norton), *Harbor King, Harbor Queen, Harbor Prince, Harbor Princess,* and the new *Harbor Countess.* You embark at Pier 43½ Fisherman's Wharf for the Bay tour, lasting one and one-quarter hour with taped historical narration. Tours leave all day, every day, at 30 to 45-minute intervals from 10 am. Tickets: $4, children (5-11) $2. (546-2810)

Alcatraz Guided Tour

In conjunction with the National Park Service, the "Red & White Fleet" operates this short cruise to "The Rock." It's a combination trip — you get some sightseeing from the boat and then a guided tour of Alcatraz, which is now part of the Golden Gate National Recreation Area. The tour is about two and one-half hours (dock to dock), conducted by National Park Rangers. Be prepared for lots of hiking and a cold wind (good shoes and a warm coat). This unusual tour departs from Pier 43 every day, all year, at 45-minute intervals from 9 to 5. No reservations in summer (ticket office opens at 8 am, usually sold out by 10 am); reservations advised the rest of the year. Tickets: $2, children (5-11) $1. (546-2805)

Marin Tours

Golden Gate Transit offers another combination trip that opens up many recreational opportunities, a two-hour ferry/bus excursion to scenic parts of Marin County. You catch the Larkspur Ferry (GT *Marin* or GT *Sonoma)* at the Ferry Building in San Francisco, then sail north up the Bay past many notable landmarks (including San Quentin), and finally transfer at the Larkspur Terminal to a bus either to Muir Woods or to Point Reyes National Seashore. Once there you can explore the redwood gulch, or the trails and beaches of Pt. Reyes (there are even hike-in campgrounds). Buses return and connect with the ferries. Operates on Saturdays, Sundays and holidays: ferries leave — 10 am, noon, 1 pm (Muir Woods only), and 3 pm. Tickets: $1.50 each way, $2 in summer.

Also, you can make a special expedition to the Renaissance Pleasure Faire using buses that meet the ferries at Larkspur. This festive amusement is held at Black Point on September weekends. Golden Gate Transit (San Francisco 332-6600 — Marin 453-2100)

Sacramento Cruises

Delta Travel, 1240 Merkley Avenue, West Sacramento 95691 (916-371-6711)

An even longer trip is the all-day cruise up the Bay and Sacramento River combined with a bus ride back to the City. Re-creating the busy San Francisco Bay/river boat route of the 1850s and '60s when most of the commerce of the Bay was trans-shipment of goods to the "diggings" and the agricultural Central Valley via Sacramento, this excursion takes you into the Delta region's islands, levees and sloughs. The old river boat pilots saw naval vessels en route to Mare Island, grain ships going to Port Costa, and other river boats. Now you may see oceangoing freighters bound for Sacramento and Stockton, tankers for the Contra Costa refineries, and hundreds of pleasure boats. One of the old customs you won't have to worry about: the old Sacramento night boats could not sell liquor until up the Bay past Red Rock (San Francisco's county boundary), so the passengers vied to get a drink and quaff it with a toast to East Brother Lighthouse as they passed. Now you can hoist one before the boat even leaves the dock.

As you cruise north you can expect good sightseeing. Note the Point Blunt Lighthouse on Angel Island (the last manned light on the Bay), the old-fashioned light on East Brother, and the old Carquinez Strait Lighthouse that was moved one-half mile east of the Carquinez Bridge on the north shore. You head through Carquinez Strait, past the waterfront of Benicia, the industry of Martinez, bridges, the naval mothball fleet in Suisun Bay, and then up the Sacramento River and the unnaturally straight Sacramento Deepwater Ship Channel. The "Red & White Fleet" boat *Harbor Emperor* makes this eight-hour trip from San Francisco. At the other end a bus takes you to the historically re-created Old Sacramento then returns you to San Francisco.

In 1978 three San Francisco to Sacramento trips were scheduled, Saturdays early in October and the last day of the year. The trips departed from Fisherman's Wharf in San Francisco. Boat cruise and return by bus cost $22.

Cruises in the reverse direction, down the Sacramento to San Francisco, were also scheduled. The arrangements were similar and the cost the same. In 1978 these were on Saturdays and Sundays in September and October.

Scheduled Dinner Cruises

For a real floating party, these three voyages offer a great way to see the Bay (all by moonlight). All cruises are on boats of the "Red & White Fleet." From this list you may select a cruise that gives you a scenic tour of the Bay or that takes you to a destination for dining at a waterfront establishment. Prices given are subject to change.

Jack London Wine & Dine Cruise

Offers two cruises:

2670 Leavenworth Street, San Francisco 94133 (441-5205)

The wine and dine cruise leaves San Francisco's Fisherman's Wharf and presents a choice of five restaurants at Jack London Square in Oakland. Aboard the boat there is music for dancing and a complimentary glass of champagne during the one-hour (each way) cruise. You have two and one-half hours at Jack London Square for dining and exploring. Season: every Friday night, May through October. Departure — 7 pm from Pier 43½ Fisherman's Wharf, return — 11:30 pm. Tickets: $13.50.

The Jack London champagne cruise is for residents of the East Bay. It is almost the reverse of the one above, leaves Oakland from Jack London Square for a two-hour sightseeing tour of the Bay with music and champagne. Then it's back to the Square for a 10 pm dinner at a choice of five restaurants. Season: every Friday night, May through October. Departures — 8 pm from Jack London Square. Tickets: $13.50.

Harbor Tours

Pier 43, San Francisco 94133 (546-2810)

A Thursday evening "bar-b-que on the Bay" is a three-hour moonlight cruise with dinner and music for dancing. Departure — every Thursday night at 7:30 from Pier 43½ Fisherman's Wharf, return — 10:30 pm. Tickets: $16.50 (no personal checks).

Helicopter Tours

Commodore Helicopters

Pier 43, San Francisco (981-4832)

For a quick overview of the City's waterfront and a sweep around Alcatraz, this trip can't be beat. It's a great place for cameras. The trip is very short, but charters are available for more extensive tours over the City. The choppers lift off from the end of Pier 43 at Fisherman's Wharf, daily, 10 am-sunset, year-round. Tickets: $7.50, children $4.

Helicoptours

Pier 46, San Francisco 94107 (495-3333)

Another flight tour takes off from the south end of The Embarcadero near Berry Street. Trips range from five minutes to one-half hour, and charters for longer times are possible. They fly every day, 9 am-sunset, weather permitting. Tickets: $8/person up to $48/person.

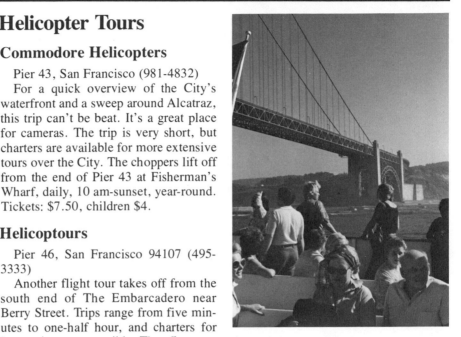

Seaplane Tour

You are offered a complete tour of the central Bay from the seaplane port in Sausalito. The twenty-minute scenic ride starts out over the mountains to the coast, then circles over the Golden Gate Bridge, the Presidio, San Francisco's Financial District, Treasure Island, Alcatraz, Angel Island and Belvedere. The planes carry three passengers maximum, every day on weekends and intermittently on weekdays. Tickets: $9.50, children half price. They also offer instruction and air taxi service; they can go anyplace that has access to water — Jack London Square, the Delta (fishermen note). Command Seaplane Service, 242 Redwood Highway, Mill Valley (north end of Sausalito, Highway One exit from 101). (332-4843)

Festivals and Events

San Francisco Bay fairly teems with intriguing events. For diversion there is a wide selection of festive occasions for enjoyment either as a spectator or participant. You will find exhibitions, contests and aquatic feats, colorful and traditional commemorations, and regattas varying from the sublime to the submerged. Foremost on the calendar of Bay activities is the yacht parade on Opening Day, and then follow all the races of the yachting season sponsored by the various yacht clubs. These regattas are too numerous to mention, but some, like the Midnight Moonlight Maritime Marathon, are imbued with tradition dating back to the 1930s. The Yachting Yearbook provides some information about these contests. All the sailing enthusiasm of summer season, mid-winter series, one-design regattas and ocean racing, taking place on weekends and week nights, as well as powerboat and hydroplane racing, seem to keep the Bay filled with pleasure boats. There are some shoreside fêtes to enliven your experience also. To be very sure about the days and times of these happenings, check the newspaper for notices.

January

New Year's Day Swim

Last year was at least the 42nd repetition of this saltwater frolic. Sponsored by the South End Rowing Club, the course is from the cold waves off Alcatraz to Aquatic Park in San Francisco. The record time is under thirty-three minutes, and 1977 saw the first woman competitor. If you can't be a spectator on New Year's Day, any other day of the year you will see swimmers taking a dip and doing their laps in the Aquatic Park lagoon.

March

Women's Invitational Cup Race

Sailing races for skippers and crews of the female persuasion are sponsored by Bay yacht clubs on successive Saturdays. The Corinthian Yacht Club hosted its third annual on Raccoon Strait early in the month in 1978. The Sausalito Cruising Club had its fourth annual Lorelei Perpetual Trophy Race in the middle of the month. The Richmond Yacht Club sponsors a race late in the month. More women's races are held in September and October.

April

Bullship Race

On a Saturday morning in the middle of the month a colorful sight can be found on the central Bay. Hundreds of tiny El Toros, eight-foot cat-rigged sailing dinghies, toil across restless waves, racing from Sausalito to the St. Francis Yacht Club at San Francisco's marina. These small boats on the immense Bay make them something to see. The event was originated by Barnaby Conrad, and the silver anniversary of the annual race was held in 1978.

Sailboat Show Afloat

A sales exhibition of boats and equipment is held at Mariner Square on the Estuary in Alameda. The thing that differentiates this from other boat shows is that most of the boats are outdoors and in the water. You can also sail to the show and moor in the Estuary. Held on the first two weekends of the month, the sixth annual was in 1978.

Opening Day of Yachting Season

As mentioned elsewhere, this is the biggest Bay event of the year for yachtsmen. The opening day water parade that marks the beginning of the six-month summer boating season attracts thousands of participants. The tradition began in the 1890s, and now the spectator appeal is so great that many thousands turn out, attracted by the colorful carnival atmosphere of the affair. The parade begins with the blessing of the fleet off Tiburon, and the course goes from Sausalito, across the Golden Gate to Fort Point, then along the San Francisco Marina and down the waterfront. Along the way there are salutes from the Bay's fireboats and the Coast Guard and the Navy. For several years a local newspaper has sponsored a Boat Décor Competition in conjunction with Opening Day. Both power and sailboats are bedecked with elaborate trimmings for the amusement of the crowd. These floating floats vie for valuable prizes. Opening Day is the last Sunday of the month.

May

Master Mariners' Regatta

This event has a grand tradition behind it. Originated in 1867 as part of the ostentatious Fourth of July celebrations, it is the oldest sailing event in the West. It was discontinued in 1892, revived in 1965, and now occurs on the closest Sunday to Maritime Day (May 22), usually the Sunday before Memorial Day. The fourteenth renewal in this century was in 1978. The historic regatta began as competition between coastal lumber schooners and Bay freight scows. Now it honors this salty merchant marine tradition with classic sailing ships. The old-fashioned flotilla has vintage craft — schooners, sloops, yawls, ketches, cat and cutter rigs. There are perennial entrants, many from the early 1900s, and a place of honor is reserved for the *Alma* (1891), a hay scow from the Maritime Historic Park. This is one regatta that can clearly be enjoyed from the shore as the central Bay course takes it by the San Francisco Marina. However an even better vantage point is from one of the Harbor Tour boats which are generally full of spectators for the event.

June

Sand Castle Contest

The only place where this contest could be held is the largest beach on the Bay, Crown Memorial State Beach in Alameda. In 1978 the twelfth annual contest was co-sponsored by the Alameda Recreation and Park Department, the Alameda Junior Women's Club and East Bay Regional Parks. Among the fanciful creations have been sunbathers, mermaids, the Statue of Liberty, a BART train, dragons, sea otters and space ships. Prize ribbons are given for sand castles and sand sculpture, and there is a perpetual trophy. The contest is on a Saturday in mid-month.

July

The Fourth of July Fireworks Display

This highly traditional celebration of the holiday with illuminations takes place on our Bay shore. The night of the Fourth, the extravaganza can be seen from the parking lot of Candlestick Park in San Francisco. A special view point is furnished by the Harbor Tours sightseeing boats that wander offshore. Embarkation at either Berkeley Marina or San Francisco's Fisherman's Wharf. There are other shoreside locations for fireworks and entertainments in the East Bay and South Bay.

August

Bathtub Regatta

For a different kind of race, where it's definitely sink or swim, try the Estuary on a Saturday in the middle of the month. The object is to make a bathtub float and win a race in it. The imaginative, funky designs sometimes make for submerged contestants. The fifth annual race was in 1978, co-sponsored by the Rusty Scupper restaurant (in Oakland, where the race is held) and a local radio station.

September

Fort Point Programs

These special programs happen only occasionally, so you have to watch for newspaper notices of them. On weekends at Fort Point in San Francisco various military and musical entertainments have been offered: Jazz concerts, traditional and Dixieland; military band music, with historic uniforms and traditional instruments; as well as other music has been heard here. Soldiers in uniforms from the last century with fifes, bugles and drums have performed military retreat ceremonies. Some of these programs occur in other months.

October

The Procession of Maria del Lume and the Blessing of the Fishing Fleet

In San Francisco the Italian community of North Beach opens ten days of Columbus Day celebrations with a parade on the first Sunday of the month. The procession is headed by a painted portrait of Sicily's patroness of fishermen, Madonna del Lume (Most Holy Mother of Light), and traces its tradition to the Italian Middle Ages. The parade from Saints Peter and Paul Church to Fisherman's Wharf features a flowered float and colorful costumes. The priest blesses the fleet for the protection of fishermen, and after the ceremony, there is Italian entertainment and folk music.

Columbus Day Celebration

A continuance of the above ceremonies, this Festa Italiana gets down to the business of saluting Columbus' discovery of the New World with verve. Many diversions, including rowing and swimming contests, coronation of a "Queen Isabella," a church bazaar and street fair with food, troubadors and music concerts, lead up to the big weekend celebrations. On Saturday a waterfront pageant, a costumed portrayal, recreates the landing of Columbus — from a fishing boat at Aquatic Park in San Francisco. On the following day is the grand parade of floats through the City to North Beach.

Golden Gate Swim for Women

The race course is through the chill waters and swirling currents of the Golden Gate from San Francisco to the Marin shore. On a weekend in mid-month, the sixth annual swim was held in 1978. This women-only race may be discontinued as more women are admitted to the heretofore men-only Dolphin Club, San Francisco Rowing Club and South End Rowing Club.

Golden Gate Swim

Sponsored by the Aquatic Park swimming and rowing clubs, the 42nd annual event was held on the last weekend of the month in 1978. The race is from Fort Point to Lime Point in Marin, and the record is just over nineteen minutes. Other notable swims of the Golden Gate: a horse swam the Gate in 1928 to settle a bet; Jack LaLanne, a fitness fanatic, swam across underwater in 1955.

All Year

Fort Mason

Now that the warehouses and piers have become part of the Golden Gate National Recreation Area, they are the site of a profusion of activities throughout the year. In developing this as a waterfront/urban park many events inviting public participation are scheduled — classes, concerts, art and craft shows, ecology exhibitions, children's festivals. In the past a kite-flying contest, the Fourth Annual Great Paper Aeroplane Derby, and Oceans Day have been held. For an activities calendar brochure, contact: Fort Mason Foundation, Building 310, Fort Mason, San Francisco 94123. (441-5705)

Visiting Ships

For all of us mere landlubbers, the sight of tankers, container ships, freighters, cruise liners and naval vessels heading out the Golden Gate produces dreams of voyages that may be more vivid than the real thing. You can conjure up visions of foreign ports, South Sea islands, unlimited ocean horizons, starry nights and rushing seas. To abet these fantasies, the best opportunity to see any of these big ships is while they are tied up on the San Francisco waterfront. Some ships making a stopover in the harbor welcome the public as visitors. When very special ships come to call, they usually get a very special reception — a welcoming fleet of small craft, honors from spouting fireboats, and lots of shoreside spectators. Some of the ships thus saluted in the past several years have been the *Golden Hinde* re-construction when it came from England to its new home, the aircraft carriers *Coral Sea* and *Enterprise* when returning to port, the *QE2* on her first visit, and various flotillas of foreign and U.S. naval ships here for a short sojourn. A few years ago, square-rigger cadet training ships of several countries were welcomed, including some of the same ones that participated in New York's famous bicentennial Operation Sail.

Passenger Liners

San Francisco is the only port on the Bay that has passenger traffic. Cruise liners from several steamship lines stop at Pier 35 on the northern waterfront, mostly in the summertime. It's a far cry from the good old days when Matson Lines and the Presidents and others were constantly streaming in and out of the Golden Gate carrying passengers, making San Francisco the gateway to Hawaii, the Orient and all of the Pacific. Now airplanes have supplanted ships for strictly transportation purposes, and liners are for vacation voyages. Ships usually stop here only for a day (sixty-four times this year), docking in the morning and departing in the evening, giving the passengers a chance to go ashore and buy trinkets from the natives. For a couple of hours before sailing, the ships have more or less an open house. It's primarily for seeing people off, bestowing "bon voyages," but it has a public relations aspect — to entice you to take a cruise, you can go aboard a ship to look it over. If you're invited on board as a guest of a passenger, that's great. And people have been known to sidle by the attendants, up the gangplank and on board. But if you really want to see a cruise liner, keep your eyes on the shipping notices in the newspaper or on the tote board at the end of Pier 35, so you will know when a ship is stopping in port. Then call up the ship company — Princess Cruises, Royal Viking Line, Sitmar Cruises or Delta Steamship Lines (formerly Prudential Lines) — to get a boarding pass. That's your ticket to a couple of hours at a real "floating" cocktail party, walking the decks and imagining yourself far away from home on foreign shores.

Special Visits

One bright, breezy Sunday morning, as I walked down the lonely, muffled Embarcadero, no commerce disturbed my pleasant stroll. But up ahead a few people were milling around the sidewalk in front of one of the piers. Approaching, I could see the cavernous interior of the pier shed with more people wandering around and standing in line. I had discovered a ship, here on a special visit, that was open for inspection with a directed tour. If you watch the newspaper faithfully, you can find announcements of these "open houses." Usually they are held on visiting Navy ships, tied up at Piers 17, 19, 29 or 45 on San Francisco's waterfront. Within the past year I have seen a variety of ships — submarines, destroyers, guided missile cruisers, fast frigates, an Australian destroyer, a Coast Guard icebreaker, and as a special treat for the bicentennial, the aircraft carrier *Coral Sea* (San Francisco's own), the first time a carrier has docked at the City since the war.

Navy Ships

Many ships of the Navy have San Francisco Bay as their home port. The well-known ships are based at the Naval Air Station in Alameda. On Armed Forces Day (in May), there is usually open house on the base and ships, and Treasure Island Naval Base has boats that you can go on. When the aircraft carriers *Enterprise* and *Coral Sea* are berthed at home at Alameda, they usually cause a ripple of interest. To find when they are here, call the ships information number (869-2992). Ship visits are arranged with the individual ship for recognized groups, like Boy Scouts.

View Points

The most extensive recreational use of San Francisco Bay is just looking at it. This viewing may be almost subconscious, as you look out an office window or drive down a street or past on a freeway. Topography determines the best views of the Bay. Some aspiration of man is fulfilled by a bird's-eye view that commands great distance. It is fortuitous that the central Bay, where the bridges and the ports and the yachts are, is surrounded by hills that present dramatic views. At the extreme north and south ends of the Bay, the terrain is thoroughly flat, so there is almost no good place to get an overall view. The basin of hills that encircle the Bay provides several locations where highway traffic has "entrance views," initial surveys that serve to psychologically define the extent of the Bay region. Important vista points in this ring of hills are found at the summits of two of the tallest peaks, Mt. Diablo and Mt. Tamalpais. From Mt. Diablo is a view of the limits of the littoral, laid out before you like a map — from the South Bay, to the Golden Gate, to San Pablo Bay, to Carquinez Strait, and around to the meanderings of the Delta. From Mt. Tamalpais you get a long distance view of part of the South Bay, a closer outlook on the central Bay, and a prospect of San Pablo Bay all the way to Carquinez Strait. The important item about these vista points is that any appreciable view requires a clear day (perhaps the day after rainfall). Then the scene is boundless. But too many days are obscured — by fog (although, from a vantage point atop Mt. Tam, watching the waves and currents of fog slip in the Golden Gate has its attractions), or more often the product of auto exhaust which presents a smogorama. Besides the view points listed here, there is information about obtaining "artificial views" of the Bay — maps and aerial photographs.

Marin County

Golden Gate Bridge Vista Point

The highway turnoff and parking area at the north end of the bridge. A view of the islands and bridges of the central Bay, one of the best views of the City in profile, the maritime traffic and the sailboat regattas.

Waldo Grade to Marin City

Driving views on Highway 101. Glimpses of the Sausalito waterfront and Richardson Bay with Belvedere and Angel Island as backdrops.

Strawberry Point

Off Highway 101 at Seminary Drive exit and follow to end. A roadside view down Richardson Bay, past Sausalito and Belvedere to San Francisco's skyline.

Angel Island

A hiker's vantage point from Mt. Livermore (info about getting to the State Park is found elsewhere in the book). View dominated by Mt. Tamalpais over Sausalito, Belvedere and Tiburon across Raccoon Strait; through the Richmond-San Rafael Bridge to San Pablo Bay, edged by the hills of Sonoma and Napa counties; the Golden Gate Bridge and San Francisco's northern waterfront with Alcatraz set in the foreground; the central Bay with Treasure Island and the bridge cutting Yerba Buena, and the East Bay cities and hills lurking behind.

Paradise Drive

Brief glimpses while driving on the twisting road on the north side of the Tiburon Peninsula. In general you should be able to see the refineries of Richmond, the bridge connecting San Rafael and Richmond, and beyond that, part of San Pablo Bay with The Brothers Lighthouse.

North San Pedro Road

The winding road on the north side of the peninsula from San Rafael, in the area where the new state park is being developed above China Camp, has some places to pull off to enjoy the view. You can see all of San Pablo Bay with its shoreline of Sonoma, Solano and Contra Costa counties, and you should be able to identify Mare Island and Pt. Pinole.

Petaluma River Bridge

A soaring concrete bridge, one of the few elevations on the North Bay, carries Highway 37 over the river and provides a sudden and quite brief driving vista of San Pablo Bay.

Contra Costa County

Carquinez Bridge

As Highway 80 heads south and west and crosses Carquinez Strait, you are presented with a true "entrance" to the Bay region. The driving view from the bridge is of the strait below and San Pablo Bay stretching away beyond. Despite the height and significance of the terrain, no one has managed to provide any vista point parking areas so that you could partake of the views. The nearest thing to a view point is the San Pablo Avenue exit at the south end of the bridge. On San Pablo there is a pull-off that gives a panorama of the strait and up Mare Island Strait to the Naval Shipyard and Vallejo.

Highway 80

The Interstate south from the Carquinez Bridge, past Rodeo and Pinole, toward San Pablo, and its feeders — Cummings Skyway, Highway 4, San Pablo Dam Road — provide driver's views of San Pablo Bay.

Point San Pablo

The Pt. Molate exit from Highway 17 near the Richmond toll plaza of the Richmond-San Rafael Bridge will take you to the end of Pt. San Pablo. Just before the end, there is a junction to Pt. San Pablo Yacht Harbor that goes up the hill through the tank farm. At the crest you find views of the Richmond Bridge, The Brothers Lighthouse in the foreground, Pt. San Pedro across the strait, Mt. Tamalpais looming above Marin, and the stretch of San Pablo Bay.

Nicholls Knob

Off Highway 17 in Pt. Richmond on South Garrard Boulevard and through the tunnel. You can now hike to the top of Nicholls Knob which is part of the George Miller Jr. Memorial Regional Shoreline. Views of the Standard Oil Refinery, the Richmond-San Rafael Bridge, the panorama of Marin shoreline opposite, tankers at Standard Oil's Long

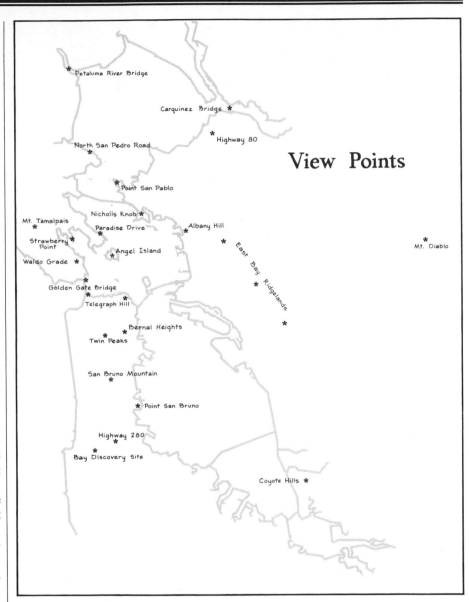

Wharf below, the industrial Port of Richmond, Santa Fe's railcar ferry operation at Ferry Point, the near-wilderness of Brooks Island, and across the teeming central Bay to the tall buildings of San Francisco.

Alameda County

Albany Hill

Turn off San Pablo Avenue in Albany on Castro Street. Relatively low-rise view of Brooks Island and the central Bay beyond, with the Port of Richmond and lots of other East Bay shoreline development.

East Bay Ridgelands

Grizzly Peak Boulevard from Berkeley (where it nearly describes the Alameda County boundary), south over the Caldecott Tunnel of Oakland, becoming Skyline Boulevard and continuing south from Oakland to San Leandro. This drive follows close to the crest of the East Bay Hills and traverses several parks. General views of the central and southern portions of the Bay, and at some points you can get a glimpse through the Golden Gate.

Coyote Hills

Regional park near Newark. A short hike to the top of Red Hill which is perhaps the only eminence that gives a good view of the South Bay. Nearby are the two southern bridges, and across the impressive length of the Bay are the hills that culminate the San Francisco peninsula, but spread out beneath you are the salt ponds, marshlands and sloughs that express the character of the South Bay.

San Francisco

Golden Gate Bridge Vista Point

Just off the highway at the toll plaza at the south end of the bridge. A very popular view of the Golden Gate with Ft. Point nestled below the bridge, the north waterfront stretching away from you, Alcatraz and other central Bay islands, the swarming shipping through the Gate, and the formations of sailboats.

Telegraph Hill

A circuitous route from the end of Lombard Street to the summit. Very popular view point, with the City as a backdrop (the night lights are especially entrancing). Near many tourist meccas, therefore it is often crowded. View of the central Bay with its islands and bridges, as well as the north waterfront very close beneath, with Aquatic Park, Fisherman's Wharf and the *Balclutha* easily identifiable. It had great historical significance as a ship-sighting location.

Twin Peaks

At the top of Market Street. This is San Francisco's premier panoramic view point. Below you the City undulates over its hills and the downtown stands tall; the Bay stretches out, the tops of the Golden Gate Bridge towers, the islands, Marin with Mt. Tam, the Bay Bridge bending to the East Bay cities and hills, San Francisco's southern working waterfront, and past San Bruno Mountain part of the South Bay can be seen; in the distance is part of San Pablo Bay to the north, across miles of ocean the Farallon Islands (belonging to San Francisco) to the west, Mt. Diablo to the east, and barely discernible Mt. Hamilton to the southeast. All this providing you are graced with a clear day for viewing.

Bernal Heights and Potrero Hill

Delightful neighborhood districts in the southeastern quadrant of San Francisco, above the freeways. Views over the industry and port workings of the City — China Basin, Central Basin, Mission Rock, Islais Creek, India Basin and Hunters Point.

San Mateo County

Point San Bruno

Off Highway 101 in South San Francisco on East Grand Avenue. There is a peak on this point which mounts a giant steel sculpture, erected to commemorate the Bay's marvelous bridges. Standing by these steel struts, you can see up to Candlestick Park and Hunters Point, across to the Oakland Airport and the shoreline of San Leandro and Hayward, and down past the San Francisco Airport and the trees of Coyote Point to the San Mateo bridge.

San Bruno Mountain

Off Highway 101 on Bayshore Boulevard, then cross the mountain on Guadalupe Canyon Road. There are places to stop a car and hike up to good vantage points. The mountain is wasted and bare, but it offers the highest place from which to view the South Bay, all the way down to the marshlands of the SF Bay National Wildlife Refuge and Alviso. Park plans would preserve at least part of the ridge top for an appropriate Bay viewing point.

Highway 280

When driving north on 280 and passing the Millbrae and San Bruno Avenue exits, there are some fleeting views of the Bay. From this height you see, across the crowded suburban streets and roaring airport, the south arm of the Bay receding to the distance as it was when the first European explorers found it.

Bay Discovery Site

Off Highway One at Rockaway Beach District of Pacifica on Fassler Avenue, and follow to end. This may seem an out-of-the-way location for Bay-viewing, but a hike of a couple of miles from the end of Fassler to Sweeney Ridge is a re-exploration of the historic route of discovery of San Francisco Bay. On the ridge is a stone indicating the point from which Gaspar de Portolá and his party made the first confirmed discovery by Europeans of the Bay (pace Sir Francis). From this vista point on the bare ridge, the immense size of the Bay can be perceived — the entire southern arm bends down toward San Jose and the wriggles of sloughs show up in the sunlight; San Bruno Mountain blocks the view to the north, but some part of the central Bay is visible, and a glimpse of terrain indicates a much larger basin stretching in that direction. If you squint your eyes, the hodge-podge of modern civilization may disappear and the chemical-laden air may be replaced with the flights of birds and the sounds of wildlife that were present on that fateful day in 1769.

Cartographic Views

Another way to view San Francisco Bay is from maps and aerial photos. There are enough different kinds, so that you could paper your walls.

United States Geological Survey

There are a couple of series of USGS topographic maps that depict San Francisco Bay. Probably the most practical is the three-sheet "San Francisco Bay Region" (1970). The sheets are large (scale 1:125000), with topography and colorful man-made and political details, and cost $2 each. The area covered is from Gualala on the coast above Sonoma, to Sacramento, to Santa Cruz; and the Bay is shown at a convenient size on sheets two and three.

The 7½-minute quadrangle maps may be more familiar. They have a convenient size and large scale (1:24000), and one covers an area of almost 7 by 8½ miles. They show topography, political divisions, roads, all natural features and some Bay details, all in full color. A central map of the Bay is "San Francisco-North" — Golden Gate and Sausalito, Tiburon and Belvedere and Angel Island, San Francisco south to Pacheco and 25th streets, and a corner of Treasure Island. To acquire a set that covers the entire Bay, you'll have to get at least nineteen topo maps. These maps are for sale at the USGS office at the US Custom House (555 Battery) in San Francisco, the USGS Western Region HQ (345 Middlefield Road) in Menlo Park, and at many outdoor and map shops in the area.

National Ocean Survey

Nautical charts are used by mariners and show all the details necessary to navigation. The large yellow and blue maps were formerly known as "Coast and Geodetic Survey" charts. There are three that encompass the Bay — "San Francisco Entrance" (18649), "San Francisco Bay, southern part" (18651), and "San Pablo Bay" (18654). At a larger scale is "San Francisco Bay — Candlestick Point to Angel Island" (18650), and others cover the Delta and navigable rivers. These charts are available at most chandleries. A very good one is George F. Butler Co. (160 Second Street) in San Francisco.

Aerial and Satellite Photos

High-altitude pictures of San Francisco Bay are very attractive and have been reproduced in many magazines, as posters, and on the cover of this book. Satellite views and photos from U-2 Earth Resources Survey Aircraft (EROS) based at NASA-Ames Research Center in Mountain View provide colorful vistas, and they have incredible detail. (You can find the roof of your house and the car parked out front.) The EROS series photographs are available in false-color infrared, black+white and color, but the extra cost for color is well worth it. The format is usually 9 inches by 9 inches and is available as positive or negative film, as well as prints. Prints can be had at the 9x9 and 9x18 size, and progressively larger, 18x18 and 36x36, etc. The price for a 9x9 print is $7 in color, $3 in B+W; a 9x18 is $14 in color; with appropriate price rises for larger sizes. In general, each high-altitude frame of 9x9 film at 1:120000 scale shows an area 16 miles on a side. To get a view of the entire Bay would require many prints. Satellite photos have the entire Bay in one shot, in both "oblique" and "straight-up" views.

To get one of these photographs, you go through a complex computerized procedure. It is supposed to be simple, but it certainly is lengthy. You need a photo frame number to order the picture you want. The photo order number and information on how to order can be obtained by mail or phone from one of the places below. If you give an exact location that you're interested in (coordinates of latitude and longitude preferred), you will receive a computer print-out that presents all of the available photos of that area. The most gratifying way to learn about the photos is to visit one of the Bay region facilities where you can see them on a viewer and determine which ones you want.

The USGS Western Region Headquarters handles both satellite and EROS photos. It is at 345 Middlefield Road, Menlo Park 94025 (323-8111). If you go there, they have a film-viewer with samples of the photos available for the Bay region. Also you can get assistance in ordering.

The NASA-Ames Research Center at Mountain View handles EROS photos. For mail information: AIRP Data Facility, NASA-Ames Research Center, Mail Stop 211-8, Moffett Field 94035. By phone, for information or an appointment (965-6252). They have a film-viewer with samples of pictures of the Bay. All you have to do is pick the one you want, and they will help you order it.

Ultimately, you will have to send your order and money to South Dakota. The EROS Data Center handles all the inquiries and orders — Sioux Falls, South Dakota 57198.

Marinas

The marinas of San Francisco Bay are the focal points of most of the nautical activities and attractions of this area. Clustered around these forty-odd small boat basins are the services and facilities that create the movement and vigor that is so engaging to spectator and participant alike. For a chance to get close to the water, there's nothing like visiting a marina. Visiting a small craft harbor — to watch the boats, to picnic by the water, to wonder at a fisherman's catch, to learn about sailboat handling, to share an after-the-regatta drink — brings the pleasure of the Bay to you. Of course if you own a boat berthed at a marina, you get all these delights as well as the satisfaction of your boat.

Using these marinas as a reference, you can find in this book other marine functions for the landsman and the sailor. The listing here is generally geographical: North (Marin), East (Solano County and East Bay), and the City and South. Fishing piers, boat ramps, bait shops, party boats, sailing opportunities, public access areas and parks, even restaurants mentioned here, can be found in more detail in other sections of the book.

The acute shortage of berthing space on San Francisco Bay is no news to anyone who has gotten into idle conversation on any boat dock. The causes of this shortage are manifold, and not all the problems are political. The difficulties that face the private owner/developer include myriad government regulations and the erratic action of financial dealings. Public agencies that propose a marina project may be entitled to redevelopment and harbor improvement funds (that means tax money), but nonetheless they must conform to design and environmental controls. So the treadmill of planning and reports and hearings goes on, and in a public project it seems as though everyone wants to be involved. Nothing happens quickly, except that the berth shortage keeps expanding.

Many of the marinas on the Bay could be called "mature"; they have no place to expand. Several others have plans for upgrading facilities and adding berths, which are reported here. The dismaying stories of waiting lists to get a berth at certain marinas are legion. A wait of six to eight years with 2,000 people on the list is reported for the San Francisco Marina. (It's notable that this is one of the less expensive places on the central Bay, and its location is a big attraction.) Average waiting time at Coyote Point is three-and-a-half to four years. However, there are berths on the Bay that are available without so much delay, and at reasonable expense. Location is the main factor. A common practice, if you can afford it, is to buy the boat and the berth that it is already in. That way you have no problem.

There are at least five marina projects that are far enough under way to talk about. In San Rafael, a plan for a 600-boat harbor at Spinnaker Point at the end of San Rafael Creek has had public hearing. But it's not settled, and completion is several years away. In Richmond, an interesting parlay of maritime development, housing project and marina scheme may start building next year. An eventual 2,000 berths will start with 500, and other marine facilities will be provided at Inner Harbor Basin. After at least four years of planning, the city of Albany may start (in a couple of years) on a proposed marina to the north of the racetrack. In San Francisco, a general refurbishing of China Basin has been started, and the project is supposed to include some new small craft berths as well as parklike esplanades. The city of

Brisbane has begun getting permits for a marina plan at Sierra Point, opposite Oyster Point. The 600-berth marina could be completed in four or five years, and it would have a shoreline park extending all the way to Candlestick Point. Merely a rumor in a sailor's eye is the talk of a marina at Foster City.

NORTH —
Marin and Sonoma counties

Sausalito Yacht Harbor

In downtown Sausalito, off Bridgeway at Bay Street.

This is the mass of masts that you admire when you're on a walking tour in downtown Sausalito. After you wend your way through all the parking lots off Bridgeway (and parking is a problem here), you will be rewarded when walking on the berthing piers. There are 450 berths in the marina on Richardson Bay, as well as a boat hoist and a yacht brokerage and chandlery. Adjacent is the Marine Service yard and Spinnaker Restaurant, and nearby is the Sausalito Yacht Club. Harbormaster (332-5000)

Pelican Yacht Harbor

In downtown Sausalito, off Bridgeway at Johnson Street (behind the Post Office).

This small marina has a very particular ambience. At the 90 berths you will find sailboats exclusively, and at least 90 percent of these are wooden hulls. There are slips that will handle a boat up to 125 feet, and they have 12 feet of water at zero tide. The pleasant harbor is overlooked by Flynn's Landing restaurant. Harbormaster (332-0723)

Marinship Yacht Harbor

At the north end of Sausalito, off Bridgeway at Harbor Drive, then at the foot of Harbor Drive turn to the right on Gate 5 Road.

The 150 berths of this marina are sandwiched in the middle of the Clipper Yacht Harbor, adjacent to the fuel dock. Among the facilities here are Jerry's Yacht Service yard, a yacht brokerage, and the sportfishing boats, *Long Fin* and *Thunderbird*. Harbormaster (332-9729)

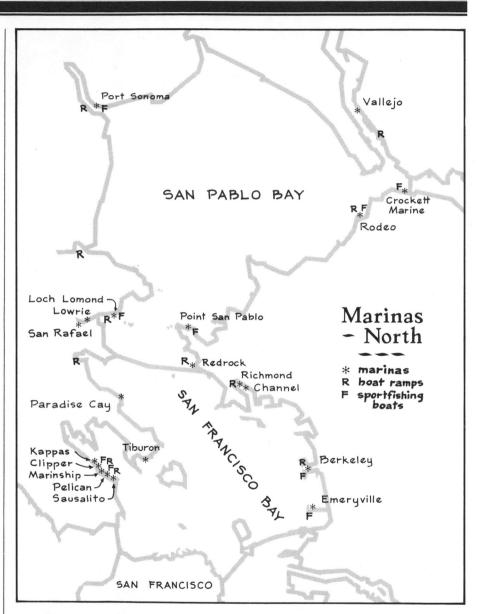

Clipper Yacht Harbor

At the north end of Sausalito, off Bridgeway at the foot of Harbor Drive.

For the time being this is the largest marina on the Bay with 1,300 berths in four basins on Richardson Bay. They also have 150 dry storage spaces, boat yards at both ends of this large area (Anderson's and Easom boat works), other marine services, a fuel dock, and an expensive boat launching ramp. In the same area are yacht sales offices, the Sausalito Food Company restaurant, and Caruso's — fresh seafood and sandwich sales, bait shop and sportfishing boat center. Harbormaster (332-3500)

Houseboat Colony

At the north end of Sausalito, off Bridgeway on Gate 5 Road, to the north of Clipper Yacht Harbor.

A community of ancient ferry hulks, rejuvenated tug boats, animated houseboats, and all manner of floating barges and beached structures for waterside residence — a controversy has hovered over this assemblage for some years. The 1972 "battle of Richardson Bay" was an illustration of this, and another confrontation took place in 1978. The latest thrust is a county low-cost housing/marina (224 berths) proposal at Waldo Point. The idea is to replace the "sub-standard" style of living with something more presentable. Construction was stymied by demonstrations, both shoreside and on the water. Despite some sinkings and fires, the Gate 5 colony remains an architectural wonder of the Western world and a well-known landmark of the Bay region. You get a glimpse of some of this variety from Gate 5 Road, but you get a better view from the north side of the huge parking lot of the Clipper Yacht Harbor.

Kappas Marina

At the north end of Sausalito, at Marin City exit from Highway 101, off Bridgeway on Gate 6 Road.

The northernmost of Sausalito's marinas is at Waldo Point. It has 125 berths and a colony of neat, trim, almost mobile-home-like houseboats. There are no other marine facilities, but back at Bridgeway is the Sausalito Boat & Tackle shop with snack bar, bait and tackle, and sportfishing party boats. Harbormaster (332-3580)

Tiburon

The yacht basin in downtown Tiburon facing Raccoon Strait and Angel Island is not a public marina. Most of the slips are occupied by boats of the Corinthian Yacht Club, one of the oldest on San Francisco Bay. There are also ferry slips and some dock space devoted to guest berthing for a few waterfront restaurants. Nonetheless, it presents a very nautical appearance and a lot of boating activity.

Paradise Cay Yacht Harbor

Off Highway 101 at Tiburon exit, then follow Tiburon Boulevard, to cross the peninsula on Trestle Glen Boulevard, then left for about a mile on Paradise Drive and down on Antilles Way to marina.

On the scenic north side of the Tiburon Peninsula, this marina has 120 berths, and that's about it — no other marine facilities. It is also the home of Paradise Harbor Yacht Club. Harbormaster (435-1652)

San Rafael Yacht Harbor

Off Highway 101 at Central San Rafael exit, then east on Second Street, then right and cross Grand Avenue bridge, then to 557 Francisco Boulevard.

Practically in the middle of San Rafael on the Canal, this marina has 140 covered and open berths. Other facilities are several spaces for dry storage, a yacht sales office, the Yacht Yard and W. C. Garvie Boat Builders, and on one side of the basin the Pier 15 Restaurant. Across the Canal is a fuel dock and several brokerages and repair yards. Harbormaster (456-1600)

Lowrie Yacht Harbor

Off Highway 101 at Central San Rafael exit, then east on Second Street which becomes Pt. San Pedro Road, to number 40.

A single basin with 109 berths on the north side of the San Rafael Canal. There is a yacht sales and brokerage and a repair shop for fiberglass, wood and engines. Nearby are other brokerages and repair yards. Harbormaster (454-7595)

Loch Lomond Marina

Off Highway 101 at Central San Rafael exit, then east on Second Street which becomes Pt. San Pedro Road for about two miles to 110 Loch Lomond Drive.

On San Rafael Bay, this marina has 450 berths, some covered, with space for more. There are 94 dry storage spaces, a marine supply and chandlery, a boat sales office and brokerage, and a snack bar. Also, it has a boat launching ramp, a fuel dock, a bait shack with the Bay charter boat *Superfish*, and it is the location of the Loch Lomond Yacht Club. Harbormaster (454-6154)

Port Sonoma Marina

Off Highway 37, near Black Point, on the east side of the Petaluma River at its confluence with San Pablo Bay.

One of the few marinas on San Pablo Bay, and the only one within many miles, Port Sonoma recently embarked on a program of active expansion and development. There are 120 berths in, and another 80 should be completed this year. Eventually the total will reach 400. Other services are a fuel dock, a bait and tackle shop, the sportfishing boat *Nobilis*, a picnic and barbeque ground, tennis and bocce courts, and an overnight guest dock. The intention is to make this a versatile recreation area, the destination of weekend cruise trips. There is no siltation problem, and it is dredged to eight feet deep at zero tide. This year Port Sonoma plans to complete a new boat shop and snack bar, 125 dry storage spaces, and the new Port Sonoma Yacht Club. In the future will come a restaurant, a pier for fishing vessels, and repair shops and boat yards. Tours to such local attractions as nearby wineries, Sears Point Raceway, and the Renaissance Faire are anticipated. Harbormaster - 250 Sears Point Road, Petaluma 94952 (897-4107)

East —

Solano, Contra Costa and Alameda counties

Vallejo Marina

Off Highway 80 at Tennessee Street West exit, then turn on Mare Island Way, then on Harbor Way into marina.

On Mare Island Strait near the causeway, this marina has 395 berths, both covered and open. Additional facilities include a fuel dock, a boat hoist and ABC Marine Service repair yard. The Harbor House Restaurant is located at the marina opposite the Mare Island Naval Shipyard. The Sardine Can is a typical marina snack bar with outside tables and a view of the docks. Open 9:30 am-9 pm every day, you can get burgers, beer and "Greek chilli." Harbormaster (707-553-4370)

Crockett Marine Service

Off Highway 80 at Crockett exit which becomes Pomona Street, then north on Port Street to end, then turn left to water.

Sitting beneath the Carquinez Bridge on the Strait, this marina has 85 covered and open berths that will handle boats up to 45 feet. Also, there is a marine railway, a fuel dock, and the Nantucket Fish Company restaurant. For fishermen, there is a bait shop with snacks, and several party boats work out of this marina, specializing in sturgeon, bass and flounder. Harbormaster (787-1047)

Rodeo Marina

Off Highway 80 at Willow Avenue-Rodeo exit which becomes Parker Avenue, then turn left at the end towards Lone Tree Point, and at foot of Pacific Avenue cross bridge to marina.

The sheds covering some 100 of the 130 boats, a serene coffee shop with good breakfasts, and lots of open dry storage scattered about combine to make this funky marina on San Pablo Bay. Sarge's bait and tackle shop next to the coffee shop arranges fishing expeditions on one of the four fishing boats that go out every day. They also have a fuel dock, boat launching ramps, and a boat and motor shop. Construction has started on dry storage sheds, and new restaurant, bar and bait shop are planned. Just to the west on Lone Tree Point is Joseph's Fishing Resort, a once thriving operation, that now offers a small beach, a snack bar, a fishing pier and a limited use boat ramp. Rodeo Marina Harbormaster (799-4435)

Point San Pablo Yacht Harbor

Follow Highway 17 through Richmond to San Rafael Bridge, then just before tollgate turn off at Point Molate exit, then follow road through Naval reservation, then turn off at sign and go up and over the tank farm hills.

Located at a very isolated point on San Pablo Bay, this marina originated years ago as a breakwater of sunken hulks of steam schooners. There are 205 berths, a few covered and some occupied by prim houseboats. Also a fuel dock, a marine railway, The Galley restaurant, and a bait shop. Fishing party boats work out of this marina, three full-time and three part-time. Harbormaster (233-3224)

Redrock Marina

Follow Highway 17 through Richmond to San Rafael Bridge, then just before tollgate turn off at Point Molate exit, then fork left at small sign toward bridge.

Sitting implacably in the middle of this ramshackle ex-ferry port, the bait shop-cum-snack bar rules the 125 berths, some covered, at this marina. You can get sandwiches and cold beer (or pop) and eat on the front door bench or out on the fishing pier. Lots of dry storage is scattered around, adding to the offhand appearance, along with a boat launching ramp and fuel dock. Occasional fishing boat charters may be arranged. An effort is being made to make the place more presentable by rebuilding the berths and adding 75 more in the future. Power and sail instruction is offered through the California Cruising Club. Harbormaster (235-0515)

Richmond Yacht Harbor (Decker's)

Follow Highway 17 through Richmond until you reach 320 West Cutting Boulevard.

Located at the end of the Santa Fe Channel, the marina has a water depth of nine feet at low tide. Some of the 60 berths will accommodate boats up to 40 feet. There is engine repair and space for trailers and dry storage. Adjacent is a public boat launching ramp, and nearby are the Richmond and Pacific boat works. Harbormaster (232-7380)

Channel Marina

Follow Highway 17 through Richmond until you reach 230 West Cutting Boulevard.

Another Richmond marina, also in the industrialized area on the Santa Fe Channel, this one has 67 covered and open berths. There is also a fuel dock. Nearby are the Richmond Boat Works and the Pacific Boat Works where you can get some bait and a pre-heated sandwich. Harbormaster (233-2246)

Berkeley Marina (City of Berkeley)

Off Highway 80 at foot of University Avenue. Can also be reached via frontage road from Ashby Avenue and Gilman Street exits.

Probably the most prominent and well-organized marina on San Francisco Bay, the large Berkeley Marina is virtually all park land. Shorebird Park is a perfect picnicking spot, the Pier is a noted fishing place, and the landfill area will eventually become North Waterfront Park. Across the freeway, at the foot of Addison Street, is Berkeley Aquatic Park where you can find more water activities, including sailing — school and rentals. At the marina there are 975 berths for boats from 20 to 84 feet and 90 dry storage spaces, as well as a one-shot fuel dock, a two-ton boat hoist, and a three-lane launching ramp. Also, limited visitor docking space, a holding tank pumpout, and a yacht brokerage. Weather warnings are flown from the marina yardarm. At the present time they are developing a new restaurant and sportfishing center, and there are plans for repair shops and a chandlery. Elsewhere in the area are three restaurants, the Berkeley Yacht Club and the Cal Sailing Club. Yacht charters and sailing lessons are available, and ferries to Angel Island ply the waters on summer weekends. The Berkeley Marina Sports Center, located in the trailer near the marina office, has a bait and tackle shop and a snack bar (open every day) — offering hot dogs, warmed-over sandwiches and beer to take out to a few tables in the parking lot. The Sports Center arranges trips on the fourteen (from 36 to 60 feet) fishing party boats that work out of the marina (call 849-2727). Harbormaster (644-6371)

Emeryville Marina (City of Emeryville)

Off Highway 80 at foot of Powell Street.

At the tip of the Emeryville peninsula, this marina has 280 berths. There is a fuel dock, a holding tank pumpout, and Hank Schramm's Sport Fishing Center with a bait and tackle shop. Nearby is the Casa Maria restaurant, and other restaurants are on the peninsula. In the future as many as 100 more berths will be added, and apparently they've been nudged to provide more landscaping and better public access to the shoreline. Harbormaster (654-6161)

Jack London Marina

Off Highway 17 at Broadway-Alameda exit to Jack London Square.

This marina is the nautical focus of the pedestrian attractions of this tourist-haven in Oakland on the Estuary. The Mast restaurant and Heinold's Saloon are beside the marina; there are more waterfront restaurants nearby; and many others on the landward side. There are 230 berths, a fuel dock, and a yacht brokerage here; next door is the Metropolitan Yacht Club and the Jack London Boatworks, where there is a travelift. The Spice Box is a typical marina snack bar (sandwiches, beer and wine — open daily 6 am-5 pm) beside Capt. Scotty's bait and tackle shop. A chandlery is nearby. Harbormaster (834-2192)

Portobello Marina

Off Highway 17 at Broadway-Alameda exit or Jackson Street exit, then follow Embarcadero West south of Jack London Square on to the Portobello development.

This marina has 55 berths on the Estuary and no other marine facilities except a yacht sales office. The Rusty Scupper restaurant is here, and a block or so south is Estuary Park which has a boat launching ramp. Harbormaster (444-8719)

Fifth Avenue Marina

Off Highway 17 at Jackson Street exit (and go south on Embarcadero), or at Sixteenth Avenue exit (and go back north on Embarcadero), then turn on Fifth Avenue to the marina.

Behind the industries and warehouses lining Embarcadero, this marina on the Estuary has 78 berths and 20 spaces for dry storage. Also the Godfather Bait and Tackle Shop (and party boat). Next door is a boat hoist, the Sommer Boat Works, and Survival & Safety Designs (safety equipment for cruising and racing). Harbormaster (834-9816)

Lani Kai Marina

Off Highway 17 at Sixteenth Avenue exit, then follow Embarcadero to number 1759.

This marina is operated by Don Wilson Yacht Sales and has 64 berths on Embarcadero Cove of the Estuary. Also there is a marine railway with a capacity of 26 feet. Nearby is Walters Engineering maintenance and repairs. Harbormaster (261-6532)

Embarcadero Cove Marina (Port of Oakland)

Off Highway 17 at Sixteenth Avenue exit to the junction with Embarcadero.

The Port of Oakland has begun a three-phase project on the Estuary to rehabilitate and expand the berthing space of the Oakland Yacht Club which lately moved to Alameda. The first phase was completed in 1978 with 150 new berths opened, and the second phase of 120 berths is scheduled for late in 1979. Public access corridors to Embarcadero Cove and shoreline pathways are included in the project. The expansion will include more than 300 berths, fishing piers, a couple of new restaurants, and new boat yards along Embarcadero. Beyond that, future plans call for redevelopment from the Ninth Avenue Pier on the north side all the way around Embarcadero Cove to Evans Radio Dock, including new commercial fishing facilities. In other words, a completely new look for all of Embarcadero Cove. For now, call the Port office (444-3188 ext. 217).

Embarcadero Cove Marina

Off Highway 17 at Sixteenth Avenue exit, then follow Embarcadero south to Embarcadero Cove.

This privately-operated marina of 150 berths wraps around the quaint cluster of

re-situated older buildings called Embarcadero Cove on the Estuary opposite Government Island. In the complex are Sailboats Inc. brokerage, marine ways at Power and Sail maintenance and repair, Quinn's Lighthouse and Victoria Station restaurants, and sailing lessons at Wayne D'Anna School and Sailor's Workshop. Next door is the Dock Café, and nearby is William J. Cryer & Sons boat repairs, in operation since 1890. The Port of Oakland's redevelopment is happening on both sides of this marina. Harbormaster (532-6683)

Mariner Square

The yacht basin at Alameda's Mariner Square on the Estuary above the Webster Tube is not a public marina. Most of the slips are occupied by boats for sale by yacht brokers, of which there are several here. Also a couple of boat yards and sailing schools — John Beery, Dave Garrett (in caboose) — use the berths. A boardwalk goes around the Barge Inn to the Rusty Pelican and presents these nautical delights, and every April a really big boat show is put on here.

Barnhill Marina

Off Highway 17 at Broadway-Alameda exit, then go through Alameda Tube, and just after getting out of the Tube turn off and follow signs back to Mariner Square at foot of Webster Street.

This is a small marina on the south side of Mariner Square on the Alameda side of the Estuary, looking across at Jack London Village. It has 70 berths, at least 40 of them serving as moorings for modern, shipshape houseboats. There is a little extra space for dry storage. Several other services are available in Mariner Square: Sea-West Yachts and Mariner boat yards, brokerage and chandlery, three restaurants — the Rusty Pelican, the Barge Inn and the Ancient Mariner. Harbormaster (523-7270)

Pacific Marina

Off Highway 17 at Broadway-Alameda exit, then go through Alameda Tube, and follow Webster Street to turn left on Lincoln Avenue, then turn left on Sherman Street and follow to the end.

An isolated marina that is on the far side of a mish-mash of railroad tracks, it may also be reached off Webster Street on Galleon Way. Operated by the Oakland Yacht Club, it has 300 berths. Other marine services in the area are Pacific Marina Boat Works (Tito Rivano) and Land & Sea Boat Repair. It is also the home to Neptune's Galleon restaurant and the Encinal Yacht Club. Harbormaster (522-6868)

Alameda Yacht Harbor

Off Highway 17 at 23rd Avenue-Alameda exit, then cross to Alameda on Park Street Bridge, then turn right on Buena Vista Avenue, then turn off near Arbor Street at 1535 Buena Vista Avenue.

On the Estuary at Fortmann Basin, this marina has 480 berths (some covered) and more are being added. There is a fuel dock, a chandlery and snack bar, and marine ways at the Alameda Yacht Repair. Harbormaster (522-9080)

Alameda Marina

Off Highway 17 at 23rd Avenue-Alameda exit, then cross to Alameda on Park Street Bridge, then turn right on Clement Avenue, then turn into marina at the foot of Schiller Street (1815 Clement Avenue).

This marina has 460 berths (some covered) on the Estuary opposite Government Island, as well as about 200 spaces for dry storage (some 50 of these covered). There is a fuel dock and a boat hoist, and just to the north, at the foot of Grand Street, is the Alameda Boat Ramp. Also in the complex is Svendsen's Boat Works for full service repairs and do-it-yourself work, the Yacht House brokerage, the Island Yacht Club, La Gondola restaurant, and sailing instruction. Harbormaster (521-1133)

Ballena Bay Yacht Harbor

Off Highway 17 at Broadway-Alameda exit, then go through Alameda Tube, and follow Webster Street to end, then right on Central Avenue, then south on Ballena Boulevard to marina.

A crescent of land on the south side of Alameda on the Bay, this marina has 500 berths, as well as a fuel dock, two boat hoists, and a holding tank pumpout station. A sailing school works out of the marina; it is the home of the Ballena Bay Yacht Club; marine services and a chandlery are available, along with two yacht brokerages; and there are two restaurants, the Whale's Tail and Beau Rivage. Harbormaster (523-5528)

San Leandro Marina
(City of San Leandro)

Off Highway 17 at Marina Boulevard West exit and follow to end, then turn on Neptune Drive to marina.

This marina has 475 berths (some covered) for boats from 21 to 60 feet, as well as a fuel dock, a boat hoist, a boat launching ramp, and a holding tank pumpout station. Also around the marina are a fishing pier, a yacht brokerage, the San Leandro Boat Works, the San Leandro Boat Club, the San Leandro Yacht Club, the Spinnaker Yacht Club, and two restaurants — Casa Maria and the Blue Dolphin, with two more planned for the future. Nearby at Marina Park, windsurfing lessons are offered. Harbormaster (577-3472)

The City and South —
San Francisco, San Mateo and Santa Clara counties

San Francisco Marina (City of San Francisco)

In San Francisco off Marina Boulevard at foot of Scott Street.

Probably the most noted marina on San Francisco Bay, surrounding Marina Green, the San Francisco Marina is one great place where City residents can drink in picture window views and realize the Bay. People come here in herds on weekends to jog, sun, frisbee, kite, play and watch the continuing unscheduled sequence of aquatic events which range from welcoming a replica of the *Golden Hinde*, to bicentennial fireworks, to yacht parades and races, to mooring a flying whale, to watching naval ships make port. The marina has 723 berths, and there is a holding tank pumpout station. Gas House Cove, which is at the east end of the marina at the foot of Laguna Street next to Fort Mason, is part of the marina and has a fuel dock, boat hoist, a small chandlery and bait shop, City Yacht Sales brokerage, and fishing on a pier at the end of the cove. Work is underway to dredge, construct a floating fender to block surge, to rehabilitate berths, and to add a few new ones at Gas House. At the west end of the marina there is a minute beach and a weekend snack stand. The marina is the home of the Golden Gate Yacht Club and the St. Francis Yacht Club (clubhouse is being rebuilt), and a few sportfishing boats. Sailing lessons are available. Harbormaster (563-8300)

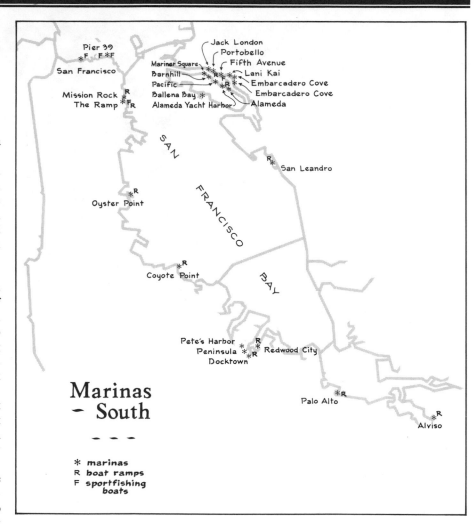

Marinas — South

* marinas
R boat ramps
F sportfishing boats

Pier 39 Marina

In San Francisco, on the north waterfront near Fisherman's Wharf.

Pier 39 is a development on The Embarcadero (it was abortively named North Point Pier) that is a "tourist/marina" with 23 restaurants, 100 shops, and a 1,000-car parking garage (horrendous thought). It seems to be a sort of "Disneyland-on-the-Bay, North," in a style which has been called "ersatz nostalgia." Apparently this "plastic" shopping complex will have boaters on display, creating a "nautical atmosphere" as a tourist visiting attraction. The tenants of the 350-berth pleasure marina and the fishing basin for commercial and charter boats will be decorative and serve as attractions in a nautical theme park. It opened late in 1978. The marina includes 21 guest berths, a couple of yacht brokers, a pumpout station, a few sportfishing boats, and a sailing club. Harbormaster (981-1796)

Mission Rock Resort

In San Francisco, off Third Street at the foot of Mariposa Street, at 817 China Basin Street.

This funky marina is a conglomerate of activities. Perhaps best known for its succulent hamburgers at the downstairs snack bar and deck, it also has a bar and restaurant with deck upstairs. There are thirty berths, a bait and tackle shop, and fishing boats for rent. The Resort is next to a fishing pier, and a couple of blocks down the street from a boat launching ramp. Besides fishermen, windsurfers sometimes hang out here. Mission Rock (621-5538)

The Ramp

In San Francisco, off Third Street at the foot of Mariposa Street, at 855 China Basin Street.

Barely able to be called a marina, this place has eighteen berths and dry storage (covered and open). There is a bait and

tackle shop with sandwiches and beer, a fuel dock, a repair shop with 40-ton crane, and of course a boat ramp. The sportfishing boat *Carol* is berthed here. The Ramp (621-2378)

Oyster Point Marina (San Mateo County)

Off Highway 101 at Oyster Point Boulevard exit, then follow to end.

This marina has 287 berths and 140 dry storage spaces. There is a fuel dock, a boat launching ramp, the Oyster Point Yacht Club. At one end of the marina is a small beach, and nearby is Bryan's Boat Yard. The marina is currently undergoing an extensive two-year expansion to around 600 berths, and will add two restaurants and a fishing pier. I hope that in all the expansion that is going on, they finally get around to opening up some space for pedestrians and developing park land that has been on the planning boards for years, so the atmosphere of the marina will be available to many more people. Harbormaster (871-4057)

Coyote Point Marina (San Mateo County)

Off Highway 101 near Burlingame at Peninsula Avenue exit, then follow Coyote Point Drive to end.

Located at the south side of this county park, the marina has 480 berths, a fuel dock, pumpout facilities, a boat launching ramp, a yacht brokerage, and is the home of the Coyote Point Yacht Club. Long-range marina expansion plans call for adding 50 or 60 new berths each year until 1,000 spaces are built. Elsewhere in the park is a long swimming beach, a restaurant, a kids' natural history museum, extensive wooded walking paths and picnic areas, and some fishing off the breakwater at the end of the marina. Harbormaster (573-2594)

Pete's Harbor

Off Highway 101 at Whipple Avenue exit in Redwood City, then follow Whipple to end, at number 1 Uccelli Boulevard.

This sprawling and interesting marina has the Harbor House restaurant as a focal point. There are 240 berths and 100 spaces for dry storage and two travelifts for the do-it-yourself repair yard. Also a marine store, chandlery and brokerage. It is the home of the Peninsula Yacht Club. Harbormaster (366-0922)

Peninsula Marina

Off Highway 101 at Whipple Avenue exit in Redwood City, then follow Whipple past drive-in movie (next door to Pete's Harbor).

This marina is brand new, the first marina to be built on the Peninsula in twenty years. When it opens in early 1979, it will have 400 berths and dry storage for 150 boats. Other facilities will be a fuel dock, a pumpout station and a boat hoist. Later amenities will include a yacht broker, two restaurants and more elaborate landscaping. For more info (591-0361 or 367-8127)

Redwood City Municipal Marina

Off Highway 101 at Harbor Boulevard exit, then follow to marina.

Located on Redwood Creek, in the midst of the industrial area and salt mountains that are the port, this marina has 150 berths (mostly filled with sailboats) and 50 dry storage spaces. Other installations are a small sailboat hoist, a boat launching ramp, a fuel dock, and chandlery/brokerage and motor repair shop. Also found here are the port's fireboat, the Sequoia Yacht Club, Charley Brown's restaurant, and the Stanford crew house and launching float. There is a fishing pier and small, cunning picnic area. Harbormaster (369-6988)

Docktown Marina

Off Highway 101 at Whipple Avenue exit in Redwood City, then follow Veteran's Boulevard on the landward side of the freeway, turn on Maple Street and take overpass to end.

At this marina there are 120 berths along Redwood Creek, and up to 350 boats can be put in dry storage. Other marina facilities include a boat launching ramp, a brokerage, a sailing center (lessons and rentals), a boat builder's supply and hoist at the South Bay Boat Works. Harbormaster (365-3258)

Palo Alto Yacht Harbor (Santa Clara County)

Off Highway 101 at Embarcadero Road exit, then follow past airport to end.

This marina is surrounded by marsh preserve and mud flats and has 118 berths. An expansion program will add 86 new berths this year, as well as a fuel dock and dry storage space, and another 140 berths next year. There is also a boat launching ramp and the Palo Alto Yacht Club. Harbormaster (323-6865)

Alviso Marina (Santa Clara County)

Off Highway 101 or Highway 17 near San Jose on Highway 237, then turn off on Taylor or Gold streets, then follow Gold and Elizabeth streets to foot of Hope Street and marina (at extreme south end of Bay).

Alviso has to be the most remarkable city of its size on San Francisco Bay. Below the levees that hold back the waters of the Bay in Alviso Slough (once the Guadalupe River), the physical remnants of its sizeable history are represented by the brick warehouses and canneries and the wooden Victorian houses and stores.

Just enough remains for you to accept that in the 1850s Alviso was one of the larger ports on the Bay and served as the Embarcadero for San Jose and the Santa Clara Valley. This waterfront activity has dwindled to a vestige that is represented by a simple marina that has recently been dredged and enlarged to 80 berths. There is a boat launching ramp and a holding tank pumpout station. Nearby is the JC Boatworks for marine repairs and fishing, as well as an antique shop and an art gallery of minor interest, and a couple of seafood ''grotto'' restaurants. At the other end of Hope Street is the nautical blue clubhouse of the South Bay Yacht Club that maintains the character of funky elegance that pervades the whole town. If it ever gets off the ground (or out of the marsh), the San Francisco Bay National Wildlife Refuge will have an environmental center near the town. Harbormaster at Palo Yacht Harbor (323-6865)

Learning to Sail

Surprisingly, one of the best ways to get away from crowded urban life is to get on to the swells and chop of San Francisco Bay. With all the water out there, it should be invitation enough to any recalcitrant landlubbers or nascent old salts who lust to be a sailor on the nautical playground right at our doorstep. The constant activity any time of the year, but particularly the regattas of large and small boats on summer weekends, quickens the interest and anticipates the thrill of encountering this wide expanse of natural environment with its intriguing conditions of weather and current. In short, if you want to learn sailing, this is the place to find your program to meet your needs.

Classes listed here should satisfy every taste in transforming you from a mere enthusiast to a sailor of whatever proficiency you desire. They range from small boats for novices who don't want complications to Bay-worthy keelboats for sailors who want a refresher course to improve their skills, and include progressive sessions for anyone bent on becoming a knowledgeable skipper. The classes can be divided into three types — fundamentals, Bay sailing and advanced.

The first type of class, many taught by parks and recreation departments in lakes and sloughs around the periphery of the Bay, are usually given in dinghies. They are susceptible to children, and some

especially for children. You learn the fundamentals of sailing and the price is exceptionally cheap. Other local recreation departments away from the Bay, not listed here — San Francisco's Lake Merced, Fremont, Milpitas, Los Gatos and Orinda — offer courses also.

The second type of class is Bay sailing taught in keelboats of various sizes in every part of the Bay. In most of them you can start out as a tyro and become competent to handle a boat on the Bay in stringent conditions. Usually there is a progression of sessions leading to racing and cruising techniques. Some classes are set up as sailing clubs — you join, take lessons, and then rent the boats to sail on your own. Several yacht brokers offer instruction as part of the deal if you are buying a boat from them. The US Coast Guard Auxiliary and the US Power Squadrons are concerned with boating classes and safety and piloting and navigation instruction, and check the local college districts for classes — the College of Alameda has good ones, and even U.C. Extension has in the past given a sailing symposium.

Finally, there are advanced courses, usually termed ''cruising'' or ''offshore.'' Many Bay sailing schools offer advanced sessions as the upper end of their curricula after basic and intermediate prerequisites are met. This instruction, plus plenty of experience, can prepare you for making that imaginary round-the-world cruise come true.

This listing should help you find a school for your taste, enjoyment and level of expectations. Prices have been included for comparison only, they have probably changed by this time. Schools are grouped geographically, but don't let that deter you from the one you want; mostly it's sailing on the Bay, which is in the middle of us all.

Sausalito

Cass' Rental Marina

Bridgeway at Napa Street (Box 643), Sausalito 94965. (332-6789) The sailing school has been offering lessons since 1961. They give three courses — basic, intermediate and advanced cruising — any time of the year, at your request. The basic course with a class of four is twenty hours, five three-hour lessons and a five-hour solo sail, for $86/person. The intermediate course for four students is twelve hours, four three-hour lessons, for $69/person. The advanced cruising course for five students on a 31-foot schooner is twenty-four hours, three four-hour lessons and a twelve-hour cruise, for $110/person. Private lessons are available, on your boat or theirs, for $38 per three-hour session. One bit of helpfulness: they freely give advice about sailing details, rigging and tides, explorations in the Delta, and because they don't sell any boats, they have unbiased opinions if you want some recommendations when shopping for one of your own. They also have rentals.

Hauser Institute

Box 281, Sausalito 94965. (388-8130) Since 1971 John Hauser has offered what is probably the most unusual sailing school on San Francisco Bay. The course combines sailing with instruction in navigation and ecology of the Bay for six students on a 26-foot sloop. The course is ten weeks long and is offered as spring, summer and fall quarters. The classes consist of five all-day sails, two evening classes and three moonlight sails where basic sailing theory is explored, short sessions in ecology are given and navigation, including celestial, is practiced under the eye of a licensed instructor. Tuition is $150/person. In addition, charters are available at $100/day.

Sausalito Recreation Department

420 Litho Street, Sausalito 94965. (332-4520) Two different courses are offered: junior sailing, for kids nine and over, at the Sausalito Yacht Club (foot of El Portal) and adult sailing at the Sausalito Cruising Club (Bridgeway at Napa Street). For juniors, the basic sailing instruction is in two summer sessions with thirty-six hours of instruction in Lasers (fourteen-foot dinghies). The cost is $45, or $25 for Sausalito residents. Adult classes are scheduled for sessions of about one month in the spring and fall and two sessions in the summer. Practical sailing experience and safety are stressed in the beginning; and intermediate courses on 30- to 35-foot boats with class size of six, given on Saturdays. The cost is $25, or $22 for Sausalito residents.

Tiburon

Sailing Center of Tiburon

21 Main Street (upstairs) (Box 678), Tiburon 94920. (435-4033) Since 1964 the Sailing Center has offered lessons: basic, advanced/racing, cruising, and offshore, at any time of year. The basic course is a class of four people in a 22- to 27-foot boat for eighteen hours, on weekdays or three consecutive weekends, for $95/person. The advanced/racing courses are classes of three students perfecting sailing skills in the demanding conditions of the Bay, as well as spinnaker and racing tactics practice for those interested in competition. Advanced, twelve hours for $85/person, and racing, fifteen hours for $145/person. The cruising course includes chart reading, planning and the experience of sailing up to the Delta and living aboard for five days for $165/person. The offshore course is four sailing trips on a 35 or 40-foot boat, primarily for the experience and to find out whether you are a bluewater sailor, for $145/person. Private lessons are available, for $20/hour, by appointment. They also have sailboat rentals and a sailing club.

Corte Madera

Corte Madera Department of Recreation

Tamalpais Drive and Willow Avenue, Corte Madera 94925. (924-1700) A basic course is offered, following the Red Cross sailing manual leading to Red Cross certification, at the lagoon behind Redwood High School. A maximum class of twelve people uses two Lasers and another (unidentifiable) boat. The course is six to eight weeks, usually on weekends in spring and fall and weekday evenings in summer. It costs $17, or $15 for Corte Madera or Larkspur residents.

Greenbrae

Canoe Trips West

2170 Redwood Highway, Greenbrae 94904. (461-1750) As you can tell by the name, this place primarily deals with canoes and canoeists, and you can find it on Corte Madera Creek by taking the Lucky Drive exit off Highway 101. However, private, individual basic sailing lessons in outrigger Go-Boats are offered, by appointment for $15/hour. These boats are also rented. Included in the canoe activities are group lessons, basic, moving water and river running, as well as naturalist excursions and guided trips on the Bay and its environs.

San Rafael

San Rafael Recreation Department

1400 Fifth Avenue, San Rafael 94901. (456-1112 ext. 261) Lessons are offered year-round at Beach Park, off Francisco Boulevard, on the San Rafael Canal in their ten Lasers, following the International Laser sailing school curriculum. Classes are sixteen hours in four weeks for ten to twelve people, on weekends, and in the spring and summer on weekday evenings. Beginning and intermediate courses are offered, and possibly advanced in the Bay, if there is demand. The cost is $32, or $25 for residents of San Rafael.

Novato

Novato Parks and Recreation Department

917 Sherman Avenue, Novato 94947. (897-4323) Lessons are offered in three seasons: spring and fall weekends; and in summer, weekday afternoons and evenings, and weekend mornings and afternoons. They use Bahia Lagoon by the Petaluma River — take the Atherton Avenue exit in Novato, then follow it east and fork left on Bugeia Lane into Bahia, then follow Topaz to the lagoon. The classes of up to ten use the six Lasers for twelve-hour courses, basic I and basic II — twenty-four hours leading to a Red Cross certificate. They also have intermediate and introduction to racing courses. The cost is $18, or $15 for residents of Novato.

Richmond

California Cruising Club

At Redrock Marina. (235-7053) This is sort of a different concept, all the advantages but none of the hassles of boat owning. The main appeal is that it works on a flat rate, $900/year. For this you get everything: there are no extra "day charges," or monthly fees, or boat charges, or anything. Neither are you buying part of a boat, or buying into a "boat-dominium." These are privately owned boats, 26 or 28 feet, for three to twelve people. All instruction is given in the boats (power and sail), by licensed skippers, individually, anytime you wish, by appointment. This instruction points towards two tests, one written and one on the water, to be "certified." Then you have unlimited use of the boats (you do have to sign up ahead of time). The only catch, which is not really a catch, is that you pay for your own fuel.

Berkeley

John Beery Sailing School

Aquatic Park (inshore of the freeway, at foot of Addison Street), Berkeley 94710. (845-6310) Practically the oldest (almost twenty years) and probably the largest sailing school on San Francisco Bay. The small boat courses are given at Aquatic Park throughout the year with an extensive schedule of classes on consecutive weekends and on weekdays in summer. Introductory classes start at the beginning and teach basic sailing skills. El Toros (8-foot catboats) are used in classes of up to twenty people for twelve hours of instruction leading to Red Cross certification (with some classroom work) for $35; instruction in the more demanding, exciting Laser for sixteen hours with a class limit of five people for $70 leads to International Laser certification. Intermediate classes are offered in Lasers and in sloop sailing on Capri 14s, with the final session of this class aboard a larger sloop on the Bay. If you are interested in competition, two advanced classes in Laser racing should whet your skills and enable you to get the maximum performance from the boat. Small boat rentals are available at Aquatic Park. Private instruction is given for up to four people in their boats for $15/hour, and in your own boat anywhere around the Bay for $10/hour. Courses in bigger boats operate out of Mariner Square in Alameda. One class that is interesting and unique is the "Day on the Bay," a basic introductory sail of six hours for $15 that lets you find out if you're cut out for that kind of life. Bay sailing is an advanced class in keelboats, usually the Ranger 23, or a Ranger 26, a Cal 34 or a Downeast 38, where you spend six hours a day for three days learning confidence in the boat, its rigging, emergency situations, heavy-weather techniques, and about the Bay's tides and currents. The unique For Women Only classes (similar to the "Bay sailing") are taught to skipper's "significant others," who are familiar with boats but have been relegated to the support role of "first (and we hope, only) mate" and would like the confidence of sailing the boat herself. Another option is the speed of catamaran sailing, taught on the Hobie 16 and Solcat 18 as private lessons. Charters are available from Mariner Square, either "bare boat," or complete with instructor/crew provided.

Berkeley Sailing Center

Berkeley Marina. (527-6592) A one-woman operation, instruction is given in a Bear, a classic 23-foot San Francisco Bay design "woodie" sloop, with no motor, so you learn practical sailing. Lessons are offered any time of the year, by appointment, for one or two people ($15 or $20) with two hours in the water. Approximately five lessons is the basic course, but you can progress through advanced experience and spinnaker, and kids are handled on a long-term, tutoring, situation.

Grisette Sailing School

Berkeley Marina (Box 855), Berkeley 94701. (849-0363) For the experienced sailor, Steve Mann offers seamanship and piloting on the 26-ton cutter *Grisette*. You get checked out on a 22-foot sloop, then move to the 40-foot bluewater beauty for two sixteen-hour weekend courses, basic familiarization and seamanship. Each course costs $50/person. Following these prerequisites a class of four to six can take the piloting course. The course runs in an informal manner, when a group can be gathered, and may last, with breaks, for six to eight months.

The assumption is that expensive electronic gear, priced out of the reach of many mariners, is not the absolute answer for piloting and navigation. The course covers compass and tables; tides and currents; speed, time and distance; charting and piloting; and concludes with a two- to three-day cruise to try out all these skills. Steve is also interested in offering other courses: celestial navigation for piloting graduates, living aboard for cruising or at berth, and perhaps even marine surveying for prospective boat buyers.

Lion Sailing School

At the Marriott Inn, Berkeley Marina. (526-4559) Priding themselves in being the Bay's most rigorous sailing school, they offer two programs of instruction. Program A is two courses, an introductory of fifteen hours, at the end of which passing the test qualifies you for their rentals, and an intermediate of twenty hours taught in a Santana. The cost comes out to $5/hour. Program B is four courses, the first two are the same as Program A — basics of handling a sailboat, emergency rescue of a man overboard, docking, and also experience of sailing on the Bay. In addition there is an advanced course and a piloting/navigation course using a Santana (two to four people in a class), a Catalina 27 (three to five people) and a 35-foot Lion sloop (three to six people). This program's seventy-five hours of class time costs $325. Backed by their great racing record, two racing courses are offered: tactics (starting and buoy), and reaching and running spinnaker. Other advanced options are a Delta cruise of three to five days and a pre-cruise indoctrination for offshore experience. Rentals are available through the Lion Sailing Club, and charters are obtainable on any of their seven boats. The fees range from $45 for a weekend day on the Santana, to $120 for a weekend day on the Lion sloop, and more for the Columbia 43. They also have charter-a-month and charter-twice-a-month plans with discounts on their fees.

Oakland

American Boating Club

55 Alice Street (Jack London Village), Oakland 94607. (763-4455) Another club with a different concept, all-inclusiveness. All the joy of boating, with a minimum of responsibility, goes with the flat rate. For $1275/year you have priority on the smaller boats, for $2075/year you have priority on the larger boats. Lessons are given on their large fleet of power boats or one of several sailboats, including a Cal 27 and an Ericson 29. For the beginner it takes about eighteen class hours to be "certified" to take out the boats any time you want. There are lots of other classes for members, both on-the-water and classroom instruction in technical subjects. The club also has facilities and boats at Pier 39 Marina in San Francisco.

Ocean Cruising School

One Fifth Avenue (Fifth Avenue Marina), Oakland 94606. (834-6877) This school has four sailing courses, and a whole raft of classroom sessions aimed at the more experienced sailor interested in cruising and technical aspects of running a boat. The courses run all year in a sort of tri-mester arrangement. Mike Brooks is in charge of the sailing classes: basic sailing in 13-foot dinghies for twelve hours on two consecutive weekends for $60/person; intermediate sailing limited to four students in a 32-foot Contessa sloop for twelve hours, also on two weekends for $60/person. The advanced classes on the Contessa are limited to four people and require a coastal navigation course or equivalent experience: offshore sailing is twenty-four hours of the more important aspects of coastal sailing for $120/person; ocean sailing training is a four-day cruise to Monterey with a realistic learning environment for $280/person. The cruising and technical courses are taught by marine-oriented experts, and include coastal and celestial navigation, weather and salt water fishing for mariners, heavy weather sailing, and survival at sea — many at both Oakland and San Rafael.

Sailors' Workshop

21 Embarcadero Cove, Oakland 94606. (533-4221) This small sailing school is at Sailboats Inc., a yacht brokerage. On their three-boat fleet, they provide individual instruction, by appointment. If you want to know if you're interested in sailing at all, the sampler course gives you two hours in the classroom and one hour on the water for only $10. Then you can progress to their regular course, twelve hours of instruction for $95; graduates of which are eligible for rentals. The three-hour cruising seminar on a 25 to 35-foot boat outside the Golden Gate trains you in planning for weekend cruises.

Wayne D'Anna Sailing School

11 Embarcadero Cove, Oakland 94606. (261-3844 direct line, or 522-7760 answering service) This sailing school offers a series of three courses, taught daily by appointment, to individuals, couples or trios, on a Santana 22, a Catalina 22 or an Ericson 23. The basic course is in four sessions, $95 for individuals and $135 for couples for ten hours, and $55/person for groups of three or four for twelve hours. The intermediate course teaches the finer points of boat handling and navigation, and lets

you move up to larger boats and be introduced to the basics of competition. You progress at your own speed, so there is no set time limitation. The advanced course concentrates on competition, including spinnaker handling or extended cruising for twelve hours. The intermediate and advanced courses are limited to individuals or couples only for $17.50/hour. They also have rentals available and a sailing club program that includes a monthly three-day coastal cruise and other benefits. Charters are available as well.

Oakland Parks and Recreation

Sailboat House, 568 Bellevue Avenue (Lake Merritt), Oakland 94610. (444-3807) Classes on Lake Merritt are offered to children and adults in an elaborate schedule of sessions from March to October. Each class is limited to twenty students, one per boat (which is usually an El Toro and sometimes a Sunfish), fifteen hours for children and eighteen hours for adults. For children twelve to seventeen years of age the classes are five consecutive days, both basic and advanced, and cost $15, or $12 for Oakland residents. Adults are offered weekend classes, week night classes, intermediate, intensive and family-learn-to-sail classes for $20/person, or $16 for Oakland residents. You can also rent the El Toros and Sunfish for sailing on Lake Merritt.

Alameda

Gray Whale

Alameda Marina, Alameda (1500 Irving Street, San Francisco 94122). (661-5622)

The skipper, Mike, and his son run this small school that offers beginning and intermediate lessons on San Francisco Bay. The licensed instructor uses an Ohlson 31 at $35/eight-hour day on weekends. They also will make Bay charter arrangements for up to six people for $130/day.

John Beery Sailing School

Mariner Square, Alameda. (845-6310) Their courses in big boats operate out of Mariner Square, but look for the listing under Berkeley for the full range of classes.

Dave Garrett Sailing School

Also known as the Northern California Sailing Center, 2415 Mariner Square (in caboose), Alameda 94501. (521-5370, offices closed Mondays) This twin school operates on both sides of the Bay, so look for their story in the listing under Redwood City.

San Francisco Sailing School

1130 Ballena Boulevard (Ballena Bay Yacht Harbor), Alameda 94501. (523-0800) This is a straight school without all the paraphernalia of clubs, or rentals, or charters. Classes are offered year-round and they start every week or two — maximum size is three people, six for offshore work. The basic course for beginners is twenty-four hours in a 25-foot sloop, concentrating on the fundamentals, for $155/person or $275/two. You may then progress through a two-day intermediate and a two-day advanced course to the offshore cruising course for experience and navigation for five days on boats up to 50 feet.

San Francisco

ABLE Sailing School

1166 Capitol Avenue, San Francisco 94112. (586-5332) Probably the oldest sailing school on San Francisco Bay; your licensed instructor, Captain Ken Greer, has been in business since 1955. Lessons in power or sail are by appointment, year-round, out of the San Francisco Marina, or Sausalito, Berkeley and other marinas. Sailing classes are in 20-footers — a Coronado 25, Rainbow 24 or Santana 22. The three courses, basic, intermediate and advanced, are twelve hours and can be taken as four-hour classes or two six-hour days if you want to do the course in a weekend. The cost is $120/course, and only one or two students are advised. Rentals are available, and skippered trips are offered on the Bay or along the coast. The trips can be just a cruise, or whale-watching or diving; a 40-foot fishing boat goes for $200/day, and a 25-foot Coronado which holds six people can be had for $22/hour for a few hours; and there are some very advantageous rates for five to seven-day trips.

Marina Green Sailing School

Marina Green, San Francisco. (992-0909, or 922-0227 on the boat) Denis Belfortie teaches out of the San Francisco Marina as a one-man outfit (though he is planning to add another couple of instructors) in a Catalina 27 sloop and a 30-foot motorboat, vintage 1931. Lessons are for one or two people at a time, although two couples who all know each other would not be too much to handle. Class times are by appointment, at your convenience, but the Bay winds normally are best for beginners in the mornings and more advanced students can use the experience of afternoon winds. Usually navigation is taught in the motorboat. A lesson of three hours costs $5/hour/person. Crewed charters on the Bay for up to six passengers are available with flexibility for individual ideas about destination for $10/hour.

Oceanic Society

Building 240, Fort Mason, San Francisco 94123. (441-5970) Crew Orientation classes help train and prepare Oceanic Society-Bay Chapter members to participate as knowledgeable crew in other society activities — water quality monitoring, field trips, environmental surveillance, whale watch and Farallon patrol. The course runs for three six-week sessions April through September. An entirely volunteer program, five to ten skippers use their boats in very individual class arrangements to convey fundamentals of sail handling, tides and docking, and to give experience in Bay conditions. The crucial participants in this program are the skipper/instructors who really love the Bay and want to share on-the-water experience by volunteering their boats to turn others on to the enjoyment of Bay sailing. If you are a boat owner, you can join others who find the reward of learning more about sailing in a teaching situation by becoming a member and volunteering your boat. Who knows, you may pick up a racing crew or some bottom scrapers. The Oceanic Society also offers celestial navigation courses in ten three-hour classes and has in the past offered a coastal navigation and piloting course.

American Boating Club

Pier 39, San Francisco 94119. (981-6551) This club gives you all the joy of boating, with a minimum of responsibility, for an all-inclusive flat rate. The annual membership fee is $1475/year, or $2375/year with priority for their larger boats. Training is included, classroom and on-the-water hours, attuned to an individual's skills and rate of learning. When you are "certified," you can take out any of their fleet of one hundred 27- to 35-foot sailing boats virtually any time you want. The club takes care of maintenance and scheduling and has other benefits for members. The club also operates out of Jack London Village in Oakland.

San Mateo

San Mateo City Recreation Division

(574-6737) Classes are given at Parkside Aquatic Park on Marina Lagoon in San Mateo — off Highway 101 at Highway 92 exit towards San Mateo Bridge, then turn left on South Norfolk Street and turn on Roberta Drive to park. They have a schedule of classes in spring, summer and fall. In the spring and fall, evening and weekend basic I and II classes are given. In the summer the basic and intermediate classes are offered on weekdays and weekends, mornings, afternoons and evenings. The fifteen-hour classes are taught on their fleet of fourteen El Toros. The cost is $20, or $16 for residents of San Mateo. They also have a Rainbow 24 at Coyote Point Marina for deepwater sailing and racing classes.

Foster City

Foster City Parks and Recreation Department

650 Shell Boulevard, Foster City 94404. (349-1200) They have a schedule of classes throughout the year using Sunfish on the Foster City Lagoon. The beginning and intermediate courses are five classes of three hours, on weekends and daily in the summer. The cost is $24, or $22 for residents of Foster City. They also offer a deepwater session out of Coyote Point Marina.

Redwood City

Dave Garrett Sailing School

Also known as the Northern California Sailing Center, Docktown Marina, 1500 Maple Street, Redwood City 94063. (368-2908, offices closed Mondays) Also located at 2415 Mariner Square (in caboose), Alameda 94501. (521-5370) Offering lessons year-round, this twin school operates on both sides of the Bay and gives instruction to individuals, couples, up to four people maximum, by appointment at your convenience. The basic course on a Catalina 22 or a Columbia 22 is eight hours of learning basic rigging, seamanship and handling. The cost is $110 for individuals and $150 for couples. The eight-hour intermediate course offers experience in more advanced techniques. The advanced courses are in an Ericson 32, seven hours for the navigation course, and a one day and one night cruising seminar on the Bay. The "Captain's Course" offers all these sessions in a package, twenty-eight hours plus a cruising weekend, for $375 individuals, $585 couples. Graduates of the sailing school are entitled to rent or charter their boats. Occasional charters are available to others, if you have visions of grandeur try their Columbia 45.

Peninsula Swimming and Sailing School

1602 Stafford Street, Redwood City 94063. (366-9211) Besides having an indoor pool for part of their aquatic activities, they also teach sailing for kids in Lasers or El Toros at Foster City and Redwood City. Lessons for adults are given year-round, weekdays or weekends, by appointment, for individuals, couples or trios. The classes go from the total tyro through advanced sailing, and the object is to strive to give you the confidence to sail on your own. For ten to fifteen (all sailing) hours the cost is $100-$150. Lessons are given on a 27-foot Quarter-Ton which holds four students out of Gas House Cove Marina in San Francisco.

Redwood City Parks and Recreation Department

1400 Roosevelt Avenue, Redwood City 94061. (364-6060) Chip Conlon has been teaching sailing in Redwood City for seven years. The schedule of classes runs from May through October, but Chip takes off the month of August to do a little sailing on his own. Class size is restricted to twelve for the six El Toros, and kids as young as ten may participate along with families or other adults. In spring and fall, two sessions are held Saturdays, mornings and afternoons, for the five-week, fifteen-hour courses at Redwood Shores Lagoon. In summer the courses switch to two-week weekday sessions at the Redwood City Marina, mornings and evenings. This basic course is very practical; you are put in the boats right from the start for a little reaching, then comes windward sailing, and you learn from your mistakes. In summer intermediate classes are added which gives you more time in a boat for some experience, and if you are progressing, you can get an introduction to racing strategies and buoy tactics. The cost is $25.50/person, or $23.50 for residents of Redwood City.

Windsurfing

Windsurfing takes the art of being on the water to its logical conclusion. It's not really like sailing or surfing, it's more a combination of sailing, skiing and hang-gliding. In fact it's such a hot, up-and-coming sport that it should be compared to skate-boarding. Anyone can be a windsurfer, young or old, and the lessons are one of the most uncomplicated things you can get into. Strength and youth are not required, wet suits will keep you warm even on the Bay, and when you try it there's no half-way, either you love it or leave it. You can see windsurfers sailing or in classes all over the Bay — the Foster City Lagoon, the Redwood Shores Lagoon, near Zack's in Sausalito, the Redwood City Marina, the Berkeley Marina, in Raccoon Strait crossing from Angel Island to Tiburon, Marina Park in San Leandro, even at Mission Rock Resort in the City. There are even a couple of annual events which are unbelievable — the "Round the Rock" race, from the San Francisco Marina around Alcatraz and return, and the "Bay Crossing" race, from the Marina to Horseshoe Bay on the Marin side of the Golden Gate. Summer finds regular gatherings of "wind-bums" at San Francisco's Marina Green on Thursday evenings, at the Berkeley Marina on Wednesday evenings, and at Alameda's Mariner Square on the first and third Wednesday evenings.

The four windsurfing schools listed here cover the Bay. Classes and arrangements are virtually the same for these schools — all equipment is provided, including wet suits; three-hour sessions on two different days get you certified; the cost is $40. They all sell windsurfers also.

Windsurfing Marin School

(383-1226) Ted McKown has been teaching windsurfing in Sausalito/Mill Valley for five years. Lessons by appointment in Sausalito or Corte Madera.

Berkeley Windsurfing School

(841-WIND) Bob Ergun, Barbara Ockel and Beth Anderson teach windsurfing at the Berkeley Marina on weekends at 8 or 9 in the morning. These are beginning lessons, but advanced lessons are also available, taught privately. Rentals are available.

Portola Windsurfing School

(Skip Voves, 351-2578) Connected with the Portola Surf Shop in Santa Cruz, Skip and other instructors give lessons in the East Bay, primarily at the sailing lagoon of Marina Park at the San Leandro Marina. Lessons are given by appointment, and they will go anywhere to teach — Crown Memorial Beach at Alameda, or the Cal Sailing Club at the Berkeley Marina, or elsewhere.

Bay Surf Windsurfers

Box 776, Menlo Park 94025. (323-7257) Glenn Taylor teaches by appointment at Redwood Shores Lagoon in Redwood City. Advanced lessons are also available, taught privately. Hourly rentals are available at lesson sites, and longer term rentals can be carted away by automobile.

Renting a Sailboat

For non-boat owners who want to get out on the exciting waters of San Francisco Bay, one feasible way to get there is to rent a sailboat. You don't have to crew for someone else to get a sail, and you can put your own group together for a voyage. If you know how to sail, or if you've recently completed a course at a sailing school and want some time on the water, the places listed here should help you get a keel under your feet and a sail above your head.

All of the rental locations (including the four small boat outfits) are connected with sailing schools, and in many cases the easiest path to rentals is to be a graduate of that school. Contained in this listing are six sailing clubs, including a couple in which the flat rate fee embraces sailing lessons. Clubs usually provide a fleet of boats to choose from and they act as a surrogate boat owner; if you're sailing quite a bit the initiation fees, yearly fees, quarterly fees and boat use fees can be a bargain.

For rentals you can find a variety of deals. The expense usually depends on the size of the boat, the length of time, and weekday or weekend use. Where prices have been included, they are for comparison only and they have probably changed by now. A deposit of $100 (cash, check or credit card) is generally required for keelboats for Bay sailing. Renters are screened for experience in boat handling, and sometimes you are given a check-out sail which may cost money.

Marin

Cass' Rental Marina

Bridgeway at Napa Street (Box 643), Sausalito 94965. (332-6789) They have a large and varied fleet that includes the following boats: Rhodes 19, Mariner 20, Cal 20, Santana 22, Tempest 24 and Bristol 27. Rates start from $17 for two hours in a Mariner 20, and go up in increments that include $29 for a weekend morning and $48 for a whole day on the weekend. The high side is a weekend day in the Bristol 27 for $87. The good deal on long-term rates is on weekdays "pay for three, sail for five," and weekly "pay for five, cruise for seven." This can turn out to be a week-long cruise up to the Delta on the Bristol 27 (which sleeps five) for $377. Another advantageous rate is the weekday after-work sail, 4 pm to sunset. Their requirements are simple: a deposit, and at least one experienced sailor on board.

Sailing Center of Tiburon

21 Main Street (upstairs) (Box 678), Tiburon 94920. (435-0265) A 50 percent deposit reserves the rental boat of your choice from among the fleet of seven to ten boats, including a Santana 22, a Coronado 23, a Columbia 26 and a Pearson 26. A deposit is required and, if they don't know you, an hour check-out sail ($5 fee). For the Santana 22, an evening sail will cost $20, a weekend morning $30, and a full weekend day $55; rates go up for the larger boats. The Sailing Center also operates a club that lets you sail with other club members at favorable rates for as low as $10/person. Club dues are $10/year plus $3/month.

Canoe Trips West

2170 Redwood Highway, Greenbrae 94904. (461-1750) Naturally, they rent canoes, either to use in the Bay or to cart off to your favorite river. In addition, you can rent one of the sailing outrigger Go-Boats for $7.50/hour and up to $35 for all day. No deposit is required to use the boats in Corte Madera Creek.

East Bay

California Cruising Club

At Redrock Marina, Richmond. (235-7053) This all-inclusive club has a flat rate fee of $900/year. After instruction and "certification," you have unlimited use of their boats.

John Beery Sailing School

Aquatic Park (inshore of the freeway, at the foot of Addison Street), Berkeley 94710. (845-6310) They have a large fleet of small sailboats — El Toros, Sunfishes, Lasers, Capris — that can be rented at Aquatic Park on an hourly basis, from $3 to $6/hour. A deposit of $10 or $15 is necessary. You will be required to demonstrate sailing ability, and if you want a Laser, an International Laser sailing course certificate will do the trick.

Lion Sailing School

At the Marriott Inn, Berkeley Marina. (526-4559) They will rent to you, if you have taken their lessons. If not, you must take a check-out cruise; a deposit is necessary. Prices range from $45/day on weekends in a Santanna 22, to $75/day in a Catalina 27, to $120/day in the Lion sloop, to $150/day in a Columbia 43, and correspondingly less for half-days and weekdays. The Lion Sailing Club, with no fees, offers members' rates for rentals of their seven-boat fleet. Members can also sail on the outfit's charters as crew.

American Boating Club

55 Alice Street (Jack London Village), Oakland 94607. (763-4455) This all-inclusive club has a flat rate fee of $1275/year with priority for their smaller boats, or $2075/year with priority for the larger ones. After instruction and "certification," you have unlimited use of their boats. The club also has facilities at Pier 39 in San Francisco.

Sailor's Workshop

21 Embarcadero Cove, Oakland 94606. (533-4221) They will rent one of their boats to graduates of their "skippers class."

Wayne D'Anna Sailing School

11 Embarcadero Cove, Oakland 94606 (261-3844 direct line, or 522-7760 answering service) They have sailboat rentals starting at $50/day for a Catalina 22, ranging up to $120/day for a Ranger 33. Weekday rates are 10 percent less. You must pass a sailing check-out ($25 fee) prior to renting. Members of their Bay sailing club have the opportunity to reserve in advance any of the boats, which include a Santana 22, a Catalina 27, a Coronado 27 and an Ericson 41. Initiation fee is $100 plus $50/year and entitles you to reduced rental rates, plus a block time discount, special cruises and seminars.

Oakland Parks and Recreation

Sailboat House, 568 Bellevue Avenue (Lake Merritt), Oakland 94610. (444-3807) If you can rig the boats, you can rent the El Toros and Sunfish for sailing on Lake Merritt. Rates are $2/hour and $3.50/hour, respectively, with a $5 deposit required.

Northern California Sailing Center

2415 Mariner Square (in caboose), Alameda 94501. (521-5370, offices closed Mondays) This twin outfit operates on both sides of the Bay, so look for their story under Redwood City.

San Francisco and Peninsula

ABLE Sailing School and Boat Rentals
1166 Capitol Avenue, San Francisco 94112. (586-5332) Captain Ken Greer has a fleet of sailboats, mostly 20-footers, with a few up to 43 feet, berthed at various marinas around the Bay — San Francisco, Sausalito, Berkeley. If you want to go out cruising, there are very advantageous rates for five- and seven-day trips.

American Boating Club
Pier 39, San Francisco 94119. (981-6552) This club berths nearly a hundred boats at the new Pier 39 Marina. The all-inclusive fee is $1475/year, or $2375/year for the larger boats. After instruction and "certification," you have virtually unlimited use of their boats. The club also has facilities at Oakland's Jack London Village.

San Mateo City Recreation Division
(574-6737) They offer classes at Parkside Aquatic Park on Marina Lagoon in San Mateo. When classes are in session, they will rent the surplus boats from their fleet of El Toros. The rentals are $3 or $4/hour, and you must verify your capability with the instructor.

Northern California Sailing Center
Docktown Marina, 1500 Maple Street, Redwood City 94063. (368-2908, offices closed Mondays). Also located at 2415 Mariner Square (in caboose), Alameda 94501. (521-5370) This twin outfit operates on both sides of the Bay and offers occasional rentals. For example, a Columbia 22 may go for $68/day on weekends and an Ericson 32 for $168/day on weekends. Graduates of their Dave Garrett Sailing School are entitled to rentals. Members of their sailing club have a choice from the fleet of twenty-five boats ranging from 20 to 45 feet. Some of these sailboats are berthed at other marinas — Jack London Square, Pacific, Ballena Bay, Berkeley and in the Delta. Club initiation is $100, with $30 quarterly charge, $25 yearly renewal and $15 one-time check-out fee. Members get 50 percent discount on rental rates.

Charter Cruises

Any group, large or small, that is looking for an exciting outing can find it on a pleasure cruise on San Francisco Bay. An intimate assemblage can mingle with the yacht action on the Bay by watching the weekend regattas, and find romantic settings by cruising the coves and landings on an evening sail. Hassle-free sailboat charters, leaving the captaining and crewing to someone else, lets your party concentrate on sightseeing at Bay landmarks or at aquatic celebrations that periodically grace our waters.

For more complicated corporate collections of people there are cruise companies that handle larger aggregations of fifty, sixty or hundreds. They are favored by businesses, conventions and others who want to throw a party that is unique to the Bay region.

Other charters can be found by looking for *Sportfishing Party Boats*, and scheduled sightseeing under *Cruising the Bay*.

Sausalito

Hauser Institute

See listing under *Learning to Sail* for information about charters on a 26-foot sloop.

Berkeley

Lion Yacht Charters

See listing under *Learning to Sail* for information about charters on their fleet of sailboats ranging from 22 to 43 feet.

Commodore Charter Cruises

200 Marina Boulevard (Marriott Inn, Berkeley Marina), Berkeley 94710. (845-7422) The elegant 65-foot motor yacht *Princess II* is available for up to fifty passengers for Bay cruises. The boat was once owned by Jerry Lewis (before you say so what, you'll have to concede that it must be a barrel of laughs). The style of accommodation is carried into the furnishing, including crystal chandeliers, and the dinner menu. Your group must supply its own alcoholic refreshment. Cruises for birthdays and retire-

ments, to celebrate weddings and receptions, tour the Bay — from Berkeley to Tiburon, Angel Island, Sausalito, San Francisco's Fisherman's Wharf, the Oakland Estuary. Arrangements can be made for boarding in Oakland or San Francisco.

Hornblower Tours

200 Marina Boulevard (Marriott Inn, Berkeley Marina), Berkeley 94710. (548-7920) This is the best-known private charter enterprise on San Francisco Bay. They specialize in private dinner cruises, but they are very amenable to your ideas about what might entertain your big group. The motor yachts *America* and *Americana* have a capacity of fifty and sixty passengers, and they double up to serve as many as one hundred. Celebrations that their cruises have made special include birthday and anniversary parties, weddings for those who want their own version of being married at sea, and holiday festivities. You can pick a destination for a river cruise, like Petaluma or Napa, or somewhere in the Delta. Even offshore fishing is accommodated on the 43-foot Hatteras sportfisher *Journey* which carries up to thirty people. Arrangements for your pleasure trip can be made by the hour (from $60), or as an inclusive package ($18/person for more than forty diners). Always part of the elegant service are a licensed captain who is glad to be bothered about what is happening with the boat and on the water, and crew, and bartenders if needed. Another part of their elaborate provisions are entertainment and dancing music, boardings at other marinas on the Bay, and connecting bus tours to spots like the wine country.

Oakland

Wayne D'Anna Charters

See listing under *Learning to Sail* for information about their sailing cruises and charters, which include a monthly three-day coastal cruise, a twice-a-summer five-day coastal cruise, and April and October trips to the Caribbean for sailing in the sun.

Mariner Yacht Charters

87 Jack London Square, Oakland 94907. (834-3052) The 68-foot luxury yacht *Mariner II* sails from Jack London Square for entertaining up to fifty passengers. The stateroom décor looks like it comes straight from *Architectural Digest* magazine. The uniformed crew will take your group on a four-hour cruise of the Bay, complete with mom-cooked gourmet ethnic food from ten menus and a bar. Customized cruises are available for weddings, receptions and other festivities. Arrangements can be made for boardings at other Bay landings, and destinations are open.

Alameda

Gray Whale

See listing under *Learning to Sail* for information about charters on their 31-foot sailboat.

John Beery Company

See listing under *Learning to Sail* (Berkeley) for information about sailing charters on their fleet of boats from Mariner Square, Alameda.

Northern California Sailing Center

See listing under *Learning to Sail* (Dave Garrett Sailing School, Redwood City) for information about charters on their large fleet of sailboats berthed at various marinas around the Bay.

San Francisco

ABLE Sailing School

See listing under *Learning to Sail* for information about charters on their fleet of sail and power boats berthed at various marinas around the Bay.

Marina Green Sailing School

See listing under *Learning to Sail* for information about charters on a 27-foot sloop.

Gold Coast Cruises

Pier 45 (Fisherman's Wharf), San Francisco. (775-9108) The sightseeing boat *Gold Coast* may be chartered for three-hour evening cruises of any part of the Bay. The capacity of the boat is 125 people, but they prefer a smaller number for private party cruises. Bar and buffet dining must be catered separately.

Harbor Tours Inc.

Pier 43½ (Fisherman's Wharf), San Francisco. (546-2826) The well-known "Red & White Fleet" of sightseeing tour boats is available for private charter. The six boats — the *Harbor King, Harbor Queen, Harbor Emperor* (Norton), *Harbor Prince, Harbor Princess,* and the new *Harbor Countess* — have varying capacities of 300, 400, 500 and 800 passengers. For huge parties or any celebration or business function, the boats can be supplied with dance music, buffet dining and bar. They can cruise from Fisherman's Wharf, the Ferry Building, Tiburon or East Bay landings and can even end up somewhere in Vallejo, Stockton or Sacramento.

Skip-A-Lou

Sportfishing boat working out of the Muny Bait Shop, 3098 Polk Street, San Francisco. (673-9815, evenings 661-0506) Offering fishing trips daily from Fisherman's Wharf; and whale-watching, bird-watching and diving day and evening cruises.

Redwood City

Northern California Sailing Center

See listing under *Learning to Sail* (Dave Garrett Sailing School) for information about charters on their large fleet of sailboats berthed at various marinas around the Bay.

Yacht Clubs

The familiar clusters of sailboats that mark Bay waters on summer weekends belong to members of yacht clubs and racing associations participating in organized competitions. The local yacht clubs exhibit a wide variety of atmosphere, expense, facilities and sailing keenness. From older clubs with elegant formality of clubhouse and exclusiveness to newer groups with less ostentatious accommodations but with sufficient corinthian (racing) zeal, there is adequate choice for any yachting spirit. The focus of the organizations may vary — kinds of boats, cruising calendar, junior seamanship, social get togethers, racing enthusiasm — but all participate in boating safety programs. Choose the benefits that coincide with your boat-owning goals. Customarily the clubs enjoy exchange privileges: members can use the berths, dining room and bar at other clubs.

There are a few winter regattas, but the kick-off of the yacht racing season is usually the last Sunday in April, with an opening day waterfront parade along the northern shore of San Francisco. The Yacht Racing Association of San Francisco Bay is the governing organization for racing on the Bay and promotes class racing of its member clubs and associations. Address: 1485 Bayshore Boulevard, San Francisco 94124 (468-0510). The Pacific Inter-Club Yacht Association is the umbrella organization for all yacht clubs in the San Francisco Bay and northern California areas — 68 Post Street, Room 417, San Francisco 94104 (392-7076). Each spring the P.I.C.Y.A. publishes the *Yachting Year Book,* which contains a yacht club membership roster of boats and skippers, listings of one-design sailboat classes and other racing associations, master racing schedule, sail numbers and other useful nautical information. The book is available from the P.I.C.Y.A. for $6 by mail, or $5 from marine dealers.

Marin County

Sausalito Yacht Club
Foot of El Portal Street (Box 267), Sausalito 94965. (332-9989) Established 1944; near the Sausalito Yacht Harbor.

Sausalito Cruising Club
Foot of Napa Street (Box 155), Sausalito 94965. (332-9922) Established 1948; very active racing club.

San Francisco Yacht Club
98 Beach Road, Belvedere 94920. (435-9133) Established 1869; oldest yacht club on the Pacific coast; very active racing club.

Corinthian Yacht Club

Corinthian Island (Box 857), Tiburon 94920. (435-4771) Established 1886; active racing club.

Paradise Harbor Yacht Club

233 Trinidad Drive, Tiburon 94920. (789-9889) Established 1965; active in youth seamanship program; at Paradise Cay Yacht Harbor.

San Rafael Yacht Club

405 Francisco Boulevard (west end of San Rafael Canal) (Box 821), San Rafael 94902. (453-9828) Established 1938.

North Bay Yacht Club

40 Point San Pedro Road, San Rafael 94901. (453-9931) Established 1959; on San Rafael Canal.

Marin Yacht Club

24 Summit Avenue, San Rafael 94901. (454-9888) Established 1935.

Loch Lomond Yacht Club

95 Loch Lomond Drive, San Rafael 94901. (453-9811) Established 1962; at Loch Lomond Marina.

Gallinas Yacht Club

Vendola Drive (Box 4087), Santa Venetia 94903. (479-7419) Established 1958.

Bel-Marin Keys Yacht Club

4 Montego Key, Ignacio 94947. Established 1966.

Solano County

Vallejo Yacht Club

Mare Island Boulevard and Florida Street (Box 311), Vallejo 94590. (707-643-9731) Established 1900.

Contra Costa County

Richmond Yacht Club

351 Brickyard Cove Road (Box 295, Point Richmond Station), Richmond 94807. (237-2821) Established 1932; very active and successful racing club.

Point San Pablo Yacht Club

700 West Cutting Boulevard (Box 307, Point Richmond Station), Richmond 94807. (234-9711 club, 233-1046 office) Established 1946; near Richmond Yacht Harbor.

Alameda County

Berkeley Yacht Club

One Seawall Drive, Berkeley 94710. (845-9277) Established 1940; at Berkeley Marina.

Metropolitan Yacht Club

89 Jack London Square, Oakland 94607. (832-6757) Established 1957; at the Jack London Marina.

Lake Merritt Sailing Club

Sailboat House, 1520 Lakeside Drive, Oakland 94612. Established 1937; active racing club.

Encinal Yacht Club

Pacific Marina (Box 401), Alameda 94501. (522-3272) Established 1892.

Oakland Yacht Club

Pacific Marina, Alameda 94501. (522-6868) Established 1913; moved across the Estuary to Pacific Marina early in 1977.

Island Yacht Club

1853 Clement Avenue, Alameda 94501. (521-2980) Established 1970; very active racing club; at the Alameda Marina.

Ballena Bay Yacht Club

1140 Ballena Boulevard, Alameda 94501. Established 1969; at Ballena Bay Yacht Harbor.

Aeolian Yacht Club

Foot of Bay Farm Island Bridge (Box 2175), Alameda 94501. (523-2586) Established 1906; active racing club.

San Leandro Yacht Club

Box 551, San Leandro 94577. (351-9666) Established 1963; at the San Leandro Marina.

Spinnaker Yacht Club

Box 244, San Leandro 94577. (351-9930) Established 1967; at the San Leandro Marina.

San Francisco

Presidio Yacht Club

Box 9046, Presidio of San Francisco, San Francisco 94129. (561-7515) Established 1959.

St. Francis Yacht Club

Foot of Scott Street, San Francisco 94123. (563-6363) Established 1927; very active racing club; at the San Francisco Marina.

Golden Gate Yacht Club

Foot of Scott Street, San Francisco 94123. (563-9716) Established 1940; at the San Francisco Marina.

Mariposa-Hunters Point Yacht Club

339 China Basin Street, San Francisco 94107. (495-9344) Established 1953.

Bay View Boat Club

429 China Basin Street, San Francisco 94107. (392-9775) Established 1963.

San Mateo County

Oyster Point Yacht Club

Box 44, South San Francisco 94080. (588-9644) Established 1964; prominent in opening day events; at the Oyster Point Marina.

Coyote Point Yacht Club

1820 Coyote Point Drive, San Mateo 94401. (347-6730) Established 1941; at the Coyote Point Marina.

Island Sailing Club

Box 4066, Foster City 94404. Established 1966.

Peninsula Yacht Club

Box 5596, Redwood City 94063. Established 1961; at Pete's Harbor.

Sequoia Yacht Club

Box 5548, Redwood City 94063. (365-9472) Established 1939; at the Redwood City Marina.

Santa Clara County

Palo Alto Yacht Club

2512 Embarcadero Road, Palo Alto 94303. (Harbormaster 323-6865) Established 1928; active racing club; at the Palo Alto Yacht Harbor.

South Bay Yacht Club

End of Hope Street (Box 102), Alviso 95002. Established 1906; near the Alviso Marina.

San Jose Sailing Club

Box 5631, San Jose 95150. Established 1958.

Bait Shops and Fishing Gear

For the fisherman bait shops are quite often the inception of any fishing expedition. Here's where you pick up any pile worms or blood worms or squid or other bait that you need. You can also find rods and reels, hooks and lines, weights and every other kind of gear to get you a story-telling fish. Most of these shops do repairs, provide licenses (if needed) and rent equipment.

Many of the bait shops are located at marinas, some near fishing piers. Commonly they have snacks and beer, and a number are the headquarters for party boat fishing fleets. These are the main bait shops on the Bay. Some are listed here without phone numbers.

Marin

Caruso's Sportfishing (Sausalito)
Clipper Yacht Harbor (foot of Harbor Drive). (332-1015) Open 5 am to 6 pm; bait and tackle; licenses; snack bar; fresh fish market; party boats.

Sausalito Boat and Tackle
Kappas Marina (Waldo Point). (332-2599) Bait and tackle (rental); licenses; coffee bar; sportfishing party boats.

Loch Lomond Bait Shack (San Rafael)
Lock Lomond Marina. (456-0321) Bait and tackle; café nearby; party boat.

China Camp (San Rafael)
On the north side of the peninsula facing San Pablo Bay, on North San Pedro Road. Open March-October; this old Chinese shrimp camp, which started in 1882 with a migration from San Francisco's Chinatown (just before 1900 more than 3,000 persons lived here), still sells shrimp bait, rents a few dories to fishermen, and has a small café serving, naturally, shrimp cocktails.

Port Sonoma Bait and Tackle
On the Sonoma side of the Petaluma River; at Black Point. Bait and tackle; snacks; party boat.

East Bay

Vallejo Pier
On Wilson Avenue, beneath Napa River Bridge. Bait and tackle (rental); snacks.

Brinkman's Marine (Vallejo)
End of Maryland Street. Licenses, bait and tackle; café next door.

Crockett Marine Service
Foot of Port Street. (787-1047) Bait and tackle (rental); licenses; snack bar; party boats.

Sarge's Bait and Tackle (Rodeo)
Rodeo Marina. (799-4076) Bait and tackle (rental); licenses; coffee shop next door; party boats.

Point San Pablo Bait (Richmond)
Point San Pablo Yacht Harbor. (233-3224) Bait and tackle; snack bar; party boats.

Redrock Marina Bait (Castro Point, Richmond)
Redrock Marina. Bait and tackle; licenses; snacks.

Pacific Boat Works (Richmond)
310 West Cutting Boulevard. Next door to Richmond Yacht Harbor; small bait shop and snacks.

Sportfishing Center (Albany)
949 San Pablo Avenue. (524-0221) Bait, tackle, repairs and rentals; party boats.

Berkeley Marina Sports Center
Berkeley Marina. (849-2727) In a trailer by harbormaster's office, may be in new building by now; bait and tackle; licenses; snack bar; party boats.

Hank Schramm's Sportfishing Center (Emeryville)
Emeryville Marina. (654-6040) Open 4 am to 7 pm; bait and tackle (rental); licenses; refreshments; party boats.

Oyster Pirates Store (Oakland)
At Port View Park, end of Seventh Street. Open 9 am-6 pm; bait and tackle; sandwiches, beer and wine.

Capt. Scotty's Bait and Tackle (Oakland)
Jack London Square, on the dock by the Spice Box snack bar. Open 6 am-5 pm; bait and tackle.

Godfather Bait and Tackle Shop (Oakland)
Fifth Avenue Marina. (465-9673) Bait and tackle; party boat.

San Francisco and Peninsula

Gas House Cove Marina (San Francisco)
Foot of Laguna Street. Bait.

Muny Bait Shop (San Francisco)
3098 Polk Street (corner of North Point), (673-9815) Full range of bait and tackle; you can get a SF Giants cap to wear on the pier; snack bar; party boats.

The Sport Fishing Center — Capurro's (San Francisco)
300 Jefferson Street (at Jones, Fisherman's Wharf). (771-2800) Bait and tackle (rental); licenses; snack bar; party boats.

Mission Rock Resort (San Francisco)
817 China Basin Street (off Third Street). (621-5538) Bait and tackle; snack bar with good burgers and beer; fishing boat rentals, $7/day and $10 deposit, no motors (bring your own).

The Ramp (San Francisco)
855 China Basin Street (off Third Street). (621-2378) Bait and tackle and refreshments; party boat.

Pete's Harbor (Redwood City)
Marine store; bait and tackle.

JC Boat Works (Alviso)
On Hope Street. Fishing tackle; rental boats.

Boat Launching Ramps

This listing of Bay boat ramps is provided so you can find a place to put your boat in the water, so you can get out in your boat for fishing or sailing. The list distinguishes between ramps that are free and ones that charge a fee. Prices are given, but assume that some of them have been raised by now.

Marin

Sausalito Boat Ramp
Foot of Turney Street (between Zack's and The Tides; on Richardson Bay; shoaled, small boats only; free.

Clipper Yacht Harbor (Sausalito)
Foot of Harbor Drive; snack bar at Caruso's; Richardson Bay; 2-lane, $4.

Canoe Trips West (Greenbrae)
2170 Redwood Highway (Lucky Drive exit); on Corte Madera Creek; $1 in and $1 out.

Loch Lomond Marina (San Rafael)
On Pt. San Pedro Road; snack bar; $2.

Buck's Landing (San Rafael)
665 North San Pedro Road (about 2 miles off Highway 101 from Civic Center exit); on Gallinas Creek; snack bar; $2.

Black Point Boat Ramp
Black Point exit off Highway 37; on the Petaluma River, beneath bridge; 2-lane, free.

East Bay

Maryland Street Boat Ramp (Vallejo)
Junction Maryland Street and Mare Island Way; on Mare Island Strait; bait shop; 4-lane, free.

Rodeo Marina
Bait shop and coffee shop; 4-lane, $2.

Joseph's Fishing Resort (Rodeo)
Adjacent to Rodeo Marina; shoaling restricts use to times of higher tides; snack bar; $1.

Redrock Marina (Richmond)
On Castro Point, under Richmond-San Rafael Bridge; bait shop and snack bar; $2.25.

Richmond Boat Ramp
700 West Cutting Boulevard (Highway 17); next to Richmond Yacht Harbor, on Santa Fe Channel; 2-lane, free.

Berkeley Marina
North side of marina; snack bar and bait shop; 3-lane, $1.

Estuary Park (Oakland)
Off Embarcadero West, on the Estuary; free.

Alameda Municipal Ramp
Foot of Grand Street (north side of Alameda Marina); on the Estuary; 2-lane, free.

Boat Mart (Oakland)
7150 Doolittle Drive (near the airport); on San Leandro Bay; $1.

Oakland Public Ramp
On Doolittle Drive (south of Boat Mart); on San Leandro Bay; 2-lane, free.

San Leandro Marina
4-lane, free.

San Francisco and Peninsula

San Francisco Boat Ramp
On China Basin Street (between Piers 52 and 54); free.

The Ramp (San Francisco)
855 China Basin Street; bait and tackle shop; $2.50-$5.

Oyster Point Marina (South San Francisco)
2-lane, $1.25.

Coyote Point Marina (San Mateo)
Peninsula Avenue exit from highway 101; 3-lane, $1.

Marina Slough Ramp (San Mateo)
Parkside Aquatic Park (off Highway 101 at Highway 92 exit, then left on South Norfolk Street, then turn on Roberta Drive to park); for small boats on Marina Lagoon; beach and kids' play area; open 6 am-10 pm; 2-lane, free.

Foster City Ramp
On Foster City Boulevard at Bounty Drive; for small boats on Foster City Lagoon; free.

Docktown Marina (Redwood City)
Whipple Avenue exit, then foot of Maple Street; $2.

Redwood City Marina
Harbor Boulevard exit; tackle shop; 2-lane, $1.

Palo Alto Yacht Harbor
Embarcadero Road exit; double ramp, $1.

Alviso Marina
Off Highway 237 (foot of Hope Street); double and single ramps, free.

Fishing from the Shore

Fishing piers and prominences of rocky shoreline offer the best possibilities for landing that captain's platter for your home dinner table. The docks and jetties usually provide proximity to deeper moving water where the best fishing is. If you want to be friends with a finny flounder, buddies with a backwater bass, sidekicks with a scaly sculpin, or chums with a crustaceous crab, there are a multitude of locations on San Francisco Bay where you can wet a line. At least forty spots are listed here, and only a few charge anything. Bait shops are usually nearby (see listing), and are your best bets for information about what's running and what bait to use. Besides supplying the bait you'll need — sardines, anchovies, ghost shrimp, grass shrimp, pile worms — they also have the tackle (and crab traps), and you may learn of a place to crawl through a chain link fence to get to an especially good spot.

Of course not everyone goes fishing for the catch. There's a lot of solitude on the end of a pier, away from the freneticity of the city. A day in the sun or fog, enjoying the Bay in your individual way, is worth a lot, whether you bring home a fish or not. But you can usually find any amount of camaraderie among the angling fraternity at any fishing location, especially if the fish are biting. There's someone around to give advice, discuss bait selection, and analyze the tides, currents and water temperature. You should be able to improve your fishing tricks, and you'll have an audience for your shaggy fish stories.

No license is required when fishing from a public pier, but other fishing regulations must be followed. A license is required for shoreline fishing ($4/year). Keep in mind, when you are casting for that prize, that most shallow water fish follow the tides — flatfish, smelt, seaperch, crab (Dungeness in season), sturgeon or sand shark. The most sought after fish are striped bass, and the best time of year is March through June and September through November.

Most of these piers and shorelines are in public parks, so you can find directions to them in the section *Finding the Bay*. Others are at *Marinas*. If you want a pleasurable family day, take advantage of the picnicking and sightseeing opportunities at these fishing sites.

Fort Baker

Pier at Horseshoe Bay

Also breakwater of yacht harbor and headland of Cavallo Point; restrooms.

Sausalito

Tiffany Beach

Along the esplanade (Bridgeway), and a small pier beside the Trident Restaurant; served by ferry.

Strawberry Point

Shoreline strip

Along Seminary Drive on Richardson Bay.

Tiburon

Shoreline strip

Along Paradise Drive just east of downtown; kids' pier beside the Caprice Restaurant on Raccoon Strait; served by ferry.

Angel Island

Fishermen wet their lines at many spots along the island's shoreline; served by ferry from Tiburon, Berkeley and San Francisco.

Paradise Beach County Park

On Paradise Drive; large pier; restrooms; parking $1 (summer; weekdays $2, weekends $4); open 7 am to sunset.

Larkspur

Shoreline strip

Exit from Highway 101 for the ferry terminal, then continue past terminal on Sir Francis Drake towards San Quentin to rocky shore beside road.

San Rafael

Beach Park

Take Central San Rafael exit, then take Francisco Boulevard parallel to the freeway and hunt for the small park sign to turn off to the left; small platform on the San Rafael Canal.

China Camp

Pier

China Camp is located on North San Pedro Road, about five miles east from the Civic Center exit, or about one mile around the point from the turn-off to McNear's Beach Park; once flourishing shrimp camp that still sells bait and has fishing boat rentals and refreshments; pier on San Pablo Bay; open March-October.

Vallejo

Vallejo Fishing Pier

From Tennessee Street, turn north on Wilson Avenue, and come to the pier almost under the Napa River Bridge (the pier is the remnant of the old bridge); lights; restrooms; fish cleaning facilities; snack bar and bait shop (tackle rental).

Vallejo Promenade

From the end of Maryland Street, along Mare Island Way; shore fishing.

Crockett

Crockett Marine Service

Small pier beside Nantucket Fish Company restaurant (50¢); restrooms; snack bar and bait shop; also a shoreline strip west of Crockett Marine by the sanitary district works has good fishing.

Rodeo

Joseph's Fishing Resort

Near the Rodeo Marina; pier open 6:30 am-6 pm (50¢); restrooms; snack bar; small beach (fee).

Richmond

Point Pinole Regional Shoreline

Popular new pier at end of point, extends a quarter mile into some of the Bay's best fishing waters; restrooms; tram operates from parking lot to point; parking $1; open 8 am to sunset.

Point San Pablo

Beyond the Naval and Standard Oil reservations to the tip of the point; this is one of those through-the-fence fishing spots; apparently it is city-owned land, and it seems that Richmond could put up a pier for fishermen.

Redrock Marina

Long pier that used to be a ferry slip, fishing costs 75¢; restrooms; bait shop and snack bar.

CalTrans Pier

Tumbledown dock that you can find on the road to Redrock Marina, through the fence beneath the Richmond-San Rafael Bridge.

Richmond Pier

Off Highway 17 and follow South Garrard Avenue through the tunnel to the end; some precarious fishing spots on the industrial pier.

Point Isabel Regional Shoreline

Park and rough shoreline for fishing on peninsula; restrooms.

Berkeley

Berkeley Pier

One of the Bay's premier fishing piers, it extends nearly 3,000 feet into the water (it was originally a ferry pier stretching more than two miles to deep water); open 24 hours, lighted; restrooms; fish cleaning station; Harry's Hut (hot dogs, chili dogs, burgers, soft drinks), weekends only; served by AC Transit.

Emeryville

Shoreline

Along outer tip of Emeryville peninsula and along the road on the neck; picnic tables; apparently something has got the city off the dime to provide better fishing access; served by AC Transit.

Oakland

Port View Park

At end of Seventh Street on the end of the Oakland Mole (which has nothing to do with the BART tunnel); lighted pier; open 24 hours; restrooms; snack bar and bait shop; served by AC Transit.

Middle Harbor Park

Fishing pier.

Estuary Park

Pier; restrooms; picnic tables.

Fruitvale Bridge

The bridge that connects Oakland with Alameda across the Estuary has piers on both sides of the channel for fishing; quay on Alameda side; lighted for night fishing.

Bay Park Refuge

Small pier on San Leandro Bay and shoreline for fishing; path and kids' play area; bird-watching.

Alameda

Ballena Bay

Shoreline along street and at end of outer edge of yacht harbor.

Shoreline Strip

Behind Encinal High School; shoreline by end of Naval Air Station breakwater.

San Leandro

San Leandro Marina

Shoreline around marina; south arm has small pier; served by AC Transit.

San Francisco

Fort Point

Fishing from seawall of Fort Point, directly beneath the Golden Gate Bridge; nearby at the foot of Long Avenue, the old mine wharf is now a fishing pier; restrooms; served by Golden Gate Transit and Muni bus (indirectly).

San Francisco Marina

Fishing from the end of the breakwater and along the seawall, plus the pier at the end of Gas House Cove; restrooms; weekend snacks at west end; served by Muni bus.

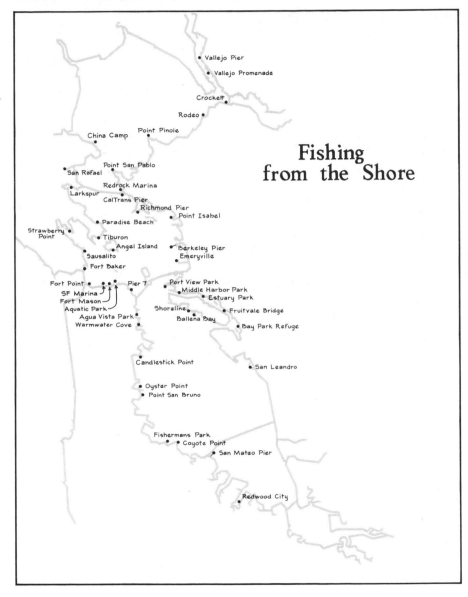

Fishing from the Shore

Pier 7

A few blocks north of the Ferry Building; fishing at end of parking lot pier; served by Muni bus.

Agua Vista Park

Pier in China Basin area, beside Mission Rock Resort; bait and tackle; snack bar.

Warmwater Cove

Foot of Twenty-fourth Street in south waterfront area; newly developed park with landscaping, restrooms and small pier; good fishing; served by Muni bus.

Candlestick Point

Rough fill shoreline on the Bay side of Candlestick Park; also small pier on south shore.

South San Francisco

Oyster Point Marina

Will be developing a fishing pier sometime in the near future.

Point San Bruno

Shoreline strip for public access and fishing at end of Forbes Boulevard.

Burlingame

Fishermans Park

On Airport Boulevard near Coyote Point Park is a small park with shoreline for fishing (closed at dusk); and to the west the rip-rap shore all the way around the Diamond Showboat restaurant and beyond.

San Mateo

Coyote Point Marina

Berm at end of marina for fishing.

San Mateo Pier

The 4,000-foot stub of the old bridge beneath the San Mateo Bridge in Foster City; open 24 hours; restrooms.

Redwood City

Redwood City Marina

Small pier beside boat ramp; restrooms; picnic area.

Fort Mason

Fishing from Piers 2 and 3, the old Army transport piers; restrooms.

Aquatic Park

The WPA-built Muni Pier with its sweeping curve into the Bay; also the adjacent old Alcatraz Pier; restrooms; snack bar; served by Muni bus.

Sportfishing Party Boats

Even if you're not a born angler, you can enjoy sportfishing, one of the notable opportunities of San Francisco, a leading party boat port on the Pacific coast. Experience some of the tradition of the 1880s, which was the heyday of the Bay's piscatorial history. Board a boat as early as 4 am and imagine that you are an ancient angler. The fish are still the same — hook, line and sinker — and pulling one aboard is just as exciting as in the past. When you leave the dock and when you return to port, you encounter the picturesque Bay scene and the nautical thrill of any big time fisherman. Then you know what world-famed Fisherman's Wharf is all about.

Sportfishing boats work out of many marinas on the Bay, most of them every day, according to demand. You can join an "open party," or your group can engage a "full boat charter." There is some specialization by the skippers depending on what they fish for and their location. Some boats even do "potluck" parties, just going around and fishing for different things — salmon or bass or whatever — to find the action spots. Neophytes are always encouraged with plenty of help and advice from crew and passengers; women and children are welcomed, so you can make it a family outing.

Basically there are three types of fishing trips. The rates for these vary from around $25 to around $19 per person for the day.

Pacific Ocean salmon trolling takes you outside the Gate to Duxbury Point, the San Francisco lightship, or off Pacifica. The king salmon season is from mid-February to mid-November, with the most numerous catch in the spring and the largest fish in the summer. You also get ten hours of relaxation, sun and pleasure. Of course if you come home early, that means that everyone aboard ''limited out'' (three apiece), or the weather got too rough.

Farallon Islands rock cod fishing may provide a glimpse of these quasi-mystical isles through the fog banks on your all-day trip. Some boats go even further out, to the Cordell Bank. The season for this deep-sea fishing is all year, and the limit can be as many as twenty fish in your sack. There are many species of bottom fish for you to catch, among them orange rockfish, lingcod, yellowtail rockfish, red snapper, green striped rockfish and bocaccio.

San Francisco Bay live bait bass drifting is in season year-round, but the hot action is from June to December. The striped bass run of SF Bay is unique on the West Coast, and the fish command top attention in the summer. Most boats make two trips a day, morning and afternoon (half-day trips cost less than prices above). Locations depend on where they're biting — from the south tower of the Golden Gate Bridge, to Alcatraz, to Treasure Island, to Raccoon Strait, to the Richmond Bridge, and on into San Pablo Bay where you can also find sturgeon fishing.

To make a comfortable expedition, you need to take several layers of clothing to remove and put on as necessary. An all-day trip can take you through a range of temperatures, and the wind that blows the damp fog away can kick up the chop. Everything else you need you can normally get at the sportfishing shop where you board the boat. If you're a beginner, the crew will help with baiting and landing your fish, and fish cleaning services are available. When you get home you can have the fish dinner of your heart's desire, or you can have your catch smoked and/or canned at several local fish companies.

When selecting a boat there are some things to keep in mind: radio and radar for navigation (almost all are so equipped), depth finder for locating fish, size of the boat (number of passengers and how it rides in the water), speed (faster boats get you to the fish quicker) — probably the most important, a congenial crew.

The sportfishing shop can supply rods and tackle (rental runs $3 to $6), bait, license for anyone over sixteen (a saltwater license is $4/year, but if you're in town for the weekend and decide to give it a try, a three-day license costs $2). Most shops have any lunch and refreshments necessary. The party boat fleets work out of bait shops, although some operate independently. Marinas and bait shops are listed in other sections of this book. A few of the boats change locations from time to time. What with skippers retiring and a wreck here and there, they can be hard to keep track of, but here is a selected list. Wake up early, get aboard and bring home the best fish dinner in the world — the one you caught yourself.

Marin

Caruso's Sportfishing

Foot of Harbor Drive (Clipper Yacht Harbor), Sausalito. (332-1015) Open 5 am to 6 pm. Fishing parties arranged; bait and tackle; snacks; and in addition they have a fish market with fresh fish daily and shell fish in season. Their fleet of approximately fourteen boats go after salmon and rock cod. To be found among their charters:

Rayann II — new 46-foot boat, 14 to 20 people, deep-sea every Tuesday, Capt. Ray Biagini (after 7 pm 584-1498);

Sandra Gal — up to 16 people (332-0372); *Ma-Ru II* — Capt. Roger Thomas (348-2107); *Speed King* — Capt. Robben Knapp; *Pacific Queen* — Capt. Ron Nass (479-1322); *Sunrise* — (435-0405); *Pattie L* — Capt. Jack Green; *Ginnie C* — Capt. Jim Robertson; *Lucky Lady; Lucy O;* and both of the boats which are listed under Jerry's.

Jerry's Fishing Trips

(Marinship Yacht Harbor), Monday-Friday 8 am-5 pm, Saturday 10 am-4 pm. (332-1912)

Long Fin — new 60-foot fiberglass boat, rock cod every Friday, Capt. Andy Cordellos; *Thunderbird*.

Sausalito Boat and Tackle Shop

North end of Sausalito, Marin City exit from Highway 101 (Waldo Point). (332-2599, evenings 883-6550) Fishing charters arranged; bait and tackle; snacks. Four boats out of Kappas Marina for daily salmon fishing and deep-sea on Fridays, Saturdays and Sundays.

Blue Horizon — 68-foot boat, Capt. Rich Urbais; *Ina Belle* — 55-foot boat, Capt. Harold McGuire; *Bluefin* — 55-foot boat, Capt. Mike Williams; *Lynn Ann* — 40-foot boat.

Bait House

At Loch Lomond Marina, San Rafael (456-0321)

Superfish — 40-foot boat, bass and sturgeon, Capt. Dick Steinhart.

Sonoma County

Bait and tackle shop

At Port Sonoma Marina, near Black Point.

Nobilis — Capt. Jim DeLaMontanya (residence 897-4076); out of Crockett Marine Service, Crockett, in summer (787-1047).

Contra Costa County

Crockett Marine Service

Foot of Port Street, Crockett. (787-1047) From the marina beneath the Carquinez Bridge, sportfishing boats put out for all-day or half-day trips for sturgeon, bass and flounder, and summer evening bass trolling; bait and tackle; snacks. Among their party boats:

Dowrelio #6 — Capt. John Severa; *Lancer* — Capt. Mike Andrews, Sr.; *Marauder* — Capt. Mike Andrews, Jr.; *Andiamo*.

Sarge's Bait and Tackle Shop

Rodeo Marina, Rodeo. (799-4076) Every day four boats that will take up to twenty people go fishing in San Pablo Bay; bait and tackle; coffee shop adjacent. You can also make arrangements through the marina (799-4435).

Point San Pablo Yacht Harbor

Richmond (233-3224) Three full-time and three part-time boats work out of this marina; bait and tackle shop.

New Keesa — operates out of Crockett Marine Service, Crockett, in summer, Capt. Mike O'Connell (787-1720); *Jessie M* — Capt. Mike Ramirez (525-5823); *Mr. Bass* — Capt. Jim Smith (236-0813). Weekends: *Admiral* — Capt. Hank Rhodes (209-823-4743); *Kelly L* — Capt. Harvey Livingston (462-1907); *Big Ern* — Capt. Ernie Tritto (357-4390).

Occasionally fishing boats work out of Redrock Marina, Richmond, so call harbormaster for information. (235-0515)

Alameda County

Berkeley Marina Sports Center

Beside harbormaster's office, Berkeley Marina. (849-2727) More than fourteen boats work from this bait and tackle facility; snack bar and beer. Daily salmon, bass, rock cod and potluck trips on the uniquely-owned (all independent) fleet berthed at this marina:

Anna V — salmon (526-1674); *Sea Horse* — 50-foot salmon boat, Capt.

Frank Matthews (849-4926); *Hazel B* — Capt. Jack Priestly; *For You* — 40-foot boat, salmon and bass, Capt. Dale Peterson (235-6324); *Wilma H* — salmon, bass, rockfish, halibut, potluck; *Chinook* — 50-foot salmon boat, Capt. Ernie Feigenberg (521-9275); *Capt. Pete* — Capt. Pete Peterson (581-4000); *Wild Wave* — Capt. Bill Beckett; *GeGe* — Capt. George Grimshaw; *Cherokee* — Capt. Joe De Silva; *Huck Finn* — Capt. Art Roby; *Fury; Off Shore; R. S. P.*

Lee Anderson Charter Boat Service

6702 San Pablo Avenue, Albany. (653-9778) Live bait bass, sturgeon and rockfish boats operating out of the Berkeley Marina. See above for more information about their seven boats:

Anna V; Sea Horse; Wilma H; Wild Wave; R. S. P.; Cherokee; Huck Finn.

Sportfishing Center

949 San Pablo Avenue, Albany. (524-0221) A pro shop featuring rod and reel repair and custom rod building, run by Capt. Dave, who is the agent for party boats holding 6 to 49 people fishing for salmon, bass and rock cod operating out of the Berkeley Marina. Tackle rental and bait.

Evie K — Capt. Dave Kinley; for information about the other boats — *Sea Horse; Hazel B; For You; Chinook; Capt. Pete; GeGe* — see above.

Hank Schramm's Sportfishing Center

Foot of Powell Street (Emeryville Marina), Emeryville. (654-6040, evenings 883-6443) Open 4 am to 7 pm. Open party charters for salmon, live bait bass and rock cod fishing; bait and tackle; drinks and cold sandwiches. Daily fishing reports on radio KSFO-560 AM. Their eleven-boat fleet:

Salmon Queen III — 70-foot boat, Capt. Ron Long; *Salmon Queen V* — 60-foot boat; *Salmon Queen VI* — 55-foot boat, Capt. Perry; *Linda* — 46-foot

boat, Capt. Ray Cox; *New Peggy Jane* — 50-foot boat, Capt. Joe Manzella; *New Sea Wolf* — 55-foot boat, Capt. Rex Southard; *Fisherman III* — bass, salmon, rockfish, 65-foot boat, Capt. Steve Bales (837-5113); *Sunfish* — 55-foot salmon, bass and rockfish boat, Capt. Jack Ellis (837-5113); *Gertha L* — 45-foot boat, Capt. John Traylor (568-1598); *Sea Sport II* — Capt. Bud Falkenstein (994-1062); *Fiesta* — Capt. Barney Holder.

Godfather Bait and Tackle Shop

One Fifth Avenue (Fifth Avenue Marina), Oakland. (465-9673) Bait and tackle; rock cod, salmon and bass fishing on their boat;

The Godson — two-year-old 45-foot steel boat, Capt. Herb Been.

San Francisco

Muny Bait Shop

3098 Polk Street (at North Point Street, across from Ghirardelli Square), San Francisco. (673-9815) Bait and tackle, snack bar. More than a dozen boats available for salmon, deep-sea and bass fishing. The first three listed sail from the San Francisco Marina and the rest from Fisherman's Wharf.

Bright I — (929-1654); *Kihaku* — Capt. Bill Borden (822-6760); *Argo* — 60-foot boat, Capt. Leo Bergmann (563-0816, or 321-3344); *Lovely Martha* — Capt. Nick Rescino (467-8294); *New Edibob* — Capt. Jim Phelan (751-3734); *New Holiday II* — 50-foot boat, Capt. Joe Morini (892-2353); *New Holiday III* — Capt. Fred Morini (924-5575); *New Florie S* — Capt. Al Spadaro (878-4644); *Skip-A-Lou* — Capt. Nemo (885-2298); *Miss Jody* — Capt. Sal Cresci; *Albacore*.

The Sportfishing Center (Capurro's)

300 Jefferson Street (at Jones, Fisherman's Wharf), San Francisco. (771-2800) Open party and charter fishing trips arranged; bait and tackle; snack bar. Their fleet of boats include:

Celestial 102 — full-time rock cod boat, Capt. Ron Hornlein; *Easy Rider* — Capt. Bill Mattlin (for both, call 24 hours, 285-2000).

Other sportfishing boats sailing from Fisherman's Wharf:

Bass Tub II and *Bass Tub III* — Capt. Cliff Anfinson (456-9055); *Butchie B* — Capt. Butchie Bentivegna (457-8388); *Wacky Jacky* — 50-foot boat, Capt. Jacky Douglas (586-9800); *Ketchikan* — Capt. Jerry Hunt (981-6269); *Lindy Su* — Capt. Sam Lackey (664-6014, or 387-6461); *Sundance* — Capt. Bill Miner (664-6014, or 387-6461); *New Merrimac* — Capt. Taylor W. McGee (388-5351); *Capt. Phil* — (583-9782); *Cindy Lu* — (664-4221); *China Doll* — (673-4453); *Uncle Ray* — (352-3468).

Pier 39 Sport Fishing

On The Embarcadero, near Fisherman's Wharf, San Francisco. (434-FISH, in other words 434-3474) A recently opened fishing center and marina that will be increasing their services and fleet; charter and open party trips arranged for salmon, rock cod and bass; bait and tackle; box lunches. Among their boats:

Jackpot — 50-foot boat (752-6061, evenings 989-5310).

The Ramp

855 China Basin Street (off Third Street), San Francisco. (621-2378) Bait and tackle and refreshments. Their boat:

Carol — (873-4240).

History

Bay Discovery

Sir Francis Drake's voyage to California is of small importance in a book about San Francisco Bay, unless he sailed his *Golden Hinde* within its mouth and planted a brass plate on the shore. Did he land on Point San Quentin in the Bay in 1579, or was it at what is now Drakes Bay, or even Bodega Bay, in western Marin County? The controversy of Drake's landing is left to historians as they search for further evidence to support one or another of the theories. Some of us can hope, however, that the romantic English sea dog Drake was the first Euoprean to set eyes on the Bay. In a sense, *discovery* by Drake is not the point, because there was no confirmation, no follow up by the English.

It was left to a later explorer to discover San Francisco Bay with the supporting confirmation, conquest and exploitation that secured Alta California for the Spanish. Nearly two hundred years after Drake, Captain Gaspar de Portolá led an overland expedition up the Pacific Coast from what is now Mexico. When the party came to the location that is now Pacifica, they camped and sent out scouts. When the pathfinders reported back, the expedition broke camp and climbed a nearby ridge to behold, for the first time, San Francisco Bay. It was on November 4, 1769, that the explorers looked down from what is now Sweeney Ridge to see the great body of water that they could not go around. There was no sense of a momentous occasion; instead there was disappointment. The expedition had been searching for Monterey Bay and had not found it, so they had to return to the south, frustrated. But this failure led to more expeditions that established settlements on the Bay of Saint Francis only a few years later.

You will find below a short hike that takes you to the Bay Discovery Site of the Portolá expedition, the story accepted by textbooks as the first discovery of San Francisco Bay. You will also find an article by Robert H. Power that presents evidence and argues for the thesis that Sir Francis Drake did indeed land in San Francisco Bay, and was thus the first European discoverer. Power is a past president of the California Historical Society and a member of the Sir Francis Drake Commission, but the views of the historical controversy presented here are his own opinions and judgments, not those of the organizations.

Bay Discovery Site

If you would like to retrace the steps of the Portolá expedition, you can hike to the Bay Discovery Site. A walk of less than two miles takes you along a ridge that leads up to Sweeney Ridge, which parallels the Pacific coastline and the Bay shoreline. At the site on Sweeney Ridge there is a stone monument that marks the historic spot, overlooking San Andreas Lake and the whole South Bay stretching away from the eye.

To make this trip on the up-and-up, you need to contact the Pacifica Recreation Department (355-4151). To get to City Hall, take the Francisco Boulevard exit from Highway One, and follow Francisco for three blocks parallel to the freeway, then turn right on Santa Maria Avenue. The City Hall is open 8:30 am-5 pm Monday-Thursday, and 8:30 am-1:30 pm on Friday. There you can get a key to the gate (which you won't need, if you have no qualms about walking across someone's yard to get around the fence), and a permit (since the trail crosses private land), and a charming *Descubridor* certificate.

To get to the hiking trail, turn off Highway One, at the Rockaway Beach District of Pacifica, on Fassler Avenue and follow to the end. This is a dead end residential street, so there is not a lot of parking space.

Only Sir Francis Knows for Sure

by Robert H. Power

The story of Drake's presence in California began on June 17, 1579 (June 27 on our since-revised calendar), when the sea-battered and leaking *Golden Hinde* of Captain Francis Drake made its way into "a faire and good Baye" near 38 degrees north latitude along the California coast. For three days the crew reconnoitered the bay for a suitable site to careen and repair their vessel before continuing the Pacific leg in a voyage around the world. During a thirty-six day stay, Drake and his crew of more than sixty men built a small fort, treated with the native Indians, observed the local plant and animal life, erected a brass plate commemorating the *Golden Hinde's* visit, and claimed the region for their queen, Elizabeth I.

It is known for a certainty that Drake saw the white cliffs on the south face of Point Reyes before he arrived at this anchorage, for while he was there, he named the land *Nova Albion* because "the white bankes and cliffes, which lie toward the sea" reminded him of the chalk cliffs of southern England. It is also known that upon his departure, Drake made landfall at the Farallon Islands, which he called the Islands of St. James. Somewhere between these two undisputed landmarks separated by a mere seventeen miles of sea, lies the "faire and good Baye" of Francis Drake.

Surely the question could be resolved by Drake's original journal of his voyage, but the document has disappeared, an apparent casualty of Elizabethan diplomacy. Drake's activities in Spanish colonial waters had strained relations between England and Spain to the point where Elizabeth stored Drake's booty, and perhaps the records of the voyage, in the Tower of London — on the apparent assumption that the less said, the better.

The journal has long since disappeared, and historians have had to rely on two narratives written after Drake's return. Richard Hakluyt's *The Famous Voyage of Sir Francis Drake* and *The World Encompassed by Sir Francis Drake* are quite similar in regard to the *Golden Hinde's* stay in Nova Albion, probably because both relied heavily upon the narrative of Francis Fletcher, preacher of the *Hinde*. Together, *The Famous Voyage* and *The World Encompassed* offer clues, but no definitive answers to the location of Drake's anchorage.

One definite clue to Drake's landing site is to be found on a world map commemorating Drake's world voyage entitled *Expeditionis Nauticae*, which was published at London in 1589 by the Flemish cartographer, Jodocus Hondius. On one corner of this gracefully illuminating map is a small drawing of Drake's California anchorage entitled *Portus Novae Albionis* (Port of Nova Albion). Hondius, a London resident, is known to have been associated in a publishing venture in 1589 with Thomas Talbot, keeper of the Queen's archives in the Tower of London. Apparently Talbot allowed his associate, Hondius, access to Queen Elizabeth's records of the Drake voyage, and thereby preserved for posterity the cartographic form of Drake's California anchorage.

Although small, the Portus plan is quite clear on its salient points; namely Drake's fort protected by a spatula shaped pointed island approximately half the length of the peninsula. This sectional map, the only solid cartographic evidence of Drake's landing site along the Golden Shore, has been twisted, turned, bent and manipulated in an effort to make it fit every inlet on the coast from Trinidad Head to Half Moon Bay.

Most such efforts are pointless and futile, because the anchorage must lie close by 38 degrees north latitude, offer a view upon arrival of the white cliffs for which Drake named Nova Albion, and allow for an overnight voyage to the Farallones upon departure. Within this narrowing range of possibilities lies our own "faire and good Baye" of San Francisco, which offers within its realm, a striking comparison to the uncommon geography depicted in the Portus plan.

As aerial photographs so clearly illustrate, the Tiburon Peninsula and Belvedere Island bear more than a passing resemblance to the wasp-waisted peninsula and flake-tipped island of the Portus plan. Like the peninsula of the Portus plan, as Tiburon grows from the mainland it appears pinched at the waist, building to dramatically more massive headlands near the tip. Similarly, Belvedere possesses the detailed sculpting at its tip that is so pronounced on the island of the Portus plan, while maintaining the proper proportions of size and location relative to the peninsula.

One inconsistent factor in this comparison is the solid bridge of land depicted on the Portus plan in length and position where we now know the strait leading into San Pablo Bay to lie. An aerial photograph shows how immaterial the closing of a distant strait is to the general configuration in a bay as large as San Francisco. It could have been an horizon to the original cartographer or a later error made by the engraver who simply thought a port should have only one opening. Whatever the reason for the land bridge across the Strait of San Pablo, it is a minor error in comparison with the positive forms of Belvedere, Tiburon and the Contra Costa shore. The end result is strikingly similar to the effect achieved by the photographs taken from an airplane as the accompanying illustrations attest.

Portus Novæ Albionis

Fœda corporum laceratione & crebris in montibus sacrificijs, hujus Novæ Albionis portus incolæ, Draci, jam bis coronati, decessum deflent.

Here is the best cartographic indication to date that Sir Francis Drake anchored not on the Marin coast but on its bay side: Hondius' Portus map (top) which historians conjecture was based on the now-lost records of Queen Elizabeth I on the Drake voyage.

The Portus plan is by no means the only link in the evidential chain which anchors Drake in San Francisco Bay. In 1936, on a Greenbrae ridge overlooking Highway 101 and Point San Quentin, Beryl Shinn found the Plate of Brass which Drake left in Nova Albion to commemorate his stay and claim the region for England. The authenticity of the brass plate which Shinn found remains in dispute among authorities. The location of its discovery correlates to Belvedere Island and Tiburon peninsula in the same way Drake's fort correlates to the Portus island and peninsula.

It has been alleged that the Plate of Brass was originally found near Drake's Bay in 1933 by William Caldiera, who discarded it as worthless near the site of Shinn's discovery. Caldiera's claim is questionable, however, on several points: there is conflicting testimony over where Caldiera tossed his piece of metal; the closest point of discard is over one-half mile from the discovery site, and Shinn did not find the Plate lying on the ground, but pulled it free from the earth after moving a rock. While the possibility exists that Drake's Plate of Brass was moved over the centuries, there is a strong likelihood that the marker was found at, or near, the site where it was originally erected.

As part of the monument Drake erected, a hole was cut in the Plate of Brass to accommodate an English sixpence. This was done in order to include the visage of his Queen and her coat of arms in the memorial. Extraordinarily, a sixpence of the proper vintage was recently unearthed by Charles Slaymaker, an archeologist working at Rancho Olompali, a few miles north of Novato adjacent to Highway 101. Olompali was the site of one of the largest and richest villages of Coast Miwok Indians in the region, and would, therefore, be the most likely village from which came on June 26, 1579, the great *"Hioh*, that is their king . . . with his guard of about 100 tall and warlike men.'' While it cannot be known for a certainty that the Slaymaker sixpence is from the Plate of Brass, or whether it is a second coin that was perhaps presented to the *Hioh* on the occasion of his visit to the Elizabethan fort, the presence of the coin at this village is a striking coincidence, and certainly merits consideration in an overall evaluation.

The evidence of Drake's landing in San Francisco Bay — the geographic similarities, the discovery of the Plate of Brass, and the sixpence — are buttressed by more information that can be gleaned from the records kept by the crewmen. Because of Indian words which were remembered by members of the crew, Robert F. Heizer and William Elmendorff were able in 1942 to identify the Indians as Coast Miwoks. This fact, while definitive and useful, only narrowed the search for Drake's anchorage to Marin and southern Sonoma Counties.

The World Encompassed, based upon Preacher Fletcher's narrative, also contains descriptions of the local plant and animal life near the beach where the *Golden Hinde* was careened, which

when considered together point directly to an anchorage in San Francisco Bay. At one point the narrator remarks ''how unhandsome and deformed appeared the face of the earth it selfe! shewing trees without leaves, and the ground without greenes in those months of June and July.'' In almost any year this description applies to the San Pablo shore in late July, when the grass is already brown and the buckeye trees are beginning to yellow and lose their leaves.

At another point, the narrator describes a ceremonial headpiece worn by the Indians that was ''covered over with a certain downe, which groweth up in the countrey upon an herbe much like our lectuce; which exceeds any other downe in the world for fineness.'' Although hardly a detailed description, two clues strongly indicate that the plant was American milkweed. First, when broken this weed exudes a white milk-like sap ''much like our lectuce''; and secondly, during late July milkweed produces a soft, silky, long-stranded, supremely fine white down that must be felt to be believed. It does indeed ''exceed any other downe in the world for finenesse.'' Milkweed is found growing ''up in the countrey'' in the warm valleys north of San Rafael — or at least it was, until dairy ranchers exterminated the plant as a danger to livestock.

they had encountered earlier in their travels. The California Academy of Sciences, quite apart from any consideration of Drake has likewise selected the Barbary Cony and California ground squirrel as examples of parallel development in distantly related mammals living in similar environments.

Normally in pre-Hispanic California, ground squirrels would not be seen in epidemic proportions, but the presence of "thousands" of tule elk would alter conditions. Usually ground squirrels overpopulate only where farming or overgrazing have destroyed the land's grass cover, something the reported large tule elk herds could have accomplished eating off the grass and breaking the turf with their hoofs — in much the same way that bison herds made possible large concentrations of prairie dogs. What Drake's men saw was a natural phenomenon, Mother Nature briefly out of balance, and it was something they would have seen north of San Francisco Bay, not on the coastal slopes above Drakes Bay and Point Reyes.

The location of Drake's "faire and good Baye" has been an elusive question for almost 400 years, largely because much of the evidence must be interpreted and evaluated. But when all of the clues are examined — the Portus plan map, the Indians, the white cliffs, the Plate of Brass, the plants, the animals, and more — the port of Drake begins to lose its mystery, and becomes instead an old acquaintance, the great bay which has shaped all our lives. Go and look for yourself. Enjoy the landmarks Drake saw, the white cliffs of Point Reyes, the island of Belvedere and the peninsula of Tiburon, but stay away from the Farallon Islands, as they are now a wildlife sanctuary.

Near the end of his stay in Nova Albion, Drake took a company of his men on an excursion inland "to be better acquainted with the nature and commodities of the country." What they saw adds to the conviction that the *Golden Hinde* was careened at Point San Quentin. *The World Encompassed* described a "company of very large and fat Deere which we saw by the thousands, as we supposed, in a heard," which were the tule elk common in that time to all of Marin County. By themselves, the tule elk do not preclude the possibility of other landing sites, but the men of the *Golden Hinde* also saw another creature co-existing with the tule elk, in a combination that points directly to the inland valleys immediately adjacent to the bay.

As described in *The World Encompassed*, Drake's party saw "a multitude of a strange kinde of Conies, by farr exceeding them (the tule elk) in number." The accompanying description strongly suggests the California ground squirrel, which inhabits the warm hillsides and valleys north of Point San Quentin, but not the coastal regions of western Marin inland from Drakes Bay. To Drake's men, this earth-bound creature was unlike the tree-climbing squirrels in their native England, and so they compared it to the Barbary Cony which

San Francisco Bay Chronology

Man's influence and the history shaping the Bay. Where to discover traces of these events.

2,000 to 5,000 years ago

Indians (Coast Miwok, Costanoan and Wintun) occupied hundreds of sites on San Francisco Bay, near fresh water supplies and plentiful food from the Bay waters, as evidenced by the shell mounds that they left behind.

Sites at Coyote Hills Regional Park and Brooks Island.

1542

November:

Explorer Juan Rodríguez Cabrillo, first European to chart California coast, sailed south past Bay entrance without discovering it.

1579

June 17 (old style date):

Francis Drake, later Sir Francis, English adventurer, sailed into San Francisco Bay (as claimed by some eminent authorities). At anchorage in Marin County his ship, *Golden Hinde,* was careened, repaired and the crew refreshed. They stayed thirty-six days and claimed the land, Nova Albion, for England.

As part of the controversy surrounding the historical authenticity of this event, there is a monument and plaque concerning the discovery at Drakes Bay on Point Reyes, which is outside the purview of this book.

1595

November 7:

Mariner Sebastián Rodríquez Cermeño wrecked his Manila galleon, *San Agustín,* at what is now Drakes Bay. Cermeño named it *Bahia de San Francisco,* and then his party continued south to Mexico, but failed to find what is now San Francisco Bay. Later explorers searched for Cermeño's bay, but discovered, accidentally, our Bay to which they transferred the name.

1602-03

• Exploration voyage under Sebastián Vizcaíno surveyed the California coast, but did not discover San Francisco Bay.

1769

November 4:

Expedition of Capt. Gaspar de Portolá discovered San Francisco Bay from a ridge on the Peninsula. A couple of days before, some of the party, under Sgt. José de Ortega, had proceeded north and seen the entrance, the Golden Gate.

The Bay Discovery site, which you can hike to, is mentioned elsewhere in the book.

November 4-10:

As the Portolá expedition (which was searching for Monterey Bay, but passed without recognizing it) was returning south, a scouting party was sent out, under Sgt. José Francisco de Ortega, who was the first European to traverse the lands of the East Bay and sight San Pablo Bay.

See the section *Commemorations of History.*

1772

March 29:

First European explorer sighted what is now Carquinez Strait at the head of San Francisco Bay. The expedition was led by Pedro Fages and included Father Juan Crespí.

1775

August 5:

First European entrance into San Francisco Bay by ship, *San Carlos,* commanded by Lt. Juan Manuel de Ayala (pace Sir Francis). His pilot, José de Cañizares, explored and charted the Bay for 44 days.

Markers at Fort Point, Aquatic Park and Angel Island.

1776

March 28:

Expedition of Capt. Juan Bautista de Anza reached what is now the Golden Gate and proclaimed the sites for the presidio and the mission.

Markers at Fort Point, the Presidio and Mission Dolores.

June 29:

Celebrated as the birthday of the City of San Francisco. Presidio of San Francisco founded by settlement of Anza's lieutenant, José Joaquín Moraga, the first commandante (dedicated September 17). First mass said at Mission San Francisco de Asís (Mission Dolores) by Padre Francisco Palou of Anza's party; the first mission in the Bay Area, not formally dedicated until October 9.

Marker at the Presidio, and the reconstructed Mission building has a marker.

1777

January 17:

Mission Santa Clara de Asís established by Padres Tomás de la Peña and Joseph Antonio Murgúia, the first mission in the South Bay.

Marker in Santa Clara.

November 29:

Lt. José Joaquín Moraga founded *El Pueblo de San José de Guadalupe* (now San Jose), as first pueblo (civil) settlement in California.

Marker in San Jose.

1792

November 14:

First Englishman (after Drake) to sail into Bay, exploration voyage of Capt. George Vancouver on sloop *Discovery.*

1794

December 9:

Spanish-built adobe fortification on present site of Fort Point, dedicated as *Castillo de San Joaquín.*

Marker at Fort Point in San Francisco.

1797

June 11:
Founding of Mission San José, first permanent settlement in East Bay (today a part of Fremont), by Father Fermín Lasuén.
Marker in Fremont.

1799

May 24:
First American ship to enter San Francisco Bay, sea otter hunter *Eliza*.

1806

April 5:
First Russian entrance into Bay, Count Nikolai Rezanov aboard *Juno*, seeking supplies for Russian settlements in Alaska.

1814

March 16:
HMS *Raccoon*, British sloop-of-war, put into Bay and laid up in Strait off Tiburon for repairs.

1817

December 14:
Founding of Mission San Rafael Arcángel as an adjunct of the Mission San Francisco.

1826

• First English-speaking settler in Marin, the sailor John Reed, established himself in the vicinity of Sausalito.

November 6:
Capt. William F. Beechey of British Navy ship *Blossom* explored and charted San Francisco Bay.

1835

June 25:
Pueblo of Yerba Buena founded with erection of a tent structure on Yerba Buena Cove (San Francisco) by William A. Richardson.

December 4:
Richard Henry Dana arrived in San Francisco Bay on board the *Alert*. His book, *Two Years Before the Mast*, did much to publicize the port's potential.

1846

July 9:
American flag raised at Yerba Buena by Commander John B. Montgomery of the sloop-of-war USS *Portsmouth*.
Marker at Portsmouth Square.

1847

January 30:
The village of Yerba Buena renamed San Francisco.

March 27:
Presidio of San Francisco formally occupied by American troops.

1848

January 24:
Discovery of gold in California.

1849

February 28:
First regular steamboat service to California inaugurated by the arrival of the Pacific Mail's *California*, carrying gold-seekers from New York.

July 28:
First clipper ship, the *Memnon*, arrived in the Bay, 120 days from New York.

1850

• First regular transbay ferry operation established by Capt. Thomas Gray with the *Kangaroo* running twice a week between San Francisco and San Antonio Creek (now the Oakland Estuary).
See the pedestrian tours for information about visiting San Francisco's Ferry Building and Jack London Square.

January 3:
Bargain sale of beach and waterfront property which had to be regularized by an act of the legislature the following year, relinquishing title to water lots within San Francisco.
To find the original waterfront of the City, consult the shoreline markers mentioned in *Commemorations of History,* and consult the maps on view at the Maritime Museum.

July 1:
Abandoned vessels numbering more than 600 were lying in San Francisco Bay and contiguous harbors.

November 6:
President Millard Fillmore, by executive order, reserves Yerba Buena, Alcatraz and Angel islands and Point San Jose (Fort Mason) for the military.
Markers at Angel Island and Fort Mason.

1853

• Meiggs Wharf built near what is now Fisherman's Wharf.

1854

June 1:
Lighthouse on Alcatraz Island began operation, the first light to shine on the Pacific coast.
You can see the light still flashing on the island, and you will see it if you visit the island on a tour.

September 16:
Navy Yard established on Mare Island by Commander David Glasgow Farragut, first yard on the Pacific coast.
Marker on the Island, but Naval Shipyard not accessible to the public.

1855

March:
Second beacon on California coast, Fort Point Lighthouse, began operation, later replaced by one on top of fort.
The light has been discontinued, but the structure can still be seen atop Fort Point.

1858

- Initial fortification of Alcatraz Island completed.

1859

- Initial use of Alcatraz as unofficial military prison (see 1895).

Summer:

Richard Henry Dana returned to Bay on board *Golden Gate,* and wrote again of the city.

1860

March 24:

Clipper ship *Andrew Jackson* arrived from New York in 89 days.

April 15:

River boat *Antelope* completed first run of Pony Express by carrying mail from Sacramento to San Francisco.

1861

February 15:

Fort Point completed and garrisoned by two companies of Third Artillery.

Marker at Fort Point, which is now a National Historic Site and open to the public.

1863

March 15:

Schooner *J. M. Chapman* seized in the Bay and five men (Confederate sympathizers) arrested as privateers.

September 2:

Railroad and ferry connection between Oakland and San Francisco inaugurated by San Francisco & Oakland RR, later to become part of the Southern Pacific.

September 12:

Troops began erection of fortifications at Camp Reynolds on Angel Island.

A visit to Angel Island will let you see remnants of these.

October 28:

Telegraph cable laid across headlands from Fort Point to Lime Point.

1864

- Lighthouse structure built atop Fort Point. You can see structure by visiting Fort Point.

April 8:

Officers quarters at Black Point Battery destroyed by fire. You can see the site of these structures by visiting Fort Mason.

April 14:

Military orders issued forbidding vessels entering harbor of San Francisco to pass north of Alcatraz, on penalty of being fired upon.

June 11:

More than 300 feet of Meiggs Wharf washed away in a storm.

November 14:

The *Comanche,* an iron-clad monitor, launched by US Navy.

1865

- Capts. A. Nelson and N.E. Anderson operated California Transportation Co., ferry line from San Francisco to Alviso with stops at many landings in between.

You can recall this tule navigation venture by a walking tour of Alviso.

1866

April 24:

Steamer *Continental* arrived with 75 of Mercer's female immigrants for the Washington Territory.

1867

September 9:

Work began on first section of seawall on San Francisco waterfront.

September 27:

First steamer, the *John L. Stephens,* to sail between California and Alaska, left the Bay.

November 4:

Fill was obtained for a section of the seawall by blasting with 90 kegs of powder at Telegraph Hill.

1868

May 10:

First ferry service between San Francisco and Marin (Meiggs Wharf to Sausalito) inaugurated by the *Princess* of Sausalito Land & Ferry Co.

You can ride the ferry to Sausalito and make a walking tour of the waterfront.

1869

Summer:

Emperor Norton (San Francisco's fabulous character) ordered a bridge built across the Bay and out to the Farallon Islands.

September 6:

River Steamer *Sophie MacLane* was first ferryboat to connect with the first transcontinental passenger train (Central Pacific) to reach San Francisco Bay, Alameda to San Francisco.

Visit the Ferry Building on a walking tour of San Francisco's waterfront.

- After the coming of the railroad, Eastern oyster spat was imported and transplanted in the South Bay to create the Bay oyster industry.

1870

October 31:

Ferry service of San Francisco & North Pacific Railway began with the steamer *Antelope* running from San Francisco to Donahue Landing on the Petaluma River.

1871

April 23:

Blossom Rock (discovered and named by Capt. Beechey in 1826) in San Francisco Bay was blown up as a navigational hazard.

1872

January 20:

First meeting of the "Committee of One Hundred" to oppose cession of Goat Island to the railroad companies.

August 23:

First Japanese commercial ship ever in the Bay arrived with a cargo of tea.

1874

March 1:

First glimmer of the lighthouse on East Brother Island off Point San Pablo.

You can still see the flashes from the Richmond-San Rafael Bridge.

1875

January 7:

Inauguration of North Pacific Coast RR from San Francisco to Tomales via ferryboat to Sausalito.

October 1:

Light began shining and steam fog whistles began blowing upon completion of Yerba Buena Island light station.

You can still see the light flashing across the bay.

1877

October 27:

First ferryboat collision on the Bay. *Petaluma of Saucelito* rammed *Clinton* of Contra Costa Navigation Company and sank it.

1879

February 19:

In dense fog on the Bay, ferryboats of the Central Pacific RR, the *El Capitan* and the original *Alameda*, collided.

May 24:

First annual regatta of the Pacific Amateur Rowing Association held.

A weekend walk at Aquatic Park, San Francisco, will let you see some rowing club enthusiasts in the water.

July 8:

Steam yacht *Jeanette* left on an Arctic exploration voyage.

1880

September 21:

Ferryboat *Saucelito* carried Rutherford B. Hayes on first ever presidential visit to Mare Island Navy Yard.

1881

August 1:

U.S. Quarantine Station authorized for Angel Island.

Now a state park, you can visit Angel Island by ferry.

1882

November 25:

Fort Point renamed Fort Winfield Scott.

Marker at Fort Point, which is now a National Historic Site and open to the public.

1883

September:

Fog signal station began operation at Lime Point, to be enlarged to a lighthouse in 1900.

You can see the light, still operating under the north end of the Golden Gate Bridge.

1884

● First ferry service from San Francisco to Tiburon inaugurated by San Francisco & North Pacific Railway's boat *Tiburon*.

See section *Transportation on the Bay*, about riding the ferry to Tiburon.

1886

● Fort Point abandoned as a harbor defense installation.

November 27:

California's first Arbor Day, promoted by poet Joaquin Miller, was celebrated with ceremonies on Yerba Buena Island; Adolph Sutro planted first tree.

1887

January 16:

Schooner *Parallel*, with a cargo of powder, blew up below the Cliff House, badly damaging it.

1888

● Robert Louis Stevenson embarked on schooner yacht *Casco* from present-day Jack London Square for final home in the South Seas.

You can make a walking tour of Jack London Square in Oakland.

February 27:

Explosion of ferryboat *Julia* while tied up at wharf in South Vallejo.

1890

January 27:

First Oakland Harbor Lighthouse began operation.

September 22:

Construction of seawall at foot of Powell Street in San Francisco began.

1892

May 1:

U.S. Quarantine Station opened on Angel Island.

Now a state park, you can visit Angel Island by ferry.

December 1:

Army post on Alcatraz Island designated "saluting station" to return salutes of foreign vessels of war.

1895

July 1:

Alcatraz Island designated as U.S. disciplinary barracks.

You can see Alcatraz on a guided tour.

August 10:

Longest ferry run on the Bay inaugurated between Vallejo and San Francisco by Monticello Steamship Co.

1898

January 11:
Lightship replaces whistling buoy at entrance to the Bay.

April 12:
Army transferred Yerba Buena Island to Navy, and retained small part as a mine-layer port.

May 23:
First Philippine expeditionary troops sailed from San Francisco Bay.

July 13:
Ferry Building opened in San Francisco; construction completed in 1903; tower 235 feet high modeled after Giralda Tower at Seville, Spain.

You can visit the Ferry Building on a walking tour of the waterfront.

1899

August 24:
California Volunteers first regiment returned from Philippines.

1900

April 30:
Because it was a navigation hazard, Shag Rock in the Bay blown up.

July 6:
First transcontinental passenger train of Santa Fe arrived from Chicago to Point Richmond, then via ferry *Ocean Wave* to San Francisco.

Santa Fe still ferries railcars to Pier 52 on the south waterfront.

November 26:
Light added to manual fog bell station on Angel Island's Point Knox.

Now a state park, you can visit Angel Island by ferry and see the bell.

1901

February 22:
Inbound from the Orient, the *City of Rio de Janeiro* foundered on Fort Point ledge and sank with great loss of life.

August 15:
Arch Rock in the Bay blown up with 30 tons of nitrogelatin.

November 30:
Collision off Alcatraz of North Pacific Coast RR ferryboats *San Rafael* and *Sausalito*, with loss of *San Rafael*. Jack London vividly portrayed this incident in his novel *The Sea Wolf*.

You will find the book romantic and exciting, if you read, or re-read it.

1902

• Dredging completed that separated Alameda from the mainland to form an island.

1903

July 11:
Second Oakland Harbor Lighthouse began operation offshore from Oakland Mole. It was later moved to Embarcadero Cove.

You can find it by dining at Quinn's Lighthouse restaurant.

October 26:
The first *Yerba Buena* inaugurated Key System ferry service, carrying the electric train passengers from Oakland to San Francisco.

1904

• Defense batteries on Angel Island were completed.

1905

July 8:
Land on Angel Island allotted to Dept. of Commerce and Labor for immigration detention station.

Now a state park, you can visit Angel Island by ferry.

Late:
Southampton Shoal Lighthouse began operation.

1906

April 18:
Earthquake started the San Francisco Fire.

1907

August 26:
At Aquatic Park, San Francisco, Harry Houdini escaped from chains underwater in 57 seconds.

1908

May 6:
Great White Fleet, one of Teddy Roosevelt's big sticks, arrived in Bay.

July 7:
Great White Fleet departed from Bay.

December 6:
Southern Pacific's ferryboat *Oakland* (the second one) struck the *Newark*, but both boats survived.

1909

• First bridge of any kind, Southern Pacific's Dumbarton railroad bridge, constructed over the South Bay.

• Construction completed on main prison building on Alcatraz.

• Batteries on Angel Island decommissioned as obsolete.

April 1:
Direct ferry route from Tiburon to San Francisco discontinued.

May 22:
San Francisco's first fireboat, *David Scannell*, launched; followed within a month by the *Dennis T. Sullivan*.

December 6:
Construction began on seawall at foot of Mission Street in San Francisco.

1910

January 15:
Carquinez Strait Lighthouse first shown over the Bay.

August 22:
Last transcontinental railroad to reach San Francisco Bay, Western Pacific, carried first load of passengers by borrowed ferryboat *Yerba Buena* from Oakland terminal to San Francisco Ferry Building.

1911

January 18:
Eugene Ely landed aeroplane on deck of USS *Pennsylvania* on San Francisco Bay.

January 31:
Congress passed resolution that named San Francisco the exposition city to celebrate the opening of the Panama Canal.

1913

January 1:
Thousands took part in ground breaking for Machinery Hall of the Panama-Pacific Exposition at Harbor View.

December 8:
Construction began on Palace of Fine Arts for 1915 exposition.

You can visit the restored Palace of Fine Arts in the Marina District of San Francisco. Inside the Exploratorium there is an exhibit with pictures of the Exposition as it was in 1915.

1914

February 23:
''Year Before Opening'' celebration held on exposition site.

February 28:
Construction and erection began for Tower of Jewels for exposition.

August 29:
First vessel arrived in the Bay via Panama Canal, the steamship *Arizonan*.

1915

February 20:
Panama-Pacific International Exposition opened.

You can visit the restored Palace of Fine Arts in the Marina District of San Francisco. Inside the Exploratorium there is an exhibit with pictures of the Exposition as it was in 1915.

May 1:
Richmond-San Rafael Ferry Company service commenced on the *Ellen*.

September 20:
Submarine cable laid across the Golden Gate.

December 4:
Panama-Pacific International Exposition closed.

1918

March 14:
First seagoing concrete ship launched, built by San Francisco Shipbuilding Co.

July 4:
Issaquah put into service, inaugurated Rodeo-Vallejo Ferry Co.

December 14:
Off Pt. Pinole in dense fog, the Monticello Steamship Co. ferry *General Frisbie* collided with the *Sehome* and sank her with no lives lost.

December 31:
Ferry Building siren sounded for first time at 5 pm.

1922

May 28:
Aven J. Hanford began operation on Hyde Street to Sausalito run of the Golden Gate Ferry Co.

You can visit the old ferry slip of Hyde Street Pier which is now a Maritime Historic Park, and you can also take a ferry ride to Sausalito.

1927

● Golden Gate Ferry began route from Hyde Street (San Francisco) to foot of University Avenue, Berkeley.

January 15:
Dumbarton Bridge opened, first auto bridge over the Bay.

April 24:
Golden Gate Ferry's *Golden City* sunk in collision.

May 1:
Carquinez Bridge, second auto bridge on the Bay, opened, terminating operations of Rodeo-Vallejo Ferry Co.

1928

February 18:
Largest explosion in Western U.S. obliterated Guano Island off Little Coyote Point for construction of San Mateo-Hayward Bridge.

1929

March 3:
Third auto bridge on Bay, San Mateo-Hayward, opened.

August 25:
Graf Zeppelin arrived from Tokyo on circumnavigation voyage, and glided over San Francisco Bay on way to Los Angeles.

1931

February 20:
Congress granted the state of California the right to construct a bridge from Rincon Hill to Yerba Buena to Oakland.

June 3:
Goat Island's early Spanish name, Yerba Buena, restored by the US Geographic Board.

June 17:
First construction contracts for Golden Gate Bridge awarded.

1933

January 5:
With the digging of pit for the Marin anchorage, construction started on the Golden Gate Bridge.

April 22:
Passenger ferry service from Santa Fe's Pt. Richmond terminal to San Francisco ended.

October 12:
Alcatraz Island made a federal prison.

You can visit Alcatraz on guided tours from Pier 43 in San Francisco.

1934

January 1:
Government officially took possession of Alcatraz as a federal prison.

July 5:
Clash between police and waterfront strikers, "Bloody Thursday," left two dead and hundreds injured.

July 12:
US Army disciplinary barracks abandoned on Alcatraz Island.

July 19:
Longshoremen ended strike and went back to work.

1936

February 11:
Pumping was started to build Treasure Island.

May 20:
Cable spinning completed on span of Golden Gate Bridge.

Summer:
Near present-day Larkspur Ferry Terminal, a "Plate of Brasse" was found. The authenticity of this 5" x 8" metal marker attesting to the discovery of San Francisco Bay by Sir Francis Drake has been questioned by authorities.

The "Plate of Brasse" is on display at the Bancroft Library, on the UC campus, Berkeley.

October 28:
Cardinal Eugenio Pacelli (later Pope Pius XII) blessed the San Francisco-Oakland Bay Bridge.

November 12:
Bay Bridge Fiesta began with opening of the bridge to traffic.

November 18:
Main span of Golden Gate Bridge joined.

1937

February 17:
Ten men died when a scaffold fell from beneath the Golden Gate Bridge.

May 27:
Golden Gate Bridge dedicated with "Pedestrian Day," and opened for traffic the next day.

Every day can be pedestrian day. You can walk across the Golden Gate from vista points at either end of the Bridge.

August 26:
Treasure Island pumping ended.

1938

July 24:
Put out of business by the bridge, the last boat of the Southern Pacific-Golden Gate Ferries, the *Yosemite,* crossed from Sausalito to Hyde Street Pier.

Now a Maritime Historic Park, the old boats at Hyde Street Pier may be visited daily.

October 1:
Blackie, a horse, swam the Golden Gate in 23½ minutes to settle a bet.

1939

January 14:
Key System and others started running electric trains from East Bay to San Francisco on the Bay Bridge. The same day all of Southern Pacific and Key System's boats ceased commuter ferry service from Oakland and Alameda.

January 22:
Aquatic Park dedicated.

You can visit the beach, fishing pier and partake of the sightseeing possibilities at the park, across from Ghirardelli Square in San Francisco.

February 18:
Golden Gate International Exposition opened on Treasure Island.

You can visit the Navy Museum on Treasure Island and see exhibits about the building of the island and the world's fair held there.

October 29:
Golden Gate International Exposition closed for first year.

1940

February 9:
Retired ferryboat *Yosemite* (renamed *Argentina*) sailed for Uruguay.

May 25:
Golden Gate International Exposition reopened on Treasure Island.

You can visit the Navy Museum on Treasure Island and see exhibits about the building of the island and the world's fair held there.

September 29:
Golden Gate International Exposition closed for final time.

1941

February 28:
Last run of old-time walking-beam ferryboats to Marin, the Northwestern Pacific's *Eureka* crossed from San Francisco to Sausalito.

You can visit the *Eureka,* tied up at Hyde Street Pier, the San Francisco Maritime Historic Park.

April 1:
Navy took over Treasure Island.

1946

January 9:
Construction on Mission Rock burned off so that the rock could become the base for extension of Pier 50.

May 2-4:
Revolt by prisoners of Alcatraz, two guards and three prisoners died.

June:
Golden Gate Bridge closed briefly for security reasons.

August 26:
Sailors Union of the Pacific voted to tie up port with a strike.

August 28:
Discharge operations of Army base on Angel Island ended.

1949

April 15:
Robert L. Niles, first person to make a stunt leap from Golden Gate Bridge.

1950

August 25:
Hospital ship USS *Benevolence* sank after collision with freighter *Luckenbach* in heavy fog off the Golden Gate.

1951

May 27:
San Francisco Maritime Museum opened.

You can visit this collection of nautical artifacts and Bay history across from Ghirardelli Square.

June 10:
Goat Island officially renominated Yerba Buena Island.

December 1:
Golden Gate Bridge closed to traffic for three hours because of high winds.

1954

• Part of Angel Island dedicated as a State Park.

You can visit the park by ferry.

1955

July 19:
The old square-rigger grain ship *Balclutha* was tied up at Pier 43.

You can visit this floating museum on San Francisco's north waterfront.

October 16:
Youngest swimmer to cross the Golden Gate, Dick Poe did it in thirty-eight minutes when he was nine years old.

1956

September 1:
Richmond-San Rafael Bridge opened; eliminated Richmond-San Rafael ferry service, last run of old familiar auto ferryboats on the Bay.

You can see the remains of the old ferry terminal by visiting Red Rock Marina at the Richmond end of the bridge.

1957

June 4:
California legislature approved creation of BART District (rapid transit) of five counties.

August:
Western Pacific's railcar ferry *Las Plumas,* a modern ferryboat with nostalgic, grandiose proportions, started hauling cars from Oakland to San Francisco (she arrived in the Bay July 11).

Still in operation and ties up at the foot of Army Street in San Francisco.

October 12:
Statue of Christopher Columbus atop Telegraph Hill in San Francisco (by Italian sculptor Vittorio di Colbertaldo) dedicated.

You can see it at vista point on top of the Hill.

November 14:
First meeting of board officially established BART District.

1958

• Second Carquinez Bridge span construction completed.

April 20:
Key System's electric trains replaced by petroleum-puffing buses at 3 am.

July 29:
Last ferry run of Southern Pacific's boats that met train passengers in Oakland and carried them to San Francisco, the oldest ferry route on the Bay.

1959

July 10:
California legislature authorized use of Bay Bridge tolls to finance construction of BART's transbay tube.

1960

April 27:
Golden Gate Bridge closed for three minutes for official motorcade of French President Charles de Gaulle.

June 3:
India Bear (PFEL) plowed into the Lime Point Lighthouse beneath the Golden Gate Bridge (ship pulled off rocks, no lives lost).

1962

March:
Tiburon-San Francisco route ferry service revived.

November 6:
BART's bond issue approved by the voters.

December:
Almost entire acreage of Angel Island transferred from federal government for State Park.

1963

March 22:
Alcatraz Island evacuated as a prison.

October 5:
Hyde Street Pier in San Francisco reopened as a State Historic Park.

October 12:
Traffic went into one-way operation on each deck of Bay Bridge at 4 am.

1964

March 8:
Band of Sioux Indians claimed ownership of Alcatraz Island.

1965

August 19:
Coast Guard crew left Mile Rock Lighthouse so that demolition could begin.

1966

September 26:
First icebreaker to enter San Francisco Bay, the *Staten Island.*

1967

July 4:
Fireworks celebration held at Candlestick Park for first time, moved from Marina Green.

September 30:
Restored Palace of Fine Arts of the Panama-Pacific Exposition of 1915 reopened.

1968

October 19:
Tolls collected southbound only on Golden Gate Bridge.

1969

November 20:
Band of Indians seized and occupied Alcatraz Island.

1970

February 28:
Bicycles permitted for first time to cross Golden Gate Bridge.

March 24:
Steam paddleboat SS *Eppleton Hall* arrived on Bay from Newcastle-upon-Tyne, England.

May 31:
Indians celebrated ''Liberation Day'' on Alcatraz.

June 1:
Five buildings on Alcatraz destroyed by accidental fire.

July 20:
First baby born on Alcatraz Island, during Indian occupation.

August 15:
Sausalito-San Francisco ferry service revived by Golden Gate Bridge District's *Golden Gate*.

1971

January 19:
Two Standard Oil tankers collided just inside the Golden Gate and released millions of gallons of oil into Bay.

April 14:
Fort Point dedicated as National Historic Site.

June 11:
U.S. marshals recaptured Alcatraz Island from Indians.

July 1:
Golden Gate Bridge paid off its $35 million bond debt.

December 14:
Golden Gate Bridge lights out all night due to power failure.

1972

October 12:
Congress established Golden Gate National Recreation Area, which includes Bay shoreline, headlands of the Golden Gate, and Alcatraz Island.

November 9:
Golden Gate Bridge closed for two hours to install scaffolding.

December 18:
Ferry Building siren replaced by electronic chimes with Westminster Peal.

1973

January:
Incident where almost 200,000 gallons of oil leaked into the water on the Oakland Estuary.

October 14:
Dedication of Golden Gate Promenade, recreational pathway on San Francisco's north waterfront.

October 26:
National Park Service started guided tours of Alcatraz from Pier 41.

1974

September 16:
BART began regular transbay train service.

1976

December 11:
Golden Gate Bridge District inaugurated ferry service, Larkspur-San Francisco, with GT *Marin*.

1977

February:
Considerable amount of oil leaked into Bay waters from a ship at San Francisco's Bethlehem Shipyard.

September 15:
Crane being towed northward between Yerba Buena Island and Oakland struck one of Bay Bridge's main horizontal supports. If the crash had occurred only 50 feet away, the bridge might have collapsed.

1978

April 1:
World's largest passenger liner, Cunard Line's *Queen Elizabeth 2*, arrived in Bay for the first time.

April 7:
Last run of exclusively passenger ship service under US flag, Pacific Far East Line's *Mariposa* returned to her home port of San Francisco.

May 3:
Skeletal ribs of the burnt out hulk of the *Niantic*, one of the original Gold Rush ships of 1849 which was converted to shoreside use, were found during excavation for new office building in San Francisco.

Marker will be incorporated in the completed building at Sansome and Clay streets.

August:
Largest ship ever to enter San Francisco Bay, supertanker *American Spirit* (265,000 tons, 2,000 feet long), moored at Hunters Point shipyard.

September 25:
Golden Gate swim by Lorelei Morino, twelve years old, in slightly over forty minutes.

November 12:
For the first time, two lanes of the Bay Bridge were blocked to allow a seven-mile running event, from Oakland to San Francisco.

Walking the Decks

The life and history of San Francisco Bay has come from its shipping. Any log that records the story will be incomplete, but the representative selection of old ships to be found on the Bay is a living chronicle of our maritime fortunes. This remarkable collection of outdoor artifacts, most of them still afloat, forms an open-air museum where, on many of the vessels, you can walk the decks and explore below. This collection of tradition is concentrated near Fisherman's Wharf in San Francisco, but you can find indications of it scattered in all parts of the Bay. The ships range from sail to steam, from small scows to huge ferries. Perhaps the ferry lore depicted here is most vivid and realistic because the boats and routes are within recent memory. Wherever the maritime past is found, it adds still another dimension to waterfront life.

For another outdoor collection, see Castro Point Railway in the section *Collections of History.*

San Francisco Maritime Historic Park (Hyde Street Pier)

At the foot of Hyde Street, adjacent to Aquatic Park, San Francisco. Open every day 10 am to 6 pm (winter 10 am-5 pm). (556-6435)

The admirable maritime assemblage of five vessels at the Hyde Street Pier rivals ''seaports'' in other parts of the country. The collection of historic ships was built up by the Maritime Museum and the State Parks Department. Now the Park is part of the federal government's National Maritime Museum in the Golden Gate National Recreation Area. The Hyde Street Pier was a ferry slip of the Golden Gate Ferry Company. Commuters and cars embarked for Sausalito, starting in 1922, and a few years later for Berkeley. The operation was taken over by Southern Pacific/ Golden Gate Ferries and continued until both routes were ended; the last run to Sausalito was in

1938. Upon this pier are perched other nautical artifacts from the seafaring days of coast and Bay — superstructures, an ''Ark'' from Tiburon, name-boards, hardware and other ship parts. But the highlight of the Park is the carefully restored ships, three of which you can clamber aboard and explore the decks. There are photos and marine exhibits all over the vessels, and on the ferry are vintage motor vehicles. Free electronic commentary gadgets provide a portrayal that matches the phrase, ''iron men on wooden ships.'' Ranger-guided tours are offered twice daily.

The wooden ferryboat *Eureka* was permanently retired in 1957, the last walking-beam side-wheeler to operate in this country. Her last days were spent on the Southern Pacific passenger run, meeting the transcontinental trains at the Oakland Mole and bringing the passengers to San Francisco's Ferry Building. The railroad company presented her to the maritime park in 1960. Before she went to work for the SP in 1941, she had been a Northwestern Pacific boat. In 1920 she was taken out of the water and completely rebuilt to carry 2,300 passengers and 120 automobiles. At the same time, her name was changed to the *Eureka*, and the Northwestern Pacific put her on the Sausalito-San Francisco run for nearly twenty years. Originally named the *Ukiah* when built in 1890 in Tiburon, she was a double-ended railcar and passenger ferry for the San Francisco & North Pacific RR. A few years later the Northwestern Pacific took over the route, but the ferryboat lasted on the Tiburon-San Francisco run for thirty years. So you can see that the *Eureka* is a celebrity, representing nearly ninety years of Bay history, and running on three of the most important routes on the Bay.

The *C. A. Thayer* is a three-masted lumber schooner, built in 1895 across Humboldt Bay from Eureka. She was rescued off the beach in Puget Sound in 1956 and brought to San Francisco Bay. Her last year under sail was 1950, at that time the last sailing ship in commercial

use on the Pacific Coast. Since 1912 she had been, off and on, in the fishery business (salmon and cod) with some time out for wartime service with the Army. Besides these voyages to Alaska and the Bering Sea, she made a few trans-Pacific runs. Originally built for the lumber trade, she traveled to the Pacific Northwest and brought millions of board feet back to the Bay and other California ports. Somewhat bigger than the ''doghole'' schooners that twenty years earlier had made California's north coast redwoods justifiably famous, she is representative of some five hundred similar ships in coastwise trade at the turn of the century.

To replace the sailing schooners, ships like the *Wapama* were built to handle lumber cargo. This wooden-hulled steam schooner was built in Oregon in 1915 to do exactly the same job as the *C. A. Thayer*, but with the addition of berthage for as many as thirty passengers. The *Wapama* was saved from a ship junkyard when acquired for the park in 1958. She had been in general cargo and passenger service between Puget Sound and Alaska before her career ended in 1947. During

the 1930s she had carried the same shipments from San Pedro to San Francisco. When she originally went into service, she was one of some two hundred steamers that carried on lumber trade with ports, large and small, on the Pacific Coast. It is fascinating to see the cabins for crew and passengers, and to try to imagine where the cargo was put when carrying a load of one million board feet of lumber.

The *Alma* is the sweetheart of the San Francisco waterfront. She gained this special place in our affections because she is a San Francisco Bay scow schooner. In fact she is the last of the scow schooners, hard-working boats that carried the everyday commerce of the Bay. About 1900 there were more than three hundred scows in and out of all the ports and landings on the Bay — creeping up the creeks, drifting through the Delta and sliding down the sloughs. These small sailing craft were built fat and flat to carry tremendous cargoes, primarily hay, but also brick, coal, sand

and gravel, lumber, and grain. In 1958 the *Alma* was retired, and the next year she was pulled off a mudbank in Alviso and restored to sailing splendor. For the last thirty years of her practical life, she had been dismasted and was used in the South Bay as a salt barge and later as an oyster shell dredge. During this time she survived fire, grounding and a collision with the Dumbarton Bridge. Built at the historic Anderson and Cristofani shipyard (which still operates at Hunters Point) in 1891, she originally freighted bulk cargo all over the Bay until 1917. She was named for Alma Peterson Sooman whose father had a fleet of scow schooners. *Alma* is one of the ships you cannot wander on at the Hyde Street Pier, but you can see her tied up to the *C. A. Thayer*, and also watch as she proudly paces the Master Mariners' Regatta around the Bay. If you would like to sail on and help maintain the ship, membership in the Friends of the *Alma* (Hyde Street Pier, 2905 Hyde Street, San Francisco 94109) provides the opportunity.

The *Hercules* was brought to Hyde Street Pier in 1972. Still privately owned, this is one of the ships that cannot be visited. The ocean-going steam tug can be seen moored next to the *Eureka*, where work is under way on restoration and making the engine run. Support is needed in the effort to purchase her and make her a permanent part of the park. Built in 1907 in New Jersey, she came to the Pacific Coast with her sister ship, the *Goliah*. Her ocean-going towboat work included trips to ports on the Pacific Coast as far north as Puget Sound, and to Mexico and Hawaii, towing barges, log rafts and sailing ships. She even towed caissons south for use in building the Panama Canal. In 1918 the company that owned the *Hercules* was taken over by Red Stack Tugboats, and later she was sold to San Francisco's favorite mayor, "Sunny Jim" Rolph. Then she was acquired by the Western Pacific RR, and spent nearly forty years hauling barges of railroad cars around the Bay before retirement in 1962.

Balclutha

Berthed at Pier 43, foot of Powell Street at The Embarcadero, San Francisco. Open 9 am-10 pm every day. Admission: adults $2, juniors $1, unaccompanied children 25¢. (982-1886)

The most distinguished of the historic ships found on San Francisco Bay is the *Balclutha*. A prominent north waterfront landmark, the square-rigger was built in Glasgow in 1886. The three-masted sailing ship was engaged in the Cape Horn trade for many years in the 1880s and '90s, bringing manufactures and coal around South America to the Golden Gate and returning to Europe, holds filled with grain from California's Central Valley. When this traffic diminished, she spent a few years in trans-Pacific lumber trade. Then the ship became part of the Star-fleet of the Alaska Packers Association. Renamed the *Star of Alaska*, she plied the waters between San Francisco and Alaska as a salmon cannery vessel for nearly the first thirty years of this century. For the next twenty years of her life, she haunted the coast of California with a new name, *Pacific Queen*, sailing as a carnival ship and appearing in Hollywood movies.

Finally rescued by the San Francisco Maritime Museum in 1954, the windjammer survives as a worthy representative of the hundreds of vanished vessels of the grain fleet. The labor unions and shipping industry of the Bay contributed to her restoration, so that the *Balclutha* could be berthed on the waterfront as a museum ship, open for public visits. Since 1978 she has been part of the National Maritime Museum of the GGNRA. The steel-hulled vessel has ship artifacts on exhibit 'tween decks and is brightly lit at night to contribute a note of reality to the Fisherman's Wharf district. The saga of the *Balclutha* is appropriate, authentic living evidence of San Francisco's maritime heritage.

Eppleton Hall

Usually berthed outboard of *Balclutha* at Pier 43, San Francisco. Not open to the public.

For a formidable type of specialized historic ship, the *Eppleton Hall* is a choice example. She is a paddle tug with two masts, brought to San Francisco Bay in 1970 from Newcastle-upon-Tyne, England. This side-wheeler with venerable side-lever steam engines is a type that brought 49ers to San Francisco from Panama during Gold Rush days (although she was built in 1924).

If you are an extreme old ship freak, you might be interested in becoming a member of the Friends of the *Eppleton Hall* Society (c/o SF Maritime Museum, Aquatic Park at foot of Polk Street, San Francisco 94109). Membership supports work on the ship and provides the opportunity to be a crew member on Bay voyages.

Vicar of Bray

Exhibition of the *Vicar of Bray* is, at this time, just a gleam in a museum director's eye. The hulk discovered some ten years ago in the Falkland Islands in the Atlantic east of the Strait of Magellan, where the cold climate preserved the original ship so that it is eighty-five percent intact. The small wooden English bark was built in 1841 at Whitehaven, and engaged in the copper ore trade, Chile to England, until she was laid up in the Falklands, probably in 1880. This three-masted windjammer has been authenticated as the only survivor of the Gold Rush fleet which consisted of hundreds of vessels that sailed into San Francisco Bay in 1849.

Properly displayed, the *Vicar of Bray* would be one of the most celebrated historic ships in the world — one of the armada that carried the argonauts to the Gold Rush and California into US history. Public and political support are needed to bring the bark back from the Falklands and, according to Maritime Museum plans, install her in the Haslett Warehouse, near the cable car turntable in San Francisco.

Golden Hinde II

No longer berthed at Pier 41 in San Francisco. Since 1977 she has been tied up at a shipyard on Embarcadero Cove, Oakland. Not open to the public.

The controversial re-creation of Francis Drake's flagship, the *Golden Hinde,* was initially berthed on the north waterfront in 1974. The wrangle concerns the authenticity of the replica. No records or description of the vessel exist, so it was built on the strength of inspired speculation and research into sixteenth century maritime ways. Certainly there is nothing antique about the three-masted, high-sterned ship, since it was built in England and completed in 1973. However, it appears that lack of public interest was the reason the vessel was prematurely retired to Oakland. Perhaps it was because the re-creation was a colorful but not altogether satisfactory ship to visit, and perhaps English history of 1579 (even if it is also California history) was too remote for San Francisco visitors.

Drake began his circumnavigation voyage with a fleet of five ships; his flagship was the *Pelican.* By the time he rounded the southern end of South America, four of the ships were gone, and he started the voyage north in the tiny flagship, rechristened the *Golden Hinde.* On this solitary foray, besides disrupting Spanish treasure traffic in the Pacific, Drake landed somewhere in Marin County, California, providing the sparks for yet another controversy.

A sidelight: digging is currently under way at London's Thameside in an effort to discover the remnants of the *Golden Hind* (as it is spelled in England), the first English ship to circle the globe. As a reward for this feat, the vessel was on display at Deptford Dockyard from 1581 to about 1650, before deteriorating and disappearing in the mud.

Dolphin P. Rempp

This ship is parked at the south end of The Embarcadero, at Pier 42, in San Francisco. It now serves as a dry-land restaurant, so information about it is found in the section *Dining and Drinking on the Waterfront.*

Master Mariners' Regatta

The Master Mariners' Regatta is a good opportunity to see some of the vintage sailing ships, most of them private yachts, that are berthed at various locations on the Bay. Traditionally the parade of old-time ships is headed by the *Alma* from the San Francisco Maritime Historic Park. Refer to the section *Festivals and Events* for more information.

Ferryboats

Of the fleet of hundreds of ferryboats of some twenty-odd lines that plied the Bay waters for more than a hundred years, there are a pitiful few left. Scattered at berths in all parts of the Bay, in various conditions, are just one more than a dozen that can be ferreted out and seen. Other than the *Eureka,* which is mentioned above at the Maritime Historic Park, there is only one that can be visited, and only under certain circumstances. Also noted here are some of the old ferry slips and a listing of the boats that were sent away to be born again elsewhere.

Sausalito seems to be the graveyard of Bay ferryboats. There are five beached at the Gate Five houseboat haven at the north end of Sausalito. The hulks are more or less deteriorated, some used as residences, including some of the oldest surviving ferries.

Vallejo: Side-wheeler, built in 1879; service on Mare Island Ferry; retired 1948.
City of Seattle: Side-wheeler, built in 1888; service on Martinez-Benicia and Mare Island Ferry; dismantled 1948.

Issaquah: Known as the "Squash"; built in 1914; service on Rodeo-Vallejo, Martinez-Benicia and Mare Island Ferry; retired to Sausalito since 1948.

Charles Van Damme: Side-wheeler, built in 1916; service on Richmond-San Rafael and Martinez-Benicia Ferry; after retirement in 1958 used as floating restaurant and night club in 1960s.

City of San Rafael: Side-wheeler, built in 1924; service on Richmond-San Rafael and Martinez-Benicia Ferry; largest of ferryboats beached at Sausalito.

The *Garden City* is one of the ferryboats that was put to sporting use after retirement. It has been lying on the shore near Port Costa, slowly rotting away for nearly fifty years. Initially it was used as a fishing resort, and a recent plan was proposed to haul the superstructure to Fisherman's Wharf as a restaurant.

Garden City: This side-wheeler is one of the oldest survivors, built in 1879; service on South Pacific Coast and Southern Pacific ferries; retired 1929.

The *Fresno,* one of the more recent ferries, was sent to Puget Sound, and has returned. When service on the Bay was discontinued, the boat changed locale and name. In Washington she was known as the *Willapa.* Recently she came back to the Bay, and with her original name can be seen at the Martinez Marina. But she is not yet open to the public.

Fresno: Built in 1927, service on Southern Pacific and SP/Golden Gate Ferries; sent to Puget Sound in 1937, now returned home.

The *Sausalito* is another of the sporting ferryboats. It has been used as a private sports clubhouse near Antioch at the mouth of the San Joaquin River.

Sausalito: Side-wheeler, built in 1894; service on North Pacific Coast, North Shore, and Northwestern Pacific ferries; retired 1933.

The *Klamath* is a vintage vessel that has been wonderfully restored and remodeled to serve as the floating office and studio of the industrial design firm of

Walter Landor and Associates. Since rebuilding in 1964 she has been moored at The Embarcadero in San Francisco. There is a close-up view at the gate of Pier 5 where she is berthed, or a better look from the parking lot and fishing spot on Pier 7.

Klamath: Built in 1925; service on Southern Pacific, SP/Golden Gate, and Richmond-San Rafael Ferries; retired 1956.

The story of the *San Leandro,* one of the Bay's finest ferryboats, is supremely tragic. Built for the Key System, the boat ran until the end of the world's fair on Treasure Island. Then she was operated by the Southern Pacific and made the final run from the Ferry Building to the Oakland Pier to pick up transcontinental railroad passengers. In this role she was one of the last big, impressive ferries on the Bay when she made her last run in July 1958. Then she was maintained in serviceable condition until 1975 when the tragedy of fire struck. Now she sits as a burnt out case at San Francisco's Pier 42 at the south end of The Embarcadero.

San Leandro: Built in 1923; service on Key System and Southern Pacific ferries; retired 1958.

While not exactly a vintage boat, the *Las Plumas* is the one large ferry still crossing the Bay, reminiscent of old-time

operations. The Western Pacific RR runs a railcar ferry much as several lines did for years before and after the turn of the century. The only self-propelled car ferry on the West Coast, she has a capacity of sixteen cars, but she has one deficiency — she will only handle the old-fashioned fifty-foot boxcars. When she came down from the builders in Portland, Oregon, she replaced the prior tugboat and barge arrangement. (The retired tug, the *Hercules,* is now at the SF Maritime Historic Park.) The modern-looking railcar ferry crosses the Bay from San Francisco to the Western Pacific Mole in Oakland, where the industrial district precludes any view of her operation. You may see her crossing the Bay early in the morning, and she usually ties up at the railyards at the end of Twenty-fifth Street in San Francisco between ten and noon. In the afternoons, you can find her by following Army Street to the end, about three blocks past Third Street, and then turning left into the large gravel parking lot.

Las Plumas: Self-propelled car ferry, built in 1957 for Western Pacific RR; still in operation.

Besides the one at Hyde Street Pier, there is one other ferryboat that you can actually visit, the *General Frank M. Coxe.* Originally built for the Army, she cruised between Alcatraz, Fort Mason, Angel Island and other posts. Very unferry-like in appearance, she had the lines of a harbor tour boat, which service she performed for several years after 1946. Then she became a floating restaurant, in 1955 in Stockton, and in 1958 as the "Showboat" at Jack London Square. Now beached in Burlingame near Airport Boulevard, she is the Diamond Showboat restaurant. (If you want to visit, you should check the information in *Dining and Drinking on the Waterfront*.)

General Frank M. Coxe: Built in 1921, service to US Army; retired from ferry and excursion boat work in 1955.

Of the many ferry routes that operated during the long and colorful heyday of paddle wheels on San Francisco Bay, only two have been revived. You can find evidence of four (I guess, four and a half) terminals from these former ferry lines. Hyde Street Pier is now preserved as the home of the San Francisco Maritime Historic Park with its collection of classic ships tied up at the ferry berths. Golden Gate Ferries crossed from the pier to Sausalito and Berkeley until the late 1930s.

The terminal at San Francisco's Ferry Building is so completely re-arranged and modernized that it bears no resemblance to any ferry-fancier's remembrance, so it can't really count. The only similarity of the former terminal to the modern ferry operation is the location.

In Sausalito the ferry slip is the same, probably even the original pilings. Currently, the Golden Gate Bridge District's ferry service runs to Sausalito from San Francisco.

The long wharf thrusting into the Bay almost three miles from the Berkeley Marina was, in the 1920s and '30s, the pier for the Southern Pacific/Golden Gate Ferries. It was extended across the shallows to deep water, and cars would sometimes be waiting in line all the way back to the shoreline. Now it has been chopped off, about one-third is the Berkeley fishing pier. You can walk to the end and see the decaying remnant across the gap of water.

Another ferry terminal, just north of the Richmond-San Rafael Bridge, is now occupied by the Red Rock Marina. A visit to the marina reveals some buildings, a gateway and the pier of the Richmond-San Rafael Ferry which ceased operations in 1956.

Expatriate Ferryboats

Many of San Francisco Bay's ferryboats were sent elsewhere to continue their careers when their days on the Bay were done. The bridges that connected all points of the Bay region and the automobile traffic they carried killed the ferries. Now, in fair play, the ferries need to kill the bridges. Most of the boats shipped out in 1937, but a few stayed until the early '40s, and a couple hung on until 1956.

At least a dozen ferryboats went to Puget Sound. Some may still be sailing the waters of the Pacific Northwest. A couple have returned to San Francisco Bay, including the *Fresno* mentioned above.

Golden Poppy: Built in 1927, service on Golden Gate and Southern Pacific/GG Ferries; went north 1937, renamed *Chetzemoka*, in service until 1973; lost at sea while being towed back for display in SF, summer 1977.

Asbury Park: Built in 1903, service on Monticello Steamship; renamed *City of Sacramento* (1925), service on Golden Gate and Southern Pacific/GG Ferries; went to Puget Sound 1942, renamed *Kahloke*; went to British Columbia 1961, renamed *Langdale Queen*.

San Mateo: Built in 1922, service on Southern Pacific and SP/Golden Gate Ferries; went north 1940.

Shasta: Built in 1922, service on Southern Pacific and SP/Golden Gate Ferries; went to Puget Sound 1940 for service as ferry; later moved to Portland as floating restaurant, renamed *River Queen*.

Golden State: Built in 1926, service on Golden Gate and Southern Pacific/GG Ferries; went north 1938, renamed *Kehloken*.

Golden Age: Built in 1928, service on Golden Gate and Southern Pacific/GG Ferries; went north 1937, renamed *Klahanie*.

Lake Tahoe: Built in 1927, service on Southern Pacific and SP/Golden Gate Ferries; went north 1937, was renamed *Illahee*.

Mendocino: Built in 1927, service on Northwestern Pacific and Southern Pacific/Golden Gate Ferries; went north 1937, renamed *Nisqually*.

Peralta: Built in 1927, service on Key System; went to Puget Sound, rebuilt 1933 as *Kalakala*.

Redwood Empire: Built in 1927, service on Northwestern Pacific and Southern Pacific/Golden Gate Ferries; went north 1937, renamed *Quinault*.

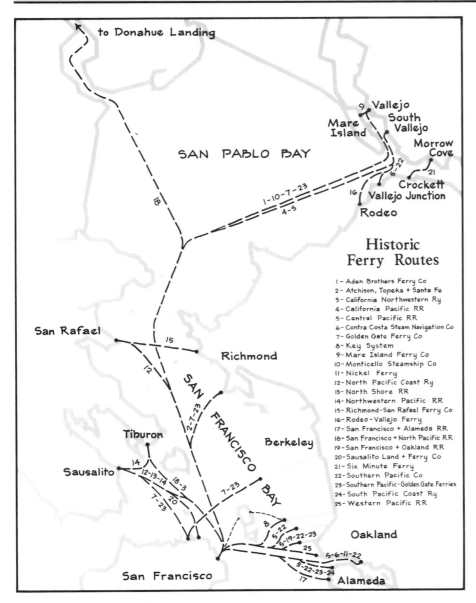

Historic Ferry Routes

1 – Aden Brothers Ferry Co
2 – Atchison, Topeka + Santa Fe
3 – California Northwestern Ry
4 – California Pacific RR
5 – Central Pacific RR
6 – Contra Costa Steam Navigation Co
7 – Golden Gate Ferry Co
8 – Key System
9 – Mare Island Ferry Co
10 – Monticello Steamship Co
11 – Nickel Ferry
12 – North Pacific Coast Ry
13 – North Shore RR
14 – Northwestern Pacific RR
15 – Richmond-San Rafael Ferry Co
16 – Rodeo-Vallejo Ferry
17 – San Francisco + Alameda RR
18 – San Francisco + North Pacific RR
19 – San Francisco + Oakland RR
20 – Sausalito Land + Ferry Co
21 – Six Minute Ferry
22 – Southern Pacific Co
23 – Southern Pacific-Golden Gate Ferries
24 – South Pacific Coast Ry
25 – Western Pacific RR

Newark: Built in 1877, service on South Pacific Coast and Southern Pacific ferries; rebuilt as the second *Sacramento* (1923), continued with SP; went to Redondo Beach in 1956; used as fishing barge, anchored offshore in summer.

Edward T. Jeffery: Built in 1913, service on Western Pacific ferries; renamed *Feather River* (1930); went to Southern Pacific service, and renamed *Sierra Nevada* in 1933; service on SP, Key System and Richmond-San Rafael Ferry; went to San Pedro in 1956, used as waterfront shopping center; she was pounded to bits in the winter storms of 1978.

Golden West: Built in 1923, service on Golden Gate and Southern Pacific/GG Ferries; went to San Diego in 1939, renamed *North Island.*

Golden Shore: Built in 1927, service on Golden Gate and Southern Pacific/GG Ferries; went to Puget Sound in 1937, renamed *Elwha;* then went to San Diego in 1944, and renamed *Silver Strand.*

Santa Rosa: Built in 1927, service on Northwestern Pacific and Southern Pacific/GG Ferries; went north 1937, renamed *Enetai,* rebuilt with many physical changes; returned to Bay 1968, berthed on Oakland Estuary; involved in as yet unconsummated plan to berth her at SF's Ferry Building as museum, theater, night club and offices.

Stockton: Built in 1927, service on Southern Pacific and SP/Golden Gate Ferries; went north 1937, was renamed *Klickitat.*

Several ferryboats were sent the other direction, to serve various functions in Southern California.

Berkeley: Built in 1898, service on Southern Pacific ferries; sold 1958, berthed on Sausalito waterfront for nearly twenty years as "Trade Fair" store; in 1974 went to San Diego to be restored as part of their Maritime Museum.

Collections of History

Representation of the history of San Francisco Bay is found in many museums. Some have gathered reminders of a specific facet of this past, and others have tried to record a complete picture. Each one offers some understanding of the forces that developed the Bay.

An account of where to find some of the old ships and a collection of Bay vessels, an even more realistic way of looking at history, is found in the section *Walking the Decks*. For information on natural history, see *Ecology Collections*.

San Francisco Maritime Museum

Beach Street at the foot of Polk Street, in Aquatic Park across from Ghirardelli Square, San Francisco. Open 10 am to 5 pm every day. (556-8177)

Among the museums that deal with San Francisco Bay, the Maritime Museum is the gem of the crop. Devoted entirely to the nautical history of the Bay, it displays a first-class accumulation of artifacts of the days of sail and steam. The building was WPA-built in a salty, art-deco style, set above Aquatic Park, overlooking historic ships and the busiest part of the Bay — the perfect location for its seafaring treasure. The building seems almost navigable, as though you could weigh anchor and go scudding across the lagoon to wreak havoc among the yacht regattas on the Bay. But the exhibits inside the building are stark reality, the reality of bygone clipper ships, paddlewheels, coasting schooners, whaling barks, Gold Rush flotillas, walking beam ferryboats, Cape Horn square-riggers, and all the scows and tugs and fishing boats that made up the traffic of the Bay.

Downstairs in a big, light room with murals covering the walls are genuine relics of seagoing life — large anchors, looming bowsprits, decorative figureheads glowering from the walls, intriguing name-boards — all pulled off ships that were rotting in the Bay. Besides this, there are buoys and intricate models representing the steamship era.

Upstairs the captivating view of the Bay is complemented by more souvenirs of the waterfront as it once was. The photos and models depict the abandoned Gold Rush fleet mouldering in the harbor and the days when San Francisco Bay was one of the world's biggest ports and the gateway to the Orient. It is also edifying to consult the maps and photos to discover the original shoreline and find out how much of the waterfront has been filled.

It is entirely appropriate that the importance of the Bay in the development and growth of the region should be represented by this fine museum of marine mementos.

Exploratorium

In the Palace of Fine Arts, Lyon Street at Marina Boulevard, San Francisco. Open Wednesday through Sunday, 1 to 5 pm, and Wednesday evening, 7 to 9:30 pm. Donations requested. (563-7337)

The Palace of Fine Arts is a majestic monument, the remnant of the Panama-Pacific International Exposition of 1915. This "world's fair" celebrated the completion of the Panama Canal and honored the 400th anniversary of Balboa's discovery of the Pacific Ocean. The exposition was built on filled Bay-front land, and most of its buildings were taken down shortly after it closed. The Palace of Fine Arts remained. Built of plaster and burlap on a flimsy wood framework, it was taken down and completely reconstructed of concrete and steel in the 1960s, largely through the generosity of Walter S. Johnson. Inside the long curving building is the Exploratorium, a very involving collection of participatory exhibits of science and technology. However, and most important from the standpoint of this book, there is also a small niche devoted to the Exposition. Displayed are large colored architectural drawings, including the Tower of Jewels and the Arch of the Rising Sun. Together with photographs of the Palace of Fine Arts, they give you some idea of the size and splendor of this waterfront project of long ago.

Presidio Army Museum

In the Presidio, Lincoln Boulevard at Funston Avenue, San Francisco. Open 10 am-4 pm, closed Monday. (561-4115)

The Old Station Hospital, a white clapboard building, looking vaguely Victorian and well guarded by a collection of cannon from different eras, houses the Presidio Army Museum. The building, dating from 1857, is the oldest of US Army construction in the Presidio. Inside are two floors of displays presenting the history of the Army at the Golden Gate — regimental flags, mannequins with a parade of uniforms, military arms, the story of Letterman Hospital, and photomurals of Army life and times. Of particular interest are maps of Bay exploration and "San Francisco Coastal Defense, 1906." Also important is the charming diorama, a large display case with a model of the Spanish fortification at *Presidio de San Francisco,* established in 1776. The diorama originally appeared at the Treasure Island world's fair, and has now been restored.

Fort Point National Historic Site

At the end of Long Avenue and Marine Drive, beneath the south end of the Golden Gate Bridge, San Francisco. Open 10 am-5 pm every day. (556-1693)

Fort Point itself is a piece of history. It was constructed from 1853 to 1861 as a sentinel to defend the entrance to San Francisco Bay. The three floors of intricate brick arched casements and the top floor barbette, surrounding an open courtyard, mounted guns to repulse a seaborne invasion which never came. Interpretive tours and demonstrations conducted by National Park Rangers reveal the history of this fort. Or you can wander on your own to discover the dramatic views of the Golden Gate Bridge and the Bay, the 1864 lighthouse atop a stairwell and the historic exhibits in the rooms that housed powder magazines. The displays of models and photomurals portray *Castillo de San Joaquín,* the original Spanish fort on the site; guns and cannon that armed the fort; a flashing "defenders of the Bay" map; living conditions for the soldiers; and the role that Fort Point played in the construction of the Golden Gate Bridge.

San Francisco Public Library

San Francisco History Room on third floor, Main Library, Larkin and McAllister streets, Civic Center, San Francisco. Open 9 am to 6 pm, closed Sunday and Monday. (558-3949)

The display cases of the San Francisco History Room exhibit materials from the City Archives. From time to time the displays are changed. You can see pictures of the Expositions, photos of maritime activity, maps of the old waterfront and ship name-boards. Naturally, for anyone doing history research, the books, pamphlets, articles and clippings are a treasure chest of information.

Navy/Marine Corps Museum

At the Main Gate of Treasure Island, in the middle of the Bay, reached from either end of the Bay Bridge. Open 10 am-3:30 pm every day. (765-6056)

The Administration Building of the Golden Gate International Exposition, one of three buildings left from the fair, contains the Navy/Marine Corps Museum. The gate at Treasure Island has been moved so that the public has free access to a parking lot and can visit the museum. Under a gigantic mural are exhibits of uniforms, armaments, ship models and other records, all telling the story of the seagoing Armed Services in the Pacific. One of the exhibits is the third order Fresnel lens, over six feet tall, from Mile Rocks Lighthouse, just outside the Golden Gate. It was removed when the light was modernized. The museum also has a corner about Treasure Island itself. Photos of the dredging and

pumping that built the island and of construction of the Golden Gate International Exposition, as well as souvenirs and maps of the fair, are displayed in all their art-deco glory. The fair, celebrating the completion of the two central Bay bridges, was erected in 1938 and was open in 1939 and 1940. The Administration Building is another delightful remembrance of this significant chapter in the history of San Francisco Bay.

San Mateo County History Center

College of San Mateo, between Highways 280 and 101, off Highway 92 on West Hillsdale Boulevard, San Mateo. Open Monday through Friday, 9:30 am-4:30 pm, and Saturday 10:30 am-4:30 pm. Donations requested. (574-6441)

This small but refreshing museum with bright, interesting exhibits is in one end of the college's main building. The museum concentrates on the history of San Mateo County and, since much of this past was dependent on the Bay, the displays reflect the Bay's history also. The Costanoan Indians are represented — relics and utensils from shoreline shell mound villages, as well as a reconstructed tule boat used to navigate the Bay waters. A display shows the Spanish discovery of San Francisco Bay by Gaspar de Portolá which took place from a hill in San Mateo County. There is more about the period of Spanish settlement and Mexican rancho, and even a diorama of Mission San Francisco. After the Americans came, ports grew up on the Bay, initially for shipping products of redwood lumbering in the hills. Also shown are the lighthouse that protected vessels on the seacoast and the development of transportation routes in the county.

Oakland Museum

Oak Street at Tenth Street, between the Nimitz Freeway and Lake Merritt near the Lake Merritt BART Station, Oakland. Open Monday-Thursday, 10 am-5 pm; Friday, 10 am-10 pm; Saturday, 10 am-5 pm; Sunday 10 am-6 pm. Admission: 25¢ per gallery. (273-3401)

The Oakland Museum building is an architectural masterpiece. The plan and profile, galleries and gardens, and exhibition techniques make it one of the finest museum buildings in the entire country. The emphasis of the collections and exhibits is a comprehensive look at California, and the three gallery-floors are allotted the categories Art, History and Natural History. Each one of the galleries has brilliant displays with something to offer on the subject of San Francisco Bay. Art: an alcove of sailing scenes in oil, portraits of the schooner *Casco*, pictures of San Francisco and the Bay shoreline in the 1880s, and included among the photographs is a tugboat, "Launch of the *Monarch*." History: portraits and adornments of Indians, hunting and technology of the culture, and archaeological relics of food gathering and the investigations of "kitchen middens"; the time of Spanish exploration and settlement, with a map of the Port of San Francisco; maps and photos of shoreline settlement after the coming of the Americans; and the more recent past — an outstanding representation of Bay transportation, the port, ferryboat life, construction of the Bay Bridge, and both international expositions. Natural History: the "coastline" section is incomplete, but it is still good for bird identification and shows other shore life. The museum is worth a visit anytime, especially by a visitor to the Bay region.

Oakland Public Library

Jack London Room, Main Library, Oak Street at Fourteenth Street, Oakland. Open Tuesday through Saturday, noon-4 pm. (893-6723)

The Jack London Room has a collection that memorializes the author, who was the most famous habitué of Oakland's waterfront. The displays of books, manuscripts, letters, photographs and other personal items naturally highlight London's literary life. But you can find articles that describe his childhood roaming the Estuary, sneaking into saloons, pirating oysters in the Bay, and his later sailing and sealing adventures. All these activities were remembered later in his naturalistic stories, which contain many vivid incidents of San Francisco Bay life.

Alameda Historical Museum

In the basement of the Main Library, located on Oak Street at Santa Clara Avenue, Alameda. Open Wednesday afternoon, 1:30-4 pm, and Saturday, 11 am-4 pm. (Library 522-5413)

This is a small museum with glimpses of Alameda's past. One cabinet is filled with artifacts dug up from an Alameda shell mound when it was leveled for housing sites in 1908. The fine implements and shell ornaments found there are displayed alongside some items that are of European origin, thus proving the Indians trade with early settlers.

Castro Point Railway

Off Highway 17 at Point Molate exit, just before the toll plaza of the Richmond-San Rafael Bridge, Richmond. Open weekends; and they give rides on the rolling stock the first Sunday of the month, November through June, and on Memorial Day and the Fourth of July. (234-6473 or 653-0354)

The Castro Point Railway is a museum that is unique in the San Francisco Bay region. The hillside yard at the entrance to the Naval reservation is full of old railroad cars — freight cars, reefers, flat cars, tankers, passenger cars, mail cars, cabooses — in various stages of operability. Spectator interest is keenest in the locomotives — several steam engines, including an 1882 Central Pacific, and a couple of miniature diesels. On weekends you can wander and observe the cars, and perhaps watch restoration work. The most exciting experience occurs on a Sunday when the boilers are fired up and the steam trains are operating. Board the train at Point Molate Beach Park. The line runs two miles along the edge of the Bay, around Castro Point and Red Rock Marina, where buildings and a pier remain from Richmond-San Rafael Ferry service, to the bridge and return. For steam train buffs of the Bay region, this is the closest short line operation. There is a possibility that sometime in the future Castro Point Railway may move down the shore to a new home in George Miller Jr. Regional Shoreline at Point Richmond.

Marin County Historical Museum

At the entrance to Boyd Park, 1125 "B" Street at Mission Avenue, San Rafael. Open 1 to 4 pm, closed Monday and Tuesday. (454-8538)

The Marin County Historical Society is in an attractive little Victorian cottage. Besides items of general Marin history, there are some artifacts of Indian culture and many maps of various dates that depict San Francisco Bay. A display case illuminates the historical controversy surrounding the landing of Sir Francis Drake in Marin.

Marin Miwok Museum

In Miwok Park, 2200 Novato Boulevard at San Miguel Way, Novato. Open 10 am to 4 pm, closed Sunday and Monday. (897-4064)

The Miwok Indians inhabited Marin from prehistoric times. The Miwok Museum is devoted to the exhibition and study of the culture of the Coast Miwoks. You can find displays of baskets and food, specimens of stone tools, and artifacts from Marin shell mounds.

Commemorations of History

The words of commemorative markers present a picturesque slice of local history. Almost thirty sites have brief, suggestive accounts pertaining to San Francisco Bay.

Site of Shell Mound

"It is said that the Indians who came to this site camped just above the shoreline. The shells they threw aside from their catches of shellfish eventually covered some hundreds of thousands of square feet, marked by several cones. When the University of California excavated this site in the 1920s, they found that the mound consisted mostly of clam, mussel, and oyster shells, with a plentiful mixture of cockleshells."

No plaque, only Shellmound Street marks the spot in Emeryville.

Site of Shell Mound

"One thousand feet due west was a prehistoric mound, 400 feet long, 150 feet wide, 14 feet high. The remains of 450 Indians, with stone implements and shell ornaments, were found when the mound was opened in 1908."

Marker in Lincoln Park, Alameda.

Site of the Discovery of San Francisco Bay

"On October 31, 1769, Captain Gaspar de Portolá was camped by the creek at the south of this valley when scouting parties brought news of a body of water to the east. On November 4 the expedition advanced. Turning inland, the party climbed to the summit of Sweeney Ridge and beheld the Bay of San Francisco for the first time."

Marker at Highway One and Crespi Drive, Linda Mar District, Pacifica.

Portolá Expedition Camp

"The Portolá Expedition of 1769 camped near a lagoon now covered by San Andreas Lake on November 4. They camped here a second time on November 12, on their return trip."

Marker on Highway 280 above Millbrae facing San Andreas Lake.

Portolá Journey's End

"In 1769 the Portolá expedition of 63 men and 200 horses and mules camped near *El Palo Alto*, the tall tree. They had traveled from San Diego in search of Monterey but discovered instead the Bay of San Francisco. Finding the bay too large to go around, and deciding that Monterey had been bypassed, they ended the search and returned to San Diego."

Marker in El Camino Park, on El Camino Real in Palo Alto.

First Ship into San Francisco Bay

"On August 5, 1775, the Spanish packet *San Carlos*, under the command of Lieutenant Juan Manuel de Ayala, became the first ship to enter San Francisco Bay. A month and a half was spent in surveying the Bay from its southernmost reaches to the northern end of present-day Suisun Bay. The *San Carlos* departed September 18, 1775."

Marker at Aquatic Park on Beach Street in San Francisco.

Angel Island

"In 1775, the packet *San Carlos*, first known Spanish ship to enter San Francisco Bay, anchored in this cove while her commander, Lieut. Juan Manuel de Ayala, directed the first survey of the bay. This island, which Ayala named *Isla de los Angeles*, has been a Mexican rancho, a U.S. military post, a bay defense site, and a quarantine and immigration station."

Marker in Ayala Cove, on Angel Island State Park.

Entrance of the *San Carlos* into San Francisco Bay

"The first ship to enter San Francisco Bay, the *San Carlos* (Captain Ayala), dropped anchor off this point August 5, 1775, and Lieutenant Colonel Juan Bautista de Anza planted the cross on Cantil Blanco (White Cliff) on March 28, 1776. The first fortification, Castillo de San Joaquín, was completed December 8, 1794, by José Joaquín de Arrillaga, sixth Governor of California. In 1853 United States Army Engineers cut down the cliff and built Fort Point, renamed Fort Winfield Scott in 1882. This fort, a partial replica of Fort Sumter, is the only brick fort west of the Mississippi. Its seawall has stood undamaged for a hundred years."

Marker at Fort Point, beneath the Golden Gate Bridge in San Francisco.

Presidio of San Francisco

"Formally established on September 17, 1776, the San Francisco Presidio has been used as a military headquarters by Spain, Mexico, and the United States. It was a major command post during the Mexican War, Civil War, Spanish-American War, World Wars I and II, and the Korean War, and remains a symbol of United States authority in the Pacific."

Marker at Pershing Square, on Moraga Avenue in the Presidio.

Anza Expedition Camp

"Here on the banks of San Mateo Creek Captain J.B. de Anza camped March 29, 1776, after exploring the peninsula and selecting the sites for the Mission and Presidio of San Francisco. The party of families, soldiers, and priests on their way to establish San Francisco also camped here for three days, June 24-27, 1776."

Marker at Arroyo Court and Dartmouth Road, near Third Avenue off El Camino Real, San Mateo.

Mission San Francisco de Asís (Mission Dolores)

"The sixth mission to be founded was San Francisco de Asís. This mission was dedicated by Father Junípero Serra on October 9, 1776; construction of mission buildings was completed 1784. Mission Dolores has none of the usual arches, arcades, and towers which adorn the more elaborate sister missions, but nonetheless its massive simplicity makes it impressive."

Marker on the building at Dolores and Sixteenth streets, San Francisco.

Old Sites of Mission Santa Clara de Asís and Old Spanish Bridge

"The first mission in this valley, Mission Santa Clara de Thamien, was established at this site by Franciscan Padres Tomás de la Peña and Joseph Antonio Murgúia January 17, 1777. Here, at the Indian village of So-co-is-u-ka, they erected a cross and shelter for worship to bring Christianity to the Costanoan Indians."

Marker at Kifer Road and De la Cruz Boulevard, Santa Clara.

First Site of El Pueblo de San José de Guadalupe

"Under command of Lieutenant José Moraga, 14 settlers and their families, a company of 66 persons, founded El Pueblo de San José de Guadalupe on or near this spot November 29, 1777."

Marker on the grounds of Jefferson School, San Jose.

Mission San José

"On June 9, 1797, troops under Sergeant Pedro Amador, accompanied by Father Fermín Lasuén, set out from Santa Clara for the spot that the natives called Oroysom in the valley of San José. The following day a temporary chapel was erected, and on June 11 the father presidente 'raised and blessed the cross. In a shelter of boughs he celebrated holy mass.' On the 28th Fathers Isidoro Barcenilla and Agustín Merino arrived to take charge of the new Mission. The mission, except part of the padres' quarters, was completely destroyed in the earthquake of 1868."

Marker at Mission and Washington boulevards, Fremont.

Bateria San Jose in 1797

"The Spanish constructed on this site a gun battery known as Bateria San Jose, for the protection of La Yerba Buena anchorage. The anchorage was approximately a quarter of a mile to the east from this point and is now known as Aquatic Park."

Marker on a knoll at end of Franklin Street in Fort Mason, San Francisco.

Landing Place of Captain J. B. Montgomery

"In the early morning of July 9, 1846, 'when the water came up to Montgomery Street,' Commander John B. Montgomery landed near this spot from the US Sloop-of-War *Portsmouth* to raise the Stars and Stripes on the Plaza, now Portsmouth Square."

Marker is located on the side of a building at Montgomery and Clay, San Francisco.

Portsmouth Plaza

"Named for USS *Portsmouth*, commanded by Captain John B. Montgomery, after whom Montgomery Street was named. It was here on the plaza that Captain Montgomery first raised the American flag near the Mexican adobe custom house on July 9, 1846. Center of many early-day activities, this plaza was the site of: the first public school building, erected in 1847 on the southwest corner of plaza, where religious services and many public meetings were held; the dramatic announcement of gold discovery made on May 11, 1848, when Sam Brannan displayed glittering samples to crowds; mass meeting to urge election of delegates to Monterey Constitutional Convention on June 12, 1849; refuge for citizens following conflagrations of 1849, 1850, 1851, and 1906; citizens' assembly on July 16, 1849, to organize against depredations of a lawless body called 'The Hounds'; memoral services held August 29, 1850, following death of President Zachary Taylor; first Admission Day celebration held October 29, 1850, when the steamship *Oregon* brought the news that California had become 31st state on September 9; an indignation meeting, organized June 1, 1852, to protest against the city council's purchase of the Jenny Lind Theatre to be used as a city hall; commemorative services held for Henry Daly, August 10, 1852; and an oration delivered by Colonel E. D. Baker on September 18, 1859, over the body of U.S. Senator David C. Broderick, killed in duel with Chief Justice David S. Terry. Robert Louis Stevenson spent many hours here during his visit to the city in 1879-1880."

Marker in Portsmouth Square, at Kearny and Clay in San Francisco.

Shoreline Marker

"This tablet marks the shoreline of San Francisco Bay at the time of the discovery of gold in California, January 24, 1848. Map reproduced above delineates old shoreline."

Marker in the sidewalk beneath the Mechanics Monument, on Market Street at the intersection of Bush and Battery streets, in San Francisco.

Long Wharf

"In the spring of 1848 the old Central or Long Wharf was built 'from the bank in the middle of the block between Sacramento and Clay streets, where Leidesdorff Street now is, 800 feet into the Bay.' After 1850 it was extended 2,000 feet and the Pacific mail steamers and other large vessels anchored there. Central or Long Wharf is now Commercial Street."

Marker on the side of a building at Commercial and Montgomery streets, San Francisco.

Niantic Hotel (Building)

"The emigrant ship *Niantic* stood on this spot in the early days 'when the water came up to Montgomery Street.' Converted to other uses, it was covered with a shingle roof with offices and stores on the deck, at the level of which was constructed a wide balcony surmounted by a veranda. The hull was divided into warehouses entered by doorways on the sides. The fire of May 3, 1851, destroyed all but the submerged hulk, which later was utilized as the foundation for the Niantic Hotel, a famous hostelry that stood until 1872."

Marker on the side of a building at Sansome and Clay, San Francisco.

Telegraph Hill

"A signal station was erected on Telegraph Hill in 1849 from which to observe the incoming vessels; a tall pole with movable arms was used to signal to the people in the town below whether sailing vessels or the sidewheel vessels of the Pacific mail were passing through the Golden Gate. In September 1853 the first telegraph in California, which extended eight miles to Point Lobos, was stationed here, giving the hill its name."

Marker at the top of Telegraph Hill, San Francisco.

First U.S. Naval Station in the Pacific

"Mare Island Navy Yard was established September 16, 1854, by Commander David G. Farragut, USN, on a site selected in 1852 by a commission headed by Commodore John D. Sloat, USN. Mare Island had the Navy's first shipyard, ammunition depot, hospital, Marine barracks, cemetery, chapel, and radio station in the Pacific."

Mare Island Naval Shipyard, Vallejo.

Alameda Terminal of the First Transcontinental Railroad

"With the Pacific Railroad Act of 1862 authorizing construction of a railroad and telegraph line, the first concentration of activity was east of Sacramento. Subsequently the line was opened from Sacramento to San Jose. During June 1869 construction was started near Niles, and by August a temporary connection had been made at San Leandro with the San Francisco and Alameda Railroad. On September 6, 1869, the first Central Pacific train reached San Francisco Bay at Alameda."

Marker at Lincoln Avenue and Webster Street, Alameda.

Jack London

January 12, 1876 - November 22, 1916

"Oakland's famed native Son was the noted author of 'The Call of the Wild', 'The Sea Wolf' and 'South Sea Tales'. He was at various times a sailor, Alaskan gold miner, salmon fisher and long-shoreman.

"For a time he was politically involved in making Socialist speeches and served as a war correspondent at different periods in the Far East and Mexico."

E Clampus Vitus

Marker on a rock at Jack London Square, Oakland.

Jack London Cabin

Dedicated July 1, 1970.

"Jack London lived in this cabin while prospecting in the Klondike goldrush of 1897. The cabin was located on claim No. 151 on the North Fork of Henderson Creek in the Yukon Territory. It was found in July 1968 and authenticated by the Yukon Territorial Historic Sites and Monuments Board. The Port of Oakland acquired the cabin and brought it to Jack London Square to honor the memory of the man who enriched the world with his stories of the Klondike."

Marker on a cabin at Jack London Square, Oakland.

Jack London

"To remember Jack London — The author who immortalized this locality in 'John Barleycorn' and 'Tales of the Fish Patrol'

A.D. 1941 — George Heinold"

Rusty marker on the outside wall of Heinold's Saloon at Jack London Square, Oakland.

San Leandro Oyster Beds

"During the 1890s the oyster industry thrived until it became the single most important fishery in the state. Moses Wicks is supposed to have been the first to bring seed oysters around the horn and implant them in the San Leandro beds. The oyster industry in San Francisco Bay was at its height around the turn of the century; it reached a secondary peak by 1911 and then faded away because of polluted conditions of the bay."

Marker along the shoreline at San Leandro Marina, San Leandro.

Coyote Point

"These beautiful grounds served as a campus of the Merchant Marine Cadet Corps during the years 1942 to 1948. Together with its sister college at Pass Christian, Miss., the schools provided training for over 6000 undergraduates of the U.S. Merchant Marine Academy, Kings Point, New York. In 1948 training was consolidated at Kings Point and the grounds were returned to San Mateo County."

Marker at the overlook, near the family picnic area, in Coyote Point County Park, San Mateo.

Indian Sites

The shell mounds of the Bay region were surveyed some seventy years ago, and at least three hundred and fifty were found scattered along the shoreline marshes and fresh water streams emptying into the Bay. These and many more found in the surrounding area were, even at that time, being bulldozed by modern civilization. The Coast Miwok, Wintun and Costanoan Indians who camped at these sites may have used some of them as long as five thousand years ago. These prehistoric peoples were nomadic, moving around in search of food in different seasons, stopping at the bayshore to gather the plentiful shellfish. Their provender consisted of clams, oysters, mussels and cockles, as well as abundant fish, sea otters and waterfowl in the Bay. The debris from the food supply (mostly shells) and the rubbish from village life gradually accumulated to form mounds, some of which were very extensive — thirty feet high and hundreds of feet long. These ''kitchen middens'' were ancient garbage dumps, villages were erected on top of them, and almost all were used for burials. By 1800 most of the Indians who dwelt on the shores of the Bay had succumbed to religious conversion, and the old way of life was abandoned. About the same time the mounds, monuments to a now-vanished race, began to be demolished. Leveling for building sites, cultivating with the plow, and excavating for paving materials led to the destruction of almost all the shell mounds in the area.

Probably the largest mound on the Bay was at Ellis Landing, now completely exterminated by industrial development of Richmond's port. Another once stood where the parking lot of Spenger's restaurant is in Berkeley. Scientific excavations were made of some of the mounds and the materials analyzed and the relics carried off to museum collections. The pressure of progress virtually extinguished all evidence of the prehistoric habitations. The large and archeologically investigated mound beneath the Sherwin-Williams Paint Company in Emeryville is now remembered only by Shellmound Street which runs over the site. In Alameda, Mound Street obliterates the location of a mound that was removed and used for paving roads in 1908. It is memorialized by a plaque in Lincoln Park a couple of blocks away. Two small parks in Berkeley on Indian Rock Road, Mortar Rock Park and Indian Rock Park, mark the location of other Indian camp sites.

At two locations on the Bay, the East Bay Regional Park District has protected shell mounds and provided an opportunity to visit them. Recently the Park District took over Brooks Island, a hump of land just offshore from the harbor of Richmond. There are at least two large mounds on this island. Archaeological investigators believe the spot was occupied longer than any other place in the Bay region, from approximately 3000 B.C. to A.D. 700. Plans are being made to allow visits of guided groups by reservation. This interpretive program is moving ahead slowly, but the Park District is working to solve the problems of transportation to the island and preservation of its environment.

To hear and see the story of Ohlone, or Costanoan, Indians, visit the shell mound at Coyote Hills Regional Park near Newark (travel directions are found elsewhere in this book). This site was occupied for some two thousand years, up into the early 1800s. Each Saturday at 2 pm naturalists guide groups on a short walk to the archaeological excavation and explain artifacts and daily life of the Ohlone culture. The composition of the mound — clam, mussel and oyster shells, animal and human bones, and early tools — is interpreted. The Indian mound walks begin at the park's entrance. For information, Coyote Hills Regional Park (471-4967).

Charting the Islands of the Bay

The most notable islands on San Francisco Bay are like mountains thrown down and anchored against the currents and flood tides. They are near and familiar neighbors to any of the cities of the Central Bay. But the Bay is further sprinkled with other islands and islets, both anonymous and anomalous — some so small that they are easy to miss, some formed and deformed by man.

Some of the major islands are explored in other sections of this book, so they will be treated minimally here. Others are so obscure that the only thing commonly known about them is the name. Finally there are a few that are so incongruous that they are no longer thought of as islands at all. Among the sloughs of the South Bay, there are islands that are so indistinguishable from the surrounding marsh shorelands that they are not considered here.

Only a few of the Bay's islands may be visited; most are closed to the public. However, they are all different and interesting. Any geographical scrutiny of the Bay would be incomplete without surveying all these seamarks for sailors.

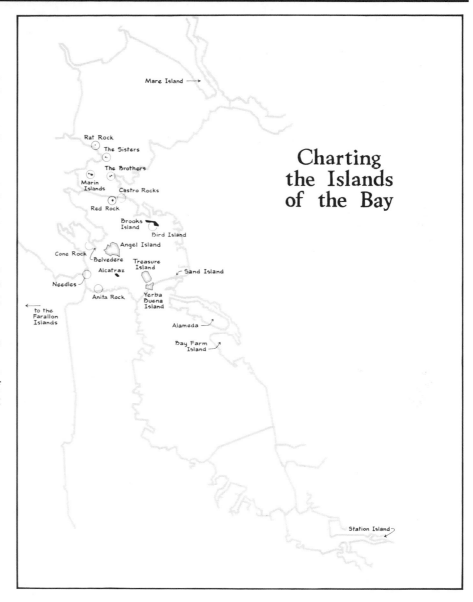

Charting
the Islands
of the Bay

Alcatraz Island

The enigmatic island of Alcatraz seems to float off San Francisco's north waterfront, a rock-like battleship with a high stone superstructure, steaming to defend the Golden Gate. Originally the Spanish name *Alcatraces*, which means pelicans, was applied to Yerba Buena Island. Later a cartographer's error transferred the name to this island and it stuck. Barely one-quarter mile long, the island was regarded as a shipping hazard in Mexican times. It was only after California became a state that a lighthouse was erected by the federal government in 1854. It is the oldest light station on the Pacific Coast. The second lighthouse building, dating from 1909, is still in operation.

In the 1850s the Army constructed a citadel making Fort Alcatraz part of the harbor defense protecting the Golden Gate. Over the years more batteries, barracks and fortifications were built. The military first used the island as a place of confinement in 1859. It achieved early notoriety as a jail for military prisoners, Civil War detainees, deserters, unsubdued Indians in the 1880s, inmates from the San Francisco jail after the '06 fire and enemy spies in WW I. Most of the present buildings were built early in this century. Military use of the island came to an end in 1934 when it became a federal penitentiary.

The shroud of mystery thoroughly enfolded Alcatraz when it was operated as a grim maximum security prison for incorrigibles of the gangster era. Sitting a little more than a mile off San Francisco, it was called "Uncle Sam's Devil's Island," or "The Rock." Many big name convicts of the 1930s served time on the island, including Al Capone. Thirteen escapes were attempted, none successful. Most escapers never got off the island. In May 1946, during the "battle of Alcatraz" it took the combined efforts of guards and U.S. Marines to subdue rioting convicts and restore order after several deaths and injuries. In an escape in 1962, one man's attempt was defeated by the cold currents of the Bay. He was captured, nearly dead, on rocks near the Golden Gate. The bitter days as a prison ended in 1963.

As surplus government property, Alcatraz was the target of numerous plans and preposterous schemes for development. Adding to the controversy was the Indian occupation from November 1969 to June 1971, asserting a claim to the island. The island is now part of the Golden Gate National Recreation Area and has been open to the public since 1973. Guided tours are detailed in the sections *Finding the Bay* and *Cruising the Bay*. The twelve-acre island is now one of the hottest tourist attractions in San Francisco. An elaborate public planning process is underway by GGNRA to determine the future of Alcatraz. Perhaps they will give it back to the pelicans.

Angel Island

The oldest haven on San Francisco Bay is Angel Island. It was the anchorage for the first Spanish ship that sailed into the Bay, in August 1775 — explorer Juan Manuel de Ayala's small *San Carlos*. Ayala sheltered his ship in the small cove, now named for him, on the northwest side of the island while his pilot, Cañizares, surveyed the Bay in a longboat and made the first charts of the whole estuary. The one square mile of mountain with rocky ridges sweeping down to the water was christened by Ayala *Isla de los Angeles*.

The long sweep of California history may be witnessed on this grassy and tree-covered island. At one time four shell mounds indicated Coast Miwok Indian fishing villages. Sailors from ships visiting *Puerto de San Francisco* (including Richard Henry Dana in *Two Years Before the Mast*) cut wood on the island until, by 1859, all the trees were gone. The Mexican governor gave permission to graze sheep and cattle there and in American times, whether this was a land grant or not was disputed all the way to the Supreme Court. President Millard Fillmore reserved the island for military purposes in 1850, and the Army finally got around to occupying it in 1863. There are hoary stories about an anti-slavery duel, the hermit Peter Casey, and ghostly apparitions (perhaps, merely angels).

The Army made long and productive use of the island, the last unit leaving in 1962. Personnel quartered there introduced plantings, including many exotic species, which gave the island its vegetative cover. Many different military scenes were played on the island — harbor defense batteries; induction center during the Indian Wars; staging areas for troops inbound or outbound overseas in the Spanish-American War, World War I and World War II; detention camp for enemy aliens; prisoner of war camp; and missile launching site. From 1900 to 1946 the island base was known as Fort McDowell. A U.S. Quarantine Station was established in 1892, and the small harbor was called Hospital Cove (since named Ayala Cove). An Immigration Station was opened in 1910 on the north shore, and it handled mostly Oriental immigrants until closed in 1940. To protect the shipping on the busy waters off the island, a fog signal bell was put on Pt. Knox in 1886, and a light was added in 1900. Two remaining light stations operate on Pt. Stuart and Pt. Blunt. Small pieces of the island are within San Francisco's city limits.

The state park was established on Angel Island with a segment of land at Ayala Cove in 1954. The remainder of the island was turned over to the park eight years later. The federal government (Park Service) has cast covetous eyes on Angel Island, and has included it within the proposed boundary of the Golden Gate National Recreation Area.

As a state park, Angel Island is now a haven for anyone who enjoys the outdoors. This mid-Bay playground is a day-use park, reserved for hikers and nature lovers. The views from 781-foot high Mt. Livermore toward Marin County and the Golden Gate are enthralling. The freedom to be found on the island is especially evoked by a view south across the miles of water to Alcatraz. Details about excursions and ferry service from San Francisco, Tiburon and Berkeley are in the sections *Pedestrian Delights, Finding the Bay,* and *Transportation on the Bay.* Recently the State Parks Department has grappled with the controversial problem of the deer herd over-grazing the vegetation on the island. The Department is still examining public opinion on future operations.

Treasure Island

An expression of the aspirations of an older time, Treasure Island was contrived by man to anchor a golden exposition shortly before the dark days of World War II. After the prodigious effort of simultaneously constructing the two largest bridges in the world, it was only fitting to celebrate the linking of the shores by building an artificial island in the middle of San Francisco Bay. The Golden Gate International Exposition not only honored the bridges, but was supposed to boost business and exhibit the contemporary fascination with science and technology. The site selected was Yerba Buena Shoals, a very shallow part of the Bay, just north of Yerba Buena Island. It was no coincidence that San Francisco favored the location as a future international airport.

Construction of Treasure Island was carried out by the Army Corps of Engineers in 1936 and 1937. Many tons of boulders were barged to the site to form a rock seawall around the 400-acre tract. Then mud from the Bay bottom was pumped in to fill up the lagoon and raise it above water level. At that time it was almost named Gold Island because of the silt that had washed down into the Bay

from Sierra gold operations. The more felicitous name was chosen — Treasure Island. The world's fair, despite its official name, was also called Treasure Island by almost everyone.

The buildings of the fair were the work of the WPA and the Public Works Administration and most were temporary, to be taken down when the fair closed. Three permanent structures were to be used by the proposed airport. The Golden Gate International Exposition opened for business in February 1939, and it finally shut down in September 1940. The lights were turned off and most of the buildings razed. The Navy borrowed the island for a temporary base, and it became known as "T. I." After the war, the island was no longer ideal for an airport — too small, too close to the Bay Bridge. So a property trade was made — the Navy received title to the island, and San Francisco acquired the nucleus of its present airport.

As a Navy base, most of Treasure Island is off limits. However, the great hall of the fair's Administration Building now houses the Navy/Marine Corps Museum which is open to the public. It may be reached from the Bay Bridge by driving down the causeway that connects Yerba Buena to Treasure Island. You can

also get there by AC Transit bus. The museum has not only Navy and Marine exhibits but also displays and photographs from the world's fair. Every spring the Armed Forces Day open house allows you to venture on more of the island, walk palm-lined avenues, visit the fountain of the Court of Pacifica, and get a better idea of what Treasure Island was like in 1939.

Brooks Island

Old-timers still call it Sheep Island — at one time it was used to pasture sheep — but Brooks Island had many uses: fishing camp, yacht club, most recently, a hunting club. The East Bay Regional Park district now owns the fifty acres of thin ridge rising abruptly out of the Bay less than one-half mile off the Richmond waterfront. The park district is planning to open the island to the public in guided groups on a limited basis. The restrictions would preserve the almost pristine condition of the island. Its solitary naturalness makes it a breeding area for Canada geese, and the slope of the 161-foot high peak is a relict native grassland. Brooks Island is also the location of the longest occupation by prehistoric people on the Bay, based on examination of the largest extant shell mound in the area.

The Brothers

Lying less than a quarter mile off the end of Pt. San Pablo are two islands, East Brother and West Brother, at the point where San Francisco Bay becomes San Pablo Bay. They are almost too small to be called islands. West Brother is a bare hump that is only visited by birds and sea lions. On East Brother is the most picturesque lighthouse on the Bay. The Victorian house and tower, automated now, first went into operation in 1874. It was a popular seamark for river boats bound up the Sacramento River. The whole station is surrounded by a white picket fence, giving it an out-of-the-past atmosphere. Owned by the Coast Guard, neither of The Brothers is open to the public.

Marin Islands

Jack London described being marooned on "one of the Marin Islands, a group of rocky islets which lay off the Marin County shore . . . fringed with a sandy beach and surrounded by a sea of mud." *(Tales of the Fish Patrol)* The two islands are prominently visible to the north of the Richmond-San Rafael Bridge, midway between Pt. San Quentin and Pt. San Pedro. East Marin is the larger, almost ten acres, tree-covered and the site of Indian shell mounds. Smaller West Marin, two and a half acres, has few trees and is a refuge for herons and egrets. The fanciful legend of defiant "Chief Marin" hiding on the islands in the 1820s had some basis in fact. Certainly there was a Bay ferryman called *El Marinero*. But the islands were named long before (1775), and the county eventually took the name. The islands were reserved by the government in the 1860s, then sold many years ago. Now owned by the head of a tugboat company, who has a weekend home on East Marin, both islands are closed to the public.

Red Rock

Looking like the fin of some species of Great Red Shark making a pass at the Richmond-San Rafael Bridge, Red Rock rises from the Bay only a quarter mile south of the bridge. It is a five-acre lump, 750 feet long and 170 feet high. Over the years it has had many uses — otter hunting by Russians camped there, tunneling for manganese in the 1870s and 1920s (extracted ore was not rich enough to be commercial), and quarrying by San Quentin prisoners. The barren shale outcrop was the home of Selim Woodworth — a Robinson Crusoe hermit who lived there for five years in the 1850s. The most intriguing tradition concerns early pirate treasure said to be buried on the rock. Most lonely islands have similar legends. Certainly no one ever found any wealth on Red Rock, although it was called Treasure Island, and Golden Island is a name still officially used. The island is a boundary corner, splitting this part of San Francisco Bay among San Francisco, Marin and Contra Costa counties. About a hundred years ago it was reserved for the military but never used by the government. Early in this century it passed into private hands, and several schemes for development of the rock have been bandied about. It is likely, however, that it will remain in its roguish, eroded state. Red Rock is privately owned and is not accessible to the public.

The Sisters

A pair of rocky islets, The Sisters lie about a quarter mile off Pt. San Pedro near McNears Beach. They are very small, too small to be islands and a little too big to be rocks — both total only two-thirds of an acre. Flat-topped, the islets are almost devoid of vegetation. They were reserved by the military in the 1860s and then were owned by the Coast Guard, although they were never marked by aids to navigation. Neither of The Sisters is open to the public.

Yerba Buena Island

In a sense Yerba Buena is the most visited island on the Bay, although it is not officially open to public visitation. The two-level tunnel bore acts as a mid-Bay splice for the San Francisco-Oakland Bay Bridge, and many thousands drive across the island each day. The island is also superlative in the matter of names. The Spanish originally called it *Alcatraces,* and it was known variously as Sea Bird Island, Wood Island, and Goat Island until a popular petition of the citizens of San Francisco convinced the U.S. Geographic Board to revert to Yerba Buena, meaning "good herb," in 1931. Yerba Buena is also the most legendary island of any on the Bay. There are romantic tales of ghosts and goats, shipwrecks and treasures, smugglers and sailors, and lighthouse keepers and soldiers. A treasure-laden Spanish galleon was shipwrecked on the island; looters and smugglers buried contraband; one resident kept a bull to patrol for trespassers; a billy goat was an inadvertent watchdog; and there were graves of soldiers, squatters, pioneers, and a favorite horse. With all the stuff supposedly buried on Yerba Buena, the most significant thing dug up has been evidence of Indian occupation. The Indians paddled across the Bay waters in barges made of bundles of tule reeds and used the island as a fishing station. Remains of a village, cremation pits, mortars and pestles have been found, and when the Bay Bridge was constructed, bones were exhumed.

Old photographs of the harbor of San Francisco show an ominous, bare island in the background. It remained treeless until the poet Joaquin Miller promoted California's first Arbor Day. On November 27, 1886, with much pomp and poetry, plantings of Monterey pine and eucalyptus were made in the shape of a huge cross over the 350-foot peak of the island. As part of the promotion for this event, Miller claimed the trees would serve as a fog break for the East Bay. Now, when the fog sweeps in through the Golden Gate, the trees seem to have little effect.

Before statehood the island was used as a goat ranch and was known as Goat Island. Then the federal government made it a reservation for harbor defense. In 1866 an Army detachment occupied the island for a while. The army stopped (in 1872) the "Goat Island grab" by the railroads, which were seeking a strategic port position for transcontinental commerce. The U.S. Lighthouse Service came to the island in the 1870s, erecting a fog signal and light, and setting up a supply depot to serve the California coast. The Navy began using the island as a training station in 1898. Now the Coast Guard reservation includes the lighthouse and a buoy tender base on a segment of the island facing Oakland. The rest of Yerba Buena belongs to the Navy and is connected to Treasure Island by a 900-foot causeway.

Some Anomalous Islands

Alameda

The present location of the city of Alameda did not start out as an island. It was a peninsula known as *Encinal de San Antonio.* It lost its peninsular status in 1902 when the Army Corps of Engineers completed dredging a channel through to San Leandro Bay. The dredging was done to improve navigation and to allow tidal action to cleanse the Estuary. Even though it is large enough to contain the city and the Naval Air Station, Alameda's island condition is confirmed by the fact that the only access is by way of four bridges and a pair of tunnels.

Bay Farm Island

Originally an island, surrounded by marshes and open water, Bay Farm was gradually drained and filled to become a peninsula. The filling was initially to create land for market gardens, hence the name. It is now more than twice its former size, and is the site of the Oakland Airport and a housing development.

Belvedere

It is still named Belvedere Island, although it is now connected to the mainland, and the lagoon has long since been filled in. The town of Belvedere is now an enclave of expensive houses. The ambiguity of Belvedere's status was established when the War Department claimed it in 1867 and called it Peninsula Island. The squatter who lived there at the time gave officials a tour, crossing a spit at low tide, to prove that it was a peninsula and therefore not eligible to be claimed when the US government took all the islands in the Bay. The dispute over land grant title, and whether it was an island or peninsula, lasted for many years in the late 1800s.

Mare Island

At one time Mare Island was about half its present size and was surrounded by the waters of San Pablo Bay, Carquinez Strait and the Napa River, with marshes lying to the north. Now its condition has changed — man-made construction and natural siltation have enlarged and made a peninsula of Mare Island. Across the river from the city of Vallejo, it has been a naval installation since 1854. It was the first Navy base on the Pacific coast, and its first commander was David Glasgow Farragut. Mare Island Naval Shipyard is off limits and rarely open to the public.

Sand Island

When the Oakland Harbor was dredged early in this century, the spoil was dumped in a shallow part of the Bay. This became Sand Island. The causeway for the Key System ferries was built across it, and at one time it was a hobo jungle. Now it is obliterated by the toll plaza of the San Francisco-Oakland Bay Bridge and is no longer an island.

Station Island

At the extreme south end of the Bay near Alviso, Station Island stands between Mud Slough and Coyote Creek. This almost forgotten island is the site of the ghost town Drawbridge. The town and island got their names when the old South Pacific Coast Railroad was built through the area. The island is virtually inaccessible.

On the Rocks

Rat Rock

Lying very close to the Marin County shore near China Camp, Rat Rock is too big to be a rock — and yet it's too small to be an island. It doesn't look like a rat — in fact, it is shaped and fringed so it looks like a man's bald head with a couple of trees growing out of the top. I have no idea why it is called Rat Rock.

Castro Rocks

The group of rocks under the eastern end of the Richmond-San Rafael Bridge are called Castro Rocks. They can easily be seen from Pt. Molate.

Needles

Lying just inside the north side of the Golden Gate, between Lime Point and Horseshoe Bay, these stony outcrops are sometimes called Needle Rocks.

Cone Rock

Just a quarter mile off Belvedere in Richardson Bay, Cone Rock can be found by careful searching from the waterfront of Sausalito.

Anita Rock

Anita Rock can sometimes be seen at low tide off the north shore of San Francisco. It stands barely a thousand feet offshore from Crissy Field.

Bird Island

Probably the least noticed island on the Bay, Bird Island is actually too small to be called an island. It stands a few hundred feet to the west of Brooks Island near the city of Richmond.

Farallon Islands

Of course, the Farallon Islands are not in San Francisco Bay. They lie west across the Gulf of the Farallones, some thirty to thirty-five miles into the Pacific from the Golden Gate. They are included here because they are considered within the city boundary of San Francisco. On a clear day, the islands are silhouetted on the horizon and are visible from San Francisco and Marin. The precipitous clusters of seven islands and collections of rocks extend for eight miles north to south, forming three main groups — North Farallon, Middle Farallon, and Southeast Farallon with Maintop Island.

Various explorers visited the Farallones — Juan Rodríguez Cabrillo in 1542; Sir Francis Drake when he sailed away from the Bay in 1579 (he was the first to land on the islands, hunting sea lion meat); Sebastian Vizcaíno in 1603; Juan Francisco Bodega y Quadra in 1775; and Capt. George Vancouver in 1792. Drake called them the Islands of St. James; but Bodega named them — *Los Farallones de los Frayles*, "little pointed islets in the sea of the friars."

Southeast Farallon is the largest of the islands, and the only one ever inhabited. Early in the nineteenth century, the Russians made a small settlement that exploited skins from sea lions, fur seals and sea otters, and the eggs from the nesting sea birds. The Americans, coming later, found the fur-bearing animals exterminated, but found a ready market for the bird eggs in San Francisco after the Gold Rush swelled the population. The lucrative business competition spawned "egg wars," with brawls and bullets, until government restrictions brought the commerce to an end in 1890.

Lighthouse keepers were stationed on the barren rocks jutting out of the ocean from 1855, when a light was put atop 350-foot high Southeast Farallon, until 1972, when the light station was automated. Now the more or less permanent residents are a team at the field station of the Pt. Reyes Bird Observatory who conduct research on sea birds and marine mammals. The middle and northern cluster of crags were protected in 1909, and in 1969 the southern islands became part of the US Fish and Wildlife Service's San Francisco Bay refuge complex. Despite past depredations, marine mammals have returned to the desolate rocks — pods of California and Stellar sea lions, and a small herd of elephant seals. The islands provide nesting for many sea birds — among them the ashy petrel, black oystercatcher, Cassin's auklet, double-crested cormorant, and tufted puffin — as well as a stop-over for migrating land birds, as many as two hundred species. The Farallones are the largest continental sea bird rookery south of Alaska.

Beacons on the Bay

The fog, strong currents and gale winds were evident to the first nautical visitors to the California coast. These early explorers literally ran into the rocks, islands and shoals that were hazards to navigation. Lt. Juan Manuel de Ayala, the first Spanish captain to pilot a ship into the Bay, was thwarted in his initial attempt by a strong ebb tide through the Golden Gate. He had to try again the next day. And the unfortunate Ayala, after weeks spent charting the Bay, managed to crack up on rocks near Lime Point when he was sailing out of the Bay.

It was to counter dangers such as this that aids to navigation were established shortly after California statehood. This protection for sailors and maritime cargo was introduced in the Bay region by the first lighthouse and the first fog signal station on the Pacific coast. The foremost peril to mariners, particularly within the Golden Gate, is fog — the summer fog that rumbles in through the Gate, and slides over the hilltops — the tule fog of winter that rises from the water and marshes, appearing gently, as if by some magic.

More than seventy fog signals operate on the Bay — the chorus of grunts and groans emanating in individual characteristic from the throats of diaphones and diaphragm horns and resounding from sirens and bells.

Two lighthouses outside the Bay guide ships safely through the entrance to the Golden Gate. Point Bonita is located on a thin, steep ridge of rock extending off the Marin headlands on the north side of the entrance. The light first flashed a warning to mariners in April 1855. A booming cannon was added as a fog signal in August 1856, the first fog device on the Pacific coast. The present lighthouse, standing for a hundred years, is the second on the site and is reached by a small suspension footbridge, a replica of the Golden Gate.

Mile Rocks Lighthouse sits atop one of a pair of menacing black rocks which

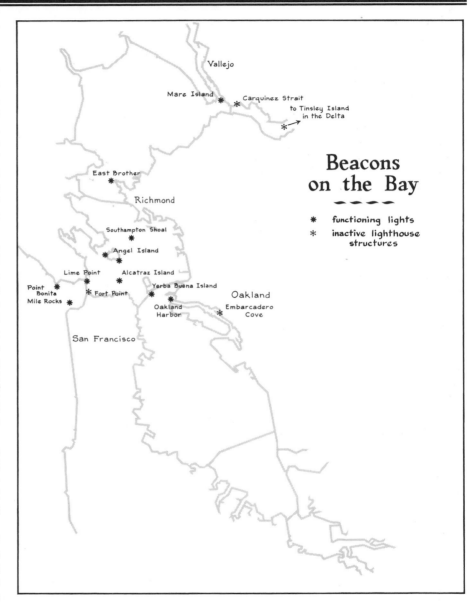

Beacons on the Bay

* functioning lights

* inactive lighthouse structures

barely show above the water. The lighthouse was a wave-swept engineering tour de force, started in September 1904 — a direct outcome of a tragic shipwreck at Fort Point three years before. Two years of treacherous toil wrought an historically magnificent beacon, seventy-eight feet tall. The light was desecrated in 1966 when the Coast Guard removed the lantern room and upper tiers to crown the remains with a helicopter landing pad. The light was automated (which means unmanned) at this time. Now it looks not so much like a lighthouse, but a Captain Nemo-esque caisson that could serve as a tide-generating machine, controlling the tides of the Golden Gate. Mile Rocks can be seen off Lands End from Lincoln Park in San Francisco.

On San Francisco Bay are a cluster of lighthouses, in all sizes and shapes, from modish little utilitarian boxes to imitation New England, including the original light station on the West Coast. These harbor lights were first overseen by the U.S. Lighthouse Service, and the authority passed to the U.S. Coast Guard in 1939. While the lights on the Bay are not so bright nor penetrating as on coastal locations, they are important seamarks even on clear, sunny days. Some of the old lighthouse buildings remain on duty, and three of them have been moved to other locations and other uses. Three of the lighthouses can be visited, only one of them is active. All of the other lights can be seen displaying their ''characteristic'' light flashes.

Lime Point

The lighthouse is on a thin projection of rocks on the north side of the Golden Gate, completely dwarfed beneath the structure of the bridge. A steam whistle fog signal station was established here in September 1883. At first it was coal fired, then powered by petroleum, then by electrically powered compressed air. A light signal was added to the station in November 1900. In June 1960, the blasts of the diaphragm horn and the flashing white light were not enough to aid the freighter *Pacific Bear*. The Pacific Far East Line's vessel hurtled through the fog and crashed into Lime Point and the light station, damaging the buildings. The ship was pulled off the rocks and repaired. Just about one year later, the station was automated and some of the buildings were removed. Lime Point is off limits to the public, but the buildings may be seen from Horseshoe Bay in Fort Baker, and from the walkway of the Golden Gate Bridge. The light can be seen from points on the Central Bay — characteristic, flashing white every five seconds.

Angel Island

For a few years Angel Island had the distinction of having three lights operating at one time — two of these remain. From atop Mt. Livermore, you can spot four other still-functioning lights on other parts of the Bay. The island and nearby Southampton Shoal represented the worst hazards to navigation on the Bay. This was especially true for the heavy traffic of grain ships to the upper Bay and Sacramento River.

Point Knox

On the south shore was the oldest station on the island. The fog signal bell was established in 1886 and light was added in November 1900. Mrs. Juliet E. Nichols served as keeper from 1902 to 1914. She became a maritime heroine in a heavy fog in July 1906 when the clockwork mechanism broke down. She pounded the bell with a hammer for twenty consecutive hours before the fog lifted, warning ships off the rocks. The station is no more, although the bell can be seen on the island. It was closed down in 1963. In what can only be termed an act of official vandalism by the Coast Guard, the little square quarters and separate bell house were burned.

Point Stuart

This station was built in 1915 on a western point of the island near Tiburon. The secondary light and fog signal, in a small house with a peaked roof, is a seamark for Sunday sailors.

Point Blunt

The station was built in 1960 on the southeast corner of Angel Island. The lighthouse itself is a very small box building with a flat roof on which sit the light and fog horn. Up the hill is a residence. The grounds are off limits to the public. Despite what other sources say, Point Blunt was the last manned light station on the Bay, being automated a year or so ago. The light characteristic, flashing green every five seconds.

Southampton Shoal

The light station was built in the middle of the Bay, a couple of miles offshore. It was a symmetrical, gabled building, three stories high with a light tower in the center and balconies around the entire building. The light and fog bell began operation in 1905. The bell was later replaced with a diaphragm horn. Keepers lived on the lonely light, and survived the San Francisco earthquake which threw several of the supporting piers out of kilter. The marvelous building was decommissioned in 1960 and the station fully automated. The St. Francis Yacht Club barged the building to Tinsley Island in the Delta where it sits on the San Joaquin River as a private clubhouse. Sharp eyes can make out the light a little north of Angel Island — its characteristic, equal interval red for six seconds (three on and three off).

Mare Island

A lighthouse was established in 1873 on the south end of Mare Island, facing Carquinez Strait, near where the Napa River empties into the strait. The very fancy Victorian building was a combination lighthouse and residence. For thirty-five years, most of the station's life, the keeper was Mrs. Kate McDougal. The station was abandoned in July 1917, and later the building was demolished. An automatic fog bell replaced it.

Carquinez Strait

In January 1910, a station was built on a very long pier jutting out into the strait off Carquinez Heights. It was on the northeast shore where the Napa River meets Carquinez Strait. The light tower and fog signal siren building were incorporated in the palatial three-story eclectic Victorian mansion, sitting on pilings.

The original building was moved in 1951 to a marina at Elliott Cove, just east of the Carquinez Bridge. The building is closed to the public although it can be seen on the north side of Carquinez Strait, across from Crockett. The light was converted to automatic operation in 1960 — its characteristic, flashing green every four seconds.

East Brother

In the strait between Points San Pedro and San Pablo, where San Francisco Bay becomes San Pablo Bay, lie two islands, The Brothers. The larger island, East Brother, is practically covered with a complex of buildings that is the light station. The light first flashed in March 1874, and a steam whistle fog signal was added two months later. The brackets and finials of Victorian splendor on the three-story tower and two-story house survive practically unaltered. The interior is succumbing to the effects of water and neglect. The paved station yard between the buildings served as a main catch basin for the drinking water cistern. The fog signal building and all the other buildings are surrounded by a prim picket fence. The light served ever-increasing shipping traffic to Mare Island and the Delta. When the Lighthouse Service closed it down in the 1930s, shipowners protested so much it was quickly reopened. The station was another victim of seagoing assault, when a tugboat ran into the island in heavy fog in 1952. No damage was done to the buildings. Ten years ago, a committee for Contra Costa shoreline parks convinced the Coast Guard to preserve the station as an historic landmark. The light was automated in 1969, and it has an air horn diaphone. No one lives on the island now, but it it is off limits to the public. It lies north of the Richmond-San Rafael Bridge, and you can have a good look at it offshore from Point San Pablo. Its light characteristic, flashing white every five seconds.

Oakland Harbor

The first light was constructed in 1889 one hundred yards offshore, completely surrounded by water. Operation began in January 1890. It protected shipping in San Antonio Creek before the creek became the Oakland Estuary. The small house on pilings had a fog bell and a fifth order lens in the lantern atop it. Shipworms undermined the pile foundation, so the building was removed and replaced with a more steadfast light. The second lighthouse was built further out into the Bay; it began operation in July 1903. The big, hip-roofed building had balconies around its two floors and a lantern room in the middle of the roof. Eventually the port facilities (the Western Pacific ferry mole) extended out to surround it. The light was electrified and the bell replaced by a diaphone horn. The third light is an automatic one put up in front of the building in 1966. Later the lantern was taken off and moved to Santa Cruz. The building was barged down the Estuary to Embarcadero Cove, where it sits as Quinn's Lighthouse restaurant. You can visit the relic and pretend you're a lighthouse keeper enjoying Sunday brunch on the veranda. The third light is still operating — its characteristic, flashing green every five seconds.

Alcatraz Island

Alcatraz has a strategic position in the middle of San Francisco Bay, and its lighthouse, the first on the Pacific coast, is a major beacon. The light was built to protect the influx of shipping to the Gold Rush harbor. It was completed in the summer of 1852, but not lit until June 1854. Two years later a hand-rung fog bell was added. The original small dwelling, built around a short tower looked like a transplant from New England's rockbound coast. The military prison buildings eventually overshadowed this first lighthouse, so a new one was built. The second lighthouse, completed in 1909, was a concrete tower eighty-four feet tall, which put the light

two hundred and forty feet above the Bay. Another fog bell, with clockwork mechanism, was added to the northwest point of the island in 1901. Despite the light and fog signal, the two ferryboats *San Rafael* and *Sausalito* collided just off the island in 1901. The *San Rafael* went down with the loss of three lives. A Northwestern Pacific ferry ran aground in 1931, and a freighter hit the island in 1946. In early 1963, the federal prison on ''The Rock'' was evacuated, and the lighthouse keepers had the island to themselves for a few months until the station was unmanned and the light automated. During the Indian occupation of the island, in 1970, the Coast Guard cut off power to the light. Mariners howled in disgust, and the Indians relit the light in June. During this period of occupation, part of the lighthouse was damaged by fire. Alcatraz is now part of the Golden Gate National Recreation Area, and the Park Service is considering restoring the damaged building. You can visit the island and see at least the exterior of the (second) lighthouse. The light can be seen from many points on the Central Bay — characteristic, flashing white every five seconds.

Yerba Buena Island

From 1873, the island served as a depot for buoys, equipment and tenders of the Lighthouse Service. On the southeast shore, facing Oakland, steam whistles (with a bell backup) and a light began operation in October 1875. The complex of lighthouse, fog signal building and picturesque keeper's dwelling are virtually unchanged in a hundred years. The white Victorian house, which some sailors have termed the perfect place to live on the Bay, is the residence of the commanding officer of the Twelfth Coast Guard District. Part of the island is a Coast Guard base for buoy tenders, patrol boats and rescue craft. The lighthouse was automated in July 1958. Its light characteristic, occulting white every four seconds (three on and one off).

Fort Point

Atop the shadows and forgotten military sounds of Fort Point, a lighthouse no longer shines. Fort Point was the second of the Bay's lighthouses to be built, the third to be lighted, and the first to be torn down. The first station here was built at the same time as the Alcatraz light (1852), it was completed a few months later than Alcatraz. Meanwhile, the Army decided it needed to fortify the Golden Gate, so the lighthouse was torn down before it began operation. When the Army completed Fort Winfield Scott, a small metal lighthouse tower was built beside it. This second light started flashing in March 1855. It was removed in 1863 in order to repair the seawall. The third light, an iron tower only twenty-seven feet tall, was put on the battlements in 1864. The total elevation from the water is eighty-three feet. After some wrecks nearby, a compressed air fog trumpet was added in 1904. Construction of the Golden Gate Bridge obscured the light and fog horn, so it was closed in September 1934. The bridge construction also called for the razing of the keepers' houses that stood on a ledge above the fort. You can visit the lighthouse, at least to see it, if not to climb on it. It is at Fort Point National Historic Site, which also has lighthouse photos and artifacts in its museum.

Buried Treasures, Fanciful Legends and Sunken Ships

The lore of San Francisco Bay is rich in legends of easy wealth and hidden fortunes, and for treasure hunters, the Gate of the legends is truly *Golden*. Each island became a site for buried treasure; each ship that was wrecked carried a valuable prize in the hold. All you have to do is find the precious trove. The legends claim that it is still there to be found — some are based on truth, others are merely myth. Usually a lot of negative information adds up to a good treasure story — wrecks not found, logbooks not explained, manifests not believed,

unclear narratives, rumors made into history. These elements are fermented by the desire to make a good story and brewed with dollar signs. Actually, the only fully authenticated tale of buccaneer plunder in all of California is the pirate Bouchard's raid on Monterey in 1818.

Bret Harte either started or perpetuated a fanciful fable of treasure in one of his short stories. The yarn has Francis Drake so successfully looting Spanish ships on his foray into the Pacific that the *Golden Hinde* becomes overburdened. Faced with the uncertain voyage across the Pacific Ocean to return to England, Drake lightened the load and buried part of the treasure on an island (which one?)

on the Bay. There is no other record of the treasure, except in Harte's narrative.

In the year 1595, the Manila galleon *San Agustín,* Captain Sebastián Cermeño, was wrecked in Drakes Bay near San Francisco. Treasure hunters have mixed names and dates (Camenon and 1599), and they have long claimed that there was a large gold and silver hoard aboard. Authentically, almost the entire cargo was silks and spices.

The *San Carlos,* another Spanish galleon en route from the Philippines to Acapulco, came a cropper in March

1797. Moorings parted in a gale, and the ship went down near the entrance to the Bay. An unknown amount of treasures was aboard, or maybe no treasure at all.

Red Rock, in the middle of the Bay, had a persistent legend concerning a pirate's buried treasure. The story gave birth to many expeditions that dug around the island and gave it the name Golden Rock.

The naming of the Marin Islands (which is recounted elsewhere in this book) has to be looked upon as just one more fanciful legend.

Several legends attach to Yerba Buena Island. One of the earliest sprang from the time of the secularization of the Missions by the Mexican government during the 1830s. Supposedly the treasure and plate from Mission Dolores in San Francisco was put aboard a ship by the Mission fathers to carry it out of the grasping hands of the government. The treasure-laden ship was caught in a storm and piled up on the shore of Yerba Buena (perhaps the year was 1837). Lives were lost, but the chest was saved and buried on the island to be recovered later. There is no record of the assets ever being retrieved. Just as there is no record of there ever having been a treasure in the first place.

In the 1830s and '40s seagoing smugglers cached goods on Yerba Buena, avoiding the import taxes. Confederates of the smugglers would row out to the island under cover of darkness and bring the contraband articles and opium ashore. At one time it was claimed that not all the illegal trade goods were found.

Yerba Buena Island popped up in treasure topics again at a slightly later date. An American ship stopped off in Peru en route to the whaling grounds of the Pacific. The notables on the losing side of a revolution besought the whaler's captain to take aboard money and jewelry for safe-keeping. After tarrying for a while, the ship sailed north. The captain intended to return later to Peru and restore the treasure. When the ship reached San Francisco, the valuables were buried (it is presumed on Yerba Buena), and the whaler continued to the Arctic, never to return. The story is supposed to have started with a crewman who jumped ship but never revealed the hiding place.

After one of the City's early fires, looters buried stolen gold and silver on Yerba Buena. Most of it was recovered rather quickly by the police. But that did not stop hopeful treasure seekers from wondering about the island.

Clairvoyants sent many prospecting parties to Yerba Buena Island in the 1870s. They were searching for the pirate treasure of Don Abecco Monte Janeiro, who raided the Manila galleons. The amount of buried gold grew to be as much as twenty millions. The treasure seekers did not find any money, but some of them had the pleasure of meeting Don Abecco in the spiritual flesh, as it were.

Another entry in the treasure tale sweepstakes was the account of a great treasure on Angel Island in the 1840s. A Mexican landowner had a Negro servant who helped the early Californian bury the fortune. Of course, the master died. Then the black servant died, leaving the death-bed story, but refusing to give a precise location of the hoard. Nevertheless, the beach at Hospital Cove (now Ayala Cove) was dug up often in the 1860s.

At about the same time, a hermit, Peter Casey, was residing on Angel Island. There were also reports from around 1869 of apparitions walking the paths of the island. Perhaps they were merely quires of angels. (Did anyone check up on Peter the Hermit?).

Off Angel Island's Point Stuart, a secretive group has made dives in Raccoon Strait in more recent times (1970s). Because of the strong tides, it is possible to dive only a few days in the year. The treasure is supposed to be hidden in the hold of a clipper ship, but no one is talking about it.

There are all kinds of tales and suppositions about valuables that were buried under the San Francisco waterfront as it was filled in during the Gold Rush. When new high-rises go up near the waterfront, there is a lot of curiosity but not much real treasure. Only copper rivets and zippers were found in excavations for the Two Embarcadero Center building.

A pair of robbers were rumored to have buried their loot at Adams Point on Lake Merritt in Oakland. One of the men was caught and died in San Quentin. The story leaked out and occasioned a spate of digging in the 1890s. Somehow the value climbed to eighty millions, in gold of course. No one ever came forward to say that he had found it.

By all accounts the Bay should be full of the hulks of wrecked ships. But the Bay is its own master, the treacherous currents have swept many of the wrecks out into the Pacific. At any rate, the stories of the wealth that many of these ships took down with them are mostly spurious, or mightily exaggerated.

The worst maritime disaster on San Francisco Bay was the wreck of the *City of Rio de Janeiro*. Early in the morning of February 22, 1901, the Pacific Mail Steamship passenger vessel, inbound to the City from the Orient, struck the rocks of Fort Point ledge and foundered. The dense fog blinded the ship; the master had already anchored twice before proceeding. The fog also hampered rescue efforts, although the vessel went down quite close to shore. Of the passengers and crew, 130 people were lost, including the captain. Within days the wreck had slipped off the underwater ledge and disappeared. As divers were going down and finding no trace, rumors and myths were floating to the surface, creating one of the longest-lived legends on the Bay. The manifests stated that the cargo was opium and silk worth hundreds of thousands of dollars. Rumors claimed the *Rio de Janeiro* was carrying silver bullion in a safe. The amount grew very quickly from a quarter million to two millions to six millions. But with no trace, where is the treasure hunter to look? Wreck debris restimulated the legend in 1916 and 1920. Wreckage from as far away as Carquinez Strait, and south down the coast, has been linked to the 1901 disaster. There were even reports that some of the treasure had been recovered. Theories about where the hulk was drifted are fascinating. Could there be a cave beneath Fort Point? Or a bottomless pit in the middle of the Bay to swallow up the ship? What about a tunnel that goes from Fort Point all the way to the Carquinez Strait, beneath the Bay? Or, more believably, some species of sea serpent that carried it away? Or was it merely swept out to sea? Searches have been made in 1956 and as recently as a few years ago.

Outside the Golden Gate is a literal ships graveyard, particularly at Lands End. The *City of New York* went down near Point Bonita in October 1893. The steamer *Katherine Donovan* was stranded on Seal Rocks in January 1941. Among the ships lying at Lands End is the tanker *Lyman Stewart,* built in San Francisco in 1914, which went down in October 1922. The wreckage of the sister ship, *Frank H. Buck,* which collided

with the *President Coolidge* in March 1937, ended up in the same spot. The lumber steamer *Coos Bay* went down in October 1927. The *Ohioan* ran aground there in October 1936.

The USS *Benevolence* was having a hospital ship shake-down cruise on August 25, 1950, when the dense fog closed in and the ship was struck by the freighter *Mary Luckenbach*. The *Benevolence* sank quickly, and 28 were lost of 526 hands aboard. The fog hampered rescue efforts, most of which were effected by Italian fishing boats in the vicinity. Fisherman John Napoli was the hero of the hour, rescuing fifty-four people.

The small coastal steamer *City of Chester* went down off Fort Point in August 1888. The cargo was merchandise. Searchers in the 1950s, who were trying to recover an inflated treasure of thirty millions in gold, were working from a figment of the imagination.

The *Valparaiso* was another lost ship that had people scouring the Bay bottom and titillated imaginations for many years. No one knew how the completely spurious story got started. The vessel was never sunk, she merely sailed away. And any hypothetical treasure aboard must have sailed with her to the other side of the world.

The sternwheel steamer *H. J. Corcoran* (which had seen service as a ferryboat) and the small *Seminole* collided off Angel Island in 1912 (stories differ, was it 1913?). Both ships went to the bottom but were later salvaged. A safe containing thirty thousand in gold ingots from the Selby Smelter in Contra Costa County slid off the deck of the *Corcoran* and was never seen again. Divers are still looking for the safe, or at least its contents. The account has become garbled over the years — somehow the *Corcoran* became the steamship *R. J. Cochrane* (no such ship) which went down off

Angel Island in 1911 with at least eighty thousand in gold aboard.

What was probably the most spirited wreck in our area occurred in 1883. The *Bremen* went down with a cargo of Scotch whisky aboard. Unfortunately it was at the Farallon Islands, too far away to do anyone any good.

With all the ferryboats and ferry traffic on the Bay for so many years, it's a wonder that there were so few fatal accidents. The worst ferry tragedy on the Bay occurred on a clear day in 1928. The *Peralta,* bound for Oakland, ran into trouble near Yerba Buena Island. The vessel suddenly nosed down and shipped water over the bow. Some passengers were swept overboard, others jumped, and five were lost. The ferryboat was not damaged.

Another ferry collision happened on a very foggy evening on the Bay — the northbound *San Rafael* was rammed by the southbound *Sausalito*. The *San Rafael* drifted to just inside the Golden Gate and went down. This tragedy of November 30, 1901, cost the lives of three people and one horse. Jack London immortalized the collision in his book *The Sea Wolf.*

A final ferry tale. Perhaps we have our own Pacific coast cousin of the Loch Ness monster. One day in 1934, passengers on a ferryboat cruising between San Francisco and Berkeley saw a creature rise out of the water nearby. The large animal surfaced and then submerged quickly, before it could be identified as anything but a sea monster. A few days later a similar denizen, or perhaps the same one, made a brief appearance off Richmond. No one was able to provide an authentic identification, or even a good description. Maybe it's time our local monster was spotted again — then Nessie will have nothing special on us.

Expositions

Two world's fairs held in San Francisco took advantage of the bountiful views, the sparkling waters, and even the freshening winds, of the Bay. The fairs also left an advantageously indelible imprint on the geography of the Bay. The Panama-Pacific International Exposition of 1915 was situated on a filled lagoon; part of the site survives as Marina Green and the San Francisco Marina on the City's northern waterfront. The Golden Gate International Exposition of 1939 blossomed on the specially man-made Treasure Island in the middle of the Bay, which became a Navy base. Both left monumental Bay-side souvenirs. Each is represented by buildings of historic value, museum exhibits, and relics of relocated art works. Both are represented by thoughtful exhibits and mementos in the Oakland Museum.

However, the first world's fair to be held in San Francisco was some years earlier. The California Midwinter International Exposition, or the Midwinter Fair of 1894, occupied the heart of Golden Gate Park. The prized legacy of that fair is the Japanese Tea Garden.

Panama-Pacific International Exposition of 1915

The International World's Exposition in San Francisco was mounted to specifically commemorate the four hundredth anniversary of the discovery of the Pacific Ocean by Balboa and to celebrate the completion of the Panama Canal and, not incidentally, to proclaim the City's phoenix-like rebirth from the ashes of the '06 fire. Civic go-getters actually conceived the idea of the Panama-Pacific International Exposition before the Panamanian treaty to build the canal was signed. The site selected was a stretch of tidelands between Fort Mason and the Presidio. The waters and marshes were filled, and President Taft presided over the groundbreaking in October 1911. After the buildings of the fair were taken down, the houses of the Marina District took their place. The seawall and yacht harbor are permanent improvements recalling the fair.

On February 20, 1915, the citizens of San Francisco and surrounding Bay communities were invited to open the Exposition. Thousands of people responded, walking blocks to the site and exploring the grounds. Attractions of the fair were many — airplane rides, transcontinental telephone hook-ups, moving pictures, equipment of the US Lighthouse Service, a working model of the Canal, the Liberty Bell from Philadelphia, and Maria Montessori educating. The buildings were a fairy fantasy of styles, on a monumental scale, with classic ornamentation on façades and colonnades. The dominant structure was the Tower of Jewels, 435 feet high, encrusted with a hundred thousand "gems" of cut Bohemian glass, lighted by searchlights at night. Other edifices were the Palace of Machinery, the Fountain of Energy, the Women's Pavilion, and the Palace of Fine Arts.

The Palace of Fine Arts, designed by architect Bernard Maybeck, was constructed as a temporary monument, of plaster and burlap on a wood framework. It remains, a majestic remembrance of the Exposition, although it was entirely rebuilt in concrete and steel in the 1960s. The philanthropy of the late Walter S. Johnson was chiefly responsible for saving the building, as well as completing the colonnade in the 1970s. The peristyle and lagoon are a park, where you may stroll, picnic, and watch a flock (more properly, a sord) of mallards on the water. Behind the peristyle, the long curving building houses the Exploratorium. Inside this exhibit of science and technology, displayed in a small nook, are drawings and photographs, reminders of the grandeur of the Exposition. Another building remains; it is inside the Presidio, across from Letterman Hospital, and is now in use as an enlisted men's club.

One of a family of sculptors, Alexander Stirling Calder, was Chief of Sculpture and created several pieces, including the Fountain of Energy, for the 1915 Exposition. He was the father of mobilist Alexander Calder and the son of sculptor Alexander Milne Calder who worked in the East. A token of the fair that was preserved is the sculpture group, two elephants and a fountain, designed by architect W. A. Faville, salvaged and located at Viña del Mar Plaza in Sausalito. Two pieces of sculpture that were exhibited in the Palace of Fine Arts wound up in San Francisco's Golden Gate Park — The Doughboy, by M. Earl Cummings, and Pioneer Mother, by Charles Grafly. The pagoda which is the centerpiece of the Japanese Tea Garden in the park was also moved there after the Exposition was over. Several murals that were painted to grace the fair's buildings have found their way into public buildings in San Francisco. From the Court of the Seasons, one remaining mural, Harvest by Milton Bancroft, is on the wall at the Academy of Stenographic Arts on Seventeenth Street. A pair of murals by Frank Vincent Dumond, Pioneers Leaving the East and Pioneers Arriving in the West, were placed in the main rooms of the Main Library. Huge wall paintings by Sir Frank Brangwyn were mounted in the Court of Abundance — a pair each of Earth, Air, Fire and Water. They now flank the auditorium of the Herbst Theater in the Veterans Building (installed when the theater was built in 1932) in the Civic Center.

Golden Gate International Exposition of 1939

Literally "on San Francisco Bay," the Golden Gate International Exposition left an impressive feature of lasting importance. Treasure Island changed the charts of the Bay. The two-year project (1936 and 1937) to create Treasure Island involved dredging and filling four hundred acres of shoals near Yerba Buena Island. The world's fair staged on the island was a party to commemorate the completion of two mighty Bay spans — the Golden Gate Bridge and the San Francisco-Oakland Bay Bridge. Also, the thought was to provide some employment and business income in troubled times. The Exposition actually ran for two years, both financially unsuccessful, from February to October, 1939, and a pepped-up, streamlined version from May to September, 1940. The buildings were another temporary set of flimsy stucco and wood, representing the grandiose imperialism of (allegedly) the Pacific empire. The Tower of the Sun, four hundred feet tall, was surrounded by courts and concourses, and the magic temples of Mayan, Malayan and Cambodian derivation.

Visitors came by car and electric train on the new Bay Bridge and by ferryboat from San Francisco and Oakland (the last run for some of the boats). The treasures and attractions of the Exposition were many — Portals of the Pacific, Vacationland, Hall of Air Transportation, Court of the Seven Seas, Lagoon of Nations, and Court of Pacifica. Visitors found pleasures and gratifications — the Gayway carnival, television, romantic Pan American Clippers, an outdoor pageant of Western history, the Levi Strauss marionette rodeo, the Aquacade water ballet with Esther Williams, and on the bandstand, Duke Ellington, Benny Goodman and Count Basie. Finally, the brilliant colored lights of the fair went out, as lights were going out all over the world in 1940, and Treasure Island became a Navy base.

Few things are left from the Golden Gate Exposition — recollections of the happy days on Treasure Island; three large buildings, built in anticipation of the island becoming an airport; a few small sculptures and some murals. The semicircular building at the foot of the causeway was to be the terminal building for the nascent airport; it served as the Administration Building of the fair, and now of the naval installation. With a parking lot in front, it is open to the public (10 am-3:30 pm daily), and houses the Navy/Marine Corps Museum. The museum has displays, as well as a mural two hundred and fifty feet wide, of the armed forces in the Pacific; there are souvenirs, mementos and photographs of the Exposition. The two buildings just behind the Administration Building never got off the ground as airplane hangars after the Navy took over. The avenues of palms and other plantings on the island are remnants of the fair. Also there is an oceanic relief map, the Fountain of the Pacific Basin, now dry, and some statuary from the Court of Pacifica.

A diverse selection of sculpture from the fair was relocated in different parts of Golden Gate Park in San Francisco. The Whales fountain by Robert Howard is now an impressive whirl of mammals in a spray of water in the courtyard of the Academy of Sciences. The bronze figure of St. Francis feeding the birds, first exhibited at the fair, is now a bubbling fountain in the Garden of Fragrance in Strybing Arboretum. The Goddess of the Forest, carved by Dudley Carter in totem pole style at the Art-in-Action exhibit at the fair, is now in Lindley Meadow. The Pioneer Mother bronze, originally from the Panama-Pacific Exposition, was resurrected for exhibition at Treasure Island, and is now in the park. Also relocated from the fair was the old-fashioned merry-go-round at the Children's Playground in Golden Gate Park. Along the ramps of the Ferry Building, you can find the most interesting art works recalling the fair. Six mural maps by Miguel Covarrubias of the culture and economy of the Pacific Basin were transported from Pacific House at the fair to the Ferry Building in San Francisco. At San Francisco City College are two further examples of the Treasure Island fair's art. Another Dudley Carter Art-in-Action redwood carving, the Ram's Head, is in front of the Student Union. A mural that Diego Rivera painted, Marriage of the Artistic Expression of the North and South of this Continent (which, incidentally, depicts Carter hewing the ram), originally in the Hall of Fine Arts, was removed to the lobby of the Little Theater on the campus.

The Treasure Island museum is heading an effort to move the dry fountain/map of the coasts and islands of the Pacific from the middle of the base to a more accessible location in front of the museum. The fountain and statuary are to be rebuilt and restored, in part with volunteer labor and materials and in part through the help of the living artists who first created the masterpiece. The Museum Association needs a hefty amount of tax-deductible "Save the Fountain" contributions. Contact the Navy/Marine Corps Museum, Building One — Treasure Island, San Francisco 94130. (765-6182)

Port Work

One of the interests of early explorers of the Pacific Coast was to find harbors for commerce. When they finally got around to discovering San Francisco Bay, they found what is now more than four hundred square miles of naturally-protected harbor. This bay and its water-borne trade made San Francisco the first metropolis on the Pacific Slope.

The Bay is a port of call for some one hundred shipping lines, and many thousands of commercial vessels pass through the Golden Gate every year. The cargo facilities on the Bay have been divided into fiefdoms of five ports. They are San Francisco, Oakland, Alameda, Richmond and Redwood City. In addition, there is tanker traffic to Standard Oil's Long Wharf (Richmond) and the Sequoia Wharf and Oleum (near Carquinez Strait). Other ships pass through the Golden Gate, bound for the refineries on Carquinez Strait and Suisun Bay and the cargo terminals of Stockton and Sacramento.

The out-moded finger piers of San Francisco unhappily wave goodbye to maritime trade as it drifts with the tide of progress across the Bay to Oakland. Some people have called San Francisco a dying port. It primarily handles the traditional general cargo and a limited amount of container cargo. Because there is so little of it, it is hard to find San Francisco's port work. Occasionally a ship puts in at one of the piers on the north waterfront (although passenger Pier 35 is fairly busy). Sometimes you will see a ship at China Basin or at Mission Rock Terminal. The container piers at India Basin near Hunters Point are almost inaccessible.

The Port of Oakland is in the forefront of container technology and has the second largest container handling facility in the United States. The colossal container cranes of the Outer Harbor have been called architectural sculpture, but when you see them in action, zipping containers on or off ships, they are all business. The many terminals of Oakland also have capabilities for "roll on/roll off" and

Port Work

traditional break-bulk cargo. You get a good look at the dynamic container operations from two small parks in the port area — Port View Park on the Outer Harbor and Middle Harbor Park (for locations see *Finding the Bay*). Comings and goings to the Inner Harbor terminals can be noted at Jack London Square and

Embarcadero Cove. The port authority has programs explaining the workings to the public — gentle propaganda. Large organized groups can get a tour of the facilities, by land (bus), or by water (Harbor Tour boat). At certain times (like the Fourth of July and during National Port Week), the port puts on an open house. The activities center on Jack London Square — yacht parades, lifeboat races, entertainments and some glimpse inside the industry.

The terminals of Alameda are the largest privately owned port operation on the West Coast. The container crane was created for use at this small port. Lack of access makes it very difficult to see any port work.

Redwood City is a deepwater port for smaller ships. Traffic is primarily salt, cement, gypsum and general cargo. The set-up is not very suitable for seeing any of the operations.

The port of Richmond extends from the Santa Fe Channel, around the Inner Harbor, and along Point San Pablo. There are several petroleum terminals, and it handles other liquid cargo and general cargo. A new container facility is planned for the port. Most of the wharves cannot be seen, but an occasional tanker (petroleum or molasses) docks at the end of Point San Pablo where you can see it (for directions, see *Finding the Bay*).

Tankers are some of the busiest ships on the Bay. Crude and refined flow in and out through the Golden Gate. When you are zipping across the Richmond Bridge, you can see Standard Oil tankers hooked up to the Long Wharf near the east end of the bridge. From the road in Rodeo, you can see tankers docked at Oleum and sitting offshore at the Sequoia Wharf, serving the refineries.

Trying to decipher the smokestack markings, and trying to determine the destination of ships plying the Bay, is an intriguing waterfront pastime.

Passenger liner service to San Francisco is shrinking. In the spring of 1978 the *Monterey* and the *Mariposa* made their final cruises, the last full-fledged passenger service under the American flag. The romantic era of regular voyages to Hawaii came to an end. Although there are a few passengers traveling on American freighters, the traditional passenger business continues on foreign ships. The South Sea voyages and cruises to Alaska and Mexico will leave from San Francisco, but on foreign-flag ships. The only passenger terminal on the Bay is Pier 35 in San Francisco. For information about the activities of passenger liners, see the section *Visiting Ships*.

Railroads were among the first to use Bay ferryboats to further commerce, and many of the early ferry lines were part of a rail operation. On San Francisco's waterfront you can see a remnant of the system of shuttling freight around the Bay. The Santa Fe car ferry slip is at Pier 52. There you can watch the transfer of railroad cars from the yards to the floats pulled by a tug. At the end of Army Street, the Western Pacific ferryboat brings cars across from the yard on the Oakland Mole. For more about the WP ferry, see the section *Walking the Decks*.

Among the marine service and repair shops on the Bay are three large shipyards. The former naval shipyard at Hunters Point in San Francisco has recently been taken over by the Triple A Machine Shop. Todd Shipyard on Alameda is the largest such facility in the region. The Bethlehem Shipyard in San Francisco with its floating drydocks, is a fascinating study in steel, and it is the only major yard that you can get a good look at. You can see it from a couple of public access view points on China Basin Street. Or you can sit on the deck of Mission Rock Resort and take in the ships with a beer and the sun.

The pilot boards a vessel ten miles outside the Golden Gate, and using the buoys and markers, guides it safely into port. The San Francisco Bar Pilots are put aboard from one of their boats, the *San Francisco*, the *California* or the *Drake*. When the boats are not in use, you can see them tied up beside Pier 7 on The Embarcadero in San Francisco, right behind The Waterfront restaurant (see *Pedestrian Delights*).

Among the towboats that you may see nosing around the finger piers or scooting down the Estuary are those from several companies, including Western Tug and Barge (Richmond) and Crowley Maritime (SF). Red Stack tugs are the most numerous and noticeable. Red Stack Towboat (Shipowners and Merchants Towboat Company) operates from Pier 9, and you can find tugboats shoaled up on both sides of the pier in San Francisco (see *Pedestrian Delights*).

The fireboats make their pleasurable presence felt when their monitors are showering a spray salute to ships on the Bay. This escort duty is performed for large Navy ships, notable vessels visiting the Bay, and for special civic functions. Two municipal fireboats guard the ports of San Francisco and Oakland, and the military has a few vessels with firefighting capabilities — Navy and Coast Guard boats stationed at Mare Island, and one small (thirty-two feet) Coast Guard boat at Yerba Buena Island. San Francisco's seventy-foot fireboat, *Phoenix* (built in 1954), docks next to Pier 24. It makes periodic pier inspections and welcomes ships to the Bay. When the *Phoenix* is out of service, the auxiliary tugboat *Frank White* fills in. The *City of Oakland*, a better looking boat one hundred feet long, is docked at Jack London Square, where you can walk right up beside it to get a good look. It was built in 1941 and served the Navy gallantly during the attack on Pearl Harbor. Every Thursday it makes a drill and inspection shakedown cruise on the Estuary to work out its hose turrets. (For finding the fireboats, see the section *Pedestrian Delights*).

Ecology

Ecology Cruising

Informative adventures — learn about the San Francisco Bay environment while you are cruising on it. You should be able to choose something just for you from this array of excursions. All the trips cost money.

Marine Ecological Institute

811 Harbor Boulevard, Redwood City 94063. (364-2760) The Institute offers programs during the academic year for school science classes, teacher workshops, trips for adults and/or kids, and does salinity research for the USGS, primarily on its boat, the *Inland Seas*. The "discovery voyage" is a four-hour cruise on the Bay between the Dumbarton and San Mateo bridges, studying fish, plankton, water quality and sediments. The "Bay discovery day" is an all-day Saturday affair. It combines a voyage with classroom study of biology and geology. The "junior marine exploration" is a four-day course. It blends cruising with classroom work, a marshland expedition, research techniques and marine discoveries.

Nature Expeditions International

599 College Avenue, Palo Alto 94306. (328-6572) Although primarily known for their expeditions to the far reaches of the globe, NEI offers a few "short course" programs on San Francisco Bay. Study the ecological relationships of the Bay on the one-day trip of the "Natural History of SF Bay" program. This is an ecologist-led cruise in conjunction with the Marine Ecological Institute. In mid-April, an all-day "Farallon Islands Symposium" serves as a classroom warm-up for NEI's cruises to the islands. History, natural history and ecology are reviewed. The "Farallon Islands Expeditions" are all-day boat trips on each weekend day from mid-April through May. The cruise to the largest continental sea bird colony (south of Alaska) departs from San Francisco and circles Southeast Farallon. Besides the abundant bird life, you probably will see seals, sea lions, whales and dolphins. Also of interest is the very popular one-day "Whale-watching Expeditions on Monterey Bay" in January.

Oceanic Society/San Francisco Bay Chapter

Building 240 — Fort Mason, San Francisco 94123. (441-5970) They offer field trips in the marine environment, as well as classroom courses in ecology, marine biology for non-scientists and water quality training. On-the-Bay activities include supply trips to the Farallon Islands and guided cruises to Bay islands. Programs are available to members and non-members.

Canoe Trips West

2170 Redwood Highway, Greenbrae 94904. (461-1750) For a different look at the Bay, try a canoe trip. Several times a year Canoe Trips West offers canoe excursions with a naturalist leader on Corte Madera Creek and Heerdt Marsh; they also offer habitat outings to find wildlife best seen from a canoe. Also, on any good day, you can make a self-guided tour of the estuaries and lagoons (a guidebook is provided).

Hauser Institute

Box 281, Sausalito 94965. (388-8120) Since 1971 John Hauser has combined ecology and navigation with sailing lessons for a unique experience on San Francisco Bay. The ten-week course consists of five all-day sails, two evening classes and three moonlight sails. If you want to learn on a 26-foot sloop, with a maximum of six students, this is for you. Tuition is $150/person.

Sierra Club/San Francisco Bay Chapter

6014 College Avenue, Oakland 94618. (658-7470) For members of the Sierra Club, a two-day weekend pleasure cruise (overnight in Stockton) is offered on a "Red & White Fleet" boat, usually in September. The large group tours the Bay and Delta with a captive crew of experts on various aspects of Bay ecology — a quick cruising seminar.

Ecology Collections and Excursions

Here are chances to whet your appetite, to investigate a little deeper, to learn more about the Bay. Here are classes and guided nature walks and museums of the Bay environment. In addition to the places listed, the Oakland Museum has finely mounted natural history displays and sponsors occasional Bay events.

Most colleges in the area have regular and extension courses with classes on various Bay-related subjects. For other expeditions, see the section *Ecology Cruising* and look for Audubon Society outings in the section on *Bird-watching*.

Richardson Bay Wildlife Sanctuary

376 Greenwood Beach Road, Tiburon 94920. (388-2524) The wildlife sanctuary is operated by the National Audubon Society and is open Wednesdays to Sundays from 9 am to 5 pm (for a small admission fee). On the grounds are a self-guided nature trail and the historic Victorian house built by Dr. Benjamin Lyford in 1876. Nature walks are available on Sundays. You can see flocks of birds, some of the thousands which visit the refuge (two hundred species have been identified), or you might see a pod of seals which winter in the bay. The community-oriented programs in the education center include films, lectures and a bookstore. Informative and entertaining programs for children, from schools all over the Bay region, include discovery field trips and Bay shore studies.

Marin Museum of Natural Science

76 Albert Park Lane, San Rafael 94901. (454-6961) Known also as the Louise A. Boyd Museum, it is open Tuesdays to Saturdays from 10 am to 5 pm. Natural history classes, workshops and field trips are available for a moderate cost. Memberships are available for $7.50/year.

East Bay Regional Park District

Tilden Park Environmental Center, Berkeley. (525-2233) The center is open daily (except Mondays) from 10 am to 5 pm. Programs include lectures, films and demonstrations. This is also the place to find out about free bird walks and nature walks scheduled in the summer at Point Isabel Regional Shoreline, Point Pinole Regional Shoreline and Robert Crown Memorial State Beach.

Coyote Hills Regional Park

8000 Patterson Ranch Road, Fremont 94536. (471-4967) Coyote Hills sends out a periodical listing its free nature walks. These weekend walks range from tidelands, to mud flats, to marshes, to salt ponds, to the Alameda Creek Trail for bikes. You can hunt for geology, weather, animals, birds and Bay ecology. Indian mound programs are held every Saturday. The Visitor Center has photo displays and slide programs. The park is open 8 am to 10 pm in summer and 8 am to dusk in winter. Parking fee $1/car on weekdays and $2/car on weekends and holidays.

San Francisco Bay National Wildlife Refuge

Headquarters at 3849 Peralta Boulevard, Fremont 94536. (792-0222) The Wildlife Refuge is building a new visitor center and administration building on a little hill beside the toll plaza at the east end of the Dumbarton Bridge. When the center opens in mid-1979 it will have wildlife exhibits and slide shows and other programs presenting the habitats of the refuge. Trails will cross the hill and follow alongside Newark Slough.

California Academy of Sciences

Golden Gate Park, San Francisco 94118. (221-5100) The museum is open 10 am to 5 pm daily (for a small admission fee) and has numerous natural history exhibits and a very large aquarium section with a fish roundabout and a touch-tank tidepool. Adult and junior academy classes and field trips on Bay-related subjects are offered to members and non-members at a moderate cost.

Bodega Bay Institute

Building 240 — Fort Mason, San Francisco 94123. (776-4449) The Institute offers education and adventure on explorations of the natural world of northern California. Some of these one-day or weekend trips concern the Bay — salt marshes, tidal life, the Fort Point Beach, Baylands and maritime history.

Coyote Point Museum

Coyote Point, San Mateo 94401. (573-2595) There is a small museum at Coyote Point with nature displays. A small zoo has some interesting animals. Classes are given for school children. The education center is open Mondays to Saturdays from 9 am to 5 pm, and on Sundays from 1 to 5 pm. Memberships are available.

Baylands Nature Interpretive Center

2775 Embarcadero Road, Palo Alto 94301. (329-2506) The Interpretive Center has displays and offers various programs — movies and slides on Indians, geology, salt marshes, birds and marine life of the Bay. Free weekend walks feature migrating birds, marsh life and bicycle excursions. There are special programs for school classes. A boardwalk over the marsh preserve presents a good opportunity for watching shorebirds. The Interpretive Center is open weekdays from 2 to 5 pm, and weekends from 10 in the morning to 6 in the evening.

Bird-watching and Sanctuaries

San Francisco Bay is an important stopover on the Pacific flyway — migratory birds find a plentiful food supply and good wintering ground; waterfowl, shore birds and many others find a home on San Francisco Bay. For more birding information:

Golden Gate Audubon Society
2718 Telegraph Avenue #206
Berkeley 94705   (843-2222)

The Audubon Society offers Bay shoreline field trips and bird trips all over northern California. Also there are spring birding cruises to the Farallon Islands and pelagic trips from Monterey for bird-watching and whale-watching. They operate a northern California rare bird alert. Dial in to find out where the rare ones have been sighted (843-2211).

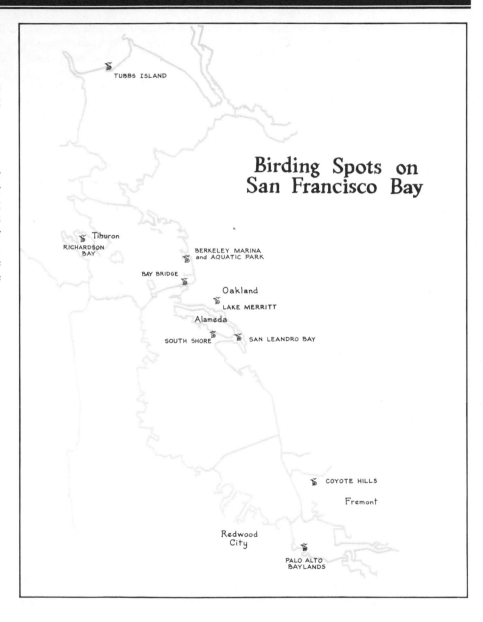

Birding Spots on San Francisco Bay

Richardson Bay

The National Audubon Society operates the Richardson Bay Wildlife Sanctuary (see the section on *Ecology Collections*). On Richardson Bay in Tiburon, the refuge has riparian habitat, open water and marsh. It is open Wednesdays through Sundays and naturalist programs are offered. It is the winter home for thousands of birds, and pods of harbor seals use Richardson Bay as a hauling ground. You can see ducks, shore birds and terns — avocets, canvasbacks, coots, willets, spotted and western sandpipers, ring-billed and California gulls, common and snowy egrets, and great blue herons.

Tubbs Island

The refuge at Tubbs Island is operated by The Nature Conservancy (see the section *Finding the Bay*). It is protected from casual entrance by a locked gate. The habitat is marsh, farmland and open water. The recent drought was hard on the marsh, but you should be able to find marsh hawks, white-tailed kites, loggerhead shrikes, short-eared owls, and wandering tattlers.

Berkeley

Along the Berkeley shoreline are some birding spots with easy access — Aquatic Park inshore from the freeway, the marsh between the freeway and the marina, and around the piers of the marina itself. Sometimes you can find short-eared owls in the marsh. Look around the waters of the yacht harbor for the Arctic, common and red-throated loons.

Bay Bridge - Radio Stations

Located just north of the toll plaza on the Oakland end of the Bay Bridge — the Port of Oakland calls this area Northport Beach (see the section *Finding the Bay*). In the late summer and fall, you can find shore birds, terns and gulls. The sand spit is a major roosting area for shore birds. You can find ducks and grebes; also Arctic and common terns, and the rare California least tern. Visiting the marsh at high tide, you may see the endangered California clapper rail which nests here.

Lake Merritt

Lake Merritt in Oakland is a controlled tidal lake. It is also North America's oldest wildlife sanctuary (designated in 1870). There is a full-time naturalist, and programs include bird-banding and caring for injured birds; fenced feeding pond and talk daily at 3:30 pm; Saturday nature walks; and Sunday programs in the Science Center. Ducks, gulls, swans, pelicans, geese and coots are found at the lake. Black-crowned night herons nest on the islands. You will find Canada geese and great and snowy egrets nesting. The best chance for deep-water diving ducks is in the winter. Snow and white-fronted geese visit; Barrow's goldeneye visits regularly in the winter; and the tufted duck (which is rare in the area) sometimes appears in the winter.

Alameda South Shore

The eastern part of Robert Crown Memorial State Beach (see section *Finding the Bay*) has good birding. You can find twenty species on the shorelands. The best time is one hour after high tide, especially in the winter.

San Leandro Bay

You will find Arrowhead Marsh on the south side and Bay Park Refuge on the east side of San Leandro Bay (see section *Finding the Bay*). The state made the area a refuge in 1931, and the East Bay Regional Parks District is planning pathways and a bird observation tower. Besides terns, plovers and avocets, you can find horned larks nesting and herons roosting. In March and April watch the courtship dance of the western grebe.

Coyote Hills

In Fremont, Coyote Hills Regional Park has a variety of habitats (see the section *Ecology Collections*). There are salt ponds, freshwater marshes (with a boardwalk), and wooded hillsides. You can find pelicans, avocets, swifts, stilts, northern phalaropes, hawks and herons. On top of the hill there is a platform for the winter nest of a great horned owl. In the freshwater marsh you can see long-billed marsh wrens, Virginia and sora rails, common gallinules, and a roost of white-tailed kites.

Palo Alto Baylands

The Baylands Nature Interpretive Center is near the Palo Alto Yacht Harbor (see the section *Ecology Collections*). The nature center has a full-time naturalist, interpretive programs and a cunning boardwalk over the marsh. Fall bird walks look for migrants and residents — sand pipers, shore birds, ducks and double-crested cormorants. The best time to look over the marsh is at high tide when the water forces the birds out of their nests and burrows. Look for large gulls, the endangered California clapper rail, the nesting blue-winged teal (rare), and the European widgeon (rare).

Endangered Species

Endangered Species

Several animals that depend on the incredibly rich and complex ecosystem of wetlands and marshlands for nesting and foraging are in danger of vanishing from San Francisco Bay. They appear on U.S. and California rare and endangered species lists, and actually face extinction. In earlier times, the pressure on these species came from hunting (meat or plumage) and habitat depredation. Now, they still face human encroachment (although they are no longer hunted) through habitat reduction, pollution of feeding grounds, and pesticides entering the food chain.

Fur seals are gone, sea otters are gone and some fish species are gone from San Francisco Bay. The black brant is merely a rare visitor, the peregrine falcon is rarely sighted. The three subspecies of salt marsh song sparrow are becoming more rare as their habitat along sloughs and marshes disappears. Maybe the trend can be reversed, particularly since more sensitivity is being shown to bayland habitat and more ecological preserves are being created — perhaps in time.

Salt-marsh harvest mouse

The harvest mouse lives in marsh areas of San Pablo Bay and the South Bay (near Alviso and Palo Alto). The little bugger is hard to spot, but you may find him when the sun warms the marshes and he comes out of the round tunnels of grasses, one inch in diameter, used as runways. The tiny brown or cinnamon mouse with reddish belly is shy, being food for owls and other predators. He lives in the pickleweed and cord grass salt marsh, eating seeds and pickleweed and drinking salt water. Only in the habitat on the Bay shoreline can his nests be found.

Brown pelican

The birth rate of the pelican has been adversely affected by pesticides. This large, bulky, brownish bird has a big bill with a pouch underneath. It is the largest fish-eater and plunges into the water to take a fish into the pouch. The peculiar flight pattern — a couple of slow-winging flaps, then a glide — easily identifies the pelican. Six-foot wingspreads flash as they flap in line or V-formation, sometimes seeming to touch the water. They perch on pilings with bill on breast. The pelican appears in limited numbers on the Bay, usually sometime between June and September.

California clapper rail

One of the largest U.S. rails, the clapper rail resembles a brown chicken and is known as a "marsh hen." It is grey-brown with speckles and a tawny breast and a stubby white patch of a tail. It is secretive and lives almost nowhere else except on San Francisco Bay. Evolution has made it almost flightless. The long bill is used to find clams, mussels and frogs in the sloughs and mudflats. High marsh ground is needed for the large nests, arched over with thick cord grass and pickleweed. This bird may be seen when high tides drive it into the open in nesting marshes near Alviso and Palo Alto and in San Leandro Bay.

California black rail

The black rail is secretive and shy — it is very difficult to find a ranting of these rails. The tidal marshes of the Bay are its principal habitat, although some migrate to southern California and inland fresh water. The smallest rail in the country, it is sparrow-size. The tiny bird is almost coal black, with white speckles on the back and a cinnamon neck nape.

California least tern

It is no longer possible to discover a torrent of these terns — they are definitely endangered. Plume-hunters almost wiped them out. They nest on southern beaches, but spend some time on the Bay, usually from April to August. Scattered colonies live on Bair and Greco islands in the Redwood City area. They may feed anywhere on the Bay, diving for minnows and shrimp in estuaries and tidal sloughs. This is the smallest tern, white and pearl grey with a black cap and a yellow bill.

Seal-watching

During the past several years, water pollution and fish loss caused seals to virtually disappear from the South Bay and to become scarce in other parts of San Francisco Bay. Improved water quality has started to restore the food chain, and now seals have started a comeback.

The seal that lives in the protected parts of San Francisco Bay is the harbor seal *(phoca vitulina)*. It grows to be four or five feet long. It is gray with white, yellow or dark spots like a leopard (which it is sometimes called). It feeds on fish, squid and crustaceans. The breeding season occurs in winter and early spring. Unlike most other seals, it is merely polygamous, but does not collect harems. Hind flippers are the identification characteristic that differentiates the harbor seal from sea lions. The rear flippers always extend behind in tail-like fashion, they cannot be folded up alongside the body. This makes it difficult for the harbor seal to clamber over rocks, restricting it to beaches and mud flats where it can "haul out."

Other marine mammals are sometimes seen on the Bay. The California sea lion *(zalophus californianus)* is familiar as the "trained seal" of animal shows. It can reach a size of eight feet. The male is dark brown, the female lighter. The sea lion (as opposed to the harbor seal) finds it easier to climb over rocks and ledges because the hind flippers rotate back to front and can be folded under the body. You are much more likely to see a California sea lion scrambling over Seal Rocks (along with the larger Stellar sea lion) on the Pacific Ocean side of San Francisco than in the Bay. Occasionally you may see harbor or bay porpoises on the open Bay waters. Historical footnote: There is even a reported instance of a killer whale being taken as far inland as Benicia.

In a couple of rather inaccessible locations on the South Bay, harbor seals retreat for R & R on the slough banks. There are several other places that seals are likely to be found cavorting. And

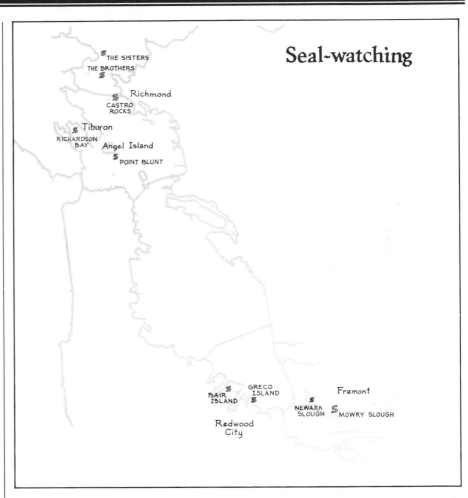

Seal-watching

there is one sure-fire spot where it is easy to do a little seal-watching at almost any time.

South of the San Mateo Bridge, major and minor breeding areas for harbor seals are to be protected in the SF Bay National Wildlife Refuge. A colony of as many as two hundred seals uses the mud flats of Mowry Slough near Fremont for hauling and pupping. A small nursery is located at the mouth of Newark Slough. Other minor rookeries are on Bair Island (Corkscrew Slough) and Greco Island near Redwood City. All of these hauling grounds are protected by their inaccessibility, so they do not offer any seal-watching.

On the Central Bay, there are several places where harbor seals hang out. In winter a pod of seals migrates from the South Bay to Richardson Bay. The Audubon Society's wildlife sanctuary in Tiburon protects not only migrating birds, but offers a place to find the seals resting on the mud flats. Sometimes you can see hauled harbor seals on The Sisters and The Brothers and on Angel Island's Point Blunt.

Castro Rocks is the place where you are almost certain to find seals basking in the sun. The rocks are beneath the Richmond-San Rafael Bridge. Approaching from Richmond, take the Point Molate exit and look for Redrock Marina. Directly under the bridge is a public fishing pier which provides close-up views of the rocks.

Sharks in the Bay

Sharks are probably the most abundant fish in San Francisco Bay. Several species are common to these waters and are not considered dangerous to man. When you see fishermen on a fishing pier, they may be hoping to hook a shark because it is a good food fish. The largest shark caught on the Bay was taken near Sausalito — an eleven-foot, 464-pound sixgill cowshark. The largest ever seen on the Bay was a basking shark. The eighteen-foot creature fouled fishermen's nets near Hunters Point sometime in the 1950s.

The brown smoothhound shark is the most abundant shark in the Bay. It is less than three feet in length. Easily caught from boats and piers, it is good eating meat. One of the largest kinds of shark found in the Bay is the sevengill cowshark. The largest recorded catch was eight and a half feet, but it is reputed to reach fifteen feet in length. The flesh is edible, in fact it may be the most palatable of sharks. The dogfish swims in schools as a scavenging predator and is food for larger sharks. It grows up to five feet long and gives birth to live pups. The very attractive leopard shark is light gray with dark bar markings on its top and spots on the sides and tail. It is less than four feet long and has tasty flesh. Other sharks found in the Bay are the soupfin and the thresher.

Sharks have an evil charisma that inspires credulous stories. In his inimitable style, Mark Twain reported on startling San Francisco sharks in the 1860s.

The story goes that Alexander Badlam, nephew of San Francisco's erstwhile civic leader Sam Brannan, created a furor using the newspapers — a shark scare. A ferocious shark was harpooned in the Bay of San Francisco by Italian fishermen. It was brought ashore and displayed to a wondering populace; actually, the fish had been cleverly imported from Mexico. Badlam earnestly went around to the newspapers with a written-up item about the shark excitement. A few days later, fishermen hooked another shark (it was the same one). It, too, was exhibited and followed up with another news story. This sequence of events continued periodically for several weeks — sometimes every three days, sometimes every day. Badlam, who was the importer of the sharks, occasionally had to vary his methods to sustain the sensation. When the carcass became too moth-eaten, a fresh fish was brought in. The team of shark-killers would tow the live one ashore and dispatch it before interested spectators.

Then back to the water (surreptitiously) for a few more harpoonings. One shark was towed into the Bay, fed some pigs, and then brought to the dock. It was killed and cut open, accompanied by wailings and gnashings about the terrible creature having eaten a child as the young pork was removed from its stomach. The onslaught of shark items in the local press had a curious effect on San Francisco's citizens. They showed distinct signs of uneasiness about their daily dip in the Bay and swimming became exceedingly unpopular. It didn't seem healthy to bathe there, and so they stopped. The aversion to swimming in the Bay did not cease, even when it turned out that Aleck Badlam was the manipulator and that he had recently erected a swimming bath on Third Street, opposite South Park. It was advertised as the largest of its kind in the United States. (It seems that Mark Twain must have fabricated, or at least embroidered, his report because no shark scare items appeared in any contemporary newspapers.)

Regulatory and Planning Agencies for the Bay

These major governmental agencies control development and influence planning on the Bay and its shoreline. City, county and regional planning departments also have authority over Bay projects. All are good sources of information about Bay protection.

San Francisco Bay Conservation and Development Commission (BCDC)

30 Van Ness Avenue, San Francisco 94102. (557-3686) The Bay Commission was created by the McAteer-Petris Act in 1965 as a regional body to regulate filling and building on the shoreline and wetlands. The commission's public hearing and permit process applies to private and public development. The goal is to protect the Bay as a natural resource and to develop it for public benefit.

US Coast Guard

630 Sansome Street, San Francisco 94111. (556-3530) Responsible for aids to navigation on the Bay, rescue of sailors in distress and monitoring oil spills.

US Army Corps of Engineers

100 McAllister Street, San Francisco 94102. (556-0595) The Corps has authority over navigable waters and flood control projects. They issue permits for dredging and filling. They also operate the Bay Model in Sausalito, doing research on water problems of the entire Bay system.

US Department of Interior — Fish and Wildlife Service

2800 Cottage Way, Sacramento 95825. (916-484-4748) Protects wildlife (i.e., migratory birds) and wildlife habitats for public enjoyment, interpretation and education.

US Environmental Protection Agency

215 Fremont Street, San Francisco 94105. (556-3232) Concerned with environmental pollution and water quality of the Bay.

US Geological Survey (USGS)

345 Middlefield Road, Menlo Park 94025. (323-8111) Engaged in studies of Bay water and geology. It is the best source for maps of the Bay. Also, Public Inquiries Office, Custom House (Room 504), 555 Battery Street, San Francisco (556-5627).

California Department of Fish and Game

1416 Ninth Street, Sacramento 95814. (916-445-3531) Protects wildlife and habitats, and classifies certain land and water areas as refuges.

California Department of Water Resources

1419 Ninth Street, Sacramento 95814. (916-445-9248) Establishes policy for water quality and quantity, and water pollution control.

Water Quality Control Board — San Francisco Region

1111 Jackson, Oakland 94607. (464-1255) Authority over water quality and pollution control.

California Department of Transportation (CalTrans) — Division of Toll Bridges

Box 3366, Rincon Annex, San Francisco 94119. (557-3692) Jurisdiction over the bridges crossing the Bay, except the Golden Gate.

Golden Gate Bridge, Highway and Transportation District

Box 9000, Presidio Station, San Francisco 94129. (921-5858 / 434-2086) The District was formed in 1928, of the counties of San Francisco, Marin, Sonoma, Del Norte and parts of Mendocino and Napa, to build the Golden Gate Bridge. Operates buses across the bridge, and ferryboats from San Francisco to Sausalito and Larkspur.

Port of San Francisco

Ferry Building, San Francisco 94111. (391-8000) Operates the maritime piers of San Francisco and is responsible for some waterfront development.

Port of Oakland

66 Jack London Square, Oakland 94607. (444-3188) Operates the maritime piers of Oakland and is responsible for some waterfront development.

Golden Gate National Recreation Area (GGNRA)

Fort Mason, San Francisco 94123. (556-2920) The GGNRA is a park unit that has lands on the Bay shoreline on both sides of the Golden Gate.

California Department of Parks and Recreation

Box 2390, Sacramento 95811. (916-445-6477) Preserves the natural environment of the Bay shoreline in several state parks.

San Francisco Bay National Wildlife Refuge

3849 Peralta Boulevard, Fremont 94536. (792-0222) Responsible for wildlife habitat and protection in a Bay refuge complex that includes the Farallon Islands and a portion of San Pablo Bay, as well as assembling what will eventually be 23,000 acres of refuge on both sides of the South Bay. It is also developing facilities for interpretation, education and public enjoyment of these South Bay lands.

East Bay Regional Parks District

11500 Skyline Boulevard, Oakland 94619. (531-9300) Administers parks in the East Bay with recreational opportunities and ecology programs. Lately there has been more emphasis on acquisition and development of beaches and shoreline on the Bay.

San Mateo County Parks and Recreation Department

Government Center, Redwood City 94063. (364-5600) Administers a couple of parks on the Bay shore.

Environimental Organizations

Here are some of the most active groups participating in the ecological issues facing San Francisco Bay. Their protection and conservation programs are certainly worth supporting.

Save San Francisco Bay Association

Box 925, Berkeley 94701. (849-3053) In the 1950s San Francisco Bay — shoreline, wildlife and beauty — was threatened by uncontrolled dredging and filling — too much development. It seemed the Bay was in danger of being diminished to the size of a river. The response was an upsurge of conservation concern, probably the first citizens' ecological crusade. The saltgrass-roots movement, led by Mrs. Clark Kerr of Berkeley, became the Save San Francisco Bay Association in 1960. The outcome of this agitation was the bill introduced in Sacramento by Senator Eugene McAteer and Assemblyman Nicholas Petris which created the Bay Conservation and Development Commission. Don Sherwood, who was a radio station KSFO personality, is credited with arousing public interest and creating a flood tide of mail on this issue in a pre-environmental era (1965), which caused passage of the BCDC legislation. Save the Bay still works to protect open water, to preserve wildlife and views, and to monitor the shoreline for compliance with filling and dumping regulations. Membership contributions start at $1.

Sierra Club

530 Bush Street, San Francisco 94108. (981-8634) The main office of the club has a bookstore of environmental and outdoor books. Members receive a bi-monthly magazine and a newsletter. Memberships in the Sierra Club start at $25/year.

San Francisco Bay Chapter. 6014 College Avenue, Oakland 94618. (658-7470) The largest regional chapter with many legislative interests and outdoor activities. Bookstore of environmental and outdoor books at chapter office.

Loma Prieta Chapter. 1176 Emerson Street, Palo Alto 94301. (327-8111) Regional chapter for San Mateo and Santa Clara area.

Audubon Societies

Golden Gate Audubon Society. 2718 Telegraph Avenue #206, Berkeley 94705. (843-2222)

Marin Audubon Society. Box 441, Tiburon 94920. (479-0258)

Santa Clara Valley Audubon Society. 1176 Emerson Street, Palo Alto 94301 (328-5313)

Of course, the Audubon Society is interested in birds, but they have other Bay concerns — East Bay Regional Parks, marine mammals, Corps of Engineers, fish and game habitat, and the GGNRA. Members participate in outings and receive a beautiful bi-monthly magazine and a newsletter. Memberships start at $18/year.

The Nature Conservancy

425 Bush Street, San Francisco 94108. (989-3056) Preserves significant ecological and environmental areas by means of acquisition and management. They have protected many acres of shoreline, including the Tubbs Island refuge. Memberships from $10/year.

Marin Conservation League

1330 Lincoln Avenue, San Rafael 94901. (456-1912) Protection of the natural environment of Marin County. Prominent in preserving Richardson Bay and creating the wildlife refuge. Memberships from $7.50/year.

Friends of the Earth

124 Spear Street, San Francisco 94105. (495-4770) A bunch of very active and scrappy environmentalists. FOE has a San Francisco regional group. Memberships start at $25/year.

Oceanic Society/San Francisco Bay Chapter

Building 240 — Fort Mason, San Francisco 94123. (441-5970) Dedicated to education, research and conservation of the marine environment. Offers films, lectures and courses; and monitors water quality in conjunction with other agencies. Opportunities for nautical field trips — winter whale-watching cruises, evening Bay sails and Farallon patrols. They publish *Oceans*, a beautiful magazine. Membership $10/year.

San Francisco Bay Gazetteer

(Locations noted by counties.)

Alameda (County and Creek):

Derived from *Alamo*, "poplar, or cottonwood." The southern part of the county was called *la Alameda*, "grove of poplar trees," probably by explorer Pedro Amador (1795); then the creek was called *Rio de la Alameda*; and a land grant in the area was named *Arroyo de la Alameda* (1842). The peninsula was known as *Encinal de San Antonio*, "oak grove on San Antonio Creek." When the city of Alameda was founded there by W.W. Chipman and Gideon Aughinbaugh (1853), it got the name of the creek some distance to the south; later two other towns appeared on the peninsula, Woodstock and Encinal. With the dredging of a tidal channel through to San Leandro Bay in 1902, Alameda became the island it is today.

Albany (Hill):

Part of the area that was called O'Shean's View, which was incorporated as Ocean View (1908). It got its present name (1909) by transfer from the city in New York, birthplace of Albany's first mayor. The Hill was first known as *El Cerrito*, "little hill." *(Alameda)*

Alcatraz Island:

The name *Isla de Alcatraces*, "Pelican Island," was bestowed on the much larger Yerba Buena Island by Juan Manuel de Ayala when he charted the Bay (1775); a later map-maker transferred the name to the smaller Alcatraces Island (1826). It was also known as Bird Island. The name took its present form (1851); because it was used as a prison, it became known as "The Rock." *(SF)*

Almonte:

Means "at the woods." A rail stop name that was changed from Mill Valley Junction by the railroad (1912). *(Marin)*

Alvarado:

See Union City.

Alviso (Slough):

From Ygnacio Alviso who was in the group of settlers that came to northern California with Capt. Juan Bautista de Anza. Originally called *El Embarcadero de Santa Clara*, the landing for the Mission Santa Clara (1777). A land grant was given to Alviso (1838), and he settled there (1840), and a short time later the name was changed. The town was laid out (1849) by Chester S. Lyman at the request of Jacob D. Hoppe; about this time Alviso was one of the busiest ports on the Bay; for some time it was known as Port San Jose. *(Santa Clara)*

Angel Island:

Named *Isla de Nuestra Señora de los Angeles*, "island of Our Lady of the Angels," by Juan Manuel de Ayala whose expedition first charted the Bay. This name was Anglicized on maps as Angel Island (1826); but was also known as Wood Island (until 1859) because of wood-gathering there; and in the 1850s was known as Los Angeles Island. The oldest extant place name on the Bay. When military post was established (1863), the island was called Camp Reynolds; then the army renamed it Fort McDowell (1900); but all along it was still known as Angel Island. *(Marin)*

Anita Rock:

Named by Capt. Joseph L. Folsom (after 1848), for the small barque *Anita*, the first armed ship to patrol the Bay (for the Army). It shows above water at low tide off Crissey Field. *(SF)*

Arch Rock:

Name often given rocks because of their formation shape. It was some distance to the west of Alcatraz, showing above the water, until blown up (1901) to clear the harbor of navigational obstructions. *(SF)*

Arroyo Viejo:

Name, "old creek," for a stream that flows into San Leandro Bay. *(Alameda)*

Avisadero:

See Point Avisadero.

Ayala Cove:

Named for Juan Manuel de Ayala, captain of the *San Carlos*, the first ship to enter San Francisco Bay, in August 1775 (pace Sir Francis); the ship anchored in the cove while the Bay was being explored. The US government opened a quarantine station there which caused the name to be changed to Hospital Cove (1880s). The name reverted to the present one when Angel Island became a state park (1955); officially rededicated (1969). The old name, Hospital Cove, still appears on many maps. *(Marin)*

Bair Island:

Named for a certain Bair, chief oysterman of the South Belmont Oysterhouse (1880s-90s). It received name when the area was drained to form an island (1910). Near the port of Redwood City. *(San Mateo)*

Ballena Bay:

Rather recent name for a man-made fill development of houses and a marina on the south shore of Alameda. The name derives from the Spanish for whales and whaling. *(Alameda)*

Bay Farm Island:

Originally an island, until filled for development and the Oakland Airport; used for a long time as market gardens. *(Alameda)*

Bay Slough:

Named, of course, for the Bay; near Redwood Shores development. *(San Mateo)*

Beards Creek:

Named (1873) for E.L. Beard who acquired some mission lands and settled there (1846). A trace of the creek may be found alongside the Dumbarton Bridge. *(Alameda)*

Belmont (Creek, Slough and Channel):

Used because it is an attractive-sounding name that is a variant of the French *beaumont*, "beautiful mountain." The area was named because of a symmetrically rounded eminence near the resort hotel of Steinburger and Beard (1851). Originally Angelo's Creek, then Belmont Embarcadero Creek (1850s), the watercourses were then given the present names (1860s). *(San Mateo)*

Belvedere Island (Lagoon and Cove):

Of Italian origin, "beautiful view"; name bestowed by land company as part of the real estate promotion (1890), although they used Belvedere Peninsula. Called *El Potrero de la Punta del Tiburon*, "pasture of Point Tiburon," when it was used for cattle as part of John Reed's rancho (1830s-40s). Known as Kashow's (or Kershaw's) Island for a squatter Israel Kashow (or Kershaw or Kashaw) who lived there for many years (1855-85). Anomalously called Peninsula (or Peninsular) Island when U.S. War Department claimed it (1867); mentioned as Promontory Island in an Army report (1879). Codfishers anchored in Stillwater Bay, which is now the Lagoon, and so the island became Still Island (1864). The Cove was named *Ensenada del Santo Evangelio*, "bay of the Holy Gospel," by Ayala (1775). *(Marin)*

Berkeley (Pier):

Named for George Berkeley (1685-1753), Irish, Bishop of Cloyne and philosopher, author of "Westward the course of empire takes its way . . . ." The name was selected about the time the university was getting started (1866). The shoreline community was called Ocean View (1860s); the vicinity of the marina was known as Jacob's Landing (1873). *(Alameda)*

Bird Island:

Named for birds nesting there; close by Brooks Island, just off Richmond. *(Contra Costa)*

Black John Slough:

Some confusion exists about the name of this slough and the nearby Black Point, but it was probably named for a man known as Black John who lived there (1850s). *(Marin)*

Black Point (at Petaluma River):

Named for James (or John) Black who settled in the area in 1832 and owned ranchos there in the 1840s and '50s. Another man, J. Black (or Black John), came to the area later (1870s). Or perhaps explorers called it black because of the dark appearance of its forests which were timbered (1860s); as you can see, some confusion exists about how it got the name Black Point (1865). Then the name was changed to Grandview Terrace for a community there (1905); but it reverted to the present name (1944). *(Marin)*

Black Point (San Francisco):

Part of the military reserve which is now Fort Mason, it was known as Black Point (1861) and still appears on maps; named for dark scrub brush growing there. The adjacent lagoon, now Aquatic Park, was called Yerba Buena Anchorage (until 1870). See Fort Mason. *(SF)*

Blossom Rock:

Named by English cartographer W. F. Beechey for his ship, *Blossom* (1826). Between Alcatraz and Yerba Buena Island. Blown up in 1871 because it was a hazard to navigation. *(SF)*

Bluff Point:

Named because of its terrain, a steeply rising cliff or bank. Earlier known as Reed's Point; located on the rancho of John Reed, Marin pioneer. Facing Angel Island across Raccoon Strait. *(Marin)*

Bonita:

See Point Bonita.

Brewer Island:

Named for Frank M. Brewer when he put up levees and drained the area for a dairy ranch (1905); now occupied by Foster City. *(San Mateo)*

Brooklyn Basin:

Towns of Clinton (1853) and San Antonio (1854) combined to form Brooklyn (1856), southeast of Lake Merritt, alongside the basin; William Heath Davis said that, like NYC, Oakland would be San Francisco's Brooklyn. The town was annexed to Oakland (1872). Historically, the location of shipyards and dry docks: many square-riggers tied up there, including whalers, sealers, cod fishermen, and salmon ships of the Alaska Packers Association. *(Alameda)*

Brooks Island:

Originally called *Isla del Carmen* by Ayala (1776); called Rocky Island (1850). It was on a map with its present name, probably from the owner (1854); but it was also known as Sheep Island (1870), which it is still sometimes called today. It has been, through history, an Indian camp site, sheep grazing land, a quarry, an orchard, a piggery, a shrimp fishing camp, a hunting club; and now the island just offshore from Richmond has been acquired (1969) by the East Bay Regional Park District as a preserve. *(Contra Costa)*

The Brothers:

It is an international custom of long standing to name a group of two or more orographic features of similar appearance brothers or sisters. These were perhaps known at one time as *Islas de Pajaro*, "eagle islands." Lying just off the tip of Point San Pablo, the smaller West Brother is bare, and the East Brother is the location of a picturesque lighthouse which began operation in 1874. The light was automated in 1970, and was *not* the last manned lighthouse on the Bay. *(Contra Costa)*

Burlingame:

Named by William Ralston (1868) for his friend Anson Burlingame, orator and diplomat, US minister to China and advisor to the Chinese government (1860s), who never lived there. *(San Mateo)*

Calabazas Creek:

In Spanish it means "pumpkins, squash or gourds," and was a popular place name in the South Bay area. The creek runs in Santa Clara and feeds Guadalupe Slough. *(Santa Clara)*

Calaveras Point:

Means "skulls," and refers to human skeletons; an Indian holy place where skulls and bones were found was mentioned, *parage de las Calaveras* (1809). Coyote Creek was called Calaveras, thus Point C. (1820s); and the name was at one time applied to what are now Coyote Hills (1855). *(Alameda)*

Candlestick Point (Cove):

Named for a tall rock offshore (1890). The Highway Department considerately acknowledged the name Candlestick Cove (1954) before fill operations for the freeway obliterated most of it. *(SF)*

Carquinez Strait (Heights and Bridge):

Name derived from villages of Karquin Indians found there, first used for descriptions, *Rancheria de los Karquines* and *Estrecho de los Karquines* (1807). The spelling remained Karquines until 1905. The first explorers, the Fages expedition, named the place *Boca del Puerto Dulce,* "mouth of the fresh-water port" (1772). *(Contra Costa and Solano)*

Castro Creek (Point and Rocks):

Named for Joaquín I. Castro, owner of land grant *Rancho San Pablo;* first granted to his father, Francisco, a Spanish pioneer member of Anza's expedition. The creek was named first. The rocks are beneath the Richmond-San Rafael Bridge. *(Contra Costa)*

Cavallo Point:

Name shown on land grant *Punta de los Caballos,* "point of the horses," (1845). Horses were kept at this point just inside the Golden Gate for travel in Marin. The name was corrupted to its present spelling (1850s). *(Marin)*

Central Basin:

Named because of its location on the southern San Francisco waterfront. *(SF)*

China Basin:

Ships of the Pacific Main Steamship Line, the "China Clippers," tied up here, hence the name (1860s). The watercourse known as Mission Creek originally extended inland for two miles to Market Street in the vicinity of Valencia Street (early 1800s). *(SF)*

China Camp:

Fishing village above Point San Pedro, settled by migration from San Francisco's Chinatown (1882). Estimated population from 3,000 to 10,000 at the height of fishing activity, mostly shrimp netting; dwindled when the State made prohibitive fishing laws (1910). *(Marin)*

Codornices Creek:

Name from *Codorniz,* "quail," which were found there (1818); forms part of the boundary between Albany and Berkeley. *(Alameda)*

Colma Creek:

Took its name from the town, which was called Station on early maps because of the railroad, then School House Station (1860s). Current name was possibly coined from Coleman (1872). *(San Mateo)*

Cone Rock:

Named because of its shape. Ayala originally named it for another shape, that of a Carmelite friar (1775), and he called what is now Richardson Bay *Ensenada del Carmelita.* *(Marin)*

Contra Costa County:

Name used by early Spanish residents of Yerba Buena for "opposite coast." It applied to Marin and the East Bay (as early as 1797); then it commonly came to mean East Bay (1835). When Alameda County was formed (1853), the name became meaningless.

Cooley Landing:

Named for Lester P. Cooley who settled there and ran a dairy ranch and a landing on the Bay (1867). *(San Mateo)*

Corinthian Island:

Named for the Corinthian Yacht Club, established 1886, which chose a site on the island beside Tiburon for its clubhouse. Named Valentine's Island for owner Thomas B. Valentine (1892). Present name taken in 1907. *(Marin)*

Corkscrew Slough:

Named because of its meandering course (before 1860). Slough originally meant muddy place. Near the port of Redwood City. *(San Mateo)*

Corte Madera Creek:

Name came from *Rancho Corte de Madera del Presidio,* "place where lumber is cut for the presidio," pioneer John Reed's land grant (1834); he built first sawmill in Marin. The shortened name was used (1846). *(Marin)*

Coyote Creek:

Western American adaptation of *coyotl,* the Aztec word for "prairie wolf." Coyotes also were prominent in the mythology of California Indians. Name mentioned as *Arroyo del Coyote* by Anza (1776), the oldest place name in Santa Clara County. The name Calaveras was applied to creek for a time (1820s). *(Alameda and Santa Clara)*

Coyote Hills (Slough):

Derivation as above. In early Spanish days it was part of *Potrero de los Cerritos,* "pasture of the little hills." The name Calaveras was applied to the hills for a time (1855); then the area received its present name. *(Alameda)*

Coyote Point (and Little Coyote Point):

Derivation as above. Called *la punta de San Mateo* (1818), *Punta San Matheo* (1827), *San Mateo Point* (later), The Coyote (1850), Big Coyote (1851), Big Coyote Hill (1853). Received present name (1890), and is now a county park. Little Coyote is at the end of the San Mateo Bridge in Foster City. *(San Mateo)*

Crissy Field:
Named for Major Dana H. Crissy, an Army flyer killed in a transcontinental air race (1919). Built on Bay fill as a race track for the Panama-Pacific International Exposition (1915); then chosen as an airfield along San Francisco's northern waterfront. *(SF)*

Crockett:
Town laid out in 1881 by Thomas Edwards, and named for Judge J. B. Crockett of the California Supreme Court who lived there (1860s). Originally one of the wheat ports; but sugar came (1898), first beets, then C+H cane. *(Contra Costa)*

Cypress Point:
Named for trees on the hillside at Point Richmond. *(Contra Costa)*

Davis Point:
Named for prominent Californian William Heath Davis, who settled here in 1838. He was a trader, merchant, ship owner, and ran a store in Yerba Buena (1846), and later became a noted historian of the state. The point is near Rodeo. *(Contra Costa)*

Deepwater Slough:
Named for its navigability; across the channel from the port of Redwood City. *(San Mateo)*

Devils Slough:
Named for its twisting course, which has since been channelized. Near Moffett Field. *(Santa Clara)*

Double Rock:
Named for shape; located off Hunters Point in South Basin. *(SF)*

Drawbridge:
This fascinating town was founded in 1876 by Senator James G. Fair and Alfred E. Davis, executives of the South Pacific Coast RR, as a construction center when the railroad was being built. It is at the extreme southern tip of the Bay, on Station Island, between Mud Slough and Coyote Creek; it took its name from the bridges over these waterways. It is now virtually inaccessible, a ghost town of many structures sinking into the marsh because of the amount of ground water pumped out in the surrounding territory; the population left more than twenty-five years ago, and the last resident pulled out about ten years ago. *(Alameda)*

Dumbarton Point (and Bridge):
When the railroad line came through (1876), a station here was given the name of a county in Scotland. Subsequently the name was transferred to the freight landing, the Point; then it was given to the Bridge (1927). *(Alameda)*

Dutchman Slough:
Named for a settler on the slough. Years ago "Dutchman" was a nickname for a German immigrant, *Deutsch,* but it was at times applied to almost any European. Located near the Sears Point Bridge in Vallejo. *(Solano)*

East Marin Island:
See Marin Islands.

El Campo:
From the Spanish for "field." In California it was more literally translated as "camp." It was an area for weekend outings from San Francisco, picnicking at a stop on the railroad (1890s). Near Paradise Cove. *(Marin)*

The Embarcadero:
In the early days, every settlement on the Bay had an embarcadero, Spanish for "landing place." The name has survived on streets all over the region, but the only one of consequence that remains is The Embarcadero that curves along San Francisco's downtown waterfront. A portion of this street was once called East St. (1906). *(SF)*

Emeryville:
Named for Joseph S. Emery, who came to California (1850) from New Hampshire and bought the land (1859). The town received its name (1897). Part of the area was known as Shellmound, for the Indian shell mound that stood there with an amusement park on top of it (until 1924). *(Alameda)*

Encinal Basin:
Derived from Spanish *encinal,* "oak grove," which was part of the original name for Alameda, *Encinal de San Antonio.* Now the location is a shipping port on the Estuary; in times past it saw a lot of square-rigger sailing ship activity. *(Alameda)*

The Estuary:
Now it is the Oakland Estuary, stretching from the Middle Harbor at the Oakland Mole, through the Inner Harbor, past all the maritime hurly-burly, past Brooklyn Basin, and through the Tidal Canal to San Leandro Bay. It was originally known as San Antonio Creek (1830), taking its name from *Rancho San Antonio,* a land grant to Luis María Peralta (1820). Starting in the 1850s the ferry route up this channel from San Francisco was known as the "Creek Route." In the 1890s this narrow waterway between Oakland and Alameda was dredged all the way through to San Leandro Bay to facilitate navigation, making Alameda an island (completed 1902). For some time (1880s) this was the greatest haven for three- and four-masted sailing ships on the Pacific — it was the world's biggest whaling port, ships were tied up from the cod and salmon fisheries, and there were shipyards and ferryboats scattered about. *(Alameda)*

Estudillo Canal:
Channelized creek that passes through San Leandro; named for José Joaquín Estudillo who settled on a land grant there (1839). *(Alameda)*

Ferry Point:
Ferry terminal of the Atchison, Topeka & Santa Fe transcontinental train service (1900) at Point Richmond; freight cars are still barged across the Bay to San Francisco. *(Contra Costa)*

Fleming Point:
Named for J.J. Fleming (1873) who settled there in 1853; site of Golden Gate Fields racetrack. *(Alameda)*

Fort Baker:

Named for Col. Edward D. Baker, who commanded a Union regiment in the War Between the States and fell at Balls Bluff. He was a veteran of military service, had been a Congressman, lived in California, and was elected senator from Oregon. This army land on the north headland of the Golden Gate was called Lime Point Military Reservation until it received the present name (1897); it is now becoming part of the Golden Gate National Recreation Area. *(Marin)*

Fort McDowell:

Military installation built on Angel Island; named for Maj. Gen. Irvin McDowell (1900), commander of Union Army at First Manassas. At that time the name applied to the entire island Army base; now the fort is known as East Garrison (built 1899), named because there was already a West Garrison. See Quarry Point and Angel Island. *(Marin)*

Fortmann Basin:

Shipping basin on the Oakland Estuary across from Government Island, now occupied by a marina. It was once the home of the sailing fleet of the Alaska Packers Association, engaged in salmon fishing in northern waters. *(Alameda)*

Fort Mason:

From early days this was a military reservation on San Francisco's north shore; it is now the headquarters for the Golden Gate National Recreation Area. It was named (1882) for Col. Richard B. Mason who was military governor after American occupation and during the time of gold discovery in California — his reports to Washington confirmed the discovery and set off the 49er gold rush. Earlier the place was known as *Punta Medanos*, "Sandy Point" (1797). When it was reserved for the military, it was called Point San Jose (1850); defenses there were known as *Batería de San José* and Battery at Yerba Buena. Part of the area was known as Black Point (by 1822, through the 1860s), probably because of vegetation. *(SF)*

Fort Point:

Name was first applied (1851) because of ruins of an old Spanish fort on the point. When Ayala sailed into the Bay, he named it *Punta de San José* (1775); and when Anza founded San Francisco, he planted a cross there on *Cantil Blanco*, "white cliff" (March 1776). The Spanish built a small adobe fort, *Castillo de San Joaquín* (1794). The cliff was cut down and the U.S. Army built the fort that is now there (1853-61); it was named Fort Winfield Scott (1882), for a former commander-in-chief of the Army. The fort was used for construction offices during the building of the Golden Gate Bridge, part of which was designed particularly to preserve it (1930s). Recently Fort Point became a National Historic Site (1970). *(SF)*

Foster City:

Named for Jack Foster, Sr., the developer of this "new town" residential and commercial community on diked and filled Bay land (1964). When it was still mud and marsh, it was called Brewers Island. *(San Mateo)*

Fremont:

Named for Lt. Col. John C. Frémont. In his checkered and controversial career, he led two army exploring expeditions into California, participated in the Bear Flag Revolt, was governor of the state, was a senator, and was a candidate for the presidency. But perhaps most significant of all, he gave the name to the Golden Gate. Early settlements there were called Centerville and Hardscrabble; several districts were incorporated as Fremont (1956). *(Alameda)*

Gallinas Creek:

Name mentioned as *sitio de las Gallinas*, "place of the hens" (1819); then the name was incorporated into Don Timoteo Murphy's land grant, *Rancho San Pedro, Santa Margarita y las Gallinas* (1844); subsequently the creek was mapped with its present name (1873). *(Marin)*

Gas House Cove:

Named for various gas and electric companies that once were in the area; now a marina, part of the San Francisco Marina, adjacent to Fort Mason. *(SF)*

Giant:

Named by the Giant Powder Company which built a plant on Point Pinole (1870s); "Giant powder" was a common early name for dynamite. *(Contra Costa)*

Golden Gate (Bridge):

Named by Lt. Col. John C. Frémont (1846), in a fortuitous prophecy which came true two years later when the Gold Rush started. Of course, being a proper geographer, he bestowed the name in Greek — "I gave it the name Chrysopylae, or Golden Gate, for the same reason that the harbor of Byzantium was called Chrysoceras or Golden Horn." The Indian word for the place was *Yulupa*, "Sunset Strait"; the Spanish name was *Boca del Puerto de San Francisco* (1775). The Bridge spontaneously received the name when the project was being envisioned (1923). *(SF and Marin)*

Government Island:

Named because the federal government built it (1916), by dredging and filling a marshy flat in the Oakland Estuary, even covering over a couple of derelict 1880s square-riggers that were rotting there. *(Alameda)*

Greco Island:

Named for V.C. Greco who had a salt works there from 1910 to 1923; offshore from the port of Redwood City. *(San Mateo)*

Greenbrae:

A ranch with this eudemonic name was in the area (1870s); and the Northwestern Pacific RR had a station there (before 1911). *(Marin)*

Green Point (Landing):

Named for Talbot H. Green, a San Francisco merchant, who had a trading wharf there (1850s). When it was revealed that he was an embezzler back East, he returned to face the music. Landing on Mowry Slough near Newark. *(Alameda)*

Guadalupe Slough (River):

Named by Anza (1776) *Rio de Nuestra Señora de Guadalupe*, for the patron saint of Catholic Mexico and principal patron of his expedition. Also known as *Rio de San José* (later). Americans abbreviated the name, making it meaningless. *(Santa Clara)*

Hayward (Landing):

Named for William Hayward who settled there (1851), and built a hotel (1852). The town was laid out (1867); the name was spelled Haywards (until 1900). *(Alameda)*

Hercules:

Named for the Hercules Powder Company which built a plant on Point Pinole (1880). The company town was later incorporated (1900). *(Contra Costa)*

Horseshoe Bay:

Popular descriptive name to indicate the shape of a geographical feature; just inside the north side of the Golden Gate. *(Marin)*

Hospital Cove:

See Ayala Cove.

Hunters Point:

There are two stories about this name. It could have been named for Robert Hunter and his brother Philip, who tried to establish South San Francisco here (1849); but it was known as Hunter Point before that time, because sportsmen went hunting there — so this is more likely. It was called *Punta de Concha*, "seashell point" (1775); known as *potrero viejo*, "old pasture" (early 1830s). *(SF)*

India Basin:

Named for the ships in Indian trade which tied up there (1870s-80s); north side of Hunters Point. *(SF)*

Islais Creek (Channel):

Named for the shrubs which lined the creek draining the slopes of what is now Twin Peaks. The Salinan Indian word was *slay* for "hollyleaf cherry"; in Spanish it became *yslay*. Mentioned in a land grant, *Los Islais* (1834); also in a land grant, *El Arroyo de los Yslais* (1835). In American times it was Islar (1851), then Islais (1853). Then it became known as Du Vrees Creek, for a settler who lived there when it extended a mile and a half inland to the south of Bernal Heights. The present spelling was restored (1859). *(SF)*

Jack London Square:

Relatively recent name for a commercial area of restaurants and offices on the Oakland Estuary at the foot of Broadway, honoring Oakland's most well-known resident; the area has historic associations with his delinquent boyhood. The area was involved in controversy for many years as Oakland sought to regain control of its waterfront. This was the terminus of the first regular ferry service on the Bay — San Francisco to Oakland (1850). *(Alameda)*

Jagel Slough:

Named for Ozymandias P. Jagel, who settled there (1859), and set up a still to carry on an illegal liquor business. He perfected the first submarine, for use in rum-running, but on its initial trial discovered his feet stuck in the clay of the slough bottom. He was never heard from again and never received proper recognition for his invention. *(Santa Clara)*

Johnson Landing:

Named for John Johnson, first American to set up a salt extraction business on the Bay. Salt was shipped to San Francisco and mining country during Gold Rush days. Located on Hayward's shoreline. *(Alameda)*

Keil Cove:

Named for David Keil who bought land and settled there (1890s). Earlier it was called Lyford's Cove for Dr. Benjamin Lyford who lived nearby. Located on Raccoon Strait at Tiburon. *(Marin)*

Larkspur:

Misnamed for a profusion of blue larkspur in the vicinity when the town was established (1887). The confusion about the profusion was that the flowers were actually lupines. Site of a new ferry terminal (1976). *(Marin)*

Lime Point:

Named by British cartographer Capt. W.F. Beechey (1826) in an outburst of modesty (it just wasn't done to call it Guano Point — and no, this has nothing to do with the British being called "limeys"). When Ayala mapped the Bay (1775), he called it *Punta de San Carlos*, for his ship. Beneath the north tower of the Golden Gate Bridge. *(Marin)*

Lion Creek:

Named because of the presence of sea lions. Runs into San Leandro Bay near the Oakland Coliseum. *(Alameda)*

Little Coyote Point:

See Coyote Point.

Long Wharf:

Wharf built by Standard Oil after moving its refinery to Point Richmond (1902) from its original site in Alameda. *(Contra Costa)*

McNears Beach:

Named for John A. McNear who established McNear and Brothers brickyard (1898) on the nearby point, which was then known as Point San Pedro (since 1811). McNear tried to build a railroad to the point; later the family operated the beach (1930s). The name came to be associated with the landing and the point. The Chinese developed a large shrimp fishing industry nearby (1880s-90s). *(Marin)*

Manzanita

Former railroad stop on Richardson Bay. The word is from the diminutive of Spanish, *manzana*, "apple," for the little-apple appearance of the fruit clusters on the shrub. *(Marin)*

Mare Island (Strait):

A somewhat romantic story claims that the peninsula received its name when one of General Vallejo's mares fell off a boat and swam to the then island; thus it became *Isla de la Yegua*, "island of the mare" (1840). This name was embodied in a land grant (1840s). Another story concerns gangs of wild elk that roamed the island, led by a wild horse — of course this wild horse and the escaped mare could be the same (1840s). Called *Isla Plana*, "flat island," by Ayala (1775); called Yegua Island (1850s); translated to present name (1850s). It is actually a peninsula, across the Strait from Vallejo, where the Naval Shipyard was established (1854). *(Solano)*

Marina Slough:

Recent name for a couple of sloughs that have been joined and cut off from the Bay. Name derived from Spanish for "shore, or seacoast." O'Neill Slough was named for Capt. Owen O'Neill who established a landing there (1860s); Seal Slough was named for the abundance of seals found there (before 1890), and was at one time called San Mateo Slough. Located inshore from Foster City. *(San Mateo)*

Marin County (and Peninsula):

A very romanticized version of the naming of Marin has to be viewed as apocryphal. Geographical advisor to the state, General Vallejo, reported the story of Chief Marin (1850). The story — an Indian (perhaps a chief) fought Mexican soldiers, and in defeat sought refuge on what are now the Marin Islands (1824). Finally captured (1826), he was pacified and took up a job as a Bay ferryman. The Spanish called him *El Marinero*, "mariner, or sailor"; the Americans made him a chief and shortened the name to Marin. Name first applied to the islands, then to the Peninsula, and finally to the County. There really was an Indian boatman, but that's about all there is to the legend. Non-legendarily, Ayala gave the name *Bahia de Nuestra Señora del Rosario la Marinera*, for the patron saint of his boat, the *San Carlos*, to what is now San Rafael Bay (1775). This was long before there were any other settlers in the area to make up stories about Indian chiefs; thus the name was given to the islands and later to the county.

Marin Islands (East and West):

A discussion of the origin of this place name is given above. The bay where the islands are was named by Ayala; in some cases this name was shortened to *Bahia del Rosario*. On a land grant the name *Ysla de Marin* was applied to the islands (1834); then they were charted as Marin Islands (1850). The largest island, East Marin, was called *del Oro*, "of gold" (1819). *(Marin)*

Mayfield Slough:

Pioneer Elisha O. Crosby bought land in the area which he named "Mayfield Farm" (1853); name was transferred to the settlement, railroad station and slough. Located near Palo Alto Yacht Harbor. *(Santa Clara)*

Meadowsweet:

Named for a dairy operated in Corte Madera (1930s); cows pastured in the area, on the Bay side of Corte Madera. *(Marin)*

Menlo Park:

Named for the birthplace (Menlough, County Galway, Ireland) of brothers-in-law D.J. Oliver and D.C. McGlynn when they established ranches there (1854). A railroad station took the name (1863). *(San Mateo)*

Mile Rock:

Actually there are two, the smaller is called Little Mile Rock. They were charted as One-mile Rocks (1826), because they were one mile south of the main shipping lane through the Golden Gate; later the name was changed to its present form. The rocks lie outside the Golden Gate, surmounted by an automated lighthouse. *(SF)*

Millbrae:

Named for Darius O. Mills, San Francisco banker and promoter and charter member of the Sierra Club, who bought land and settled there (1860s); it is a combination of his name and the Scottish *brae*, "hill slope." *(San Mateo)*

Mills Creek:

Named for the same man as Millbrae; it runs into the Bay south of the San Francisco Airport. *(San Mateo)*

Milpitas:

Derived from the diminutive of Spanish *milpas*, "corn patches." Mentioned in a land grant (1835). The original settlement was called *Penitencia*, for the nearby creek; then the town received its present name (1850). *(Santa Clara)*

Mission Dolores:

Popularized name of the mission that Anza sited on the spring and stream that he called *Arroyo de Nuestra Señora de los Dolores*, "Our Lady of Sorrows." The first mass was said at *Misión San Francisco de Asís* on June 29, 1776, celebrated as the birthday of San Francisco. *(SF)*

Mission Rock:

A tidal channel called *Estero de la Misión* (1842) originally extended from the Bay to Mission Dolores. Now it is called Mission Creek, but more often China Basin. The whole area south of this creek was water, and was known to the Americans as Mission Bay. It had on its shore a Potrero Point and a Point San Quentin, which have long since been covered by fill. Mission Rock stood out in the bay and was a landmark for mariners; encroaching industrial fill gradually moved toward the Rock until it was buried under the waterfront at Pier 50 (1946). *(SF)*

Mission San Jose:

Established by Father Fermín Lasuén, who celebrated the first mass on June 11, 1797. The first permanent settlement in the East Bay; the town later took the name (1851). *(Alameda)*

Mission Santa Clara:

Fathers Tomás de la Peña and Joseph Antonio Murgúia established *Misión Santa Clara de Asís* on January 17, 1777. *(Santa Clara)*

Mountain View (Slough):

Named when settled (1850s) because of views of the Santa Cruz Mountains and Mt. Diablo; name was also used for the railroad station (1864). *(Santa Clara)*

Mount Eden Creek (and Slough):

Named for an Eden Landing, established by the Mount Eden Company (1850). *(Alameda)*

Mowry Slough (and Landing):

Named for an early settler, Origin Mowry, who established a landing there; below Newark. *(Alameda)*

Mud Slough:

Named for the looks of the slough, which is a little bit anomalous since one use of "slough" was to describe a muddy place; at the southern tip of the Bay, near Drawbridge. *(Alameda)*

Mulford Landing:

Named for Thomas W. Mulford, one of the first settlers of San Leandro (1849), who established Mulford's Landing for shipping grain and dairy products to San Francisco; now the location of the San Leandro Marina. *(Alameda)*

Napa (County, Slough and River):

Derived from dialect of Patwin Indians, *napo,* or *napa,* which apparently meant "houses, or villages." First used by the Spanish (1795) as a name for the Indians of what is now the Napa Valley; the name was later used for the area (1830s), then for the city (1848), and finally for the Creek and River (1850). *(Napa, Solano and Sonoma)*

Needles:

Sometimes called Needle Rocks; just inside Lime Point on the north side of the Golden Gate. Named by British cartographer Capt. W. F. Beechey (1826). *(Marin)*

Newark (Slough):

Named for the New Jersey home of the Davis brothers, early settlers. The town was established by the Newark Land Association (1875); also the name of a station on the South Pacific Coast RR (1876). Once called Dumbarton, it was a shipping point for produce to San Francisco. *(Alameda)*

Nitro:

Once was an explosive rail stop on Point Pinole; see Giant and Hercules. *(Contra Costa)*

Novato Creek:

Possibly named for a chief of the Hookooeko Indians who was baptized as Novatus (for the saint). The area where mission cattle grazed (1828) was called *Cañada de Novato;* name used in a land grant, *Rancho de Novato* (or *Novata*) (1836). *(Marin)*

Oakland:

The land grant to Luis María Peralta (1820), *Rancho San Antonio,* encompassed the sites of Berkeley, Oakland and Alameda. In Spanish times the area that is now Oakland was known as *Encinal del Temescal,* "oak grove by the sweat house," and a settlement was called *Temescal.* When the city was laid out (1850), the present name was selected. *(Alameda)*

Oakland Estuary:

See The Estuary.

Oakland Mole:

Because of constant industrial development, the area has been filled and extended further into the Bay; now it is part of Oakland Harbor. Once known as Gibbon's Point (1850s); a railroad, later the Southern Pacific, built a ferry connection to San Francisco there (1863). Long since covered by the port, the first Oakland Harbor Lighthouse was built (1890). The Western Pacific ferry point, which is still in operation, was built around the second lighthouse. *(Alameda)*

Oleum:

Name contrived from pet*roleum* when the Union Oil Company built a refinery near Rodeo (1912). *(Contra Costa)*

O'Neill Slough:

See Marina Slough.

Oyster Point:

Named for oyster beds laid out in the Bay (1872), which were still in operation as late as 1935. The name has appeared on maps since 1900. *(San Mateo)*

Palo Alto:

Early Spanish used *palo alto,* "tall tree," for *sequoia sempervirens;* and especially noted a particular one on the bank of San Francisquito Creek where the expedition of Portolá camped (1769). A land transaction used the name (1857); and the town name followed (1892). *(Santa Clara)*

Paradise Cay (and Cove):

Named for its presumed resemblance to the abode of the blessed. The area fronting on the Bay was chosen as a site for a real estate venture, California City, by Benjamin Buckelew (1852). Paradise Cove was a resort and picnic area (see El Campo) for San Franciscans (1860s-80s). It was also called Ring Point for George Ring who owned the land (1880s-1900s). Now Paradise Cay is an area of residential lagoons with marina on Bay fill. *(Marin)*

Patterson Creek:

Andrew Jackson Patterson and two brothers settled in the vicinity (1850s); Patterson Pass in the hills above Fremont was named for the spot where his wife broke her leg; then the Creek was named. Near Coyote Hills Regional Park. *(Alameda)*

Peninsula Point:

Named for the landform, but also involved in the saga of the appellations of Belvedere Island (which see). *(Marin)*

Petaluma Point (and River):

Name derived from an Indian village located near the river; the Coast Miwok word, *petaluma,* meant "flat back." Mentioned as *El llano de los Petalumas,* "the plain of the Petaluma Indians" (1819); and used in a land grant name (1834). The city later adopted the name (1851). *(Marin and Sonoma)*

Phelps Slough:

Named for Timothy Guy Phelps who established a landing there (1850s); near San Carlos Airport. *(San Mateo)*

Pinole (Creek and Shoal):

Name derived from the Aztec word for toasted and ground grain or seeds. The Spanish got provisions from the Indians and called the place *El Pinole.* The name was used in a land grant to Ignacio Martínez (alcalde of Yerba Buena), *Pinole y Cañada de la Hambre* (1836). Later mentioned as *Boca de la Cañada del Pinole* (1842). Sometimes misspelled as Penoli and Penole. The Point was once called *San Andreas. (Costa Costa)*

Point Avisadero:

Originally the whole of Hunters Point, the name now refers just to the tip. Called *Punta Avisadera* prior to 1844; other versions were Avisada and Alvisadera. Then came to the present spelling (1873). *(SF)*

Point Bonita:

Named by Ayala *Punta de Santiago* (1775). Later it received the name *Punta de Bonetes,* "hat point," because the three hills resembled the *bonete* of a Spanish clergyman. Misspelled *Punta de Bonetas* (after 1800), or *Punta Boneta* (1826); then the present spelling was adopted (1850s). Through the misspelling, a new definition was arrived at — *bonita* became "pretty point"; spelled Bonito (until 1900). A lighthouse has been located there since 1855. *(Marin)*

Point Isabel:

Named by the Spanish, *Santa Ysabel,* for Saint Elisabeth. The Vigolite Co. powder works moved there from Tiburon (late 1890s). Located just north of Golden Gate Fields, in Richmond. *(Contra Costa)*

Point Lobos:

Outside the Golden Gate near Lands End. Name derived from Spanish for "wolf," *lobo marino,* "sea wolf," meaning seal or sea lion. Name *Punta de los Lobos* was mentioned (1816); later mentioned in a land grant, *Punta de Lobos* (1846); then the present name was used (1826). *(SF)*

Point Molate:

This name has a screwy history. In Mexican times, Red Rock was called *Moleta,* which was the Spanish for the conical stone used by painters to grind colors, for the shape resemblance. Then the name was misspelled Molate (1826). The name was transferred from Rock to Point (1854); also used for the reef offshore (1864). The site was used as a large weekend resort (people from San Francisco were ferried over for galas) called Winehaven (1906), which was wiped out by Prohibition (1921). Now the site is a Naval Supply Depot on Point San Pablo. *(Contra Costa)*

Point Orient:

An oil pier was built there shortly after Standard Oil moved to the area (1902). *(Contra Costa)*

Point Pinole:

Now a Regional Shoreline; see Pinole.

Point Potrero:

From the Spanish *potrero,* "pasture"; part of the land grant in the area. Known as Shoal Point (before WW II); at the end of Richmond Harbor. *(Contra Costa)*

Point Richmond

Known as Point Stevens (1851), then Richmond Point (1852). When the Santa Fe RR decided to build there, the place became Point Richmond (1897). The community that grew up there was called Santa Fe, and now Point Richmond, part of Richmond. When the Santa Fe ferry service started, the terminal became Ferry Point (1900). See Ferry Point and Richmond. *(Contra Costa)*

Point San Bruno:

Named for the nearby mountain; called *Punta San Bruno* (1844) and Point San Bruno (1851). See San Bruno. *(San Mateo)*

Point San Pablo:

The twin peninsulas facing each other across a strait were named for Saints Peter and Paul; the name *Punta de San Pablo* appeared as early as 1817. The large land grant on the eastern shore took its name from the point. See San Pablo. *(Contra Costa)*

Point San Pedro:

Named as above. Name mentioned as *Punta de San Pedro* (1811), then put on a map (1831); a land grant later took the name. It is sometimes still called McNears Point (since the turn of the century). See San Pedro. *(Marin)*

Point San Quentin:

Named for a renegade Indian, Quintin, who was captured on the point (1824). A land grant was named for him, *Rancho Punta de Quintin* (1834). The name was changed to its present spelling and the "San" added by American cartographers who were into saint-izing names (1850). The site of a failed real estate venture, Marin City, by Benjamin Buckelew (1852). The nearby prison has adopted the name. *(Marin)*

Point Stuart:

It is just barely possible that this name was a corruption of Stewart from the defense post, Battery Stewart, which the military built on Angel Island (1864), named for the first commanding officer of Alcatraz, Capt. Joseph Stewart. A secondary light station operates there. *(Marin)*

Point Tiburon:

Derived from Spanish, *Punta de Tiburon,* "shark point." Mentioned (1823), and put on a map (1826). Misspelled as Tiburn Point on a later map (1873). *(Marin)*

Potrero Point:

Derived from Spanish for "pasture." It took its name from the land grant that includes what is now Potrero Hill; the Point is below the hill on the south waterfront. *(SF)*

Presidio:

The Spanish word for garrison or fortified barracks. The Presidio of San Francisco was established in 1776 and has been a military post continuously since that time. *(SF)*

Pulgas Creek:

A favorite Spanish place name meaning "fleas." The name was used in some early land grants. The creek runs through San Carlos to the Bay. *(San Mateo)*

Quarry Point:

Location of East Garrison on Angel Island; named for the quarry there that supplied rock for building on Alcatraz and Mare Island (operated from 1851 until the hill was leveled in 1922). See Fort McDowell. *(Marin)*

Raccoon Strait (and Shoal):

Named for the British sloop-of-war *Raccoon* which was careened and repaired in the Strait (1814). *(Marin)*

Rat Rock:

Named for the animals found there; one of the smallest islands on the Bay, near China Camp. *(Marin)*

Ravenswood Slough (Point):

Name probably transferred from somewhere else. The land purchased and town laid out by Woods, Rowe, Haskell, Hackett and Judah (1853) in anticipation of a railroad bridge crossing the Bay. Some time later the two South Bay points were called West Point and East Point (1880s), now Ravenswood and Dumbarton. A long wharf was built for the shipping of lumber. When the railroad bridge finally came (1910), the town of Ravenswood had disappeared; East Palo Alto is now located there. The north part of the Slough was called "the Elbow." *(San Mateo)*

Red Rock:

The early Spanish name was *Moleta,* for the conical stone used by painters to grind colors; then the name was misspelled Molate (1826). The name Red Rock was used as early as 1849 for the red stone color of the rock, and is still the authorized name. The term Molate Rock was also used (as late as 1897). The name Golden Rock is another official term used on surveys; it is a boundary corner for the counties of San Francisco, Marin and Contra Costa. Pirates were supposed to have buried treasure there, so the name *llamada del oro,* (island) "called golden," was mentioned (1819).

Redwood City (Creek and Point):

Originally an embarcadero for the commercial exploitation and shipping of redwood lumber to San Francisco (1850s). A town was established by Simon M. Mezes (1854), which came to be called Mezesville; but it was still known as Redwood Landing or Embarcadero until it became Redwood City (1860). *(San Mateo)*

Redwood Highway:

The name of Highway 101, north from the Golden Gate Bridge. It took its name from the Redwood Empire (1915), the counties from Marin to Del Norte.

Richardson Bay:

Named for William A. Richardson, a mate of an English whaler, who jumped ship in California (1822). He built the first house in Yerba Buena, now San Francisco (1835), and was appointed captain of the port. He received a land grant and settled in Sausalito (1838). Originally the Bay was called *Ensenada de la Carmelita* by Ayala (1775), because there was a rock that resembled the shape of a friar of the Carmelite order (now Cone Rock). At one time it was known as Whaler's Cove or Whaler's Harbor, a translation of *Puerto de los Balleneros* (1825), because of whaling ships anchored there; later maps used the term Richardson's Bay (1850). *(Marin)*

Richmond:

A good guess is that the town name was transferred from Virginia, the birthplace of Edmund Randolph, a California pioneer. The town was laid out near Point Richmond by Augustin Macdonald (1899). The harbor was known as Ellis Landing (1890). See Point Richmond. *(Contra Costa)*

Rincon Point:

Derived from Spanish *rincón,* "corner, or angle." The name was used (as early as 1850) for a "corner" on the waterfront, a prominent early Bay landmark, that disappeared as downtown San Francisco was filled and built up. The elevation above the point was cut down for the City terminus of the Bay Bridge. *(SF)*

Roberts Landing:

Named for Capt. William Roberts who settled on the shore near San Leandro (1850) and freighted hay and grain from there to other Bay landings (1870s-80s). *(Alameda)*

Rodeo (Creek):

Derived from the Spanish for an enclosure where cattle are kept. The name appears on the Pinole land grant (1860); later the creek was mapped (1865). *(Contra Costa)*

Sacramento River:

Early Spanish expeditions named it for the Holy Sacrament. The lower river was called *Rio de San Francisco,* for the Bay (1811); but the name, which was already being used for the upper river, was moved down to include the whole river, *Rio de Sacramento* (1817). Later Hudson's Bay men called it Bonaventura, or Buenaventura, River (1830s).

San Bruno (Channel and Mountain):

The padres of the earliest Spanish expeditions usually named a place for a feast day — so the German eleventh century saint, founder of the Carthusian Order was commemorated. The name was first used for a creek on the side of the mountain (1774). The hillside was used as cattle range for the Presidio, *Cerro de San Bruno* (1826). *Cerro,* "hill," was later misunderstood as *Sierra,* "mountain." Also *Montes San Bruno* (1844); finally got the present name (1850s). *(San Mateo)*

San Clemente Creek:

Named for St. Clement, the third Pope and Bishop of Rome, probably for its discovery on the saint's day. *(Marin)*

Sand Island:

The location is now the toll plaza and Oakland end of the Bay Bridge. It became known as Sand Island when Oakland harbor improvements were carried out and the dredging spoil was dumped in a shallow spot in the Bay (1927). At one time it was a hobo jungle, and after the Bridge was built it became the home of some radio transmission towers. *(Alameda)*

Sand Point:

Named by early explorers *Punta de Arenas,* "sand point." Located near Palo Alto Yacht Harbor. *(Santa Clara)*

San Francisco (Bay):

Probably the oldest place name in California. Cartographers honored St. Francis of Assisi by putting his name on maps shortly after Sir Francis Drake voyaged to California (1590); essentially the name applied to an imaginary bay that no one had yet discovered. Later another map showed *Bahia de San Francisco* where Drakes Bay is today (1595). Even when the explorer Portolá came along (1769), he was looking for today's Drakes Bay which he knew as "San Francisco," and so he was not satisfied with his discovery. The other side of the political story was presented by an English map which showed Port Sir Francis Drake (1753) for the present San Francisco Bay. Finally it received the name *Puerto de San Francisco* as a result of Ayala's ship entering the Bay (1775) and in conjunction with the founding of *La Misión de Nuestro Serafico Padre San Francisco de Asís a la Laguna de los Dolores,* "mission of our seraphic father St. Francis of Assisi at the lake of (Our Lady of) the Sorrows" (1776). The shortened name applied only to the mission and the presidio; the settlement itself was called Yerba Buena (1835), and an early Spanish nickname was *las lomitas,* "little hills." The name only came to be applied to the city with American occupation (1847). See Yerba Buena. *(SF)*

San Francisquito Creek:

From Spanish *Arroyo de San Francisquito,* "Little San Francisco Creek," which was an anomalous meaning (evidently the creek was little, because the saint was not). The creek was first named *Arroyo de San Francisco* (1776); the present name then appeared on land grants (1840s) and was applied to the creek (1850). *(San Mateo and Santa Clara)*

San Joaquin River:

Named for Saint Joachim, the father of Virgin Mary. The earliest expedition called it *Rio Grande de San Francisco* (1772); later it was *Rio de San Juan Baptista* (1775); until it received the present name (1805).

San Jose:

Named for Saint Joseph, the husband of Virgin Mary. When *El Pueblo de San José de Guadalupe* was established by José Moraga (1777), it was named for the river (see Guadalupe). *(Santa Clara)*

San Leandro (Bay and Creek):

Named for Saint Leander, Bishop of Seville. The creek was named *Arroyo de San Leandro* (1828); then José Joaquín Estudillo applied the name to his rancho and incorporated it in his land grant (1839). *(Alameda)*

San Lorenzo (Creek):

Creek was called *Arroyo de San Salvador de Horta* by Father Juan Crespí (1772). The current name came into use in the area (1820s), and appeared on land grants (1840s). The community that grew up was originally called Squatterville (1850s). *(Alameda)*

San Mateo (County and Creek):

Named for Saint Matthew, apostle and evangelist. The creek was called *Arroyo de San Matheo* by Anza (1776), and this spelling persisted until 1850. Also mentioned were *Estero de San Mateo* and *Punta de San Mateo* (1810). Later the city was laid out (1863).

San Pablo Bay (Creek and Strait):

Named for Saint Paul. First Point San Pablo received the name, then the large land grant of Francisco María Castro was called *Rancho San Pablo* (1823), then the strait was known as *Estrecho de San Pablo* (1824). The earliest explorers used the name "Round Bay," later it was *Bahia de Sonoma* (1824). Points San Pablo and San Pedro were mapped (1831); and the Bay finally received its present name (1844). It is also traditionally called the North Bay, to indicate that is a portion of San Francisco Bay. *(Contra Costa)*

San Pedro Hill:

The hill that is a quarry on Point San Pedro. The name was mentioned as early as 1807. The area is sometimes known as McNears Point, for the quarry operator. See Point San Pedro. *(Marin)*

San Rafael (Creek and Bay):

Named for Saint Raphael, the archangel, when *Misión San Rafael Arcángel* was founded (1817) as a "branch" of Mission Dolores. The Bay was called *Bahia de Nuestra Señora del Rosario la Marinera* by Ayala (1775). *(Marin)*

Santa Clara (County):

Named for Saint Clare of Assisi, cofounder of the Franciscan Order of nuns, The *Misión de Santa Clara de Asís* was founded (1777). The name was used in a land grant (1844).

Santa Fe Channel:

Named for the Atchison, Topeka & Santa Fe Railroad, when it came to town (1897). The channel was dredged by Henry Cutting as part of building the port of Richmond (after 1912). *(Contra Costa)*

Saratoga Creek:

The present name for the town was taken (1876) because the waters at Pacific Congress Springs resembled those at Congress Springs in (Saratoga) New York; when the community was founded (1851), it was called McCarthysville. The creek feeds Guadalupe Slough. *(Santa Clara)*

Sausalito (Point):

Derived from Spanish *sauce,* "willow," which Juan Manuel de Ayala used in referring to the place (1775). The correct Spanish, *Saucelito,* "little grove of willows," was mentioned in 1826 and was used for the land grant to William A. Richardson (1838). With the American occupation came the corruption of the spelling into English, with at least nine different versions (Saucilito, Sausolita, Sauzalito, Sausolito, Sousoleto, South Salieto, Sausaulito, Sauselito), including the present spelling. Finally the railroad and the post office settled on Saucelito (1870); but then the post office changed it to the present spelling (1887), which was used when the city was incorporated (1893); but the old spelling persisted until after 1900. *(Marin)*

Seal Slough:

See Marina Slough.

Sears Point:

At one time a landing for Bay commerce, named for Franklin Sears, a California pioneer who settled in the Sonoma Valley (1851). The name was applied to the railroad station (before 1888). *(Sonoma)*

Selby:

Named for the Selby Smelting Works which was established by Thomas H. Selby, an early mayor of San Francisco, at what is now Fort Mason, and was moved by his son, Prentiss, to the location near Rodeo (1885). *(Contra Costa)*

Semple Point:

Named for Robert Semple, a pioneer Californian and crony of General Vallejo. He was also active in business, was founder of Benicia, started ferry service between Benicia and Martinez, and was involved in the Mount Diablo coal boom. The Point is at the north end of the Carquinez Bridge. *(Solano)*

Sierra Point:

Name was a misunderstanding of *Cerro de San Bruno,* "San Bruno Mountain," which was made into "Sierra" (1851). See San Bruno. *(San Mateo)*

The Sisters:

Lying just off the tip of Point San Pedro. At one time they were called Two Sisters (1870). See The Brothers. *(Marin)*

Skagg Island:

Named for William and Alexander Skaggs who acquired land in the area (1856); first used on a map (1873). *(Sonoma)*

Smith Slough:

Named for William C.R. Smith who established a landing on the slough (1854); sometimes considered part of Steinberger Slough. Near the port of Redwood City. *(San Mateo)*

Sobrante:

Derived from the Spanish term for surplus land left over from a land grant, that land usually became part of another grant with the term used as its name. Because it was on El Sobrante grant, a railroad stop at Point Pinole was named Sobrante (1878); later "El" was added to the town name (1945). *(Contra Costa)*

Solano County:

Name used when the county was established (1850), at the request of General Vallejo for the chief of the Suisun Indians, Francisco Solano, who was baptized for Saint Francis Solano.

Sonoma County (and Creek):

Derived from Patwin Indian dialect *sono,* "nose," which was the nickname of a chief with a noticeable nose. The Spanish named Indian villages after the chief, so it became "land or tribe of Chief Nose." Name of the Indian tribe, *Sonomas* or *Sonomi,* used (as early as 1815). Attribution of the meaning as "Valley of the Moon" is complete romantic fiction.

Southampton Shoal:

Named by the Coast Survey (1850) for USS *Southampton,* which led the fleet of Commodore Jones to anchorage at Benicia in 1849. Located between Angel Island and Point Richmond; a lighthouse was established there (1905). *(SF)*

South Basin:

Named because of its location, on the south side of Hunters Point. *(SF)*

South Bay:

The south arm of San Francisco Bay was called *Estrecho de San José* by the early Spanish; also *Estero de Santa Clara* (1824). Before the turn of the century, anything south of Yerba Buena Island (including Oakland) was known as the South Bay.

South San Francisco:

Named by G.F. Swift, meatpacker, who set up business there; he thought it was analogous to South Chicago and South Kansas City as a meatpacking area. *(San Mateo)*

Steinberger Slough:

Named for John Beal Steinberger who was a settler in Belmont (1850s). The name sometimes extended to include Smith Slough. Near Redwood Shores development. *(San Mateo)*

Stevens Creek:

Named for Capt. Elisha Stevens (or Stephens), who came to California in 1844 and once had a ranch in the area. Originally called *Arroyo de San José Cupertino* by Anza (1776); later it was mapped as "Stephens or Cupertino Creek" (1873); later the present spelling was used (1899). *(Santa Clara)*

Strawberry Point:

Named in good pioneer humor, "because there weren't any strawberries on it." Once the home of Dr. Benjamin Lyford (1870s-80s), whose house was barged across Richardson Bay to the Audubon preserve in 1957. *(Marin)*

Sunnyvale:

A name born of real estate euphoria, applied by W. E. Crossman to a subdivision in the area (1900); originally the settlement was called Murphys Station for the rancher who owned the land. *(Santa Clara)*

Temescal Creek:

The Spanish brought the word *temescal,* derived from Aztec for "sweat house," to California and applied it to Indian constructions. The name was mentioned in the San Antonio land grant (1820), *Arroyo de Temescal o Los Juchiyunes,* and also (where the Oakland Mole is now) *Encinal del Temascal.* The landing place became known as *Embarcadero Temescal* (by 1844); what's left of the creek runs into the Bay at Emeryville. *(Alameda)*

Tiburon:

Taken from the Spanish, *Punta de Tiburon,* "shark point," name first mentioned (1823). It is one of the oldest place names in the county. *(Marin)*

Tolay Creek:

Named for an Indian chief or a lake, now drained; mentioned as *Laguna de Tolay así llamada del capitan de los Indios,* "Tolay Lake so called for the chief of the Indians" (1823). It flows into the Bay near Sears Point. *(Sonoma)*

Tormey:

Named for John and Patrick Tormey who bought part of the Pinole grant and set up ranching (1860s); between Selby and Oleum. *(Contra Costa)*

Treasure Island:

Artificial island site of 1939-40 Golden Gate International Exposition. When pumping was started to build the island (1936), the name was selected "because it expressed a glamorous, beautiful, almost fabulous island that would present the treasures of the world," although there was some sentiment for calling it Gold Island. *(SF)*

Turk Island:

Named for Frank Turk, who came to San Francisco in 1849, was elected second alcalde, and had business dealings across the Bay. The island is another land-locked mound near Coyote Hills. *(Alameda)*

Union City:

A relatively recent incorporation of the districts of Alvarado and Decoto. The town of Alvarado was originally called New Haven (1851) and was the first county seat of Alameda County. In 1853 the name was changed to honor Juan Bautista Alvarado, the Mexican governor who led opposition to American occupation. Union City was founded by J.M. Horner (1851), and was called Uniontown for a while, after a transbay transport vessel, the *Union. (Alameda)*

Vallejo:

Named for and laid out by General Mariano Guadalupe Vallejo, who was commandante of the northern Mexican frontier and who established Sonoma. The city was proposed as the state capital with the name Eureka (1850); when that fell through, the present name was adopted. *(Solano)*

Visitacion Point:

Name mentioned as *la Visitacion,* a cattle ranch of San Francisco's Presidio (1798); later embodied in a land grant to Jacob Leese, *Cañada de Guadalupe, la Visitacion y Rodeo Viejo* (1841). Now the Point is land-locked by Bay fill; near the SP yards at Brisbane. *(San Mateo)*

Waldo Point:

Several of the streets in Sausalito are named for towns (perhaps this is for Waldo, Oregon); Waldo Street appeared on a map (1869), and a railroad station was called that (1891). *(Marin)*

West Garrison:

The first Army post on Angel Island was called Camp Reynolds (1863); then the post took the name of the island and at that time the specific location got the name West Garrison (1866). From this derived the names East Garrison and North Garrison. By now West Garrison and Camp Reynolds are synonymous. See Angel Island. *(Marin)*

West Marin Island:

See Marin Islands.

Westpoint Slough:

In earlier times there were two points, West Point and East Point, which correspond to today's Ravenswood and Dumbarton points. The Slough was named for the Point (1880s); near the port of Redwood City. *(San Mateo)*

Wildcat Creek:

Probably named because wildcats were encountered, seen or killed at that place. Runs through San Pablo to the Bay. *(Contra Costa)*

Winslow Cove:

Named for Charles Winslow who worked for thirty years to preserve Angel Island as a state park. Located at North Garrison. It was known as China Cove when the Immigration Station was there to handle the Oriental influx. *(Marin)*

Yerba Buena Island:

From Spanish for "good herb," *Micromeria chamissonis,* sometimes called California mint. Originally the island was called *Isla de Alcatraces* by Ayala (1775), but that name was transferred to an entirely different island. Later it was called *la Ysla de la Yerba Buena* (1795), part of the name being used when what is now San Francisco was settled (1835). Early settlers went through a variety of names for the island, Sea Bird Island, Wood Island (1847), Goat Island (1836), because of a goat ranch there. The first state legislature used Yerba Buena (1850); the US Geographic Board changed it to Goat Island (1895); and finally they changed it back to Yerba Buena (1931). *(SF)*

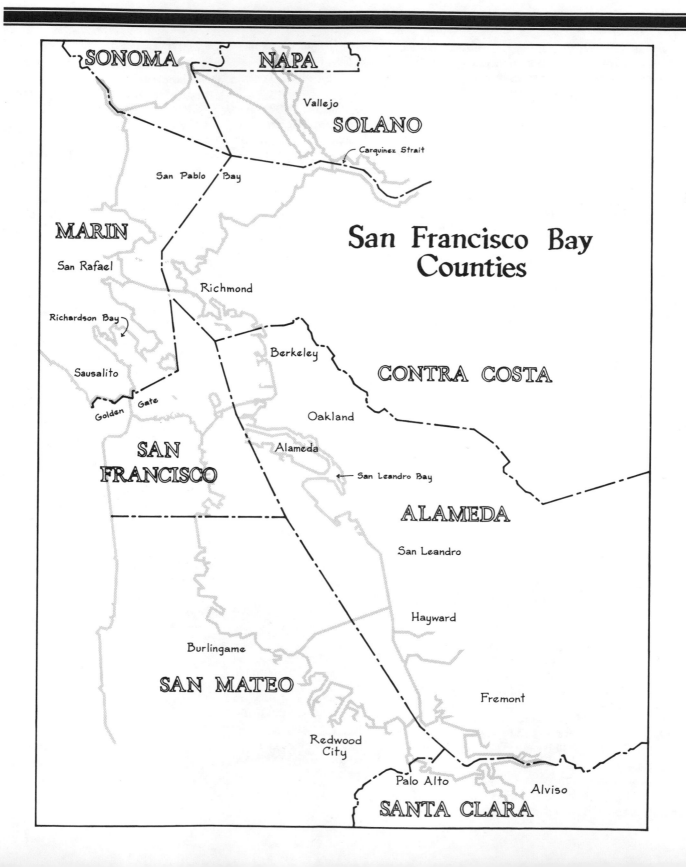

SONOMA   NAPA

Vallejo

SOLANO

Carquinez Strait

San Pablo Bay

MARIN

San Rafael

Richardson Bay

Sausalito

Golden Gate

SAN FRANCISCO

Richmond

Berkeley

Oakland

Alameda

San Leandro Bay

San Francisco Bay Counties

CONTRA COSTA

ALAMEDA

San Leandro

Hayward

Burlingame

SAN MATEO

Fremont

Redwood City

Palo Alto

Alviso

SANTA CLARA

Freeway Index

For the convenience of visitors or residents who wish to make driving explorations, activities and places are listed for your discovery by freeway exits around the Bay.

The list of exits generally follows a clockwise circuit of the Bay. Starting from the Golden Gate Bridge, the index follows Highway 101 north through Marin County, then it follows Highway 37 east through Sonoma and Solano counties, then Highway 80 south across the Carquinez Bridge and through Contra Costa County into Alameda County, then Highway 17 south through Alameda County to Santa Clara County. Then there is a sort of reversal, the index returns to the Golden Gate Bridge and takes in San Francisco and follows Highway 101 south through San Mateo County and into Santa Clara County.

Marin County

North from the Golden Gate Bridge on Highway 101. (for Golden Gate Bridge information, look under San Francisco)

Vista Point exit

(no exit southbound)

Recreation. *Bike route:* down to Sausalito 78. *View point:* bridge vista 101, 74, 161. Below the vista point is the north anchorage of the Golden Gate Bridge and Lime Point. *Events:* Golden Gate Swim 97.

History. *Chronology:* Lime Point 157, lighthouse 158, bridge 160, ship collision 162. *Islands:* Needles 186. *Lighthouse:* Ayala 187, Lime Point 188.

Alexander Ave exit

(this is actually the first of four exits to Sausalito, but in order to prevent traffic congestion on the streets of the town, the name has been left off the exit sign, and it is recommended you drive over the hill to the marked Sausalito exit)

An overview of Sausalito with many of its highlights is offered in *Pedestrian Delights* 9-11.

Recreation. Some of the restaurants of Sausalito may best be reached from this exit — *Dining:* Valhalla Inn, The Trident, Ondine, and Scoma's 27; Slinkey's El Monte and The Spinnaker 28. *Parks:* Fort Baker and Sausalito city parks 50. *Ferry:* Sausalito 68. *Bridge:* Emperor Norton 73. *Buses:* Golden Gate Transit 77. *Bike route:* down to Sausalito 78. *Events:* Bullship Race 95, Opening Day of Yachting Season 95. Some of the *marinas* of Sausalito may best be reached from this exit: Sausalito Yacht Harbor and Pelican Yacht Harbor 108. *Yacht club:* Sausalito 134. *Shore fishing:* Fort Baker and Sausalito's Tiffany Beach 141.

History. *Chronology:* John Reed 156, first ferry 157, ferry run 158 & 160, last ferry 161, ferry revived 163. *Old ferryboat:* Eureka 165-166. *Exposition:* preservation of relics at Viña del Mar Plaza 196.

Spenser Ave / Montemar Dr exit

(an exit that leads to residential parts of Sausalito but not very handily to the waterfront)

Rodeo Ave exit

(an exit that leads to residential parts of Sausalito but not very handily to the waterfront)

Sausalito exit

(the fourth of four, and the official Sausalito exit)

An overview of Sausalito with many of its highlights is offered in *Pedestrian Delights* 9-11.

Recreation. The rest of the restaurants of Sausalito — *Dining:* Flynn's Landing and Zack's 28; The Tides and Sausalito Food Co. 29. *Parks:* Sausalito city parks 50, Bay Model 11 & 63. *Ferry:* Sausalito 68. *Bridge:* Emperor Norton 73. *Buses:* Golden Gate Transit 77. *Bike routes:* down to Sausalito 78, Sausalito to Mill Valley 79. *Events:* Opening Day of Yachting Season 95. *View Point:* Waldo Grade to Marin City 101. Other *marinas* in Sausalito: Marinship Yacht Harbor and Clipper Yacht Harbor 108; Houseboat Colony and Kappas Marina 109. *Learning to sail:* Cass' Rental Marina, Hauser Institute, and Sausalito Rec Dept 121; windsurfing 128. *Sailboat renting:* Cass' Rental Marina 130. *Charter cruises:* Hauser Insitute 132. *Yacht clubs:* Sausalito Yacht Club and Sausalito Cruising Club 134. *Bait shops:* Caruso's and Sausalito Boat & Tackle 137. *Boat ramps:* Sausalito and Clipper Yacht Harbor 139. *Shore fishing:* Sausalito's Tiffany Beach 141. *Sportfishing boats:* Caruso's, Jerry's, and Sausalito Boat & Tackle 145.

History. *Chronology:* John Reed 156, first ferry 157, ferry run 158 & 160, last ferry 161, ferry revived 163. *Old ferryboats:* Eureka 165-166, *Vallejo, City of Seattle, Issaquah, Charles Van Damme, City of San Rafael* 169; ferry terminal 170; *Berkeley* 171. *Island:* Cone Rock 186. *Exposition:* preservation of relics at Viña del Mar Plaza 196.

Ecology. *Cruising:* Hauser Institute 201.

Mill Valley / Stinson Beach / Highway One exit

Recreation. *Bike routes:* from Sausalito to Mill Valley 79, Mill Valley to Strawberry Point 79. *Cruising:* seaplane tour 93. *View point:* exit inland for Mt. Tamalpais 100.

Seminary Dr exit

Recreation. *Parks:* Strawberry Point 50. *Bike route:* from Mill Valley to Strawberry Point 79. *View point:* Strawberry Point 101. *Shore fishing:* Strawberry Point shoreline 141.

Tiburon / Belvedere exit

(everything in Tiburon, Belvedere and the whole Tiburon Peninsula can be reached from this exit, as well as ferry connections to Angel Island)

An overview of Tiburon and Angel Island with many of their highlights is offered in *Pedestrian Delights* 12 & 13-14.

Recreation. *Dining:* Tiburon Tommie's, Thirty-nine Main, Sweden House, Sam's Anchor Café, and The Dock 30; Sabella's, Windjammer, and Caprice 31. *Parks:* Richardson Bay Wildlife Sanctuary, Richardson Bay Park, Belvedere Park, and Tiburon 51; Angel Island State Park and Paradise Beach Park 52. *Ferries:* Tiburon and Angel Island 68. *Bridge:* to Tiburon 69. *Bike routes:* Strawberry Point 79, Tiburon 80, Angel Island 80, Tiburon Peninsula 81. *Events:* Opening Day of Yachting Season 95. *View points:* Angel Island and Paradise Drive 101. *Learning to sail:* Sailing Center 122. *Sailboat renting:* Sailing Center 130. *Yacht clubs:* San Francisco 134, Corinthian 135. *Shore fishing:* Tiburon shoreline, Angel Island, and Paradise Beach Park 141.

History. *Chronology:* San Carlos 155, HMS *Raccoon* 156, military reservation 156, Camp Reynolds 157, quarantine station 158, first ferry 158, Pt Knox lighthouse 159, defense batteries 159, immigration station 157, batteries decommissioned 159, ferry discontinued 159, Army base 161, state park 162, ferry revived 162, state park 162. *Old ferryboat: Ukiah* 165. *Commemoration:* Angel Island 177. *Islands:* Angel Island 182-183, Belvedere 185, Cone Rock 186. *Lighthouses:* Angel Island 188. *Buried treasures:* Angel Island 193, sunken ships 193-194.

Ecology. *Collection:* Richardson Bay Wildlife Sanctuary 203. *Bird-watching:* Richardson Bay 205. *Seal-watching:* Richardson Bay and Angel Island 207.

Paradise Dr exit

Recreation. *Park:* Paradise Beach Park 52. *Bike route:* Tiburon Peninsula 81. *View point:* Paradise Drive 101. *Marina:* Paradise Cay Yacht Harbor 109. *Yacht Club:* Paradise Harbor 135. *Shore fishing:* Paradise Beach Park 141.

Corte Madera / Larkspur exit

Recreation. *Learning to sail:* Corte Madera Rec Dept 122, windsurfing 128.

Lucky Dr exit

Recreation. *Learning to sail:* Canoe Trips West 123. *Sailboat renting:* Canoe Trips West 130. *Boat ramp:* Canoe Trips West 139.

Ecology. *Cruising:* Canoe Trips West 201.

San Anselmo / Sir Francis Drake Blvd exit

(Ferry Terminal and Richmond Bridge)

Recreation. *Dining:* Victoria Station 32. *Ferry:* Larkspur 66-67. *Bridge:* Richmond-San Rafael 70-71. *Buses:* Golden Gate Transit 77. *Bike route:* bridge crossing 78. *Cruising:* Marin tours 91. *Shore fishing:* Larkspur shoreline 141.

History. *Bay Discovery:* "Plate of brasse" site 150, 151-152, 161. *Chronology:* Richmond-San Rafael Bridge 162, first Larkspur ferry 163.

Richmond-San Rafael Bridge / Francisco Blvd exit

(the first of four San Rafael exits, but not really useful for anything except crossing the Bay to Richmond)

Recreation. *Bridge:* Richmond-San Rafael 70-71. *Buses:* Traveler's Transit 77. *Bike route:* bridge crossing 78.

History. *Chronology:* first ferry 160, bridge opened-last ferry 162.

Central San Rafael exit

(actually the second of four San Rafael exits, but the most significant if you want to get to the waterfront)

Recreation: *Dining:* Pier 15, Dominic's Harbor, and Loch Lomond Marina Snack Bar 32. *Parks:* San Rafael, McNear's Beach Park, and China Camp State Park 52. *Buses:* Traveler's Transit 77. *Bike routes:* bridge crossing 78, San Rafael and China Camp 81. *View point:* North San Pedro Road 101. *Marinas:* San Rafael Yacht Harbor, Lowrie Yacht Harbor, and Loch Lomond 109. *Learning to sail:* San Rafael Rec Dept 123. *Yacht clubs:* San Rafael, North Bay, Marin, and Loch Lomond 135. *Bait shops:* Loch Lomond and China Camp 137. *Boat ramp:* Loch Lomond Marina 139. *Shore fishing:* San Rafael Beach Park and China Camp pier 141. *Sportfishing boat:* Loch Lomond Marina 145.

History. *Chronology:* mission founded 156, bridge opened-last ferry 162. *Collection:* Marin County Historical Museum 175. *Islands:* Marin Islands 184, The Sisters 185, Rat Rock 186. *Legends:* Marin Islands, 184.

Ecology. *Excursions:* Marin Museum of Natural Science (Louise A. Boyd Museum) 203. *Seal-watching:* The Sisters 207.

North San Pedro Road exit

(the third of four San Rafael exits, at the Civic Center)

Recreation. *Park:* China Camp State Park 52. *Bike route:* San Rafael and China Camp 81. *View point:* North San Pedro Rd 101. *Yacht club:* Gallinas 135. *Bait shop:* China Camp 137. *Boat ramp:* Buck's Landing 139. *Shore fishing:* China Camp pier 141.

History. *Island:* Rat Rock 186.

Freitas Parkway exit

(the last San Rafael exit)

Lucas Valley Road exit
Marinwood / St. Vincent Dr exit
Alameda del Prado exit
Hamilton AFB / Nave Dr exit
Ignacio Blvd / Entrada Dr exit

(these six exits do not offer access to the Bay shoreline)

Junction of Highway 101 and Highway 37

(there are a few places listed here that require going north to Novato, but the route encircling the Bay goes east on Highway 37)

Recreation. *Learning to sail:* Novato 123.

History. *Collection:* Marin Miwok Museum 175.

East from Highway 101 on Highway 37.

(until you reach Vallejo, these are not freeway exits as such, since Highway 37 is not a freeway)

Black Point / Novato exit

Recreation. *Bridges:* Petaluma River 76. *Cruises:* Marin tour 91. *View point:* Petaluma River Bridge 101. *Boat ramp:* Black Point 139.

History. *Chronology:* first ferry 157.

Sonoma County

Port Sonoma exit
Recreation. *Marina:* Port Sonoma 109. *Bait shop:* Port Sonoma 137. *Sportfishing boat:* Port Sonoma 145.

Lakeville Road exit
(the road heads inshore to Petaluma, and it only goes toward the Bay to end up on private property)

Highway 121 / Sonoma-Napa exit
(the turn-off only goes away from the Bay to the wine country)

"Tubbs Island 3 miles"
(almost immediately after the Highway 121 turn-off, you come to the gate and sign for Tubbs Island)
Recreation. *Preserve:* Robert Lee Sims (Tubbs Island) 52.
Ecology. *Bird-watching:* Tubbs Island 205.

Solano County

Skaggs Island exit
(the road goes inland, not to the Bay)

Mare Island exit
(an exit to the Navy base, which is not open to the public)
History. *Chronology:* Navy Yard 156, presidential visit 158. *Commemoration:* Naval station 178. *Island:* Mare Island 186. *Lighthouse:* Mare Island 189.

Vallejo and Wilson Ave exit (cross the Napa River Bridge)
(the first exit for Vallejo — Highway 80 which passes on the east side of town has several Vallejo exits, but the town is small enough that all exits will take you to the waterfront)
Recreation. *Dining:* Harbor House, The Wharf, and The Grotto 33. *Park:* Vallejo 53. *Ferry:* Mare Island 66. *Buses:* Greyhound 77. *Marina:* Vallejo 110. *Yacht club:* Vallejo 135. *Bait shops:* Vallejo Pier and Brinkman's Marine 137. *Boat ramp:* Maryland Street 139. *Shore fishing:* Vallejo Pier and Promenade 141.
History. *Chronology:* ferryboat explosion 158, longest ferry run 158, Carquinez Strait Lighthouse 159, first ferry 160, bridge opened-ferry ended 160, second span 162. *Lighthouses:* Mare Island and Carquinez Strait 189.

Contra Costa County
South on Highway 80 from Vallejo.

Crockett / Rodeo exit
(cross the Carquinez Bridge)
Recreation. *Dining:* Nantucket Fish Co. 33. *Bridge:* Carquinez Bridge 70-71. *Buses:* Greyhound 77. *Bike routes:* Crockett to Port Costa and to Rodeo and Pinole 82. *View points:* Carquinez Bridge and Highway 80 102. *Marina:* Crockett Marine 110. *Bait shop:* Crockett Marine 137. *Shore fishing:* Crockett Marine 141. *Sportfishing boats:* Crockett Marine 146.
History. *Chronology:* first explorer 155, Carquinez Strait Lighthouse 159, first ferry 160, bridge opened-ferry ended 160, second span 162. *Old ferryboats: Garden City* and *Fresno* 169. *Lighthouses:* Mare Island and Carquinez Strait 189. *Port work:* refineries 198-199.

Cummings Skyway exit
(only goes inland)

Martinez / Concord / Highway 4

Willow Ave / Rodeo exit
Recreation. *Dining:* Rodeo Marina Coffee Shop 33. *Park:* Rodeo 53. *Bike route:* Rodeo and Pinole 82. *View points:* (head far inland for) Mt. Diablo 100, Highway 80 102. *Marina:* Rodeo 110. *Bait shop:* Sarge's 137. *Boat ramp:* Rodeo Marina 139. *Sportfishing boats:* Rodeo Marina — Sarge's 146.
History. *Chronology:* first ferry 160, last ferry 160. *Port work:* refineries 198-199.

Pinole / Hercules exit
Recreation. *Park:* Pinole 53. *Bike route:* Rodeo and Pinole 82. *View point:* Highway 80 102.

Appian Way / El Sobrante exit
(an exit that leads to Pinole, listed above)

Hilltop Dr exit
Recreation. *Park:* Point Pinole Regional Shoreline 53. *Bike route:* Point Pinole 82. *Shore fishing:* Point Pinole 142.
History. *Chronology:* ferry collision 160.
Ecology. *Excursions:* East Bay Regional Parks 203.

El Portal Dr / San Pablo exit
(an exit that can lead to Point Pinole, listed above)

San Pablo Dam Road exit
McBryde Ave exit
San Pablo Ave / Central Richmond exit

(these three exits do not lead to the Bay)

El Cerrito / San Rafael Bridge / Cutting Blvd exit

(southbound)

San Rafael / Potrero Ave exit

(northbound)

(these exits lead through Richmond, with all its waterfront, to Pt. San Pablo and the San Rafael Bridge) ·

Recreation. *Dining:* The Galley 33. *Parks:* Point Molate Beach Park 53, George Miller Jr Memorial Regional Shoreline and Keller's Beach Park 53. *Bridge:* schemes 69, Richmond-San Rafael 70-71. *Buses:* Traveler's Transit 77. *Bike routes:* bridge crossing 78, around Pt San Pablo 83. *View points:* Pt San Pablo and Nicholls Knob 102. *Marinas:* Pt San Pablo Yacht Harbor, Redrock Marina, and Richmond Yacht Harbor 110; Channel Marina 111. *Learning to sail:* California Cruising Club 123. *Sailboat renting:* California Cruising Club 130. *Yacht clubs:* Richmond and Pt San Pablo 135. *Bait shops:* Pt San Pablo, Redrock Marina, and Pacific Boat Works 137. *Boat ramps:* Redrock Marina and Richmond 139. *Shore fishing:* Pt San Pablo, Redrock Marina, CalTrans Pier, and Richmond Pier 142. *Sportfishing boats:* Pt San Pablo Yacht Harbor 146.
History. Offshore from Richmond are several islands with historical sites. *Chronology:* Indian shell mounds 155, first explorer 155, East Brother light 158, first Santa Fe train 159, first ferry 160, ferry ended 160, bridge opened 162. *Old ferry terminal:* Redrock Marina 170. *Collection:* Castro Point Railway 175. *Indian sites:* Richmond and Brooks Island 180. *Islands:* Brooks Island 183, The Brothers 184, Red Rock 184, Castro Rocks 186, Bird Island 186. *Lighthouse:* East Brother 189. *Treasure and legend:* Red Rock 184, sea monster 194. *Port work:* refinery 198, Santa Fe Channel and Pt San Pablo 199.
Ecology. *Seal-watching:* The Brothers, Castro Rocks, Richmond-San Rafael Bridge 207.

Carlson Blvd exit

(also goes through Richmond, places listed above)

Central Ave exit

Recreation. *Park:* Point Isabel Regional Shoreline 54. *Shore fishing:* Pt Isabel Reg Shoreline 142.
History. Offshore from Pt Isabel is Brooks Island with historical sites. *Chronology:* Indian shell mounds 155. *Indian sites:* Brooks Island 180. *Islands:* Brooks Island 183, Bird Island 186.
Ecology. *Excursions:* East Bay Regional Parks 203.

Alameda County
Albany exit

(the listed places are all inland from the freeway)
Recreation. *View points:* Albany Hill and East Bay Ridgelands 103. *Bait shop:* Sportfishing Center 137. *Sportfishing boats:* Lee Anderson Charters 146, Sportfishing Center 146.

Gilman St exit

(first of three Berkeley exits, this street goes inland, the only thing on the Bay side is the race track)

University Ave exit

(the second of three Berkeley exits)
Recreation. *Dining:* The Landing, Solomon Grundy's, and Hs Lordships 34. *Park:* Berkeley Marina 54. *BART:* to Berkeley 65. *Ferry:* to Angel Island 68. *Bike route:* Berkeley 84. *View point:* (exit inland to) East Bay Ridgelands 103. *Marina:* Berkeley 111. *Learning to sail:* John Beery Sailing (exit inshore) 123; Berkeley Sailing Center, *Grisette* Sailing, and Lion Sailing 124, windsurfing 128. *Sailboat renting:* John Beery Sailing (exit inshore) 130, Lion Sailing 130. *Charter cruises:* Lion Yachts and Commodore Cruises 132, Hornblower Tours 133. *Yacht club:* Berkeley 135. *Bait shop:* Berkeley Marina 137. *Boat ramp:* Berkeley Marina 139. *Shore fishing:* Berkeley Pier 142. *Sportfishing boats:* Berkeley Marina, Lee Anderson Charters, and Sportfishing Center 146.
History. *Chronology:* first ferry 160, "Plate of Brasse" at Bancroft Library 161. *Old ferry terminal:* Berkeley Marina 170. *Indian sites:* restaurant and parks in Berkeley 180. *Legends:* sea monster 194.
Ecology. *Excursions:* East Bay Region Parks 203. *Bird-watching:* Berkeley 205.

Ashby Ave / Highway 13 exit

(the third of three Berkeley exits, this street goes only inland)
Recreation. *View point:* East Bay Ridgelands 103.
Ecology. *Cruising:* Sierra Club / SF Bay Chapter 201.

Powell St / Emeryville exit

Recreation. *Dining:* Angelina's, Charley Brown's, Trader Vic's, and Casa Maria 35. *Park:* Emeryville and "mud flats" 54. *Marina:* Emeryville 111. *Bait shop:* Hank Schramm's 137. *Shore fishing:* Emeryville shoreline 142. *Sportfishing boats:* Hank Schramm's Sportfishing Center 146.
History. *Commemoration:* site of shell mound 176. *Indian site:* Emeryville 180.

Junction with Highway 580 and Highway 17-Nimitz Freeway

Cypress St / West Grand Ave. exit

Turning toward the Bay Bridge and San Francisco, you come to the Harbor Terminals / Last Oakland exit — from the opposite direction, coming off the Bay Bridge, this is the Cypress St / West Grand Ave exit (this really should be considered an Oakland exit, even though it is not very near the rest of the Oakland waterfront)
Recreation. *Dining:* Oyster Pirates Store (Port View Park) 36. *Parks:* Bay Bridge-Radio Stations 54, Port View Park 55. *Bridge:* longest 70, San Francisco-Oakland Bay Bridge 72, Emperor Norton 73. *Buses:* AC Transit and Greyhound 77. *Bike routes:* bridge crossing 78, Oakland 84. *View points:* (take Highway 580 inland) Mt Diablo 100, East Bay Ridgelands 103. *Bait shop:* Oyster Pirates Store 137. *Shore fishing:* Port View Park 142.
History. *Chronology:* ferry route 157, Emperor Norton's vision 157, Key System ferry 159, bridge rights 160, Cardinal blessed bridge 161, Bay Bridge opened 161, end of Key System ferry-start of trains 161, Key System trains ended 162, last ferry run 162, one-way bridge traffic 162, BART transbay service 163, crane collision with bridge 163, Bay Bridge run 163. *Old ferryboat: Eureka* 165. *Island:* Sand Island 186. *Port work:* Oakland Outer Harbor and Port View Park 198.
Ecology. *Bird-watching:* Bay Bridge-Radio Stations 205.

South from the Bay Bridge on Highway 17, the Nimitz Freeway, there are ten Oakland exits, almost all of which lead to some part of the waterfront. (some of the Oakland exits also lead by tunnel or bridge to Alameda, which is listed separately, after all of Oakland, with the pertinent exits repeated)

14th St / Downtown Oakland exit

(the first of ten Oakland exits)
Recreation. *Dining:* Oyster Pirates Store (Port View Park) 36. *Parks:* Port View Park and Middle Harbor Park 55. *BART:* Oakland West Station 65. *Bike route:* Oakland 84. *Bait shop:* Oyster Pirates Store 137. *Shore fishing:* Port View Park and Middle Harbor Park 142.
History. *Chronology:* ferry route 157, first lighthouse 158, ferry route 159, end of SP ferry-start of trains 161, last ferry run 162, BART transbay service 163. *Old ferryboat: Eureka* 165. *Lighthouse:* Oakland Harbor 190. *Port work:* Oakland Outer Harbor, Port View Park, and Middle Harbor Park 198.

Broadway / Alameda Tube exit

(Jack London Square, Harbor Terminals)
(the second of ten Oakland exits)

An overview of part of the Oakland Estuary with many of its highlights is offered in *Pedestrian Delights* 15-16.

Recreation. *Dining.* Caffé Lido, Sea Wolf, The Grotto, El Caballo, and The Castaway 36; The Mast, Heinold's, Spider Healy, Sophies, and The Rusty Scupper 37. *Parks:* Middle Harbor Park and Estuary Park 55. *BART:* Oakland West Station 65. *Tunnels:* Webster Street and Posey tubes to Alameda 65. *Bike route:* Oakland 84. *Dinner cruise:* Jack London Square 92. *Marinas:* Jack London and Portobello 112. *Learning to sail:* American Boating Club 124. *Sailboat renting:* American Boating Club 130. *Charter cruises:* Mariner Yachts 133. *Yacht club:* Metropolitan 135. *Bait shop:* Capt Scotty's 137. *Shore fishing:* Middle Harbor Park and Estuary Park 142.

History. *Chronology:* first ferry 156, Robert Louis Stevenson 158, oil leak 163, BART transbay service 163. *Commemorations:* Jack London and Jack London Cabin 179. *Lighthouse:* Oakland Harbor 190. *Port work:* Middle Harbor Park and Jack London Square 198, fireboat 199.

Jackson St exit

(the third of ten Oakland exits)

An overview of part of the Oakland Estuary with many of its highlights is offered in *Pedestrian Delights* 15-16.

Recreation. *Dining:* Spider Healy, Sophies, and The Rusty Scupper 37. *Park:* Estuary Park 55. *BART:* Lake Merritt Station 65. *Bike route:* Oakland 84. *Events:* Bathtub Regatta 96. *Marinas:* Portobello and Fifth Avenue 112. *Learning to sail:* American Boating Club and Ocean Cruising School 124; Oakland Parks 125. *Sailboat renting:* American Boating Club and Oakland Parks 130. *Yacht club:* Lake Merritt Sailing Club 135. *Bait shop:* Godfather Bait 137. *Boat ramp:* Estuary Park 139. *Shore fishing:* Estuary Park 142. *Sportfishing boat:* Godfather Bait and Tackle 147.

History. *Collections:* Oakland Museum and Oakland Public Library 175. *Treasure:* Lake Merritt 193. *Expositions:* exhibits at Oakland Museum 195.

Ecology. *Bird-watching:* (inland to) Lake Merritt 205.

16th Ave / Embarcadero exit

(the fourth of ten Oakland exits)

An overview of Oakland's Embarcadero Cove with many of its highlights is offered in *Pedestrian Delights* 17-18.

Recreation. *Dining:* Ace McMurphy's, The Ark, Barclay Jack's, and Quinn's Lighthouse 38; Victoria Station and Dock Café 39. *Park:* Embarcadero Cove 56. *Bike route:* Oakland 84. *Marinas:* Fifth Avenue 112, Lani Kai and two Embarcadero Coves 113. *Learning to sail:* Ocean Cruising School 124, Sailor's Workshop and Wayne D'Anna 125. *Sailboat renting:* Sailor's Workshop and Wayne D'Anna 130. *Charter cruises:* Wayne D'Anna 133. *Bait shop:* Godfather Bait 137. *Sportfishing boat:* Godfather Bait and Tackle 147.

History. *Chronology:* second lighthouse 159. *Old ships:* Golden Hinde II 168, Santa Rosa 171. *Lighthouse:* Oakland Harbor 190. *Port work:* Embarcadero Cove 198.

23rd Ave / Alameda exit

(the fifth of ten Oakland exits)

An overview of Oakland's Embarcadero Cove with many of its highlights is offered in *Pedestrian Delights* 17-18.

Recreation. *Dining:* Quinn's Lighthouse 38, Victoria Station, Dock Café, and Pier 29 Restaurant 39. *Park:* Embarcadero Cove 56. *Bridge:* Park Street 76. *Marinas:* Lani Kai and two Embarcadero Coves 113. *Learning to sail:* Sailor's Workshop and Wayne D'Anna 125. *Sailboat renting:* Sailor's Workshop and Wayne D'Anna 130. *Charter cruises:* Wayne D'Anna 133.

History. *Chronology:* Alameda dredging 159, second lighthouse 159. *Old ferryboat:* Santa Rosa 171. *Lighthouse:* Oakland Harbor 190.

Fruitvale Ave exit

(the sixth of ten Oakland exits)

Recreation. *Dining:* Pier 29 Restaurant 39. *Bridge:* Fruitvale 76. *View point:* (inland to) East Bay Ridgelands 103. *Shore fishing:* Fruitvale Bridge 142.

History. *Chronology:* Alameda dredging 159.

High St / Alameda exit

(the seventh of ten Oakland exits)

Recreation. *Bridge:* High Street 76. *View point:* (inland to) East Bay Ridgelands 103. *Shore fishing:* Fruitvale Bridge 142.

History. *Chronology:* Alameda dredging 159.

66th Ave / Coliseum exit

(the eighth of ten Oakland exits)

Recreation. *Park:* Bay Park Refuge 58. *Bike route:* San Leandro Bay 85. *Shore fishing:* Bay Park Refuge 142.

Ecology. *Bird-watching:* San Leandro Bay 205. *Endangered species:* found in San Leandro Bay 206.

Hegenberger Rd / Oakland Airport exit

(the ninth of ten Oakland exits)

Recreation. *Park:* Bay Park Refuge 57. *Bike route:* San Leandro Bay 85. *Boat ramps:* Boat Mart and Oakland Ramp 139. *Shore fishing:* Bay Park Refuge 142.

Ecology. *Bird-watching:* San Leandro Bay 205. *Endangered species:* found in San Leandro Bay 206.

98th Ave exit

(the tenth of ten Oakland exits, it leads to Hegenberger Road and the places listed above)

Alameda exits

(these five exits are repeats of Oakland exits above, but they also lead by tunnel or bridge to Alameda — places listed below are not in Oakland, only Alameda)

Broadway / Alameda Tube exit

(the first of five Alameda exits)

An overview of part of the Oakland Estuary with many of its highlights is offered in *Pedestrian Delights* 15-16.

Recreation. *Dining:* Rusty Pelican and Barge Inn 40; Ancient Mariner, Neptune's Galleon, La Gondola, Whale's Tail, and Beau Rivage 41. *Parks:* Ballena Bay 56, Robert Crown Memorial State Beach 57. *Tunnels:* Webster Street and Posey tubes 65. *Events:* Sailboat Show 95, Sand Castle Contest 96. *Visiting ships:* Navy 99. *Marinas:* Mariner Square 113, Barnhill and Pacific 114, Ballena Bay Yacht Harbor 115. *Learning to sail:* John Beery Sailing, Dave Garrett Sailing, and San Francisco Sailing 124. *Sailboat renting:* Northern California Sailing 130. *Charter cruises:* John Beery and Northern California Sailing 133. *Yacht clubs:* Encinal, Oakland, and Ballena Bay 135. *Shore fishing:* Ballena Bay and Shoreline strip 142.

History. *Chronology:* first transcontinental train-ferry 157, last ferry 161. *Collection:* Alameda Historical Museum 175. *Commemoration:* First Transcontinental RR 178. *Island:* Alameda 185. *Port work:* Alameda 199.

Ecology. *Excursions:* East Bay Regional Parks 203. *Bird-watching:* Alameda south shore 205.

23rd Ave / Alameda exit
(the second of five Alameda exits)
An overview of Embarcadero Cove with many of its highlights is offered in *Pedestrian Delights* 17-18.
Recreation. *Dining:* La Gondola 41. *Park:* Robert W. Crown Memorial State Beach 57. *Bridge:* Park Street 76. *Events:* Sand Castle Contest 96. *Marinas:* Alameda Yacht Harbor and Alameda Marina 114. *Learning to sail:* Gray Whale 126. *Charter cruises:* Gray Whale 133. *Yacht clubs:* Island and Aeolian 135. *Boat ramp:* Alameda Municipal 139.
History. *Chronology:* Alameda dredging 159. *Old ferryboat: Santa Rosa* 171. *Collection:* Alameda Historical Museum 175. *Island:* Alameda 185. *Port work:* Alameda 199.
Ecology. *Excursions:* East Bay Regional Parks 203. *Bird-watching:* Alameda south shore 205.

Fruitvale Ave exit
(the third of five Alameda exits)
Recreation. *Bridge:* Fruitvale 76. *Yacht club:* Aeolian 135. *Shore fishing:* Fruitvale Bridge 142.
History. *Chronology:* Alameda dredging 159. *Island:* Alameda 185.

High St / Alameda exit
(the fourth of five Alameda exits)
Recreation. *Bridge:* High Street 76. *Yacht club:* Aeolian 135.
History. *Chronology:* Alameda dredging 159. *Commemoration:* site of shell mound 176. *Indian site:* Alameda 180. *Island:* Alameda 185.
Ecology. *Bird-watching:* Alameda south shore 205.

Hegenberger Rd / Oakland Airport exit
(the fifth of five Alameda exits, this leads around the airport to come upon Alameda from the back way)
Recreation. *Bridge:* Bay Farm 76. *Yacht club:* Aeolian 135.
History. *Islands:* Alameda and Bay Farm Island 185.
Ecology. *Bird-watching:* Alameda south shore 205.

Now back to the regular progression of exits of Highway 17-Nimitz Freeway having passed through Oakland, heading south.
(all Oakland exits and places are listed above, before Alameda)

Davis St / Downtown San Leandro exit
(the only thing at the Bay end of this exit is a garbage dump)
Recreation. *View point:* (head inland for) East Bay Ridgelands 103.

Marina Blvd / San Leandro Marina exit
Recreation. *Dining:* Blue Dolphin and Casa Maria 42. *Park:* Marina Park 57. *Bike route:* San Leandro Marina 85. *Marina:* San Leandro 115. *Learning to sail:* windsurfing 128. *Yacht clubs:* San Leandro and Spinnaker 135. *Boat ramp:* San Leandro Marina 139. *Shore fishing:* San Leandro Marina 142.
History. *Chronology:* oyster industry 157. *Commemoration:* San Leandro Oyster Beds 179.

Highway 580 / Castro Valley exit
Lewelling Blvd / San Lorenzo exit
A St / Downtown Hayward exit
Winston Ave exit
(these four exits do not offer access to the Bay shoreline)

Jackson St / San Mateo Bridge / Highway 92 exit
Recreation. *Bridge:* longest 70, San Mateo-Hayward 75. *Buses:* samTrans 77.
History. *Chronology:* bridge construction 160, bridge opened 160.

Tennyson Rd exit
Industrial Parkway exit
Whipple Rd exit
Alvarado-Niles Rd exit
Fremont Blvd / Centerville Dist exit
(these five exits do not offer access to the Bay shoreline)

Jarvis Ave / Dumbarton Bridge exit
Recreation. *Parks:* Coyote Hills Regional Park 58, SF Bay National Wildlife Refuge 58. *Bridges:* Dumbarton 75, Dumbarton railroad 76. *Buses:* Peerless Stages 77. *Bike routes:* Alameda Creek Trail (also accessible from Fremont Blvd exit) 85, Coyote Hills Regional Park 85. *View point:* Coyote Hills 103.
History. *Chronology:* Indian sites 155, first railroad bridge 159, first auto bridge 160. *Old ship: Alma* collision with bridge 166. *Indian sites:* Coyote Hills Regional Park 180.
Ecology. *Excursions:* Coyote Hills Regional Park and SF Bay National Wildlife Refuge 203. *Bird-watching:* Coyote Hills 205.

Thornton Ave / Highway 84 exit
Recreation. *Park:* SF Bay National Wildlife Refuge 58.
Ecology. *Excursions:* SF Bay National Wildlife Refuge 203. *Seal-watching:* (near Fremont) Mowry Slough and Newark Slough 207.

Mowry Ave exit
Stevenson Blvd exit
Durham Rd exit
(these three exits do not offer access to the Bay shoreline)

Fremont Blvd / Cushing Rd exit
Recreation. *Bridges:* Station Island (not really accessible by road) 76.
History. *Island:* Station Island (not really accessible by road) 186.

Warren Ave exit
(this exit does not lead to the Bay)

Mission Blvd exit
(this exit does not lead to the Bay, but there is a site inland)
History. *Chronology:* founding of Mission San José 156. *Commemoration:* Mission San José 177.

Dixon Landing Rd exit
(this exit does not lead to the Bay)

Junction of Highway 17 with Highway 237, Milpitas-Alviso Road
(heading west on 237 takes you to Alviso, which is covered following San Francisco and the Peninsula — there are a couple of places listed here that require going south into San Jose)
History. *Chronology:* founding of Mission Santa Clara 155, founding of pueblo of San José 155. *Commemorations:* founding of Mission Santa Clara 177, founding of pueblo of San José 177.

Note: There are some places in the book that are outside the Golden Gate, not precisely on San Francisco Bay, and also not near any freeway. They are listed here.
History. *Bay Discovery:* Sir Francis Drake — Point Reyes, Faralon Islands 150. *Chronology:* Drakes Bay 153, Emperor Norton's bridge 157, ship explosion 158, ship collision 162, Mile Rocks Lighthouse 162. *Islands:* Farallones 186. *Lighthouses:* Point Bonita 187, Mile Rocks 187-188. *Sunken ships:* outside the Golden Gate 194, at the Farallones 194. *Port work:* pilot boats 199.
Ecology. *Cruising:* Farallones 201. *Seal-watching:* Seal Rocks 207.

San Francisco — Bay Bridge, Yerba Buena Island, Treasure Island

(there are exits both directions on the Bay Bridge for both of these mid-Bay islands, although only a small portion of Treasure Island is open to the public)

Recreation. *Bridge:* longest 70, San Francisco-Oakland Bay Bridge 72. *Buses:* AC Transit and Greyhound 77. *Bike routes:* bridge crossing 78, south waterfront 87. *Visiting ships:* Navy 99.

History. *Chronology:* Goat Island hassle 157, Yerba Buena Lighthouse 158, first Arbor Day 158, Navy got Yerba Buena Island 159, Bay Bridge construction 160, renamed Yerba Buena Island 160 & 162, Treasure Island construction 161, Cardinal blessed bridge 161, bridge opened 161, electric trains started 161, Exposition opened and closed twice 161, Navy got Treasure Island 161, trains stopped 162, bridge one-way traffic started 162, crane collided with bridge 163, Bay Bridge run 163. *Collection:* Navy/Marine Corps Museum 174. *Islands:* Treasure Island 183, Yerba Buena Island 185. *Lighthouse:* Yerba Buena Island 190. *Treasures and shipwrecks:* 193-194. *Exposition:* Golden Gate Exposition and surviving relics (Oakland Museum, Treasure Island, Navy/Marine Corps Museum, Fountain of the Pacific Basin, Golden Gate Park, Ferry Building) 195 & 197.

South on Highway 101.

San Francisco — Army St exit

Recreation. *Dining:* The Bounty 47. *Parks:* south waterfront 61. *Bridge:* Islais Creek 76. *Bike route:* south waterfront 87. *View points:* Twin Peaks 103, Bernal Heights and Potrero Hill 103. *Shore fishing:* Warmwater Cove 143.

History. *Chronology:* Western Pacific ferry 162. *Old ship: Alma* built at Hunters Point 166. *Ferryboat: Las Plumas* 170. *Port work:* India Basin 198, Western Pacific ferry 199, shipyard at Hunters Point 199.

San Francisco — Third St exit

(Candlestick Park can be reached by Harney Way exit — northbound only)

Recreation. *Park:* Candlestick Point 62. *Events:* Fourth of July Fireworks 96. *View point:* San Bruno Mountain 104. *Shore fishing:* Candlestick Point 143.

History. *Chronology:* fireworks at Candlestick Park 163, largest ship in Bay 163.

San Francisco — south waterfront, Bay Bridge to China Basin

Recreation. *Dining:* Carmen's, The Boondocks, and Red's Java House 46; Java House, Pier Head, and *Dolphin P. Rempp* 47. *Bridges:* Third Street 75-76, Fourth Street 76. *Bike route:* south waterfront 87. *Cruising:* helicopter tour 93.

History. *Old ships: Dolphin P. Rempp* 168, *San Leandro* 169. *Port work:* China Basin 198, Pier 24 fireboat 199.

San Francisco — waterfront south of China Basin

Recreation. *Dining:* Wharfside, Blanche's, and Mission Rock Resort 47. *Parks:* south waterfront 61. *Bridges:* Third Street 75-76, Fourth Street 76, Islais Creek 76. *Bike route:* south waterfront 87. *Marinas:* Mission Rock Resort and The Ramp 117. *Yacht clubs:* Mariposa-Hunters Point and Bay View Boat Club 135. *Bait shops:* Mission Rock Resort and The Ramp 137. *Boat ramps:* SF Ramp and The Ramp 139. *Shore fishing:* Agua Vista Park and Warmwater Cove 143. *Sportfishing boat:* The Ramp 147.

History. *Chronology:* Santa Fe ferry 159, Mission Rock burned off 161, Western Pacific ferry 162, oil leak 163. *Ferryboat: Las Plumas* 170. *Port work:* China Basin, Mission Rock, and India Basin 198, Pier 52 Santa Fe ferry 199, Bethlehem Shipyard 199.

San Mateo County

South on Highway 101.

Oyster Point Blvd / South San Francisco exit

Recreation. *Park:* Point San Bruno 62. *View points:* Pt San Bruno and San Bruno Mtn 104. *Marina:* Oyster Point 117. *Yacht club:* Oyster Point 135. *Boat ramp:* Oyster Point Marina 139. *Shore fishing:* Oyster Point Marina 143, Pt San Bruno 143.

Grand Ave exit

Recreation. *Park:* Point San Bruno 62. *View point:* Pt San Bruno 104. *Shore fishing:* Pt San Bruno 143.

South Airport Blvd exit

(does not go to the Bay)

Freeway 380 junction

(does not go to the Bay — head west to Pacifica for the Bay Discovery Site)

Recreation. *View point:* Bay Discovery Site 104.

History. *Bay Discovery Site:* hike to Sweeney Ridge 149. *Chronology:* Bay Discovery Site 155. *Commemoration:* Bay Discovery Site 176.

San Bruno exit

(goes only inshore)

Recreation. *View point;* Highway 280 104.

San Francisco Airport exit

(does not give access to the Bay)

Millbrae Ave exit

Recreation. *Dining:* Saluto's, Casa Maria, Charley Brown's, and The Fisherman 48. *Parks:* Burlingame 62. *Bike route:* Burlingame and San Mateo 88. *View point:* (inland to) Highway 280 104.

History. *Chronology:* Bay discovery expedition 155. *Commemoration:* Portolá expedition 176.

Broadway / Burlingame exit

(Old Bayshore Highway)

Recreation. *Dining:* Saluto's, Casa Maria, Charley Brown's, The Fisherman, Kee Joon's, and Diamond Showboat 48. *Parks:* Burlingame 62. *Bike route:* Burlingame and San Mateo 88. *Shore fishing:* Fisherman's Park 143.

History. *Old ferryboat: General Frank M. Coxe* 170.

Poplar Ave / Coyote Point Dr exit

(northbound it is Peninsula Ave)

Recreation. *Dining:* Diamond Showboat and The Castaway 48. *Parks:* Burlingame 62, Coyote Point Park 62. *Bike route:* Burlingame and San Mateo 88. *Marina:* Coyote Point 117. *Yacht club:* Coyote Point 135. *Boat ramp:* Coyote Point Marina 139. *Shore fishing:* Fishermans Park 143, Coyote Point Marina 143.

History. *Old Ferryboat: General Frank M. Coxe* 170. *Commemoration:* Coyote Point 179.

Ecology. *Collection:* Coyote Point Museum 203.

Third Ave exit

Recreation. *Bike route:* Burlingame and San Mateo 88.

History. *Commemoration:* Anza expedition 177.

Highway 92 / San Mateo Bridge exit

Recreation. *Parks:* Foster City 62. *Bridge:* longest 70, San Mateo-Hayward 75. *Buses:* samTrans 77. *Bike route:* San Mateo and Foster City 89. *Learning to sail:* San Mateo City Rec 127, Foster City Park & Rec 127. *Sailboat renting:* San Mateo City Rec 131. *Yacht club:* Island Sailing Club 135. *Boat ramps:* Marina Slough and Foster City 139. *Shore fishing:* San Mateo Pier 143.

History. *Chronology:* bridge construction 160, bridge opened 160. *Collection:* San Mateo County History Center 172.

Hillsdale Blvd / Foster City exit

Recreation. *Parks:* Foster City 62. *Bike route:* San Mateo and Foster City 89. *Learning to sail:* San Mateo City Rec 127, Foster City Park & Rec 127. *Sailboat renting:* San Mateo City Rec 131. *Yacht club:* Island Sailing Club 135. *Boat ramps:* Marina Slough and Foster City 139. *Shore fishing:* San Mateo Pier 143.

History. *Collection:* San Mateo County History Center 174.

Ralston Ave / Marine World Parkway exit

Recreation. *Park:* Redwood Shores 63. *Learning to sail:* Peninsula Sailing and Redwood City Park & Rec 127, windsurfing 128.

Holly St exit

(does not offer access to the Bay shoreline)

Whipple Ave / Veterans Blvd exit

Recreation. *Dining:* Harbor House 48. *Marinas:* Pete's Harbor, Peninsula, and Docktown 118. *Learning to sail:* Dave Garrett Sailing 127. *Sailboat renting:* Northern California Sailing 131. *Charter Cruises:* Northern California Sailing 133. *Yacht club:* Peninsula 135. *Bait shop:* Pete's Harbor 137. *Boat ramp:* Docktown Marina 139.

Harbor Blvd exit

Recreation. *Dining:* Charley Brown's 48. *Park:* Redwood City Marina 63. *Marinas:* Docktown and Redwood City 118. *Learning to sail:* Dave Garrett Sailing 127, Redwood City Park & Rec 127. *Sailboat renting:* Northern California Sailing 131. *Charter cruises:* Northern California Sailing 133. *Yacht club:* Sequoia 135. *Boat ramp:* Docktown Marina and Redwood City Marina 139. *Shore fishing:* Redwood City Marina 143.

History. *Port work:* Redwood City 199.

Ecology. *Cruising:* Marine Ecological Institute 201. *Endangered species:* near Redwood City Marina 206. *Seal-watching:* near Redwood City Marina 207.

Marsh Rd exit

(leads only to a garbage dump by the Bay)

Willow Rd / Highway 84 / Dumbarton Bridge exit

Recreation. *Bridge:* Dumbarton 75. *Buses:* Peerless Stages 77. *View point:* cartographic views (USGS inshore) 105.

History. *Chronology:* first railroad bridge over Bay 159, first auto bridge over Bay 160. *Commemoration:* Portolá expedition 176.

University Ave exit

(does not lead easily to the Bay)

History. *Commemoration:* Portolá expedition 176.

Santa Clara County

Embarcadero Rd exit

Recreation. *Parks:* Baylands Nature Center 63. *Marina:* Palo Alto Yacht Harbor 118. *Yacht club:* Palo Alto 135. *Boat ramp:* Palo Alto Yacht Harbor 139.

Ecology. *Cruising:* Nature Expeditions International 201. *Excursions:* Baylands Nature Center 203. *Bird-watching:* Palo Alto Baylands 205. *Endangered species:* near Palo Alto Baylands 206.

San Antonio Rd exit

(leads only to a disposal site by the Bay)

Rengstorff Ave exit

(leads only inland)

Stierlin Rd exit

(leads to a landfill site by the Bay)

Recreation. *Park:* Shoreline Regional Park 63.

Moffett Blvd exit

(access to the Bay is blocked by Moffett Naval Air Station)

Recreation. *View points:* cartographic views — aerial photos 105.

Junction of Highway 101 with Highway 237, Mtn View-Alviso Road

(heading east on 237 takes you to the Alviso turn-offs, Gold Street and Taylor Street — continuing south takes you to San Jose)

An overview of Alviso with many of its highlights is offered in *Pedestrian Delights* 24-25.

Recreation. *Bridges:* on Station Island (not really accessible by road) 76. *Marina:* Alviso 119. *Yacht clubs:* South Bay and San Jose Sailing Club 135. *Boat ramp:* Alviso Marina 139.

History. *Chronology:* ferry to Alviso 157. *Old ship: Alma* rescued from mudbank 166. *Island:* Station Island (not really accessible by road) 186.

Ecology. *Endangered species:* found near Alviso 206.

Notes

Notes

Notes

Notes

<u>**Explicit**</u>   TERRY MILNE